ROUTLEDGE LIBRARY EDITIONS:
BUSINESS AND ECONOMICS IN ASIA

Volume 30

STATE, MARKET AND PEASANT IN COLONIAL SOUTH AND SOUTHEAST ASIA

STATE, MARKET AND PEASANT IN COLONIAL SOUTH AND SOUTHEAST ASIA

MICHAEL ADAS

Routledge
Taylor & Francis Group

LONDON AND NEW YORK

First published in 1998 by Ashgate Publishing Limited

This edition first published in 2019
by Routledge
2 Park Square, Milton Park, Abingdon, Oxon OX14 4RN

and by Routledge
52 Vanderbilt Avenue, New York, NY 10017

Routledge is an imprint of the Taylor & Francis Group, an informa business

© 1998 Michael Adas

British Library Cataloguing in Publication Data
A catalogue record for this book is available from the British Library

ISBN: 978-1-138-48274-6 (Set)
ISBN: 978-0-429-42825-8 (Set) (ebk)
ISBN: 978-1-138-61820-6 (Volume 30) (hbk)
ISBN: 978-1-138-61821-3 (Volume 30) (pbk)
ISBN: 978-0-429-46130-9 (Volume 30) (ebk)

Publisher's Note
The publisher has gone to great lengths to ensure the quality of this reprint but points out that some imperfections in the original copies may be apparent.

Disclaimer
The publisher has made every effort to trace copyright holders and would welcome correspondence from those they have been unable to trace.

Michael Adas

State, Market and Peasant in Colonial South and Southeast Asia

Ashgate
VARIORUM

Aldershot · Brookfield USA · Singapore · Sydney

This edition copyright © 1998 by Michael Adas.

Published in the Variorum Collected Studies Series by

Ashgate Publishing Limited
Gower House, Croft Road,
Aldershot, Hampshire GU11 3HR
Great Britain

Ashgate Publishing Company
Old Post Road,
Brookfield, Vermont 05036–9704
USA

ISBN 0–86078–696–X

British Library CIP Data
Adas, Michael
    State, Market and Peasant in Colonial South and Southeast Asia.
    (Variorum Collected Studies Series: CS616)
    1. Peasantry – South Asia. 2. Peasantry – South Asia – History.
    3. Peasantry – Asia, Southeastern. 4. Peasantry – Asia, Southeastern –
    History. 5. Colonies – Asia – History. 6. South Asia – Civilization –
    Foreign Influences. 7. Asia, Southeastern – Civilization – Foreign
    Influences. I. Title
    305.5'633–0954

US Library of Congress CIP Data
Adas, Michael
    State, Market and Peasant in Colonial South and Southeast Asia /
    Michael Adas
        p.   cm. — (Variorum Collected Studies Series: CS616).
    1. Peasant Uprisings – Asia – History. 2. Peasant Uprisings – Asia,
    Southeastern – History. 3. Peasantry – Asia – History. 4. Peasantry –
    Asia, Southeastern – History. I. Title. II. Series: Variorum Collected
    Studies: CS 616.
    HD 1536.8.A33 1998   98–19002
    305.5'633'00959–dc21   CIP

The paper used in this publication meets the minimum requirements of the
    American National Standard for Information Sciences – Permanence of
    Paper for Printed Library Materials, ANSI Z39.48–1984. ∞ ™

Printed by Galliard (Printers) Ltd, Great Yarmouth, Norfolk, Great Britain

VARIORUM COLLECTED STUDIES SERIES CS616

CONTENTS

PEASANT RESISTANCE: FROM FOOTDRAGGING TO REBELLION

This volume consists of xiv + 332 pages

PUBLISHER'S NOTE

The articles in this volume, as in all others in the Collected Studies Series, have not been given a new, continuous pagination. In order to avoid confusion, and to facilitate their use where these same studies have been referred to elsewhere, the original pagination has been maintained wherever possible.

Each article has been given a Roman numeral in order of appearance, as listed in the Contents. This number is repeated on each page and quoted in the index entries.

PREFACE

Prompted by the decolonization movements that swept Asia and Africa following World War II as well as growing popular resistance to United States interventions in Latin America, the victory of the Communist forces in China's decades-old civil war, and especially the debacles of French and then American wars against the Marxist-nationalist regime in Vietnam, peasants and peasant protest movements became a major focus of research and scholarship in 1960s and 1970s. Numerous scholars, but most cogently Eric Wolf, sought to define the once-vague concept of the peasant with precision, and to challenge the conflation of peasants with farmers that had much to do with the Western, particularly American, policy disasters in the vast and diverse zone designated in cold war parlance as the Third World. A prodigious flood of monographic studies, and a more modest flow of comparative works (most of the latter written by political scientists, anthropologists, and history-minded sociologists rather than historians), sought to reveal the workings of peasant-based societies. Often applying cross-disciplinary methods and sources, peasant specialists explored topics ranging from systems of social stratification and religious beliefs and rituals to the mind-sets and motives that drove peasants to open rebellion against both their indigenous, non-Western elites and alien colonizers.

The essays collected in this volume are very much a product of several waves of scholarship on peasant cultures and peasant behavior that were among the dominant preoccupations of historians during the peak decades of the cold war. But they also incorporate a number of additional concerns that preoccupied scholars in the aftermath of World War II. Though some deal with precolonial conditions and patterns, the bulk of the articles included here address the profound changes and disruptions wrought in peasant societies as a result of European colonial domination and the spread of the capitalist world economy from its western European base, beginning in the sixteenth century.

The time frame for most of the articles spans the late-eighteenth, nineteenth, and early twentieth centuries, with particular emphasis on the middle period, which proved to be a watershed era in virtually all of the areas that are the focus of different studies. Some essays focus on the structure of the colonial empires themselves and the agents, both European and Asian, who served them. These examine the ways in which these forces affected peasant societies in a number of locales, particularly Bihar in north India, and lower Burma and central and west Java in Southeast Asia. Throughout the collection various sorts of peasant responses, from enthusiastic production for the market to different forms of resistance to what were seen to be excessive colonial demands and market setbacks, are examined. A number of the articles also explore the movement of merchants, moneylenders, and peasant migrants between European colonies, and the importance and impact of this circulation of resources and labor power on the receiving societies and European colonial systems as a whole.

Although detailed case study evidence from a number of areas is included in most of the essays, all are aimed at delineating broader patterns and addressing general questions and debates regarding peasant responses to the impact of colonialism and capitalism in the various guises it took in different locales. Those in the first section of the collection concentrate on testing theories regarding the origins of peasant protest, from the concept of the moral economy to the methods and perspectives of the subaltern approach to peasant societies pioneered by South Asian specialists. These articles also contribute to a larger concern, which gained prominence among some scholars of peasant societies and agrarian protest in the 1980s, to reorient our thinking regarding peasant *mentalités* and responses to colonialism and its concomitant market forces. Scholarship in the 1960s and 1970s had given rise to a quasi-romantic image of the peasant as revolutionary, ever vigilant to injustice and always prepared to rise up in violent protest against perceived oppressors. Drawing in part on the wealth of evidence provided by the fine and detailed studies produced in those decades, but also reading that evidence in new ways and employing rather different sources, some peasant and protest specialists sought to emphasize the everyday and non-confrontational modes of peasant response to injustice and exploitation that have been pervasive in and endemic to peasant societies throughout history in contrast to more dramatic, but relatively rare, instances of violent peasant protest, including much studied peasant-based revolutions.

The essays included in section one, explore both the historical and sociocultural contexts in which these everyday or avoidance modes of peasant response are embedded, and the variety of forms they take in different societies and time periods. They also examine the relationships between these modes of peasant resistance and more confrontational responses, including Gandhian *satyagraha*, millenarian rebellion, and peasant support for Marxist-inspired revolutionary movements.

The contributions included in the second half of the collection cover a broader range of related themes. Here a good deal of attention is given to precolonial conditions, or perceived conditions, that formed the contexts in which colonialism and capitalism wrought their transformations. Questions relating to the structure and imperatives of empire are also addressed in considerable detail, with particular attention to the connections between various parts of the vast and diverse British empire that have often been considered in isolation. Here stress is placed on the ways in which comparisons and a consideration of various locales within the context of a larger imperial structure provide a different vision of the workings and impact of colonialism and insights into the history of the post-colonial world in Africa and Asia. Like the essays in section one, each of those in part two are intended to enhance our understandings of an era of unprecedented change and disruption in the post-neolithic peasant societies where the vast majority of humankind have lived out their lives.

MICHAEL ADAS

Rutgers University at New Brunswick
January 1998

ACKNOWLEDGEMENTS

Grateful acknowledgement is made to the following persons, editors, publishers, institutions and journals for their kind permission to reprint the articles included in this volume: Cambridge University Press (I); Frank Cass and Company Ltd., London (II); *Journal of Social History*, Pittsburgh (III); The University of Michigan Press (IV); Duke University Press, Durham, NC (V, XI); Oxford University Press, New Delhi (VII); *Journal of Southeast Asian Studies*, Singapore (IX); Orient Longman, New Delhi (XII); Association for Asian Studies, Inc., Ann Arbor (XIII); University of Hawai'i at Manoa (XIV); Westview Press, Boulder (XVI).

I

From Avoidance to Confrontation: Peasant Protest in Precolonial and Colonial Southeast Asia

Although there has been a dramatic broadening of the definition of social protest in recent years to include collective behavior that was once dismissed as criminal, irrational, or insignificant, our attention has continued to be focused on movements involving direct, often violent, confrontations between the wielders of power and dissident groups. Avoidance protest, by which dissatisfied groups seek to attenuate their hardships and express their discontent through flight, sectarian withdrawal, or other activities that minimize challenges to or clashes with those whom they view as their oppressors, has at best remained a secondary concern of students of social protest. Although specific forms of avoidance protest, such as the flight of slaves in the plantation zones of the Americas or the migration or serfs to the towns of medieval Europe and peasants to the frontiers of Tsarist Russia,[1] have merited a prominent place in the historical literature on some societies and time periods, avoidance protest has rarely been systematically analyzed as a phenomenon in itself. There have been few detailed studies of the diverse forms which avoidance protest may take and the ways in which these are shaped by the sociopolitical contexts in which they develop. This neglect is serious because in many societies and time periods (perhaps in most in the preindustrial era), modes of protest oriented to avoidance rather than confrontation have been the preferred and most frequently adopted means of resisting oppression and expressing dissatisfaction. Thus, rather than being treated as isolated episodes or indicators of social unrest which culminated in "major" forms of protest, such as riots or rebellions, as has been the case in the work of most scholars

I would like to thank Peter Carey, Victor Lieberman, William Koenig, and the members of the Social History Group of Rutgers University for their contributions to the original draft of this essay. I would also like to thank the participants in the Symposium on Peasant Rebellions at Johns Hopkins University and the members of the Ethnohistory Program at the University of Pennsylvania for their valuable comments and critiques.

[1] For sample discussions of avoidance protest in each of these situations, see, respectively, Eugene D. Genovese, *Roll, Jordan, Roll* (New York, 1972), esp. pp. 648-57, and Gerald Mullin, *Flight and Rebellion: Slave Resistance in Eighteenth Century Virginia* (New York, 1972); Rodney Hilton, *Bond Men Made Free* (New York, 1973), esp. ch. 2, and H. S. Bennett, *Life on the English Manor* (Cambridge, 1937), ch. 11; Jerome Blum, *Lord and Peasant in Russia* (Princeton, 1961), esp. ch. 14.

I

(including my own),[2] the various forms of avoidance protest ought to be examined in their own right.

This essay will focus on several related forms of avoidance protest found in many Asian and African societies. Although, in illustrating the different patterns of avoidance protest and examining the sociopolitical contexts which gave rise to these forms of resistance, I will rely mainly upon evidence from Burma and Java, where most of my own research has been concentrated, I will also make use of examples from Africa, South Asia, and other areas in Southeast Asia. These supplemental examples, for which parallels can be found in works on China, Europe, and Latin America, are used to indicate the widespread distribution and importance of avoidance protest and, with significant variations, the prevalence of the type of political economy found in precolonial Burma and Java which I characterize as the "contest state." A wide variety of preindustrial political systems, ranging from the warrior-dominated kingdoms of medieval Europe or Japan, at one pole of a hypothetical continuum, to relatively highly centralized empires like the Mughal in India or the Asante in Ghana, at the other, can be grouped under the general type of the contest state. Central to this form of political organization is rule by a king or emperor who claims a monopoly of power and authority in a given society but whose effective control is in reality severely restricted by rival power centers among the elite, by weaknesses in administrative organization and institutional commitment on the part of state officials, by poor communications, and by a low population-to-land ratio that places a premium on manpower retention and regulation. These conditions gave rise to polities in which there was a constant struggle between the ruler and the nobility, between factions of the elite at various levels, and between supravillage elite groups and village notables and peasants for the control of labor and the agricultural production which formed the basis of these predominantly agrarian states. Although the fortunes of the contending parties fluctuated greatly over time, their continuing struggle over revenue control and the inability of any one of the parties to dominate the others decisively on a sustained basis suggest the concept of the contest state as a useful way to characterize this form of political organization.

One of the central purposes of this essay is to examine the ways in which the coming of colonial rule transformed contest states into much more centralized, bureaucratic systems and to consider the effects of this transformation on the modes of protest adopted by peasant groups. One of the cruelest

[2] Notable recent exceptions to this trend include the work of James Fernandez, and especially his article on "The Affirmation of Things Past: Alar Ayong and Bwiti as Movements of Protest in Central and Northern Gabon," in *Protest and Power in Black Africa*, Robert Rotberg and Ali Mazrui, eds. (Oxford, 1970), pp. 427–57; A. I. Asiwaju's article on "Migrations as Revolt: The Example of the Ivory Coast and the Upper Volta Before 1945," *Journal of African History* 17, no. 4 (1976): 577–94; Allen Isaacman, *The Tradition of Resistance in Mozambique* (Berkeley, 1976), ch. 5.

contradictions of the era of colonization arose from situations in which population growth and political centralization forced the peasantry of Africa and Asia to adopt methods of protest involving confrontation with incumbent regimes, rather than relying on resistance through avoidance, at a time when vastly improved military organization and weapons technology rendered such clashes lethal exercises in futility.

In societies similar to those found in Burma and Java before the advent of European colonial rule, various modes of avoidance protest were closely related to, and in many instances merely extensions of, longstanding defense mechanisms developed by peasant communities to buffer elite demands on village production and manpower. These defenses were in turn rooted in demographic and geographical conditions and in the nature of the political economies of the societies in which they emerged. As a result, it is often difficult to distinguish between defense mechanisms and expressions of protest, and it is also impossible to understand either of these in isolation from the political and social systems in which they arose. Peasant migration from the lands of an unpopular lord, for example, was both a means by which the group in flight protected itself from what it felt to be excessive exactions and a dramatic way of protesting and drawing attention to the maladministration of the noble or official in question. The option of flight was in turn dependent upon a low population density, the availability of refuge zones or unoccupied lands in which the runaways could settle, and a relatively low level of administrative control and coercive capacity.

These examples indicate the importance of beginning the analysis of avoidance protest with an overview of the state systems of precolonial Java and Burma, the nature of elite-peasant interaction in these societies, and the ways in which these institutions and exchanges shaped the persistent defense mechanisms employed by peasant communities in each area. I will then consider the conditions under which these defenses were violated or judged insufficient to provide adequate protection and were thus superseded by various forms of collective protest. Though the focus of this essay will be on modes of avoidance protest, I will also examine the relationship between these forms of collective behavior and the kinds of resistance aimed at confrontations with, and at times fundamental challenges to, those whom the peasants viewed as their oppressors. The remaining portions of the essay will be devoted to a discussion of the political, economic, and social changes which occurred in Burma and Java as a result of European colonization, and the impact of these transformations on the modes of protest adopted by dissident groups.

In precolonial Java and Burma, as in kingdoms throughout most of Southeast and South Asia and over much of Africa, administrative and military weaknesses and poor communications provided the main checks against excessive

I

demands by elite groups on their peasant subjects. Although abstract ethical considerations set forth in religious texts or in political discourses on the attributes of a just ruler may have deeply influenced some monarchs and state officials,[3] elite rivalries, personalist patron-client ties, and poorly integrated (both vertically and horizontally) administrative systems were far more constant and secure sources of peasant protection. In the kingdoms of precolonial Burma and Java, control of political positions was determined primarily by inheritance and lineage patterns associated with Max Weber's ideal type of patrimonial domain.[4] This mode of allocating authority resulted in deep divisions among the elite and in incessant, often violent, struggles by groups allied to lineages at various levels from the court center to the local district as they vied for control of the limited resources of the state that emanated largely from the labors of the cultivating classes at the bottom of the sociopolitical hierarchy. These chronic and pervasive struggles greatly inhibited the rulers' and administrators' ability to control the village communities where the great majority of their subjects lived. The rivalries also made it possible for the peasant inhabitants of these communities to develop a wide range of techniques designed to defend their interests in the ongoing contest through the circumvention or reduction of elite demands.

Like the kingdoms and empires in the Middle East and South Asia upon which they modelled their political institutions and ideologies, the societies of Java and Burma were periodically ravaged by bloody strife that resulted from a fundamental contradiction in the sociopolitical order. In situations where monarchs were expected to, and normally did, have large numbers of wives, concubines, and children, the process of royal succession was not clearly defined or regulated. Because the royal blood line included the ruler's siblings and extended over several generations, there were usually many potential claimants to the throne of a given kingdom. Though only a few of these were likely to possess sufficient ambition and backing to attempt to seize the throne of a reigning monarch, the constant threat which his relatives, as well as members of powerful families among the nobility, posed for the ruler forced him to devote considerable time and resources to surveillance and Machiavellian maneuvers designed to prevent strong support from coalescing around promising rivals or to crush attempts at open rebellion.[5]

[3] For examples, see Soermarsaid Moertono, *State and Statecraft in Old Java* (Ithaca, N.Y. 1968), pp. 35ff.; Thaung, "Burmese Kingship in Theory and Practice under the Reign of King Mindon," *Journal of the Burma Research Society* (hereafter cited as *JBRS*) 42 (1959): 178-83; John W. Spellman, *Political Theory of Ancient India* (Oxford, 1964), ch. 8; Max Gluckman, "The Kingdom of the Zulu in South Africa," in *African Political Systems*, M. Fortes and E. E. Evans-Pritchard, eds. (London, 1940), esp. pp. 28-34.

[4] Max Weber, *Economy and Society: An Outline of Interpretive Sociology*, G. Roth and C. Wittich, eds. (New York, 1968), vol. 3, ch. 12. To a lesser degree than empires in the Islamic heartland or Mughal India, Javanese and Burmese administrative systems also contained prebendal elements.

[5] Court intrigues and succession disputes received much attention in earlier historical works on Burma and Java, as the writings of G. E. Harvey, Arthur Phayre, M. L. van Deventer, and H. J.

The rivals themselves and their supporters, which usually included many of the monarch's chief ministers and the most important nobles of the realm, were also deeply immersed in efforts to build the power of their own factions and to deprive competing groups of manpower and sources of revenue. If a ruler fell ill, suffered serious losses in wars with neighboring states or advancing European colonizers, or died, the rival claimants and their preexisting factions entered into intense, often bloody, contests for control of the throne. Though the winners of these struggles frequently conducted brutal purges to destroy rival power centers, new claimants and competing factions invariably emerged, even in the reigns of the strongest of rulers.

Rivalries centered at the court and capital city were paralleled by tensions between the monarch and the regional lords. Although regional administrators were the appointees and nominally the representatives of the ruler, even the most powerful monarchs were unable to maintain effective control over more than just the capital city and the heartland areas of the kingdom which surrounded it.[6] As one moved away from the core areas of a state, the power of the ruler diminished perceptibly and that of the regional lords became increasingly evident. Regional administrators, whether they be members of the royal family, personal retainers of the sovereign, or local lords, used their positions to build up their own power bases and amass personal fortunes. In most instances, they ruled their provinces as autonomous and self-sufficient units and posed a constant threat to the rulers of Javanese and Burmese kingdoms – a threat that was often translated into plots or rebellions aimed at seizing the throne.

Regional administrators not only vied with the ruler in their attempts to build their own bases of power and wealth, they competed with other nobles and administrators for the loyalty of client-retainers and control over peasant producers. These lords were also locked in a ceaseless contest with their own retainers and subordinates as each strove to maximize the share of the col-

---

de Graaf amply illustrate. For more recent studies which attempt to relate these phenomena to broader political analyses, see William Koenig, "The Early Kòn-baung Polity, 1752-1819" (Ph.D. diss., University of London, 1978), chs. 6,7; or Victor Lieberman, "The Burmese Dynastic Pattern, circa 1590-1760" (Ph.D. diss., University of London, 1976); and Peter Carey, "Pangeran Dipanagara and Origins of the Java War, 1825-1830," in *Verhandelingen van het Koninklijk Instituut* (Leiden, forthcoming), ch. 2. For Indian examples, see the writings of Satish Chandra or Athar Ali on the Mughal court and nobility; for Africa, see Ivor Wilks, *Asante in the Nineteenth Century* (Cambridge, 1975), esp. 12; Max Gluckman, *Custom and Conflict in Africa* (Glencoe, Ill., 1959), pp. 39, 43, 45-6, *et passim*.

[6] For discussion of regional autonomy, see Moertono, *State and Statecraft*, pp. 88ff., 104-5, 107, 134; H. J. de Graaf, *De Regering van Sultan Agung, Vorst van Mararam, 1613-1645* (The Hague, 1958), pp. 118-21; Koenig, "Early Kòn-baung Polity," pp. 34-6, 41ff.; Lieberman, "Burmese Dynastic Pattern," pp. 36, 39-40, 45, 120ff., 227ff. For a superb study of this pattern in India, see Richard G. Fox, *Kin, Clan, Raja and Rule* (Berkeley, 1971). For African examples, see Gluckman, *Custom and Conflict*, pp. 34-5, 37-44; R. E. Bradbury, "The Kingdom of Benin," in *West African Kingdoms in the Nineteenth Century*, D. Forde and P. M. Kaberry, eds. (Oxford, 1967), pp. 5-6, 9, 27; Jan Vansina, "A Comparison of African Kingdoms," *Africa* 32 (1963): 329-30.

I

lected revenue that he retained as the tribute passed upward through a complex hierarchy of administrators and tax collectors.[7] The fact that administrators at all levels were given a cut of the taxes collected, rather than a regular salary, made this contest inevitable. Institutionalized corruption in the forms of underreporting and embezzlement was rampant in precolonial Southeast Asia polities. Within certain informally prescribed limits, these practices were essential to the functioning of the administrative system because they compensated for the inadequacy of the formal remuneration of state officials. The withholding of up to 10 percent of the taxes collected appears to have been widespread and accepted. At times, however, even in periods of strong dynastic control, the amount held back illegally reached as high as 40 percent of the revenue that passed through the hands of administrators at different levels.[8]

Another key weakness of precolonial polities in Burma and Java that made it possible for cultivators to develop defenses against excessive elite demands was the failure of the administrative system to penetrate to the village level. Although village headmen had to be approved by regional officials and, in times of dynastic strength, by ministers in the capital, the local leaders gained and maintained their positions primarily through local influence and support. The village headmen of Java and Burma, who were generally drawn from the regional gentry families of these societies, were the most secure and best informed persons who exercised political authority in the precolonial era. Their control over local affairs rested on the extent of their holdings, the number of laborers and artisans dependent on the use of their land and their patronage, the wisdom they demonstated in village councils, and their ability to defend the interests of their communities in dealings with supravillage officials and their agents. In contrast to the often short-lived careers of courtiers and tax farmers, the village gentry families frequently controlled local offices for generations and, in some cases, centuries. Village headmen and the local gentry from which they came them were pivotal intermediaries between the state and the mass of the peasantry. Without their cooperation, it would have been difficult, if not impossible, for transient tax farmers and even local men appointed to administrative posts to draw revenue and manpower from village communities on a regular basis.[9]

[7] De Graaf, *De Regering van Sultan Agung*, p. 119; Peter Carey, "Origins of the Java War," manuscript, pp. 8-11; Onghokham, "The Residency of Madiun Pryayi and Peasant in the Nineteenth Century" (Ph.D. diss., Yale University, 1975), pp. 44ff., 60-61, 84; W. A. J. van Davelaar, "Middenpersonen tusschen de districts-beambten en desahoofden op Java," *Tijdschrift voor Indische Taal, Land, en Volkenkunde* (hereinafter cited as *TGB*) 34 (1891): 365-72; Koenig, "Early Kòn-baung Polity," pp. 273ff., esp. pp. 295-96, 303-7; Kennon Breazeale, "Thai Provincial Minority Elites" (Paper read at the Seventh Conference of the International Historians of Asia, Bangkok, 1977), pp. 3-4, 11-12; S. N. Hasan, "Zamindars under the Mughals," in *Land Control and Social Structure in Indian History*, R. E. Frykenberg, ed. (Madison, Wisc., 1969), pp. 17-32.
[8] Koenig, "Early Kòn-baung Polity," pp. 245-46, 311-12; Daw Mya Sein, *Sir Charles Crosthwaite and the Administration of British Burma* (Rangoon, 1938), pp. 63-4, 67-8.
[9] Mya Sein, *Sir Charles Crosthwaite*, pp. 47, 67, 69, 72; J. S. Furnivall, "Notes on the History of Hanthawaddy," *JBRS* 4, no. 4 (1914): 209; Mya Kyan, "Village Administration in

Underlying the weak political integration of precolonial states in Java and Burma were low population densities, poor communications, and a low level of achievement in military organization and technology. In Burma and Java, as in most Asian and African kingdoms, control of manpower, and not of land, was the state's chief concern. Even in regions that were fairly densely populated, like central and east Java or the Dry Zone of Upper Burma, substantial amounts of unclaimed cultivable land were available, and large tracts of scantily populated forest wilderness beckoned to disgruntled cultivators. Except in riverine or coastal areas, movement of large military forces or bulk goods was ponderous and costly. Aside from cavalry regiments manned by the nobility or special service corps and small contingents of professional soldiers stationed in the capital, the armies of precolonial rulers were primarily made up of forcibly conscripted peasants who were poorly equipped and trained. These conditions greatly restricted the ruler's capacity to control regional lords, and made it virtually impossible for him to forcibly collect taxes or mobilize labor on a sustained basis.[10]

Thus, precolonial rulers were compelled to rely mainly upon adherence to state cults centering on the ruler's powers to protect and to grant fertility, on chains of patron-client clusters extending from the court to local notables, and on the cooperation of village leaders, rather than on military clout, to ensure that taxes were collected and order maintained. Though the selective use of force and, more critical, the potential to apply force were essential to political survival, effective rulers relied heavily on bribes, diplomacy, bluffs, and intrigue to control fractious nobles and contain social unrest. In fact, a ruler's repeated use of force for internal control was normally a sign that the ruling house was in decline.[11]

The combination of low population-to-land ratios, poor communications, weakly integrated administrative systems, and elite rivalries that characterized the contest states of precolonial Java and Burma provided numerous opportunities for peasants to defend themselves from excessive exactions by their overlords. Incessant struggles between elite factions consumed a good deal of time and material resources that might otherwise have been devoted to improved record keeping, better bureaucratic and military organization, and the

Upper Burma,'' *JBRS* 52 (1969): 68; Onghokham, ''Residency of Madiun Pryayi,'' pp. 63-68; Thomas Raffles, *The History of Java* (London, 1817), vol. 1, pp. 145, 284-86; John Beattie, *The Nvoro State* (Oxford, 1971), pp. 132ff.; Gluckman, *Custom and Conflict*, pp. 35-41, 51-52; Jacques Berque, *Egypt: Imperialism and Revolution* (New York, 1972), esp. pp. 51-57.

[10] For detailed discussions of transport and communication difficulties in central Java and the Javanese military system, see Pieter Louw and E. S. de Klerck, *De Java-Oorlog van 1825-1830* (The Hague-Batavia, 1894-1909), vol. 1, pp. 23-50, 203-8. For a discussion of the population of Java in the late eighteenth and early nineteenth centuries, see Bram Peper, *Grootte en Groei van Java's Inheemse Bevolking in de Negentiende Eeuw* (Amsterdam, 1967). For Burma, see James G. Scott [Shway Yoe], *The Burman: His Life and Notions* (New York, 1963), ch. 54; Henry Burney, ''On the Population of the Burman Empire,'' *Journal of the Royal Statistical Society of London* 4, no. 4 (1842): 335-47.

[11] For an incisive discussion of these patterns, see Merle Ricklefs, *Jogjakarta under Sultan Mangkubumi, 1749-1792* (Oxford, 1974), ch. 1.

establishment of firmer controls over the village population. Elite rivalries also forced uneasy monarchs to develop elaborate devices to prevent strong coalitions of hostile nobles from forming and to limit the opportunities for regional officials or appanage holders to build up independent power bases.[12] These devices included the fragmentation of appanage holdings granted to the members of the royal family or nobility; the periodic rotation of officials appointed to high-level posts;[13] marriage alliances with powerful noble families and the requirement that members of these families reside in the capital city; periodic journeys by regional lords to the court to offer homage to the ruler or, especially in India and Africa,[14] royal tours of the provinces of the realm; and the maintenance of extensive networks of royal spies and informants.[15]

Although these devices were essential to the maintenance of a ruler's position vis-à-vis elite groups at different levels, they diminished the control which he could exert over the peasant base of the society. Appanage holders spent little or no time in the areas allotted for their support. Their residence at court, which most preferred in any case because of the vastly superior social and cultural amenities and political excitement in the capital, meant that day-to-day administration was left in the hands of subordinates. Even officials who governed in their home districts knew little about village conditions and were dependent on poorly trained and self-serving subordinates and village notables for the actual administration of the peasant population under their control. Because the time officials spent in particular posts was often limited, it was rare for them to develop a sense of identity with or responsibility toward those whom they governed. In fact, the reverse was the case. Rotation in office, in the absence of a firm commitment to an accepted code of bureaucratic ethics, meant that most officeholders were out to get all the material advantages they could before their tenure of a particular post ended. Periodic trips to the capital exacerbated these tendencies by orienting the ruling classes to events at court rather than to the concerns of their subjects.[16]

[12] Max Weber has analyzed these control devices in general terms. See *Economy and Society,* vol. 3, pp. 1042–44. For Java, see Onghokham, "Residency of Madiun Pryayi," pp. 15, 35–36, 40–43, 61ff.; G. P. Rouffaer, "Vorstenlanden," *Encyclopedia van Nederlandsch-Indie* (The Hague, 1905), vol. 4, pp. 588–90, 624–25. For Burma, see Koenig, "Early Kòn-baung Polity," pp. 40, 249ff., 312–20; Lieberman, "Burmese Dynastic Pattern," pp. 88, 129ff. For African examples, see S. R. Karugire, *A History of the Kingdom of Nkore in Western Uganda to 1896* (Oxford, 1971), pp. 64ff.; Beattie, *Nyoro State,* pp. 137–39.

[13] In the more highly developed bureaucratic system found in China, officials were prohibited, at least in times of dynastic strength, from serving in their home districts. This was not the case in Java or Burma.

[14] Beattie, *Nyoro State,* pp. 138ff.; John F. Richards, ed., *Kingship and Authority in South Asia* (Madison, Wisc., 1978), pp. iii, v.

[15] Koenig, "Early Kòn-baung Polity," pp. 35, 40–41 *et passim;* Lieberman, "Burmese Dynastic Pattern," p. 124. The most graphic account of the use of spies and subterfuge in this sort of polity remains Vishakadatta's play, *The Signet Ring of Rakshasa.* See P. Lal, *Great Sanskrit Plays* (New York, 1957).

[16] Carey, "Origins of the Java War," pp. 6–10; J.L.V., "Bijdrage tot de kennis der residentie Madioen," *Tijdschrift voor Nederlandsch Indië* (hereafter cited as *TNI*) 17, no. 2 (1855): 2–3,

I

The staffing of the lower levels of the administrative hierarchy with a motley horde of transient tax farmers who had little commitment to the ruler, or to the political system per se, further reduced the possibility of effective control over the peasant producers. Because these functionaries, like the lords who appointed them, routinely underreported the taxes they collected in order to retain as much as possible for themselves, the revenue records of precolonial regimes reflected at best rough estimates of the population and productivity of a given region. As Soermasaid Moertono has observed with reference to the kingdom of Mataram in Java, court registers recorded only "the amount of tax that the ruler expected to draw from a territory given in appanage" rather than the actual resources of the area, which normally far exceeded those that were taxed.[17]

The sorry state of precolonial record keeping left many openings for concealment and evasion. For the cultivating classes, those openings exploited by the village headmen were the most critical. Like all of the administrators and tax collectors above them, the village headmen regularly underassessed the population and cultivated acreage from which they derived revenue payments and recruited manpower for services to the state. Because taxes were paid, though not always assessed, and labor recruited on a village basis, the efforts of the headmen to minimize payments to supravillage elite groups benefitted and were supported by all members of the community. Collusion between village notables and the state's revenue collectors and the employment of a wide range of time-tested evasion techniques were the most effective ways in which cultivators were able to defend themselves against excessive elite demands on a sustained basis. Beyond the inaccuracies that abounded in original tax inquest and census statistics, any new lands brought into production or increased yields on previously assessed lands often went unreported. Portions of harvested crops were buried or hidden away outside the village. A part of the village population would settle temporarily in a nearby forest in periods of military campaigns or during labor recruitment for public works or a monarch's indulgence in monumental construction. Villages were subdivided and records compiled in ways that were sure to bewilder even the most vigilant tax collector. Bribes were usually sufficient to win the silence, and often the cooperation, of revenue officials who ought to have exposed these irregularities and demanded the ruler's full due. If a ruler appointed special revenue supervisors or ordered surveys to revise revenue estimates, their effectiveness could usually be minimized by additional bribes and more elaborate measures for concealment.[18]

7-8; "De toestand van Bagelen in 1830," *TNI* 20, no. 2 (1858): 30; Koenig, "Early Kòn-baung Polity," esp. pp. 308-12; and Lieberman, p. 186.

[17] Moertono, *State and Statecraft*, pp. 139-40, 143-44. See also Onghokham, "Residency of Madiun Pryayi," pp. 95-96; James G. Scott and John P. Hardiman, *Gazetteer of Upper Burma and the Shan States* (Rangoon, 1900), vol. 1, pp. 413, 416-18; Koenig, "Early Kòn-baung Polity," pp. 95, 312, 315-16.

[18] Onghokham, "Residency of Madiun Pryayi," pp. 167-76, 199-200; Carey, "Origins of

Although local notables paid village taxes in lump sums and strove to maximize the resources retained by the peasants themselves, the rewards garnered by collusion and evasion were not equally distributed. Precolonial villages in Burma and Java were not, as has often been claimed, egalitarian havens of communal harmony and cooperation. Village populations were divided into several socioeconomic strata, and village affairs were dominated by a small minority of large landholding families which often headed hostile factions. In central Java, for example, power and status in the village sphere as late as the first decades of the nineteenth century were monopolized by landowning families called *sikeps* which usually claimed to be descended from the founding families of the village. Most of the remaining families in the village were attached as clients, with varying degrees of dependence, to one of the *sikep* households. The clients, or *numpangs,* worked the *sikeps'* fields for a customary share of the harvest yield, performed domestic and artisanal services, and in some cases actually lived in dwellings provided by their patrons.[19] Although the *sikeps* clearly derived greater advantages from the various devices by which the village community sought to reduce the exactions of supravillage elite groups, the *numpangs,* through their patron-client links to village notables, also benefitted, usually in proportion to their families' socioeconomic standing in the village. The great majority of cultivators in precolonial Asian and African societies relied primarily upon similar patron-client ties and on the guile of local leaders and their collusion with lower-level officials as their primary defenses against oppression.

In situations where the regular village defense mechanisms failed, the peasants were forced to resort to more extreme measures to protect their interests. Despite the fact that in the literature on protest there is an emphasis on riots and rebellion, these additional measures were actually more likely to involve passive withdrawal or a search for alternative sources of patron protection than they were to foster conflict with those responsible for the cultivators' discontent. Although the quality of the source materials relating to peasant groups in most of precolonial Asia and Africa makes it impossible to determine the incidence of different forms of agrarian protest with precision, violent upheavals growing out of the grievances of the cultivators themselves appear to have been rare relative to other forms of protest expression. A careful scrutiny of many of the rebellions which have been attributed to

the Java War," pp. 6, 8–9, 37–38, 40–42, 50; J.L.V., "Kennis der Madioen," pp. 5–6, 9; Mya Sein, *Sir Charles Crosthwaite,* pp. 40–41, 52, 65, 67–69; Scott and Hardiman, *Gazetteer of Upper Burma,* pp. 415–16.

[19] M. J. H. Kollman, "Bagelen onder het bestuur van Soerkarta en Djokjokarta," *TGB* 14 (1864): 362–64, 368. For greater detail and regional variations, see W. Bergsma, comp., *Eindresume ... de rechten van den inlander op de grond op Java en Madoera,* 3 vols. (Batavia, 1876, 1880, 1896). Insofar as I am aware, information of comparable quality on precolonial conditions in village Burma is not available.

peasant unrest or labelled as agrarian risings often leads to the conclusion that these conflicts were in fact interelite feuds or dynastic struggles in which peasant conscripts and peasant communities became unwillingly involved.[20] This conclusion arises not from the fact that these movements were led by men who were not from peasant origins, for, as Gil Carl Alroy and others have correctly argued, in sustained protest movements peasants have almost always borrowed their leaders from the rural gentry, the military, or urban-based elite groups.[21] It rests rather upon an examination of the issues that gave rise to the rebellions on which we have information and the goals of the dissidents in these movements. With important exceptions of risings in which the peasantry rallied to messianic figures or charismatic leaders struggling to overthrow inept or tyrannical rulers,[22] the origins and outcomes of these struggles had little or nothing to do with peasant concerns or the condition of the cultivating classes. The peasants themselves understood that they had little to gain and very often much to lose - including their homes, crops, livestock, and lives - in these elite squabbles. It is not surprising then that the peasants' usual response to civil disturbances was flight en masse from the affected areas and a refusal to return until the conflict had been abated.[23]

Rather than riot or rebellion, the admittedly scanty and largely elite-authored evidence we have for the precolonial era suggests that peasants preferred a wide variety of alternative modes of protest that minimized direct confrontations with those viewed as oppressors. The fact that we must interpret peasant responses indirectly, through sources provided either by the very elite groups to whom they were reacting or by alien European observers, is particularly troublesome in dealing with avoidance protest because such a filter often makes it difficult to distinguish clearly between the various forms of this sort of behavior and other modes of peasant adaptation. Peasants migrated or shifted patrons not only to protest elite excesses, but also to better their economic situations or to take up new occupations. There were numerous instances, however, when migrations, shifts to new patrons, or related activities were explicitly linked to peasant grievances. In most instances, it is elite reactions, rather than peasant proclamations - which were rare - that

---

[20] For examples, see Jean Chesneaux, *Contributions à l'histoire de la nation Vietnamienne* (Paris, 1955), pp. 91ff.; Gluckman, *Custom and Conflict*, pp. 39, 43, 45; and Jan Myrdal and Gun Kessel, *Angkor: An Essay on Art and Imperialism* (New York, 1970). For a discussion of the low incidence of peasant rebellion in precolonial Java, see Moertono, *State and Statecraft*, pp. 5, 75.

[21] Gil Carl Alroy, *The Involvement of Peasants in Internal Wars* (Princeton, 1966), esp. pp. 12, 18-20.

[22] See, for examples, Koenig, "Early Kòn-baung Polity," pp. 91-92; Gluckman, "Kingdom of the Zulu," pp. 43-44; Lê Thanh Khôi, *Le Viêtnam: histoire et civilisation* (Paris, 1955), pp. 296-310.

[23] Moertono, *State and Statecraft*, pp. 5-6; Gustaaf W. van Imhoff, "Reis van den Gouverneur-General van Imhoff in het Jaar 1746," *Bijdragen tot Taal-Land-, en Volkenkunde* (hereafter cited as *BKI*) 1, no. 3 (1853): 361-62, 409.

allow us to distinguish between avoidance protest and other forms of peasant response in the precolonial era. In court chronicles, legal codes, and royal decrees, instances of peasant migration, transfer of services to new lords, and flight to the refuge of temple estates or cult centers are identified as acts of protest designed to draw attention to elite misrule and to force reductions in tribute demands or the dismissal of overly rapacious officials from office. Evidence of a direct link between these peasant responses and the expression of peasant grievances and demands is essential to the identification of examples of the type of dissidence which I have labelled as avoidance protest. Groups or individuals resorted to acts of evasion, rather than to spontaneous outbursts of violence or organization for confrontation, as a means of expressing their discontent.

The peasants' preference for modes of protest other than open rebellion was in part shaped by their vertical orientation to men of power and influence in patron-client networks. This orientation, which existed at even the subvillage level and was paralleled by the patron-client ties which linked the members of other social groups like cult communities and merchant associations, meant that horizontal links between different peasant groups tended to be weak. Thus, though the distinctions between the ruling and cultivating classes were clearly demarcated and readily apparent in differing styles of dress, housing, behavior and, in Java, even different language forms employed at each level, there was very little sense of class consciousness or peasant identity in societies like Java and Burma that were organized along the lines of the contest state. Peasants responded as members of a particular community and especially as the clients of particular landlords, local officials, or royal appanage holders. If and when cultivators rose in rebellion, they normally did so in support of these patrons or, alternatively, as the devoted followers of a holyman-prophet. They rose up not to effect fundamental changes in a sociopolitical order, which they accepted as legitimate and divinely ordained, but to back a lord or faction against rivals, to express displeasure with the excessive demands of a particular lord or, in times of dynastic collapse, to influence the outcome of contests that would determine which family and factions of the nobility would control the throne. Their vertical organization and local orientation made it difficult to mobilize widespread peasant support, and rendered most peasant risings small and ephemeral affairs. The structure and organizational patterns associated with the contest state not only reduced the level of elite efficiency and control over the peasantry but, by blocking the emergence of a strong class identification on the part of the peasantry, they reduced the possibility of mobilizing and organizing peasant protest on a scale sufficient to make modes involving confrontation effective.

Very often the first act of protest employed by dissident peasants was one that was sanctioned both by longstanding custom and official approval. In both

Burma and Java, peasants who felt that their taxes were too high or that they were being mistreated by a local lord could petition a higher official or the monarch himself for redress of their grievances. In Java, disgruntled villagers – at times led by their headmen or, in other instances, in opposition to them – organized processions to the residence of the most powerful lord in the region, which in the vicinity of the capital meant the royal palace. The participants often concluded their march with a sit-in on the *alun-alun*, or great square, in view of the royal audience hall. They remained there until the ruler or one of his advisers heard their complaints and assured them that measures would be taken to reduce their burdens and punish the offending officials.[24] It was also possible for peasants to petition local officials for reduction in tax or corvée labor demands, and there were severe penalties for administrators who were found dismissing village headmen unjustly. The fragmentary evidence which we have suggests that when these petitions failed to produce results, dissident villagers turned to other, more radical means of resistance.[25] Given the fragmentation of power and responsibility in the precolonial Burman and Javanese state systems and the great potential for official evasion, one suspects that petitions and protest processions rarely brought effective redress to aggrieved cultivators. But the very existence of these legal or quasi-legal channels of protest must have given some pause to even the most tyrannical officials.

Perhaps the most common and least risky mode of peasant defense and protest in the precolonial era involved the cultivators' transfer of their allegiance and services from lords whose demands were felt to be exorbitant to other patrons from whom they hoped to receive better treatment. The reciprocal patron-client bonds which formed the organizational backbone of the village community extended in most precolonial African and Asian societies to all levels of the sociopolitical hierarchy.[26] Like that of a village notable, the power and status of a lord depended to a large degree on the number of his clients, who themselves sought to attract retainers of their own. Conversely, an individual's career and the well-being of his family – including their physical safety in societies where "soft" states offered little protection from violent assault – depended heavily on his ability to attach himself to a prosperous, powerful, and successful patron. In states where the demand for manpower exceeded the supply and where there was a constant rivalry be-

[24] Moertono, *State and Statecraft*, pp. 76–77; H. J. de Graaf, *Geschiedenis van Indonesie* (The Hague, 1949), pp. 428–29. For Burma, see Scott and Hardiman, *Gazetteer of Upper Burma*, vol. 1, p. 432; Mya Sein, *Sir Charles Crosthwaite*, p. 67. For a form of protest similar to the sit-in on the *alun-alun*, see Howard Spodek, "On the Origins of Gandhi's Political Methodology: The Heritage of Kathiawad and Gujarat," *Journal of Asian Studies* 30, no. 2 (1971): 361–72.

[25] Carey, "Origins of the Java War," p. 10; "De toestand van Bagelen," p. 81; Rouffaer, "Vorstenlanden," p. 624; Raffles, *History of Java*, p. 284.

[26] Koenig, "Early Kòn-baung Polity," esp. 128–30; Moertono, *State and Statecraft*, pp. 104ff.; Akin Rabibhadana, *The Organization of Thai Society in the Early Bangkok Period* (Ithaca, N.Y., 1969), esp. pp. 82–89; Beattie, Nyoro State, pp. 132–33, 137, *et passim*.

tween nobles and officials at all levels, client-retainers enjoyed considerable bargaining power. Ambitious men, hoping to make their way up the chain of patron-client clusters and establish the position of their families for succeeding generations, were expected to transfer their loyalties away from patrons whose power was on the wane to those with more promising prospects for the future. Those making their way up the social hierarchy relied on their connections with powerful patrons to gain even higher and more lucrative administrative posts. If successful, they would also attract growing numbers of client-dependents and in some instances supplant the very men who had made their rise to power possible.[27]

A similar relationship existed between peasant clients and their patrons within the village and beyond. In Java, peasant tenants or laborers who felt that the share of the harvest demanded by their landlords was too great or that they were not effectively shielded from state demands for labor and produce, could exercise the right, sanctioned by the *adat*, or customary law, to transfer their services to another landowner. Tradition obliged them to give the landlord whose fields they were leaving a chicken and a basket of rice, after which they were free to attach themselves to another notable either within the same village or in another community. Instances were recorded in which a majority of the cultivators of the villages in an entire district exercised this option. There were also cases in which discontented cultivators returned to their original villages to work the lands of their former patrons when the demands of such landlords or those of the tax collector in that locality decreased.[28] The periodic visits of Javanese appanage holders and other officials to the court were apparently especially opportune times for disgruntled cultivators to attach themselves to new patrons. If the peasants who accompanied the lord felt that the demands – including the services they were expected to render during the period of residence at the court – made upon them by their present lords were too great, they could, through gossip and contacts with the retainers of other notables who were gathered in the capital, find new patrons who promised better terms of service.[29]

In Burma, the *myothugyis*, or township heads, also competed for peasants to reside in their villages and work their lands. In Lower Burma in particular, the low man-to-land ratio and the highly mobile nature of the peasant household forced the *myothugyis* to temper their revenue demands and foster the well-being of their peasant subjects or risk losing these to neighboring town-

[27] For a brilliant analysis of these patterns, see Lucien M. Hanks, "Merit and Power in Thai Social Order," *American Anthropologist* 64, no. 6 (1962): 1247–62.

[28] Carey, "Origins of the Java War," p. 19; Moertono, *State and Statecraft*, p. 76; Akin Rabibhadana, *Organization of Thai Society*, p. 87. For an African parallel, see Karugire, *History of Kingdom of Nkore*, pp. 105–6.

[29] Onghokham, "Residency of Madiun Pryayi," p. 44; Akin Rabibhadana, *Organization of Thai Society*, p. 181–82.

ships where taxes were lighter and the headmen's demands more reasonable.[30] Transfers of peasants also occurred, on a much larger scale, from the lands of one appanage holder or regional official to another. In some periods, peasants sold themselves as debt slaves to powerful ministers or rich merchants to escape the harsh conditions of service under a member of the nobility or the monarch himself. The loss of manpower from the royal domains was of special importance in Burmese history because such defections constituted one of the major causes of dynastic decline. In the more closely administered core areas of Burman kingdoms, there was a recurrent pattern of steadily increasing exactions as the needs of the royal household grew in proportion to the increase in the number of its retainers and servants and the spiralling costs of military campaigns required to hold the kingdom together. These demands resulted in a loss of manpower as peasants left the royal domains to enter the less rigorous service of princes, nobles, and powerful ministers. These defections forced even greater exactions from the population remaining on royal lands and thus further exacerbated the abuses that had led to client transfers from the ruler's domains.[31]

The intense competition between princely factions, regional lords, and members of the local gentry for client-retainers rendered the possibility of transferring one's loyalty and services an especially effective deterrent to excessive elite demands. In states where rulers went to war in part for the captives they hoped to carry home from defeated kingdoms and where local regional lords were not above resorting to open warfare with rivals over contested villages and retainers,[32] the peasants' chances of finding a new patron who offered, at least in the short term, better conditions of service were good. The possibility that absconding peasants would be returned because of the demand of their original lord was remote, unless that lord was willing to buy them back or risk an armed encounter with the new patron. The monarch found it difficult enough to keep his own cultivators in place; he had little inclination – and less means – to control population transfers between the territories allotted to his relatives or the nobility.

Shifting to a new patron was both an effective peasant defense and a potent means of protest, for the act of severing a patron-client link in itself drew

[30] Mya Sein, *Sir Charles Crosthwaite*, p. 67; Charles Crosthwaite, *The Pacification of Burma* (London, 1912), pp. 5-6.

[31] Lieberman, "Burmese Dynastic Pattern," pp. 45, 165, 189, 190, 196ff., 205-6, 221-22. For other areas, see Beattie, *Nyoro State*, p. 137; Irfan Habib, *The Agrarian System of Mughal India* (Bombay, 1963), pp. 116-17, 334ff.; Vansina, "Comparison of African Kingdoms," p. 326.

[32] Koenig, "Early Kòn-baung Polity," pp. 304-5, 321-22; Lieberman, "Burmese Dynastic Pattern," 102; Rouffaer, "Vorstenlanden," p. 624; Carey, "Origins of the Java War," pp. 9-10; Breazeale, "Thai Provincial Minority Elites," pp. 3-4; and Vansina, "Comparison of African Kingdoms," p. 326.

attention to the shortcomings or misdeeds which the defecting cultivators claimed had spurred their search for a new patron. It also represented a blow to the status and esteem and a real reduction in the power of the original lord.

A form of peasant defense and protest that was closely related to the act of changing patrons, but a good deal more disruptive of the peasants' lives and potentially more risky, was flight. Flight was, of course, one of a cultivator's principal means of defending himself and his family from the ravages of war, the depredations of marauding bandits, starvation in times of drought, and the other malevolent forces which periodically intensified his already difficult struggle to survive.[33] Although there is no direct evidence relating to the process by which peasants decided to migrate, it is reasonable to infer that they opted for flight and the search for new lands to settle only in situations where transfer to the service of other lords either was not possible or appeared unlikely to redress their grievances. It was not a step that was taken lightly, but an act that arose out of a "really desperate situation."[34] This was particularly true in areas of wet-rice cultivation where peasant households had a large investment extending over many generations in painstakingly cleared and cultivated paddy fields and intricate irrigation works. In these areas, peasant dwellings were substantial and in many cultures villagers developed deep attachments to village shrines and deities and the gravesites of their ancestors.

Although the populations of areas cultivated on a dry crop or shifting basis appear to have been considerably more mobile and thus more prone to migrate if the demands of their overlords became too great,[35] numerous examples of mass protest migrations on the part of wet-rice agriculturists can be found in the sources relating to Southeast Asia, India, and other areas. Peasant families and whole villages fled to escape corvée labor or military conscription. They migrated to avoid and to protest against what they viewed as harsh treatment or unreasonable exactions by the nobles or officials who were given jurisdiction over them.[36] In some cases, they fled from the domains of one ruler into a rival kingdom.[37] More commonly, they migrated into sparsely settled frontier

[33] M. L. van Deventer, *Geschiedenis der Nederlanders op Java* (Haarlem, 1886–1887), vol. 1, pp. 127, 158, 230, 255, 301, 313; Elizabeth Hopkins, "The Nyabingi Cult of Southwest Uganda," in *Protest and Power*, Rotberg and Mazrui, eds., p. 283.

[34] Moertono, *State and Statecraft*, p. 76.

[35] Crosthwaite, *Pacification of Bruma*, pp. 5–7; Gustaaf W. van Imhoff, "Reis van den Gouverneur-General Gustaaf Willem Baron van Imhoff in en door je Jakatrasche Bovenlanden in 1744," *BKI* 7 (1863): 234, 237, 244, 247. For another social pattern which also provided a high degree of mobility and potential for avoidance migration, see Alexander Woodside's discussion of the boat people of Cochin China in *Vietnam and the Chinese Model* (Cambridge, Mass., 1971), p. 141.

[36] For examples, see Moertono, *State and Statecraft*, pp. 75–76, 145ff.; Raffles, *History of Java*, vol. 1, p. 273; Carey, "Origins of the Java War," pp. 11, 42–43; Koenig, "Early Kòn-baung Polity," pp. 88–92, 130, 144.

[37] van Deventer, *Geschiedenis der Nederlanders*, vol. 1, pp. 155, 199; Kollman, "Bagelen onder het Bestuur," p. 354; Lieberman, "Burmese Dynastic Pattern," p. 45; Gluckman, "Kingdom of the Zulus," p. 42.

areas that bordered on or, in cases like Java, were interspersed with the densely populated heartlands of precolonial kingdoms. In Burma, peasants moved into the hills and forests surrounding the Dry Zone or travelled south into the vast wilderness of the Irrawaddy delta where they struggled to found new settlements in defiance of wild animals, disease, floods, and hostile non-Burman inhabitants. In Java, disgruntled peasants found refuge in the forest and hill terrain that fringed the volcanic peaks of the heavily populated eastern and central portions of the island. In some societies, peasant migrants gathered in fortified settlements and openly defied the leaders whose authority they had rejected.[38]

In times of scarcity or man-made hardship, large numbers of villagers simply took to the roads that linked the major towns in precolonial kingdoms. Some became porters on the routes between the capital and other centers where merchants and nobles were concentrated. Others joined wandering theatrical troops or settled in the towns as servants of courtiers or rich merchants - though the later option appears to have been less common in Southeast Asia or Africa than in more highly urbanized European kingdoms in the late Middle Ages. More adventurous peasant migrants joined bands of vagabonds or bandit gangs - a phenomenon discussed in detail below.[39]

Although the sacrifices and risks for uprooted peasants were considerable, flight was a potent means of defense and protest. Military service could be avoided and tax and corvée burdens evaded - though usually only until the state's agents also moved into areas newly settled by disaffected cultivators. Some peasant migrants gained a chance to take up other, and at times more rewarding, occupations. The importance of the threat of peasant protest migration as a check on official abuses is reflected in the numerous royal edicts in which state officials are warned to look to the welfare of their subjects or the latter would flee and their lands revert to wilderness. Lords from whose domains there were large-scale migrations not only suffered the loss of the manpower upon which they depended to meet revenue quotas and provide for their own sustenance; they also faced the danger of being accused by rival officials or the monarch's ministers of misrule and incompetence. In Thailand, the flight of large numbers of peasants was considered a key indicator of an administrator's incapacity and often led to demotion or dismissal from

[38] B. Schrieke, *Indonesian Sociological Studies* (The Hague, 1957), vol. 2, pp. 300-301; Moertono, *State and Statecraft*, pp. 5-6, 75; Onghokham, "Residency of Madiun Pryayi," pp. 154, 175, 188, 224: Lieberman, "Burmese Dynastic Pattern," pp. 45, 52; Akin Rabibhadana, *Organization of Thai Society*, pp. 73, 87-88; Robert Tignor, *The Colonial Transformation of Kenya* (Princeton, 1976), p. 66. For the fortress-defiance pattern, see I. N. Kamambo, "Mbiru, Popular Protest in Colonial Tanzania, 1944-47," in *War and Society in Africa*, B. A. Ogot, ed. (London, 1972), p. 242.

[39] Carey, "Origins of the Java War," pp. 14-15; Louw and de Klerck, *Java-Oorlog*, vol. 1, pp. 25-26; Th. Pigeaud, *Javaanse Volksvertoningen* (Batavia, 1938), pp. 35-36; Koenig, "Early Kòn-baung Polity," p. 90; Lieberman, "Burmese Dynastic Pattern," p. 45; Chesneaux, *Contributions à l'histoires*, p. 40; Berque, *Egypt: Imperialism and Revolution*, p. 130.

I

royal service. In Burma in the reign of King Tha-lun, officials considered responsible for peasant migration were liable to be executed.[40] The flight of the peasantry came to be seen in most African and Asian cultures as a sign of dynastic weakness and socioeconomic decline. Cruel and incompetent rulers were abandoned by their subjects and millenarian prophecies spoke of eras of chaos and confusion in which hordes of villagers wandered aimlessly on the roads.[41]

Cult movements and entry into monastic orders or religious schools represented major variants of another major form of peasant protest that involved transfer to a new patron-protector and often travel to distant regions. Though many peasants became the devotees of mystics and holymen for religious reasons that had nothing to do with social protest, and though numerous cult movements stressed spiritual enrichment rather than changes in the terrestrial realm, religious institutions and leaders also provided important outlets for peasant dissidence in the precolonial era. In mainland Southeast Asia, the Buddhist Sangha and extensive monastic estates served as places of refuge for disgraced ministers, thwarted princely claimants to the throne, and overburdened peasants alike. Evidence relating to Burman dynasties separated by several centuries indicates that the large-scale migration of peasants onto monastic lands and the entry of young men into the Buddhist monkhood to escape taxes, corvée labor, or military conscription posed major problems for the rulers and nobles whose fields they abandoned and for the recruiters who consequently failed to meet their manpower quotas. Some rulers, like the seventeenth-century Taung-ngu monarch, Tha-lun, issued edicts forbidding marriages with pagoda slaves and prohibiting young men from entering the Sangha to escape taxes and labor services. From the time of the Pagan Dynasty (1044–1287) to the nineteenth century, the drain of manpower from state to monastic lands was a major factor in the decline of successive Burman dynasties. Thus, disgruntled peasants, protesting the increasing demands of princes and nobles or seeking improved terms of servitude on monastic estates, played a major political role in precolonial Burma.[42]

In Java, where there was no institutionalized religious establishment in the

[40] Than Tun, "Administration under King Thalun (1629-48)," *JBRS* 51, no. 2 (1968): 177–80; Lieberman, "Burmese Dynastic Pattern," p. 120; Akin Rabibhadana, *Organization of Thai Society,* pp. 73–74; Onghokham, "Residency of Madiun Pryayi," p. 37.

[41] Pe Maung Tin and G. H. Luce, *The Glass Palace Chronicle of the Kings* of Burma (Oxford, 1923), p. 177; J. A. B. Wiselius, "Djaja Baja, zijn leven en profetieën," *BKI* 7 (1872): 185.

[42] Than Tun, "Administration under King Thalun," pp. 181, 186-87; Lieberman, "Burmese Dynastic Pattern," pp. 45, 161, 203-4, 217; Michael Aung Thwin, "Kingship, the *Sangha* and Society in Pagan," in *Explorations in Early Southeast Asian History: Origins of Statecraft,* K. Hall and J. Whitmore, eds. (Ann Arbor, Mich., 1976), pp. 205–56; Akin Rabibhadana, *Organization of Thai Society,* p. 87. Victor Lieberman argues in a recent article that Aung Thwin has overestimated the importance of this pattern in the post-Pagan period. See "The Political Significance of Religious Wealth in Burmese History: Some Further Thoughts," *Journal of Asian Studies* 39, no. 4 (1980): 753–69.

I

Islamic period comparable to the Sangha in mainland Southeast Asia, defections to religious sanctuaries proved less of a threat to the manpower reserves of the ruling classes. In both the Hindu-Buddhist and Muslim periods, however, there were religious schools and shrines which Javanese rulers endowed with a village or villages for their support. These centers of learning and worship, as well as the gravesites of renowned holymen and rulers that were often the foci of pilgrimages and popular veneration, were declared *perdikan* villages. This status, which was often retained for many generations and was usually honored by the Dutch colonizers, freed the villagers from regular tax and corvée obligations in return for their support of religious teachers or upkeep of graves and shrines. Although little has been written about conditions within these villages in the precolonial era, Dutch writers reported that *perdikan* villages were among the most prosperous in central Java in the early nineteenth century and that the sons of poor peasants were included among the students and devotees of Muslim teachers and holymen.[43] It is impossible to know the degree to which *perdikan* villages served as places of refuge for dissident cultivators in the precolonial period. It is not unreasonable to surmise, however, that *perdikan* centers may have performed a role in Javanese society analogous to that which Louis Dumont has assigned to renunciation in Indian society.[44] By attracting the more aware and articulate individuals, and by providing for them meaningful career alternatives and outlets for expression, these centers may have served as important antidotes to the build-up of discontent among both the peasants and the ruling social strata. In this way they may have greatly reduced movements of protest arising out of the tensions and constrictions inherent in the highly stratified Javanese sociocultural order.

In both Java and Burma, cult movements that coalesced around mystics, holymen, and religious seers also provided important outlets for peasant protest expression. The size and character of these movements and the nature of their leaders varied widely, but a number of general patterns can be discerned. Most leaders claimed, and their followers believed, that they possessed magical powers which usually included protective and healing abilities. Many propagated ideologies built around divine revelations or millenarian prophecies that sometimes posed direct challenges to the legitimacy of reigning dynasties. The majority of the adherents to these movements were illiterate peasants who were normally required to undergo rather elaborate rituals of initiation, provide material support for the holyman-leader, and swear oaths of

---

[43] F. Fokkens, "Vrije Desa's op Java en Madoera," *TGB* 31 (1886): 477-517; J.L.V., "Kennis der Madioen," pp. 10-11; Onghokham, "Residency of Madiun Pryayi," p. 46. For a somewhat different view of *perdikan* conditions late in the nineteenth century, see K. W. van Gorkom, "Over het desabestuur op Java," *Indische Gids* (hereafter cited as *IG*) 27, no. 2 (1905): 1028-29.

[44] Louis Dumont, *Homo Hierarchius* (London, 1970), pp. 230-33.

unswerving allegiance to the leader and the cult rules. In some movements ecstatic dancing, mesmerism, and drugs provided important sources of release for discontented peasants. In times of political strife and social breakdown, the number of these cults proliferated and the size of their followings increased dramatically. Some movements became openly hostile to local officials or the reigning monarch and ended in bloody but futile outbursts of violence. Most, however, stressed passive withdrawal and avoidance of contacts with state officials or nonbelievers. In some instances, local officials and even kings gave special honors and positions of authority to cult leaders in order to win their cooperation and support. The communities that formed around the hadjis (Muslims who had made the pilgrimage to Mecca) and *kyais* (Muslim religious teachers) in Java or the *sayas* (necromancers) and *gaing* (sect) leaders in Burma provided temporal relief for dissident peasants. The eschatological revelations of these cult leaders promised eternal salvation in the age of bliss that was to come.[45]

Burmese and Javanese theatrical entertainments also provided a form of protest that paralleled cult formation in its mystical and magical orientation and in its attempt to create, in a very different fashion, fantasy worlds in which the peasantry could find release from their afflictions. As Moertono has observed, the *wayang kulit* (puppet shadow plays) and *wayang wong* (plays staged by actors) were "weathervane[s] of public opinion" in Javanese society. The able *dalang* (puppeteer) cleverly wove commentary on current conditions and political satire into his dramatic narration of the great Indian epics that the Javanese have so brilliantly employed in their plastic arts and theatrical entertainments. The *dalang*, who, like the clowns in the *garabeg* (court festival) processions, was considered immune from punishment, was able to give voice to peasant complaints and to transmit them from one region to another. In Burma, as in Java, peasant grievances and frustrations also found expression in folk songs and popular stories that often criticized elite failings and excesses and contained thinly veiled ridicule of prominent political figures.[46]

Another form of peasant protest that involved both flight and attachment to a new leader was banditry. Given the paucity of reliable sources on bandit organization and aims in precolonial Java and Burma, it is difficult to determine whether, and to what degree, brigandage was a genuine vehicle of

---

[45] On the traditions of cult and eschatological protest in Java and Burma respectively, see Michael Adas, *Prophets of Rebellion: Millenarian Protest against the European Colonial Order* (Chapel Hill, N.C., 1979), pp. 97-99, 101-2.

[46] Moertono, *State and Statecraft*, pp. 77-79; Margaret J. Kartoni, "Performance, Music and Meaning of Réyog Ponorogo," *Indonesia* 22 (1976): 114-15; Benedict R. O'G. Anderson, *Mythology and the Tolerance of the Javanese* (Ithaca, N.Y., 1965), p. 28; Maung Htin Aung, *Burmese Law Tales* (London, 1962), esp. pp. 68-71, 94-95, 103-4, 120-21, 146-47; *idem, Epistles Written on the Eve of the Anglo-Burmese War* (The Hague, 1968), p. 27; *idem, Burmese Drama* (Oxford, 1937), pp. 19-20, 50-51, 74, 77, 86-87, 107-8.

popular protest or was simply an organized form of criminal behavior. This dearth of information compounds the already considerable degree of ambiguity and the problems of interpretation identified by investigators studying bandit groups in Europe or China where relevant evidence is far more abundant. The extent, for example, to which the images projected in folk legends about the heroic deeds of the Javanese *rampoks* (bandits) - like Ken Angrok, who went on to found the Majapahit dynasty - or the *Bohs* of Burma correspond to the actual behavior of these men is impossible to determine. Information compiled in police reports in the colonial period is helpful, but it is heavily biased and rarely focused on questions relating to group composition and motivation that need to be answered in order to determine whether or not a particular gang or individual was truly an exponent of popular protest - a "social bandit" in Eric Hobsbawm's usage.[47]

The sources we do possess on banditry in precolonial Java and Burma indicate that it was widespread and that in certain periods, particularly those of civil conflict or dynastic decline, brigand gangs played important political roles. Banditry was popularly regarded as a regular occupation - however disreputable - in both of these societies. Bandit leaders were stereotyped as men of great physical courage, as evidenced by the attributes of the *jago* (literally, fighting cock) personality usually associated with brigands in Javanese society. Some bandit gangs were large enough to form their own communities which often controlled the villages in surrounding areas. Bandit leaders assumed official-sounding titles, like that of *Boh* or lieutenant–colonel commonly adopted by brigand chiefs in Burma, and they staked out territorial claims and divided their zones of operation among their subordinates in the manner of a feudal lord. Though many bandits were professional criminals, some of whom inherited their way of life from their fathers as one would a trade, others became brigands to escape the hardships of peasant life. The numbers of the latter swelled in periods of political strife when many agriculturists' households found mere survival difficult. In Java and Burma, as in China and Vietnam, the growth of banditry beyond its normal endemic proportions was one of the key signs of dynastic decline. Peasant refugees from drought, famine, and excessive taxation often joined established bandit gangs. In these they became members of new patron-client hierarchies extending downward from the bandit chief and his inner circle of followers.[48]

---

[47] For the original formulation of this concept, see Eric Hobsbawm, *Primitive Rebels* (New York, 1959), ch. 2. For a later elaboration, see *idem, Bandits* (New York, 1969), and the incisive critique by Anton Blok, "The Peasant and the Brigand: Social Banditry Reconsidered," *Comparative Studies in Society and History* 14 (1972): 494-503.

[48] On banditry in precolonial Java and Burma, see Moertono, *State and Statecraft*, pp. 85-86, 185; Onghokham, "Residency of Madiun Pryayi," pp. 16-17, 65-69, 86; de Graaf, *Geschiedenis von Indonesië*, pp. 102, 205; Lieberman, "Burmese Dynastic Pattern," pp. 223-28; Koenig, "Kon-baung Polity," pp. 15, 88-90, 132, 166; Crosthwaite, *Pacification of Burma*, pp. 6-7; Mya Sein, *Administration of Burma*, p. 88; Scott and Hardiman, *Gazetteer of Upper*

With the few exceptions of the runaway slaves or peasants who took up banditry and eventually emerged as major political figures or popular heros in the Robin Hood tradition,[49] it is not possible to follow the careers of peasants who became bandits, and therefore no determination can be made as to whether or not they acted to avenge the wrongs they had suffered or to assist peasant communities in their struggles with the state. The initial flight, however, and the decision to join brigand gangs were acts of protest. It is important to note that these were responses oriented to evasion or avoidance of the sources of their suffering rather than confrontation with them. Though some bandits may have struck back at the tax collectors or landlords who were responsible for their decisions to become criminals, most appear to have been indiscriminate in their choices of targets. Merchants, who usually had few links to village communities in the precolonial era, were favorite targets, but the peasants themselves were often the prey. Rather than challenging the state and its agents, brigands very often cooperated with local officials or were persuaded to assume quasi-administrative roles that their fame and influence in a particular locality well suited them to fill. In Java, successful bandit leaders rose to high rank, and the greatest of all founded a dynasty. In Burma, brigand gangs played important roles in succession struggles and in resistance campaigns against foreign invaders. Thus, though banditry was very often a career chosen by local bullies and ne'er-do-wells and constituted a source of peasant oppression, it was also a means through which peasants could escape intolerable elite demands and, if they were competent and fortunate, rise to positions of wealth and influence.

In addition to banditry, other, less well-organized activities that were also considered crimes by those in power provided more sporadic and transitory ways in which peasants could react to excessive demands. The burning of standing crops or, in Java, of the toll stations that made travel in the interior so costly and unpleasant was a mode of peasant reprisal for which we have good documentation from the early colonial period. It is probable that peasants had also resorted to these measures in much earlier time periods. In periods of extreme political and social dislocation, rebellious villagers were known to join the burning and pillage of the residences of the nobility and, on at least one occasion in Burma, the royal palace itself.[50] Excepting hit-and-run arson incidents, these acts were likely to lead to direct confrontations with those whom the peasants saw as their oppressors, rather than to the evasion which I have argued was the preferred orientation of peasant dissidence in the pre-

---

Burma, vol. 1, p. 512. For parallels in other areas, see Lê Thanh Khôi, *Le Viêtnam,* pp. 259, 261-62; Berque, *Egypt: Imperialism and Revolution,* pp. 130ff.; Wolfgang Franke, *A Century of Chinese Revolution 1851-1949* (New York, 1971), esp. pp. 6-12.

[49] Van Deventer, *Geschiedenis der Nederlanders,* vol. 2, pp. 6-8; E. Sarkisyanz, *Buddhist Backgrounds of the Burmese Revolution* (The Hague, 1965), p. 70.

[50] Koenig, "Early Kòn-baung Polity," pp. 90-91.

I

colonial era. They indicate the danger of overstating the case for avoidance protest. Although village riots and peasant risings were usually localized and short-lived affairs, they did occur. When linked to the campaigns of ambitious and able nobles or princes seeking to carve out their own kingdoms or usurp power in existing ones, peasant rebellions could and did have considerable political impact. Nonetheless, the paucity of references in the precolonial sources to jacqueries or peasant riots, and the availability of a wide range of defense techniques and less hazardous modes of resistance stressing evasion rather than confrontation, suggest that peasants resorted to violent resistance only out of sheer desperation in situations where severe dislocations undermined the effectiveness of village defenses and rendered avoidance protest an insufficient response to excessive elite demands.

The coming of colonial rule to Java and Burma did not bring a sudden end to village defense mechanisms and peasant protest oriented to avoidance. Collusion and concealment, flight, banditry, and sectarian withdrawal persisted as modes of peasant resistance and protest throughout the colonial period and, in many cases, into the era of independence. In Burma, for example, bandit groups spearheaded postconquest resistance to the advance of British colonial control throughout the nineteenth century. Large bandit gangs continued to operate, in some regions with impunity, until well into the twentieth century. Guerilla resistance by dacoit bands proved the most difficult aspect of the agrarian rebellions of the 1930s for the British to suppress. Large-scale bandit activities and, in coastal regions, pirate raids were reported in Java in areas like Banten throughout the nineteenth century, and bandit leaders assumed lofty titles and set up petty chiefdoms as late as the 1940s.[51] In colonial Burma, peasants seeking to escape obligations to moneylenders, or the chance to work their own holdings free from the control of large landowners, migrated by the hundreds of thousands into the fertile but undeveloped expanses of the Irrawaddy delta where the booming rice-export economy was centered. In Java, peasants migrated from areas controlled directly by the Dutch to those that remained under Javanese rule or vice versa, depending on where tax demands were lower. They also fled to escape Dutch census inquests, which they rightly suspected were linked to Dutch efforts to increase tax revenues and corvée labor quotas.[52]

---

[51] Crosthwaite, *Pacification of Burma*, pp. 14, 17, 23, 27, 31ff.; Grattan Geary, *Burma after the Conquest* (London, 1886), pp. 46-47, 71, 232, 276, 292-93; Government of Burma, *Report[s] on the Police Administration in Burma* (Rangoon, 1888—1913), esp. those for 1888, 1894, 1902, 1909, 1910, 1912, 1913; Sartono Kartodirdjo, *The Peasants' Revolt of Banten in 1888* (The Hague, 1966), esp. pp. 24, 110-16; "Binnenlandsche onlusten op Java," *TNI* (1861): 288-300; D. H. Meijer, "Over het bendwezen op Java," *Indonesië* 3 (1949-50): 178-84.

[52] Michael Adas, *The Burma Delta: Economic Development and Social Change on an Asian Rice Frontier, 1852-1941* (Madison, Wisc., 1974), ch. 2, 3, 6; J.L.V., "Kennis der Madioen," p. 6; Onghokham, "Residency of Madiun Pryayi," pp. 194, 215-18, 222; van Imhoff, "Reis

In both societies, there was a great proliferation of sectarian movements and local cults. Many of these movements stressed withdrawal from rather than challenges to the colonial system, but often they ended in police repression or bloody clashes with the colonial authorities.[53] Particularly in the early decades of colonial control, peasants also relied on evasion techniques and on collusion between village leaders and local officials to buffer European demands for cash revenue and produce.[54] The persistence of these modes of defense and protest underscores the need for caution against drawing too sharp a distinction between the precolonial and colonial periods. European conquest in both Java and Burma was gradual and advanced by stages spread over nearly two centuries in the former and several decades in the latter area. The extension of effective control over local areas and the village populace came only decades after formal annexations in most regions, and in some areas it scarcely came at all. As late as the 1880s, Sir Charles Crosthwaite could write that large areas in the vicinity of the colonial capital of Burma at Rangoon were controlled by bandit gangs or local leaders rather than by the British.[55]

In the contested transition period between the defeat of indigenous states and the advance, but not yet full establishment, of colonial authority, many of the conditions - poor political integration, weak military control, and low population-to-land ratios - that had made avoidance protest possible still persisted. As a result, underreporting, flight, and brigandage remained viable and often the preferred modes of protest for peasant dissidents in this period. However, as precolonial contest states were gradually transformed into highly centralized bureaucracies which increasingly impinged on local and village affairs, the usual peasant defense mechanisms were greatly reduced in effectiveness or rendered completely impotent. Fundamental transformations of the political economies of Burma and Java and major demographic and social changes in these and other colonies also altered the conditions that had been essential to peasant reliance on avoidance protest. Though some forms remained viable, particularly in inaccessible frontier areas,[56] for the great majority of colonized peoples, stratagems of flight, banditry, and sectarian withdrawal were no longer effective responses to excessive elite demands. In these

van 1774," p. 230. For African parallels, see Hopkins, "Nyabingi Cult," and J. M. Lonsdale, "Political Associations in Western Kenya," in *Protest and Power*, Rotberg and Mazrui, eds., pp. 283 and 592, respectively.

[53] For examples, see Adas, *Prophets of Rebellion*, esp. ch. 5.

[54] Adelante, "De ontwikkeling van de inlandsche hoofden op Java," *IG* 14 (1892): 683-84; Government of Burma, *Report on the Settlement Operations in the Bassein and Thongwa Districts, 1888-9* (Rangoon, 1890), p. 23. For Africa, see Isaacman, *Tradition of Resistance in Mozambique*, pp. 103-5.

[55] Crosthwaite, *Pacification of Burma*, p. 23.

[56] For examples, see Allen Isaacman, "Social Banditry in Zimbabwe (Rhodesia) and Mozambique, 1894-1907: An Expression of Early Peasant Protest, *Journal of Southern African Studies* 4, no. 1 (1977): 1-30; David Sturtevant, *Popular Uprisings in the Philippines 1840-1940* (Ithaca, N.Y., 1976), pp. 94-95, 127ff.

circumstances, peasant unrest, which rose sharply in the colonial period in response to the profound dislocations that accompanied far-reaching political and socioeconomic change, was increasingly channelled into collective protest expression that involved confrontations, and often violent clashes, with the European colonizers and their allies.

As the limited control exercised by indigenous lords over the peasant population gave way to colonial bureaucracies which penetrated to the village level, collusion and evasion, which had formed the first line of defense for the precolonial peasant community, were eliminated or took on new forms that served the interests of village leaders and large landholders and not those of the community as a whole.[57] In many areas, peasant settlements were reorganized in ways which were often arbitrary. In all cases, they were gradually integrated into a bureaucratic hierarchy that was geared primarily to the efficient collection of revenue and the mobilization of labor, the maintenance of law and order, and the promotion of commercial expansion. Though the colonizers' priorities varied somewhat by region and time period, far less effort was expended on community development and peasant welfare than on tax collection or keeping the peace. Village leaders, even though they were still chosen by the peasants themselves in some areas, were transformed into agents of the state. The frequency with which village headmen were the targets of peasant risings in the colonial period indicates the degree to which they became alienated from the village population as a whole and to which they came to be perceived, usually quite justifiably, as tools of the European colonizers.

Costly and time-consuming cadastral surveys, special training for revenue assessors, more sophisticated methods of record keeping, and more effective administrative surveillance greatly reduced opportunities for tax evasion or bribery of revenue officials. Even though colonial officials argued that they took a smaller share of the cultivators' harvest than had the indigeneous rulers who preceded them, the reality was often very different. The Europeans had far more accurate assessments of what and how much was actually produced than did the precolonial lords, and the Europeans also had the capacity actually to collect a far larger proportion of what they claimed as their due. Precolonial rulers, by contrast, demanded a greater share of the peasants'

---

[57] The following discussion of integration of peasant villages into the colonial systems of Java and Burma is based primarily upon J. S. Furnivall, *Colonial Policy and Practice* (New York, 1956), pp. 71-77, 241-43; Mya Sein, *Sir Charles Crosthwaite*, pp. 81-115, 157, 161, 165-75; D. H. Burger, ''Structuurveranderingen in de Javaanse samenleving,'' pt. 1, *Indonesië* 2 (1948-49): 381-94. For sample parallels in Subsaharan Africa, see Lonsdale, ''Political Associations in Western Kenya,'' and Rene Lemarchand, ''The Coup in Rwanda,'' in *Protest and Power*, Rotberg and Mazrui, eds., pp. 589-96 and 889-90, respectively. In some areas, the reach of the colonial bureaucracy was more limited until well into the twentieth century. See D. A. Washbrook, *The Emergence of Provincial Politics: The Madras Presidency, 1870-1920* (Cambridge, 1976).

production, but lacked the means of accurately determining the output on which their claims were based and of ensuring that the revenue that was collected actually reached the royal coffers.[58] Of course, embezzlement and bribery at the village level continued in the colonial era, but on a much reduced scale and for the benefit of individuals – mainly petty officials – and not peasant communities as a whole.

Not only were village defenses eroded in the colonial period, but peasant communities were exposed to new influences that often had adverse effects on the majority of their households. The uneven, but greatly intensified, involvement of the peasantry in many regions of Java and Burma in production for the market sharpened competition and exacerbated existing divisions within the village. Local notables became increasingly involved in financial enterprises that transcended or had little to do with production in their home villages. They were also capitivated by the more exciting social life that came with residence in the towns that grew up in response to bureaucratic and commercial expansion. These shifts and the growing reliance of the landed classes on the state for political backing dissolved or greatly distorted the patron-client bonds that had once been a key source of peasant protection.[59]

Merchants and moneylenders came to play major roles in all but the most remote village communities, and many peasant households were reduced to debt servitude to these outsiders, against whom they had little bargaining power. Though Samuel Popkin is correct in arguing that the peasants responded to these altered circumstances by establishing new links to landlords, merchants, and government officials,[60] the advantage in the new networks of dependence rested overwhelmingly with landed and mercantile groups. Landlords and moneylenders controlled the resources and market outlets essential to peasant production and economic well-being. They were also tied into financial networks and became members of political associations that gave them financial and legal support should disputes arise with their tenants or laborers. These associations exerted in many cases considerable influence over colonial administrators and policy decisions regarding agrarian affairs. The wealth of landed and mercantile groups and their connections with members of Western-educated, professional families – particularly lawyers and judges – made it possible for them to exploit fully the openings that the property-oriented courts and legal codes of the European colonizers provided for them. Thus, they were able to beat back the challenges of tenants or laborers and strengthen their hold over the cultivating classes.[61]

[58] Scott and Hardiman, *Gazetteer of Upper Burma*, vol. 1, p. 416; Government of Burma, *Report on Settlement Operations in the Mandalay District, 1892-93* (Rangoon, 1894), p. 24; Onghokham, "Residency of Madiun Pryayi," p. 416ff.

[59] For a comparative discussion of this process, see James C. Scott, "The Erosion of Patron-Client Bonds and Social Change in Southeast Asia," *Journal of Asian Studies* 33 (1972): 5-37.

[60] Samuel Popkin, *The Rational Peasant: The Political Economy of Rural Society in Vietnam* (Berkeley, 1979), pp. 61-66, 71-72, 76, 80-82, *et passim*.

[61] Adas, *Prophets of Rebellion*, esp. ch. 3.

Paralleling the decline of defense mechanisms centered on the village were a number of developments which greatly reduced the efficacy of various forms of avoidance protest. The more effective horizontal integration of the colonial bureaucracy rendered peasant transfers from one patron-official to another difficult, if not impossible. Greater uniformity of tax demands from one administrative division to another meant that there was little relief to be found in attaching oneself to another official because the new patron was obliged to follow the same rules and enforce the same policies as the one whose jurisdiction was abandoned.

The decrease in effectiveness of patron transfers also resulted from fundamental demographic changes that eliminated the option of protest through flight in many areas. For a number of reasons, some of which remain in dispute, European colonization brought first gradual and then increasingly rapid population growth in Java and Burma, as in many areas of Africa and Asia. As early as the first decades of the nineteenth century in some parts of central and east Java, and by the last decade of the same century on the Lower Burma rice frontier,[62] unclaimed cultivable lands were no longer available. The loss of frontier regions as areas of refuge was accelerated by a penchant on the part of European officials for closing off vast forest reserves from peasant occupancy and use. This policy not only further reduced the number of areas to which peasants might migrate, it deprived them of the firewood, materials for housing and tools, and supplementary foods that they had once gathered free in the forest. These measures increased peasant reliance for household necessities on market exchanges, which was usually one of the effects that their colonial overlords intended. The closing of forest regions often contributed to peasant protests which ended in violent clashes with forestry officials and the police or which led to movements that rejected the colonizers' restrictions and advocated the founding of settlements in the frontier wilderness.[63]

Unless peasant groups were located in border regions from which they could migrate into other colonial territories,[64] the possibility of using flight as an effective response to excessive tax or debt burdens was also limited by the greatly increased bureaucratic and military reach of the colonial state. Only those dissidents who fled into the most inaccessible, and therefore most inhospitable, areas were likely to find relief from oppression.

The greatly enhanced military power and communications technology of colonial regimes rendered banditry a much more hazardous, and usually less

[62] Carey, "Origins of the Java War," p. 15; Adas, *Burma Delta*, ch. 6.

[63] Harry Benda and Lance Castles, "The Samin Movement," *BKI* 125, no. 2 (1965): 222-23; and Government of Burma, *The Origin and Causes of the Burma Rebellion 1930-1932* (Rangoon, 1934), pp. 33-34.

[64] Isaacman, *Tradition of Resistance in Mozambique*, pp. 98ff., 101, 105-6; Asiwaju, "Migration as Revolt," *passim;* Lonsdale, "Political Associations in Western Kenya," in *Protest and Power*, Rotberg and Mazrui, eds., p. 592.

I

rewarding, outlet for peasant protest than it had been in the precolonial era. The activities of brigand gangs clashed sharply with the maintenance of law and order - or the passive acceptance of alien rule - that was so cherished by colonial administrators. European officials were less apt than their predecessors to look the other way when merchants or moneylenders were robbed, landlords' estate houses sacked, or villages raided. Considerable resources - including machine guns and, by the 1920s, airplanes - were mobilized to eradicate the bandit gangs that were endemic to most colonial areas. Given the bias of the colonial observers who have provided virtually all the information we possess on these campaigns and the Europeans' habit of indiscriminately labelling anyone who resisted colonial rule as a bandit or decoit, it is very difficult to determine the extent to which different bandit groups were the exponents of popular resistance or were merely common criminals. The widespread support provided for many brigand gangs by peasant communities in Burma, Java, and other colonial areas suggests, however, that like the social bandits studied by Hobsbawm, these men were viewed by large numbers of the colonized peasantry as allies and proponents of the precolonial order[65] Though some bandits enjoyed fairly long and lucrative careers and others even managed to work their way into the colonial administrative systems,[66] most peasants found brigandage a high risk, short-lived occupation that very often ended with imprisonment or violent death. Banditry continued, but the coming of the colonial order had vitiated its potential as a vehicle of avoidance protest and transformed it into a pursuit that was sure to force direct and often violent confrontations with the European overlords and their allies.

As a career as a full-fledged bandit became less attractive, it is likely that aggrieved peasants increasingly resorted instead to arson, vandalism, and other more spontaneous criminal acts to strike back at onerous landlords, moneylenders, and officials. Because the information on such forms of protest in the precolonial era is extremely limited, it is difficult to know if peasant reliance on them increased in the colonial period, but many incidents were reported and it is probable that there were many more than the official records indicate. Favorite targets were telegraph and railway lines, standing crops in the fields of large landowners, and the homes and offices of moneylenders, tax and toll collectors, and headmen who collaborated with the colonial authorities. In some cases, acts of vandalism, such as the uprooting of crops grown for export by forced labor or the severing of communication links between colonial administrative centers, were the signals for widespread agrarian rebellions. In these instances, the mode of protest shifted from avoidance

[65] See Government of Burma, *Reports on Police Administration:* Sartono, *Peasants' Revolt of Banten.* For other areas, see Isaacman, "Social Banditry," pp. 15-16, 19, 23; Sturtevant, *Popular Uprisings,* pp. 121ff., 135-36.

[66] Sartono, *Peasants' Revolt of Banten,* pp. 135-36; Berque, *Egypt: Imperialism and Revolution,* pp. 134ff.

to direct confrontation, and frequently to violent clashes with the colonial authorities.[67]

Like banditry, sectarian protest became much more likely to provoke forcible repression in the colonial era than it had in the precolonial period. Cult groups, whose leaders initially stressed withdrawal from rather than clashes with the colonial authorities, were very often eventually drawn into direct and bloody conflict with the police and local officials. In part, these clashes were inevitable in a situation where passive withdrawal meant, among other things, the nonpayment of taxes and a refusal to give deference to colonial administrators, behavior which the latter found an intolerable affront to their authority. Equally critical was the intense suspicion, often verging on paranoia, that colonial officials felt toward specific cult movements and the more devout followers of the indigenous religions in general. Religious teachers, holymen, or monks who gained large numbers of adherents among the peasantry quickly came under police surveillance. Administrators viewed even the most innocuous cult groups as seedbeds of sedition and as conspiracies to overthrow the colonial regime. Colonial investigators into civil disturbances tended to stress the roles of "fanatical" hadjis or "perfidious" monks in formenting every outburst of protest.[68] These attitudes and the persistent overreaction on the part of colonial administrators to cult movements were not completely without foundation. Before the emergence of nationalism in Burma and Java, the monks, holymen, and religious teachers were in fact the main catalysts of popular resistance to colonial rule. Their teachings implicitly, if not openly, posed direct challenges to the legitimacy of the rule of European colonizers, who were branded as infidels and aliens. Thus, even sectarian movements that stressed passive withdrawal and refuge in the community of believers presented major political challenges that similar groups did not in the precolonial era. Consequently, colonial officials believed that they had to curb or crush movements that the indigenous rulers and officials had been able either to ignore or to enlist in actual support for their efforts to control the peasant masses. Tragically, for the peasants of Java and Burma, yet another major mode of avoidance protest had been transformed into a likely cause for forcible repression and violent conflict.

Given the limited acquaintance of most colonial officials with the languages

[67] Onghokham, "Residency of Madiun Pryayi," pp. 226, 230; Louw and de Klerck, *Java-Oorlog*, vol. 1, pp. 267, 269, 273; Adas, *Burma Delta*, pp. 149-50, 203-4; Isaacman, "Social Banditry" p. 23; idem, *Tradition of Resistance in Mozambique*, pp. 100-101, 107, 115-16; John Iliffe, "Organization of the Maji Maji Rebellion," *Journal of African History* 8 (1967): 499.

[68] For a superb illustration of these fears applied to several colonized areas, see W. J. Schoemaker, "Het Mohammedaansche fanatisme," *IG* 20, no. 2 (1896): 1517-537. For discussions of actual government overreactions, see G. W. J. Drewes, *Drie Javaansche Goeroe's: Hun Leven, Onderricht en Messiasprediking* (Leiden, 1925), esp. pp. 39-40, 49; E. Michael Mendelson, *State and Sangha in Burma* (Ithaca, N.Y., 1975), pp. 173-79; Berque, *Egypt: Imperialism and Revolution*, pp. 233, 262.

I

of the peoples they ruled and their disinterest, or contempt, toward the cultural expression of colonized peoples, it is not surprising that the tradition of peasant protest through theatrical satire and other vehicles of ridicule flourished in the colonial era. Gestures of contempt and mockery that were incomprehensible to or passed unnoticed by the Europeans were also added to the peasant arsenal of impromptu protest. Messianic and nationalistic leaders exploited the colonizers' lack of familiarity with the local culture; they worked double entendres into speeches to peasant gatherings and made references to legendary heroes and stirring events from the past that had great emotional impact on their audiences but meant little to police observers. Peasant grievances were also articulated in literary form by members of the emerging bourgeois intelligentsia who penned novels and plays that drew attention to the miserable condition of the majority of the cultivating classes under colonial rule. Pamphlets, vernacular newspapers, and satirical cartoons (which were the most accessible of these forms to the illiterate or semiliterate peasantry) were additional means by which peasant awareness was aroused and the problems of the rural masses brought to the attention of the emerging nationalist elite.[69]

The proliferation of new literary and cultural vehicles to express dissidence was symptomatic of a wider search for effective modes of protest to sustain peasant groups in their increasingly unequal struggle with the European colonizers and their non-European allies, both immigrant and indigenous. As village defenses disintegrated and community autonomy gave way to bureaucratic interference and control, peasant reliance on evasion, patron protection, and avoidance shifted to forms of protest expression that involved more direct challenges to and clashes with the wielders of power. The adoption of modes of protest involving confrontation was also influenced by a gradual, but definite, shift in the locus of peasant identity and orientation from the landlord or noble patron to their fellow cultivators. As vertical patron-client ties were transformed in ways that worked increasingly against the cultivators' interests, and new patterns of property ownership and market demands turned large numbers of village dwellers into migrant laborers and tenants without land or strong community roots, horizontal links and a sense of class consciousness began to emerge. At the same time, the European colonizers failed

For examples of these forms of protest see, respectively, Raden Adjeng Kartini, *Letters of a Javanese Princess* (New York, 1964), p. 60; James R. Brandon, *Theatre in Southeast Asia* (Cambridge, Mass., 1964), pp. 259, 284–88; James L. Peacock, "Anti-Dutch, Anti-Muslim Drama among Surabaja Proletarians: A Description of Performances and Responses," *Indonesia* 4 (1967): 44–73; Kartomi, "Performance, Music, and Meaning," pp. 115–16; Bernhard Dahm, *Sukarno and the Struggle for Indonesian Independence* (Ithaca, N.Y., 1969), esp. pp. 102–5; Thein Pe Myint, "Her Husband or Her Money," "Oil," "Bittersweet," and "A Song to Make One Weep," in *Selected Short Stories of Thein Pe Myint*, P. M. Milne, trans. (Ithaca, N.Y., 1973); Ngo Vinh Long, *Before the Revolution: The Vietnamese Peasants under the French* (Cambridge, Mass., 1973); Adas, *Burma Delta*, pp. 193–96; and Mendelson, *State and Sangha*, pp. 214–21.

I

to surround themselves with the symbols and roles that had given legitimacy to the precolonial rulers. Fertility ceremonies were no longer performed; sacred shrines and palace centers were neglected or turned into museums or European social clubs; religious or customary strictures regarding the behavior of the ruling classes had no influence on the policies of alien and infidel European overlords.

These changes not only gave rise to ideologies of rebellion that were more radical than those associated with precolonial peasant dissidents, they made it more possible to mobilize and organize large numbers of peasants over wide areas. The awesome organizational and technological superiority which the colonizers could bring to bear in the confrontations that often resulted and the heavy casualties these clashes inflicted forced peasant dissidents to seek new allies and new ways of redressing their grievances. Although protective magic and millenarian solutions proved capable of mobilizing large numbers of peasant supporters for anticolonial resistance movements in many areas, numbers alone were no match for European howitzers and machine guns. In some colonies, like India and Ghana, peasants became deeply involved in constitutional agitation and passive resistance campaigns that sought to challenge the colonizers without provoking violent repression. In other areas, like Algeria and Vietnam, those who sought to arouse the peasantry turned to ancient traditions of guerilla warfare. When combined with tactics modified for postindustrial military technology, well-articulated revolutionary ideologies, the discipline of cadre organization, and broad military strategies, guerilla warfare proved capable of offsetting the advantages of superior firepower and mechanization enjoyed by the conventional colonial armies. Though guerilla resistance failed in many colonies, and for reasons which often differed widely, victories in China, Vietnam, and other areas have elevated guerilla tactics to the position of the preferred mode of peasant protest and resistance in the twentieth century. Avoidance and selective confrontation have been combined to erase many of the advantages that industrialization had given to colonial elite groups in their incessant contest with the cultivating classes.

II

From Footdragging to Flight: The Evasive History of Peasant Avoidance Protest in South and South-east Asia

In the late 1840s, large numbers of peasants from the Demak and Grobogan areas of the Semarang Residency on Java's north-east coast fled from their villages which were situated in areas where the Dutch had introduced the forced production of tobacco in the previous decade. In March of 1850, Dutch officials questioned a group of refugee peasants in an attempt to determine the grievances that had led to their flight and, if possible, convince them to return to their home villages, where severe labour shortages were making a shambles of colonial production quotas. After repeated assurances that they would not be harmed if they spoke freely, the refugees (or a particularly vocal and courageous one; it is not clear from accounts of the inquiry) related a long list of grievances. They claimed that they had once lived in a state of well-being that had been undermined by the introduction of the compulsory cultivation of tobacco which was one of the most demanding and time-consuming of the export crops that the Dutch collected in the era of the Cultivation System. The peasants' complaints – excessive production quotas, the disruption of rice cropping routines, intermittent demands for special services for which there was little or no pay, forced deliveries of tobacco at far below its market price – included many of the critical defects that Dutch pamphleteers cited in their hotly fought campaigns beginning in the 1840s to reform or abolish altogether the Cultivation System [*Fasseur*, 1978]. The peasants asserted that their families had been threatened by starvation as a result of the excessive demands of Dutch and Javanese officials. They fled in order to survive. They declared that they would not return unless the Dutch promised that they would no longer have to grow tobacco. In fact, in succeeding years many of these same peasants migrated *en masse* yet again in response to Dutch attempts to re-establish their control and reintroduce the compulsory production of export crops into the areas where the peasants had originally taken refuge [*Pierson*, 1868: 153–5; *Soest*, 1869: 3, 205].

　　These events – the large-scale flight of Javanese peasants and the impromptu Dutch inquiry – provide a rare instance of avoidance protest in

II

From Footdragging to Flight   65

which peasant dissent was not merely recorded by government officials, but those who committed the acts of protest were given the opportunity to explain the motives for their resistance in some detail. If we assume that the peasants' responses were reasonably accurately recorded -- admittedly a problematical supposition -- it is possible to gain a sense of the more fundamental values and underlying sense of justice by which they evaluated the elite demands and defined the grievances that provoked their dissidence. The peasants' mistrust of all officials ('De kleine man klagt nooit openlijk');[1] their conviction that subsistence cultivation must take precedence over production for state or market demands; their belief that a man's labour ought to be fairly rewarded (even by the state); and their deep-seated belief that flight was an effective, although costly, means of combatting the excessive demands of local and colonial officials, are all readily apparent in the refugees' angry responses to the Dutch inquiry. The peasants' flight itself was an act of defence; Dutch questions had tranformed it into a vehicle for social protest.

Even in this 'best case' situation, the perils of avoidance protest as a subject of historical inquiry are strikingly illustrated. Careful examination of the questions asked and the peasants' replies reveals a wide range of problems relating to this rather rare encounter between European officials and peasant dissidents. Were the Dutch officials posing the right questions? To what degree were the questions posed and the responses actually recorded shaped by the Dutch administrators' personal feelings about the Cultivation System which was the object of great controversy at the time. Were the Javanese, whose mistrust of even apparently sympathetic officials is clear from their testimony, expressing their feelings fully or concealing deeper grudges and motives, or alternatively personal shortcomings and animosities that may have driven them to flee? In the available published accounts of this incident, we are told little about the composition of the peasant groups which fled or even the actual numbers involved. We do not know what measures they may have taken short of migration to defend themselves; why some peasants fled and others chose to remain; why the former migrated to the areas where the Dutch found them; or whether or not they considered more confrontational modes of protest, including those involving violence, as alternative means of countering what they perceived to be exploitative demands. These and other questions arise even in this instance where we have relatively hard evidence. For most incidents of avoidance protest the evidence is much more sketchy; the process of interpretation necessarily based more heavily on inference and speculation.

In recent years those who work with peasant social systems in a variety of disciplines have in a sense rediscovered these critical modes of protest for they have long been a central concern of those who study plantation societies or agrarian systems based on serfdom.[2] From passing references to foot-dragging or evasive protest as precursors of major riots or rebellions, we have moved (perhaps too quickly) to the position that these forms of 'dissent from within' [*Last*, 1970: 350ff] have been major -- perhaps the most pervasive – modes of peasant protest to excessive elite demands. The importance of this shift in perspective cannot be overemphasised, for it may ultimately force a major rethinking of our approaches to the study of social protest, both rural and urban, more generally. Because they are embedded in established institutions and ongoing exchanges between patrons and clients at various levels, serious analysis of peasant defences and avoidance protest forces us to deal with *whole* social and political systems,[3] rather than concentrating on peasant conditions and responses to vaguely delineated and caricatured elites. It requires that we examine in depth the ongoing interaction and day-to-day contests over scarce resources between elites and peasants, taking into account the impact of institutions and ideologies on these processes. The study of peasant resistance in this wider perspective cannot be successfully accomplished unless we break down crude categories like elite/peasant and coloniser/colonised in order to unravel the complex layering of socio-economic hierarchies in rural societies and identify the bewildering varieties of exchanges and responses between individuals and groups at different levels. This approach accentuates the vertical dimensions of rural socio-political and economic relations, centred on patron–client interaction [*Scott*, 1972a, 1972b; *Scott and Kerkvliet*, 1973], and may force us to alter the way we look at peasant communities which, as Jan Breman has recently argued [1982], were more likely to have been elite-infiltrated and deeply divided by factions and variations in wealth than the closed, corporate entities that are often assumed in the literature on peasant societies.[4] Serious study of avoidance protest requires that we examine more fully the important links that have existed between ongoing or quasi-institutionalised modes of peasant resistance and specific outbursts of rural riot or rebellion, as well as the connections between peasant movements as different points in time.

An approach to peasant resistance that emphasises ongoing defences and modes of avoidance protest may well lead to the conclusion that, contrary to the impression conveyed by the great attention given in recent decades to rural conflict and peasant risings, outbursts of confrontational protest are exceptional occurrences and riots and rebellions are rare events, and revolutions even more so. This realisation will in turn require major alterations in the approaches that have dominated peasant protest studies for decades – studies in which topics are selected, arguments premised, and data organised on the assumption that the history of whole societies over considerable periods of time was inexorably shaped by and targeted towards major outbursts of societal conflict. Not only is this perspective narrow and crisis-centric; it promotes a wrong-headed approach to historical analysis – backwards from conflicts and confrontations that are viewed in retrospect as 'main events'.

In our enthusiasm to embrace this new vision of the dynamics of agrarian societies and peasant social protest, we should exercise great caution. We should do so not because this is a less viable way to study rural history than the major confrontation approach, but because the sources available for the study of the protest of avoidance, at least those extant for the pre-independence period, are limited and often difficult to interpret with precision or even the assurance that the investigator has understood the real meaning of the invariably scanty information that is available. The paucity and low quality of the source materials dealing with peasant defences and avoidance protest compounds the difficulties that would be encountered even if better documentation were available. The problems of distinguishing peasant defences from peasant protest and individual acts of resistance from reprisals resulting from personal quarrels; of determining whether peasant activities like banditry and arson are criminal acts or expressions of *social* protest; or of analysing the links between avoidance protest and peasant/ elite confrontations are greatly complicated by the lack of sufficient information.

The many problems associated with the study of rural protest, beginning with the scarcity of sources produced by peasants themselves, that have been identified by numerous authors are greatly magnified in the analysis of avoidance resistance because incidents of peasant footdragging or evasive reprisals are very likely not to have been recorded at all. The success of this form of protest has often depended on its clandestine nature. Officials must be deceived; 'cheating' must pass unnoticed, or at least its perpetrators must remain undiscovered. In addition, measures and activities that state officials condemned as illegal were often viewed by members of village communities as essential defences or just retribution for elite excesses and thus 'covered up'. In many instances, local officials themselves collaborated with village leaders or local men of influence to resist state demands for tribute or manpower. The collusion, deception and subterfuge that have been central to most forms of avoidance protest serve to frustrate the eager social scientists' efforts to understand this form of resistance every bit as much as they made it difficult for state officials to detect and punish it.

Even if evidence of peasant cheating or reprisal reached local or regional officials, it is likely to have been suppressed. In both the pre-colonial and colonial periods, the superiors of local officials were likely to view expressions of peasant unrest as signs of administrative incompetence or corruption on the part of their subordinates. Due to the disruptions that resulted and the need for military support from the court or district centre in times of violent peasant risings, it was virtually impossible to conceal incidents of confrontational protest, however much local leaders may have wished to cover them up. Pilfering, arson, crop concealment, adulterated tribute deliveries, verbal abuse and gestures of contempt, on the other hand, could be overlooked or dealt with by a local leader's hired toughs. If these expressions of discontent and resistance were reported, an official's reputation and career could be badly damaged or he could be exposed to attacks by his rivals. Evidence of misrule could bring dismissal, imprisonment or in some instances – as in seventeenth-century Burma [*Than Tun*, 1968: 177–80] – execution. Even if they reported incidents of avoidance protest, threatened and obviously hostile officials were unlikely to relate accurately the grievances, demands or aspirations of peasants driven to flight, footdragging or sectarian withdrawal.

The evasive, often clandestine, nature of most forms of avoidance protest means that there has historically been a very low ratio between the number of occurrences of this mode of dissent and those that have actually been recorded, much less described in detail. It is impossible to estimate this ratio with any precision, but it varied widely by time period, area, type of regime, and according to the form of protest involved from rarely recorded (but perhaps ubiquitous) incidents of peasant footdragging to frequently recorded instances of peasant protest migration *en masse*. The available evidence, however, makes it possible to delineate several broad categories of avoidance protest and to discern the conditions that caused them to change over time. Often the conditions that influenced peasant decisions to adopt particular forms of avoidance protest also have had a bearing on the extent to which these expressions of agrarian dissidence were recorded. The 'soft' state structures and poor communications systems of pre-colonial South and South-east Asian societies, for example, provided openings for a wide range of peasant avoidance responses. Low population-to-land ratios, the presence of large tracts of unoccupied land, and vigorous elite competition for limited supplies of manpower reinforced these tendencies and at the same time led to an official obsession with large-scale protest migrations or the transfer of peasant services from one elite patron to another. This concern resulted in fairly abundant documentation of these peasant responses. In the colonial era, detailed official reports on small-scale sectarian movements like those which made possible works like Drewes' classic account of Javanese chiliasm [*Drewes*, 1925], reflected the great anxiety felt by colonial officials regarding this sort of activity which they little understood or cared to tolerate. Better bookkeeping, improved communications and tighter bureaucratic control in the colonial period also forced peasants to rely more heavily on different forms of resistance than those they had favoured in the pre-colonial era and produced the sorts of records that make it possible for us to study elusive modes of protest like concealment, arson, feigned ignorance and production boycotts in some depth for the first time.

The bulk of this study is focused on an examination of the historical and situational factors in pre-colonial and colonial South and South-east Asia that influenced peasant preferences for different forms of avoidance protest and also often determined the extent to which these activities would be recorded. For the purpose of analysis, I have grouped the many forms of non-confrontational or avoidance resistance into three main types: (1) the protest of denial – everyday resistance; (2) the protest of denial – exit; and (3) the protest of retribution. The major distinction between types one and two, both of which are centred on the efforts of peasant cultivators to deny material resources or labour services to local notables or government officials whose demands are viewed as excessive, are structural. Modes of the protest of denial belonging to the first type are endemic to rural social systems and occur on an ongoing, day-to-day basis. Avoidance protest of the second type, which involves flight or transfer of peasant services and loyalties, are more dramatic and perilous and thus more rarely adopted by hardpressed peasants, usually when everyday defences are not sufficient to hold elite exactions at a tolerable level. As its name implies, in contrast to either type of the protest of denial, the protest of retribution consists of modes of peasant resistance that involve attempts to strike back at those who are viewed as sources of oppression. As distinguished from modes of confrontational protest, such as riots or rebellion, however, these forms of avoidance protest centre on anonymous reprisals or clandestine acts that are not intended to bring on direct confrontations between dissident tenants or labourers and those who are the targets of their retribution.

Most modes of avoidance protest are rooted in everyday peasant patterns of work, social action and even amusement. They overlap with, and are therefore often difficult to distinguish analytically from, other peasant strategies for survival such as crime, collusion with patrons or government officials, or various forms of confrontational protest, both violent and non-violent. In order to be meaningfully classified as protest, however, each mode of avoidance response must involve a conscious and articulated intent to deny resources or services or do injury to those who are perceived as the sources of their suffering, while minimising or altogether evading direct clashes with their adversaries.

THE PROTEST OF DENIAL I: EVERYDAY PEASANT RESISTANCE FROM WITHIN

By far the most difficult type of avoidance protest to study is also that which is the most pervasive. In fact, everyday forms of peasant resistance frequently straddle the nebulous zone between ongoing peasant defences and protest to such a degree that it is difficult, and perhaps unnecessary, to distinguish sharply between them. Everyday or footdragging resistance typically involves individual rather than collective action; it is normally aimed at specific demands rather than grand reforms; and in most instances it involves calculated errors or incompetence rather than sustained protest efforts. The aggrieved party seeks to deny labour or produce to those who are viewed as exploiters, although curses or malicious gossip represent perhaps the minimal forms of this type of protest. Everyday resistance is by definition localised and endemic to particular agrarian systems. It plays an integral role in the ongoing exchanges between elite and cultivating groups at different levels. It is characteristically so pervasive and specific that it has rarely been recorded and, until recent decades, almost never been described in detail. Indeed, our awareness of these forms of peasant response has resulted to a large degree from contemporary village studies. We have of necessity interpolated patterns of everyday protest from recent fieldwork by gleaning the bits of historical information available, borrowing heavily from studies of non-peasant societies where evidence of footdragging and cheating is more abundant [*Genovese*, 1972: 285–324, 599–657], and ultimately resorting to a good many inferences based on circumstantial evidence.

For the pre-colonial era, the only forms of everyday resistance through denial that we can discuss with any degree of certainty are collusion and concealment. Even so, we must approach these indirectly through a more general analysis of state structures and revenue collection patterns. The often substantial difference between the tribute that South or South-east Asian rulers claimed as their fair share and the amount of revenue that actually reached their coffers or labour that was actually performed in their fields or workshops provides vivid testimony of the degree to which concealment and cheating were endemic in these states. Collusion, deception and denial, however, were found at all levels from the village to the royal palace. Thus, it is difficult to know how much cultivators of different standings from landholders to landless labourers benefited from the weak communications and low level of bureaucratic organisation and commitment that made these practices so widespread and effective. It is probable that the greatest advantages derived from the denial of revenue and labour to the state went to those of highest position and power and that the returns diminished as the contest for control of scarce resources descended the social scale. Above the village level, these gains would primarily benefit the families and clients of local lords. However, the villages in many areas of South and South-east Asia were assessed and paid their taxes on a communal basis. This meant that even the most vulnerable cultivators, landless labourers, received some protection through collusion and concealment as long as they were attached to patron notables. Recent superb studies, such as those by Moertono [1968] and Lieberman [1984], have illuminated the various devices by which villagers collaborated, often with local officials, to bury harvested crops, under-report the amount of village land under cultivation, overestimate crop losses due to flooding or drought, or relocate young men in the forest when government recruiting parties were in the vicinity. Although it is highly probable that smaller-scale concealment in the form of pilfering and petty hoarding occurred on an individual basis, as yet little evidence has been uncovered to empirically validate this assumption.

Despite the fact that pre-colonial sources rarely mention them, it is reasonable to assume that other forms of everyday resistance – feigned incompetence, calculated mishaps, gestures of anger or contempt, etc. – were widespread in South and South-east Asia. In the colonial period, information on these forms of protest through denial, as well as colusion and concealment, becomes more abundant, although still thin relative to data on other types of avoidance protest. As bureaucratic control grew tighter (although not nearly as tight as was once assumed); population growth reversed population-to-land ratios once favourable to the peasantry; and European military preponderance made banditry or violent risings ever more dangerous, everyday resistance may well have increased greatly in importance.

Although highly variable in coverage and accuracy [*Dewey*, 1979], colonial revenue records make it possible for us to estimate with some degree of precision the amount of revenue lost to the government through collusion, concealment and under-reporting. These estimates in turn can give a fairly accurate picture of the nature and extent of these practices in different societies and regions under colonial rule. Special inquests into official 'corruption', such as that which forms the basis for Frykenberg's detailed study of Indian influence in the British colonial administration [*1965*], also make it possible to study in some depth the techniques and circumstances that enabled local officials and villagers to deny colonial regimes substantial sums of revenue. However, the extent to which under-reporting or cheating on tribute payments represented corruption for individual gain, as opposed to resistance to demands that were perceived to be excessive, is difficult to determine. Because colonial taxes were often levied on individual households, the elements of community co-operation and (very unequally) shared benefits which characterised pre-colonial concealment devices tended to be diminished. Those who suffered the most from the erosion of village and patron–client collusion were the growing numbers of landless labourers who were perhaps the hardest hit (in proportion to their meagre incomes) by regressive head taxes or levies on salt and other essential items that were standard sources of colonial revenue.

The topics of concern and the detail of reporting found in the colonial police and revenue records and political correspondence from local officials make it possible for us to study more than collusion and concealment among everyday forms of protest. Feigned incompetence or ignorance – the very essence of footdragging protest – is reflected, for example, in innumerable revenue officials' complaints about peasant indolence or carelessness; their 'reactionary' stubborness in refusing to adopt new crops or implements; and their suspicion of, and open hostility to, public works projects, campaigns for improved village sanitation and hygiene and census taking. One of the more revealing expressions of peasant mistrust of these sorts of measures was a handbill issued by the anti-separationists in Burma in the 1920s. The flyer warned that if Burma became a Crown Colony (as the separationists wanted), no prostitutes would be allowed, every house would have to have a lavatory and it would be inspected three times a day, only government-approved water could be drunk, and the meat of animals which had died of old age or disease could not be eaten [*Christian*, 1942: 332–3].

In times of heightened social tension and conflict, such as the decade after the First World War in India, fairly abundant evidence about everyday forms of agrarian protest is available. Cultivators' refusals to work the lands of European or Indian estate-owners, peasant rejection of demands that they grow certain crops or that their plough teams be used to work estate lands, their illegal and surreptitious use of landlords' fields to pasture their cattle or plant subsistence crops, and their outright refusals to co-operate with tax or rent collectors are all recorded in considerable detail.[5] In Burma in roughly the same period, hardpressed tenants resorted to very different measures to counter landlord power and demands. Pilfering, surreptitious harvests and absconding with crops produced on landlords' fields were widespread. Some tenants took crop loans from both landlords and money-lenders and then made off with the cash they had received after working the fields they had rented for only a week or two [*Burma, RAP*, 8633, 1911: 178; *Couper*, 1924: 21; *Tin Gyi*, 1926: 11–12]. Recent oral research among cultivators who had been subjected to Portuguese cotton tribute demands during the last decades of colonial rule in Mozambique reveals the wide-spread adoption of additional forms of everyday protest. The adulteration of cotton shipped to government warehouses, the cooking of cotton seeds before planting in order to convince government officials that certain areas were unsuitable for cotton cultivation, the clandestine cultivation of food crops on fields designated for cotton, late planting, and laxity about weeding cotton fields were among the techniques adopted to frustrate Portuguese tribute demands [*Isaacman*, 1980].

Because it has often been the response of individuals or small groups, usually clandestine and localised, everyday resistance involves ideology only minimally and represents a very constricted state of peasant consciousness. Although concealment or feigned incompetence express, in a rather rudimentary form, core peasant convictions that, for example, the cultivation of subsistence crops should take precedence over market production, various forms of everyday resistance have tended to be more defensive and remedial than expressions of conscious and clearly articulated protest. Footdragging tactics are integral parts of the Hobbesian struggle between elites and cultivators that has been central to both pre-colonial and colonial political economies in South and South-east Asia, as in virtually all pre-industrial societies. All parties to elite–peasant exchanges have been aware of concealment, feigned ignorance and deception; members of elite groups habitually assume that peasants will resort to these measures to buffer tax and rental demands. Because they have been so individualised, so embedded in pre-colonial and colonial systems of social control, everyday forms of the protest of denial have rarely provided, if ever, a suitable basis for collective protest, even though the cumulative effects of production sabotage or crop concealment can be seen as modes of collective response. Except in situations of extreme social dislocation and political breakdown, everyday resistance is the peasants' preferred means of defence and protest. It is effective, however, only in situations where political institutions and social structures remain viable. Conditions of social and political deterioration and severe economic scarcity force peasants to turn to more radical, and risky, measures to protect their interests, and often, merely to survive.

THE PROTEST OF DENIAL II: EXIT

Of the many forms of avoidance protest, the most disruptive and, largely for that reason, the best documented, are those that involve the denial of labour or resources as a result of individual and collective decisions to quit positions that are no longer considered tenable or abandon particular social systems altogether. The chronic scarcity of labour and the availability of large amounts of arable, unoccupied land in pre-colonial South and South-east Asia led to continuous contests among elite groups at various levels for manpower control. This rivalry in turn provided cultivating groups with institutionalised checks on elite excesses and effective means of protest. Because these contests and potential modes of peasant resistance were so central to the dynamics of statebuilding and power maintenance in indigenous South and South-east Asian states, they are perhaps the best documented of all forms of peasant resistance in the pre-colonial era, including those involving mass peasant violence. Four main forms of the protest of denial through exit can be identified from the available sources: (1) the transfer within existing social and state systems of services from one lord to another or from nobles (including the ruler) to religious institutions; (2) flight, often *en masse*, to unoccupied areas beyond the state's control; (3) the abandonment of routine agrarian tasks in favour of membership in sectarian communities; and (4) the rejection of peasant status altogether in order to join a bandit gang or theatre troupe, enter the domestic service of a powerful lord, or become a porter or urban labourer.

Because the second form of avoidance protest by denial through exit, flight, was the most likely to be collective and hence the most disruptive of regular production routines and social control networks, it is perhaps the form of pre-colonial peasant resistance that we know the most about. It is also the form of avoidance response in which protest can be the most clearly distinguished from purely defensive measures on the one hand and the pursuit of personal advantage on the other. Although peasants migrated by individual households or whole villages to find food in times of flood or drought, to escape the depredations of warring armies, or to settle more fertile areas, abundant evidence exists that indicates that migration was also a major means of protest. Royal proclamations and bureaucratic regulations from numerous societies make it clear that large-scale peasant migrations were often regarded as signs of misrule and peasant discontent. In Thailand, for example, the migration of peasants or townsmen was linked to the very meaning of the term 'oppression'. Royal officials were ordered to ascertain whether migrant groups had in fact been oppressed and, if so, report those responsible to the king or his ministers who regarded these abuses as criminal acts [*Rabibhadana*, 1969: 73–4]. It is clear that the threat of migration gave client peasants substantial leverage in their dealings with elite patrons throughout most of South and South-east Asia.

The other form of protest through exit that is well documented for the pre-colonial era centred on the transfer of a cultivator's services from one patron to another. In working with the sources available for this sort of response, however, it is more difficult than in the case of migration to distinguish actions taken out of a desire for personal advancement from those taken to protest abuses. Frequently the two motives were intertwined, but the practice of shifting patrons was apparently so common in some pre-colonial societies that customary procedures developed by which a peasant client notified his lord of his decision to transfer his services to another patron and – in Java at least [*Carey*, 1987, Ch. 2] – provided symbolic recompense in the form of material gifts. That personal advantage was a common cause for elite transfer cannot be doubted, as the following stylised request for acceptance by a patron employed by the Ankole of East Africa makes dramatically clear:

> Give me milk; make me rich;
> keep me in mind; be my father;
> I will be your child [*Mair*, 1966: 169].

The problems of distinguishing protest expression from opportunity seeking is compounded by the fact that individual acts of client transfer are rarely recorded and never (in so far as I am aware) recounted from the viewpoint of the client. Evidence provided by Habib [1963], Onghokham [1975], Lieberman [1984], Moertono [1968] and others, however, leaves no doubt that client transfer was a major form of avoidance protest. As in the case of peasant migration, labour services (and thus potential material support) were denied in situations where obligations to royal patrons had become overly burdensome relative to that for individual nobles or religious establishments. This pattern was also followed in instances where patrons had proven incapable of protecting their clients from excessive state demands [*Onghokham*. 1975: 44]. Even though clients' decisions to transfer their services were normally made on an individual household basis, they could do considerable harm to the reputation and material base of power of the abandoned patron, particularly if other clients became convinced that the lord or notable had lost his aura of authority (*wahju, pon*, etc.) and promise of continued success [*Hanks*, 1962]. As Lieberman [1984] and Aung Thwin [1976] have convincingly shown, the cumulative effects of individual and small group client defection could mortally wound the strongest of pre-colonial states.

The existence of sectarian movements in pre-colonial South and Southeast Asia is, of course, well documented. Mysticism, millenarianism, guru–chela attachments and sectarian communities were prominent, at times central, features of pre-colonial societies. Surviving sources have told us a good deal about the beliefs, organisation and activities of these communities, as well as their relations with more 'orthodox' religious leaders, local notables and pre-colonial states [*Tai*, 1983; *Mendelson*, 1975; *Ahmad*, 1964; *Eaton*, 1977]. What is virtually impossible to determine and yet crucial to the identification of avoidance protest, is the degree to which these sects as movements or the decisions of individual members to join represented acts of protest, expressions of philosophical and religious conviction, calculations of personal advantage, or a combination of all three. Even though peasant participation in these movements has been documented, we know little in detail about the composition of their adherents or how this changed over time. None the less, chronicles of dynastic decline and the pattern of sectarian recruitment and behaviour suggest that there were important connections between misrule, popular unrest and millenarian prophesies in the pre-colonial period. Because many sectarian movements stressed passive withdrawal from the wider society and the severance of ties to the existing state, they can be seen as expressions of the protest of denial through exit.

Although some evidence relating to bandit activities in the pre-colonial period has been uncovered, this form of peasant response falls more properly into the third category of avoidance discussed below, clandestine retribution, if indeed it can be classified as avoidance protest at all. Nevertheless, the initial acts of peasants who opt for banditry as a means of resistance to oppression involve flight and the denial of labour and potential productivity to members of elite groups. Unfortunately, because we have virtually no information as to why individuals in the pre-colonial period became bandits, excepting those who inherited this calling from their fathers or other relatives and were trained in much the same way a craftsman learned his trade, it is impossible to know the extent to which decisions to run away and join a bandit gang were acts of protest. This is a different question from that which has proven such a source of contention between Blok and Hobsbawm [1972], focusing on the degree to which bandits were social advocates for and defenders of exploited social groups like peasants, or simply criminals out for personal gain. It is based on the premise that an individual's decision to become a bandit may be a different form of protest than that adopted in his subsequent career, or that one may be an act of protest and not the other.

All of the major forms of protest of denial through exit persisted into the colonial period. As improved communications, an awesome advantage in military strength, and more and better trained administrators give the colonisers and their indigenous allies an ever greater preponderance of power and control over the peoples of South and South-east Asia, the various forms of avoidance protest through exit were altered in major ways and, in some cases, utterly transformed.

For decades after the imposition of colonial rule in most areas, flight remained a major response of disgruntled peasants. Large tracts of unoccupied land were still available and the European overlords found themselves heavily dependent on highly porous indigenous systems of social control. In addition, new places of refuge were added as more carefully defined boundries and territorial jurisdictions were established both within colonies and between colonial possessions and the lands of rump indigenous princedoms that survived on the fringes of most colonised areas. As new market demands and incentives multiplied, however, and European policy-makers actively sought to stimulate the settlement and cultivation of new areas that had previously been underpopulated and poorly developed, migrations became increasingly oriented to opportunity, even on the part of hardpressed, landless cultivators, and diminished as an effective mode of protest for most peasants. Population growth combined with the settlement of more accessible frontier tracts reduced the potential areas to which peasants might flee, while colonial regimes improved their capacity to monitor peasant movements and to catch and punish those who sought to escape corvée labour or revenue demands through flight. Despite these trends, migration *en masse* remained a viable peasant defence and protest option for peasants on the edges of heavily forested areas or those living in regions bordering on territory belonging to rival colonial powers or indigenous princes [*Asiwaju*, 1976; *Henningham*, 1979]. To a limited degree, migration was also adopted as a protest response by Indian nationalist leaders who encouraged peasants to abandon their villages rather than submit to British revenue demands that the nationalists had made the focal issue in their anti-colonial campaigns [*Pandey*, 1978: 173].

At the same time that protest migration diminished as a viable response for most colonised peasants, the transfer of client services also lost much of its former meaning and effectiveness. Under colonial rule contractual, cash nexus relationships increasingly supplemented or supplanted the personalist, quasi-reciprocal patron–client exchanges that had dominated pre-colonial political economies. Although patron–client links persisted in many areas changing political and socio-economic conditions and most especially population growth that resulted in population-to-land ratios that were decidedly unfavourable to cultivators at all levels, rendered these ties increasingly advantageous for patron landholders, often to the point where they could exploit and humiliate 'client' tenants or labourers with impunity [*Scott*, 1972b]. Consequently, a client's decision to transfer his services to a new employer, rather than an alternative patron, gradually became a matter of market calculation and virtually disappeared as a mode of protest. As labour was transformed from personal dependency into a depersonalised commodity, especially in the case of land– and villageless workers, it became less and less possible for the weak to use the denial of labour services as a weapon against landlord adversaries. On the contrary, the oversupply of labour in most colonised areas gave those who controlled capital and land overwhelming advantages in their everyday dealings with labour over how to apportion the increasingly scarce resources available. From lords competing, and at times clashing violently, for control of scarce manpower in the pre-colonial era, the situation had been utterly transformed into one in which increasingly impoverished tenants and labourers vied for a proportionately decreasing number of jobs.

It is probable that sectarian movements increased considerably in number and size in the colonial period in response to the imposition of 'infidel' rule and social and economic dislocations [*Tai*, 1983; *Kartodirdjo*, 1972]. Although the often substantial accounts of these movements by colonial officials need to be read with great caution due to the Europeans' (often well-founded) paranoia regarding sectarian activities and their lack of understanding with or sympathy towards the socio-cultural contexts in which these movements arose, elements of hostility towards colonial regimes and their discredited collabateur allies are often unmistakable. As studies of these movements have shown [*Drewes*, passim; *Benda* and *Castles*, 1969; *Sturtevant*, 1976: 94–5, 110–11, 176], however, the adherents of these sects often intended to register their dissent through passive withdrawal, and thus the themes of denial and exit persisted in the colonial period. These intentions were often frustrated by overly zealous cult members or the insistence of European or indigenous officials that passive sectarian movements posed threats to the colonial order. Preemptive arrests or other repressive measures were often attempted that put an end to the sect's activities or drove its adherents to violent clashes with those in power [*Holt*, 1958: 54–8; Adas, 1979: 122–30]. Thus, the protest of denial through exit was transformed into violent peasant riots or rebellion.

A peasant's decision to leave his village and join a bandit gang involved much greater risks in the colonial period than earlier times, due to many of the same changes that had transformed other modes of avoidance protest. Forest refuges were cleared and settled or regularly patrolled; police and military forces were larger and better trained and armed. They were also less likely to collude with bandit leaders and conversely more committed than pre-colonial officials to hunting down those who threatened property or the peace and order that were so treasured by colonial officials. Banditry remained an exit option in some areas [*Berque*, 1972: 127–36; *Isaacman*, 1977; *Meijer*, 1949–50], but, despite romantic legends of outlaw resistance, one that was more and more likely to lead to a life of harassment and flight, and very often a violent death.

The protest of denial through exit has never been undertaken lightly. All of its forms involve the abandonment of homes, villages, grave sites and fields that represent years, often generations, of hard work, personal commitments, and associations with kin and community. All of its forms expose those who adopt them to great risks of physical harm during their passage to new lands, patrons or communities where they hope to find a better life. Of all of the types of avoidance protest, denial through exit requires the greatest preparation, the strongest commitment, and the most pronounced break with the peasant's past life. Because many of its forms also involve collective decisions and action, from small groups of young men who set off to join a bandit gang to entire village communities which flee to escape rapacious officials, the protest of denial through exit also demands a higher level of group consciousness and ongoing commitment than other types of avoidance protest. Excepting the transfer of client services, which as noted above had much in common with everyday forms of denial protest, all forms of protest through exit force those who participate in them outside the existing socio-political system. However, the calculations, risks and common commitments of denial protest through exit create only a very constricted sense of identity that is vertically orientated to group leaders and bounded by the migrant band, sect or bandit gang. Dissident organisation remains rudimentary; group goals are narrow, remedial and specific.

Although sectarian movements can coalesce around leaders with broad visions and radical aspirations, as well as a deep-seated sense of group identity and commitment, they have rarely achieved the scale that might allow them to force major reforms in or pose as viable alternatives to precolonial or colonial regimes. Peasant migrants, bandits and sect members have been able in some instances to win concessions from elite adversaries or enjoy brief periods of freedom from taxes or corvée labour, but they have been ultimately repressed or recaptured by the state and social systems which they fled. Co-option, violent assault or the extension of state control into newly settled areas have invariably cut short episodes of the protest of denial through exit. Thus, forms of avoidance protest involving denial through exit can temporarily ameliorate the sources of peasant hardship, but they cannot force the sorts of changes that promote the long-term well-being of peasants.

THE PROTEST OF RETRIBUTION

If the clear delineation of categories of everyday protest and the protest of denial through exit is made difficult by the potential overlap between these responses and purely defensive measures taken to enhance personal opportunity, the protest of retribution is often difficult to distinguish from modes of peasant resistance aimed at confrontation. Like confrontational protest, avoidance protest through retribution often involves violent assaults that may not be directed against the actual source of the peasants' discontent. Unlike confrontational protest, the protest of retribution is covert. Its perpetrators hope to do injury to those whom they view as their oppressors, but to avoid an open clash with their intended victims or the agents of the state that backs their adversaries. Although confrontational protest can involve numbers of peasants that vary from a handful of dissidents to millions of supporters of a revolutionary movement, the protest of retribution is usually carried out by individuals or small groups of peasants linked by kinship or personal acquaintance. Like everyday resistance and protest through exit, the protest of retribution is a weapon of the weak. It poses, however, a more direct threat to those who are in power and is a good deal more dangerous than most forms of the protest of denial. Although peasants who adopt any form of avoidance protest seek to prevent overt clashes with bureaucratic or landed adversaries, those who engage in the protest of retribution run the highest risk of provoking violent repressive measures.

Although the most prevalent forms of the protest of retribution – arson, vandalism, crop destruction and bandit raids – are rarely recorded in precolonial records, it is reasonable to infer that they were widely employed. Based on the experience of other societies where evidence is available [*Berque*, 1972; *Le Roy Ladurie*, 1974; *Thompson*, 1972], it is also probable that community modes of reprisal such as shaming, ridicule, cursing and the use of sorcery against powerful individuals who violated customary checks and ignored reciprocal obligations were employed by peasant groups throughout South and South-east Asia[6] we know, for example, that criticism of unpopular leaders frequently found its way into folk stories and songs, and especially into the splendid dance drama performances that exemplify so well the cultural ideals and worldview of South and South-east Asian peoples. As Margaret Kartoni [*1976*] has shown in her detailed analysis of the popular *reyog* dance drama of the Ponogoro region in central Java, songs and plays can be used to mock the arrogance of powerful figures, including kings. Through drama deep-seated resentment of the *priyayi* elite is also given voice through the transformation of characters who ought to be refined or *alus* into coarse, vulgar bullies. At the same time, peasant values and '*kasar* earthiness' can be affirmed.

In the colonial period, incidents of the protest of reprisal are more readily documented. Arson – the burning of crops, toll stations, estate houses or factories, and government records depots – is widely recorded in many areas of India, Java and Burma. In times of crisis widespread arson often served as the prelude to open peasant rebellion, as in the case of the burning of Chinese toll stations in Yogyakarta at the start of the Java War [*Louw* and *Klerck*, 1894, 267–73]. Clandestine incendiary attacks were also combined with non-violent forms of confrontational protest such as mass meetings and petition campaigns in areas like Bihar during the Champaran disturbances of the early 1920s to serve notice to colonial officials and nationalist leaders alike of the depth of peasant dissatisfaction and their determination to force reforms [*Henningham*, 1976: 62; *Misra*, 1963: 116, 121, 138, 140, 152]. Cases of peasant vandalism – the calculated destruction of buildings, tools, livestock, and crops – are also widely documented for the colonial period. Of particular concern to colonial authorities were acts of vandalism aimed at railways and telegraph lines that European officials rightly perceived as vital to the maintenance of colonial control [*Gillion*, 1971: 142; *Harcourt*, 1977: 319–20].

The problems of distinguishing between crime and protest identified for the pre-colonial period remain for the colonial era due to the sketchiness of most police reports on matters relating to motivation and the colonisers' penchant for labelling all manner of disturbances illegal. Even colonial officials were forced on occasion to concede, however, that robberies and assaults on landlord and moneylending groups were peasant retribution for what were perceived as exploitative practices on the part of key agents and allies of the European colonisers [*Adas*, 1982, 159ff]. Although it is a fictionalised account, Thein Pe Myint's 1934 short story, 'Her Husband or Her Money', vividly captures one instance of the protest of retribution through crime. Having killed the miserly moneylender, Me Sein, the dacoit, Kan Htaik, removes his disguise and reveals his true identity to her husband and his uncle, U Kyauk Lon. U Kyauk Lon gasps in astonishment: 'So it's you, my nephew! How could you have done such a thing?' Kan Htaik's reply epitomises the sorts of causes that drove peasants to the protest of retribution, just as his actions, clandestine and aimed at a familiar and specific target, typify this form of avoidance response:

> If it had been anyone else, I wouldn't have, Uncle. I did it because I simply couldn't stand that wife of yours. All I know is that I was poor because of her. I was nearly starving, but she never gave me a helping hand. You never realised how much we contributed to her riches, did you? I don't want to talk about it. She was a mean bitch [1973: 34].

As I have argued above, banditry remained an important peasant response to oppression or opportunity throughout the colonial era. Very often bandit gangs targeted rich, but unpopular, individuals or groups that the peasantry of a given area found especially exploitative. The Chettiars in Burma, the Chinese in Java, the *vanis* of western India were favourite targets of bandit gangs during times of relative peace and the object of mob assaults in periods of crisis and social unrest [*Kumar*, 1968: Ch. 5; *Adas*, 1982: 96–8]. The degree to which bandits selected moneylenders or landlords as targets because they were vulnerable and lucrative or to avenge their harsh treatment of cultivating groups varied widely from one instance to the next and is difficult to determine in most cases. A blend of both motives may have been present on many occasions, even though colonial records tend to stress the pursuit of individual gain as the cause of criminal acts.

As overt, especially violent, protest grew more dangerous, retribution through clandestine criminal acts may have increased in importance as a response of dissident peasants. Individual, small-scale robberies and assaults were less likely to be intensely investigated and punished than ongoing bandit operations which were seen by the colonial authorities as potential political threats. It was easier for those involved in specific acts of retributive protest to return to their everyday roles as peasants and law-abiding community members than was the case for full-time, professional bandits. 'Part-time' avengers were also less likely to be compelled to attack peasant communities for the means to survive, which appears to have been the case with hard-pressed dacoit gangs [*Vitalis*, 1851: 7–9; *RPAB*, 1913: 18; 1918: 17, 19]. The former were thus more likely than full-time bandits to be accepted, supported and protected by villagers who could take vicarious satisfaction in the humiliation, and even the bodily harm done to, tight-fisted moneylenders or unyielding landlords. 'Social' banditry, therefore, may have been more likely to be a part-time, or even one-shot, activity than a full-time career which is the sense in which Hobsbawm [1959, 1969] usually applies the term.

As regional elite groups and local estate owners grew more reliant on the backing of the European colonisers and more prone to live in urban areas, the power of inter-community sanctions like shaming and sorcery inevitably declined. The frequency of criminal assaults on landlords and moneylenders may indicate that stronger measures of retribution – poisoning, physical aggression, arson – became more common, but the available sources and the paucity of information the pre-colonial period, make it difficult to verify these trends. One form of the protest of retribution that almost certainly became more widespread in the colonial era was mockery. In a wide variety of forms, from gestures of contempt like the sneers Raden Adjeng Kartini observed on the faces of Javanese commoners who hastened to make way for a pompous Dutch official parading under a gold umbrella [1964: 60], to a great proliferation of vernacular pamphlets, stories, cartoons, sayings and plays, ridicule grew in importance in the colonial period as a vehicle of avoidance protest. The following description by James Peacock of a scene from a popular Javanese play performed in Surabaya illustrates the range of issues that could be captured in popular entertainments:

> A fat Dutchman appears, with much bold braid and other decorations on his uniform, blustering out pompous gutteral instructions in Indonesian to Amat. He waits for Amat to answer. Amat utters a crude Surabaya Javanese word (laughter). The Dutchman is infuriated. He gives Amat some more orders but Amat suddenly gives his shoulder a comradely shove (great laughter). The Dutchman is further enraged. Amat leaps away, smiles tensely. Now the Dutchman commands Amat to bring in the prisoners. He does so acting tough (incongruously so, since he is puny in appearance and ordinarily passive in manner); he makes them kneel to him, rattles his gun at them. The Dutchman bustles up, pats Amat on the shoulder. 'Ah yes,' he says, 'That is good. You must show your power' [1967: 48].

The coarse and insensitive Dutch bureaucrat, his puny and posturing Javanese lackey, the empty pomp, the uneasy relationship between coloniser and indigenous ally, the importance of a show of physical power are all captured in a very few words and meaningful gestures. Although the plays that Peacock describes were produced in the post-independence period, similar treatment of many of these same themes must have delighted Javanese audiences throughout the colonial era. As Peacock's summaries indicate, not only the Dutch were subjected to ridicule through popular drama. Pretentious *modins* (mosque officials who call the faithful to prayer) and corrupt and hypocritical *hadjis* are also caricatured and exposed [56].

The cultural distance that separated the Europeans from their subjects would have rendered the colonisers oblivious to most gestures of contempt or other forms of popular satire, but their indigenous allies could not have remained unaware of the bitter criticism and perhaps the implicit threats expressed by the characters and themes portrayed by travelling dance and drama performers. Detailed study may well show that these performances were major means of arousing anti-colonial sentiments and mobilising the peasantry for struggles aimed at achieving independence throughout South and South-east Asia.

Excepting ridicule through songs and plays, the protest of retribution involves perhaps the least developed consciousness of the three main types of avoidance protest. Although there is the satisfaction of revenge, of being able to injure their enemies, peasants, acting in small groups, engage in acts of retribution that are clandestine, transitory and aimed at individual material or human targets. Thus, most forms of the protest of retribution represent very limited responses that flaunt laws and threaten individuals, but have little lasting impact on existing systems of peasant–elite exchange and social control. This is not true, however, of ridicule through popular arts and entertainments which reaches the widest audience, is the most genera- lised of the forms of the protest of retribution in terms of targets, and is a potent means of articulating peasant grievances and more fundamental ethical values. Not surprisingly, of all of the forms of avoidance protest, ridicule in its various guises has been the most readily harnessed to more broadly based, more ideologically sophisticated peasant protest movements, both nationalist/anticolonial and Marxist/revolutionary [*Ngo Vinh Long*, 1973; *Anderson*, 1965, 1966].

BEYOND AVOIDANCE PROTEST

It is difficult to know with any certainty the degree to which avoidance protest in its many forms either obviated against or served as a prelude to more aggressive, better organised modes of peasant resistance involving direct confrontations with those who are viewed as oppressors. It is probable that the nature of these connections varies by the general type and particular form in question. Forms of everday protest through denial are likely to prevent the adoption of more radical measures as long as they provide effective defences for cultivating groups and, concomitantly, the systems of exchange and control in which they are employed remain viable. Severe social dislocations or sudden increases in the power of elite groups that allow them to override customary restraints and peasant buffers can force cul- tivators to turn to other types of avoidance protest – exit or retribution – which are less embedded in existing institutions or to modes of overt confrontation from petition processions to jacqueries.

Even though most forms of the protest of denial through exit place aggrieved peasants outside existing state systems and elite/peasant exchange networks at least temporarily, they are unlikely to bring about solutions to the underlying causes of agrarian unrest. Flawed political economies are abandoned rather than reformed or overthrown and reconstituted. In fact, because forms of denial protest through exit are orientated to evasion, they often have effects that act against amelioration of the conditions that lead to peasant unrest. They release pent-up anger and disperse those who are disgruntled, at times rendering them more vulnerable to reprisals by their elite adversaries. In the case of client transfer or individual flight, protest through exit may dampen mounting collective discontent by drawing highly conscious and vocal individuals out of situations of frustration and hu- miliation and offering them alternative, and potentially more rewarding, careers.

It is difficult to document convincingly, but there is some evidence that cultivators who engage in the protest of retribution are those most likely to become involved in direct confrontations with elite adversaries. Police reports, special enquiries into peasant risings and related sources indicate that a high proportion of peasants who join in mass demonstrations, riots or rebellions had previously been convicted of acts which those in power labelled 'crimes'. It may be that agriculturists who are willing to risk capture and bodily injury while committing surreptitious acts of reprisal, are also those most willing to brave the counter-reprisals of incumbent elites who are openly challenged. However, the individual or small group orientation and the limited consciousness associated with most forms of the protest of retribution mean that recruiting and organisational skills and ideological sophistication must come from beyond poorly educated, provincially minded peasant groups who are too much caught up in daily efforts to survive to formulate grand revolutionary designs. Avoidance protest in its many forms can protect, win specific concessions or exact revenge, but it cannot reform in major ways or transform unjust socio-political systems. Only modes of confrontational protest can achieve the latter and, if the history of agrarian revolution is any guide, non-peasant, elite allies are essential to the mobilisation and success of peasant resistance once it moves beyond the protest of avoidance.

NOTES

1. 'The common or little man never complains publicly'. A peasant's response to Dutch queries as to why the migrants had not complained about worsening conditions earlier while they were still in Semarang [*Pierson*, 1868: 155].
2. For examples, see the essays in the volume on Maroon societies edited by Richard Price [1979] and the studies by Mullin [1972], Hilton [1973] and Blum [1961].
3. Including environmental factors and modes of peasant adaptation to these which Elizabeth Perry [1980] has shown may greatly influence the modes of defence and protest that peasants adopt.
4. For a fine discussion of these patterns in a very different historical and societal setting see Beqiraj [1966].
5. For examples of these forms of resistance see Government of Bihar and Orissa, *Police Proceedings*, 17 Jan. 1913, enclosure A2; Vol. 9793, 1915, No. 28, p. 3; Vol. 10291, 1918, No. 37, p. 2; Vol. 11383, 1924, No. 8, pp. 2–3. See also Pandey [1978: 172, 181]; Hardiman [1977: 56, 58ff].
6. This assumption is supported by numerous anthropological accounts based on research conducted in recent decades which relate the existence of these practices in the post-independence era.

REFERENCES

Adas, Michael, 1979, *Prophets of Rebellion: Millenarian Protest against the European Colonial Order*, Chapel Hill: University of North Carolina Press.

Adas, Michael, 1982, 'Bandits, Monks, and Pretender Kings: Patterns of Peasant Resistance and Protest in Colonial Burma, 1826–1941', in Robert P. Weller and Scott E. Guggenheim, *Power and Protest in the Countryside*, Durham, NC: Duke University Press.

Ahmad, Aziz, 1964, *Studies in Islamic Culture in the Indian Environment*, Oxford: Oxford

University Press.

Anderson, Benedict R. O'G., 1965, *Mythology and the Tolerance of the Javanese*, Ithaca, NY: Cornell University Press.

Anderson, Benedict R. O'G., 1966, 'The Languages of Indonesian Politics', *Indonesia*, Vol. 1, No. 1.

Asiwaju, A.I., 1976, 'Migrations as Revolt: The Example of the Ivory Coast and the Upper Volta before 1945', *Journal of African History*, Vol. 17, No. 4.

Aung Thwin, Michael, 1976, 'Kingship, the *Sangha* and Society in Pagan', in Kenneth Hall and J. Whitmore (eds.), *Explorations in Early Southeast Asian History: Origins of Statecraft*, Ann Arbor: University of Michigan.

Benda, Harry and Lance Castles, 1969, 'The Samin Movement', *Bijdragen tot de Taal-Land-en Volkenkunde*, Vol. 125, No. 2.

Beqiraj, Mehmet, 1966, *Peasantry in Revolution*, Ithaca, NY: Cornell University Press, 1966.

Berque, Jacques, 1972, *Egypt: Imperialism and Revolution*, New York: Praeger.

Blok, Anton, 1972, 'The Peasant and the Brigand: Social Banditry Reconsidered', *Comparative Studies in Society and History*, Vol. 14, No. 4.

Bihar and Orissa, Government of, 1913–22, *Police Proceedings*, India Office Records, London, England.

Blum, Jerome, 1961, *Lord and Peasant in Russia*, Princeton: Princeton University Press.

Bremen, Jan, 1982, 'The Village on Java and the Early Colonial State', *The Journal of Peasant Studies*, Vol. 9, No. 4.

Carey, Peter, 1987, *Pangeran Dipanagara and the Origins of the Java War, 1825–1830*, Leiden: forthcoming.

Christian, J.L., 1942, *Modern Burma*, Berkeley: University of California Press.

Couper, Thomas, 1924, *Report of Inquiry into the Condition of Agricultural Tenants and Labourers*, Rangoon: Government of Burma.

Dewey, Clive, 1979, '*Patwari* and *Chaukidar*: Subordinate Officials and the Reliability of India's Agricultural Statistics', in Clive Dewey and A.G. Hopkins (eds.), *The Imperial Impact in Africa and South Asia*, London: Institute of Commonwealth Studies.

Drewes, Gerardus W.J., 1925, *Drie Javaansche Goeroe's: Hun Leven, Onderricht en Messiasprediking*, Leiden: Vros.

Eaton, Richard, 1977, *Sufis of Bijapur, 1300–1700: Social Roles of Sufis in Medieval India*, Princeton: Princeton University Press.

Fasseur, Cornelis, 1978, *Kultuurstelsel en Koloniale Baten: De Nederlandse Exploitatie van Java 1840–1860*, Leiden: University of Leiden.

Frykenberg, Robert E., 1965, *Guntur District 1788–1848: A History of Local Influence and Central Authority in South India*, Oxford: Oxford University Press.

Genovese, Eugene, 1972, *Roll, Jordan, Roll: The World the Slaves Made*, New York: Pantheon.

Gillion, K.L., 1971, 'Gujarat in 1919', in R. Kumar (ed.), *Essays on Gandhian Politics*, Oxford: Oxford University Press.

Habib, Irfan, 1963, *The Agrarian System of Mughal India*, Aligarh: Aligarh University Press.

Hanks, Lucien, 1962, 'Merit and Power in the Thai Social Order', *American Anthropologist*, Vol. 64, No. 6.

Harcourt, Max, 1977, 'Kisan Populism and Revolution in Rural India: The 1942 Disturbances in Bihar and East United Provinces', in D. A. Low (ed.), *Congress and the Raj*, London: Heinemann.

Hardimann, David, 1977, 'The Crisis of the Lesser Patidars: Peasant Agitations in Kheda District, Gujarat, 1917–34', in Low, *Congress and Raj*.

Henningham, Stephen, 1976, 'The Social Setting at the Champaran Satyagraha: The Challenge of an Alien Elite', *Indian Economist and Social History Review*, Vol. 13, No. 3.

Henningham, Stephen, 1979, 'Agrarian Relations in North Bihar', *Indian Social and Economic History Review*, Vol. 16, No. 1.

Hilton, Rodney, 1973, *Bond Men Made Free*, New York: Viking.

Hobsbawm, Eric, 1959, *Primitive Rebels*, New York: Norton.

Hobsbawm, Eric, 1969, *Bandits*, New York: Dell.

Holt, P.M., 1958, *The Mahdist State in the Sudan 1881–1890*, Oxford: Oxford University Press.
Isaacman, Allen, 1977, 'Social Banditry in Zimbabwe (Rhodesia) and Mozambique, 1894–1907: An Expression of Early Peasant Protest', *Journal of Southern African Studies*, Vol. 4, No. 1.
Isaacman, Allen, Stephen, Michael, *et al.*, 1980, ' "Cotton is the Mother of Poverty": Peasant Resistance to Forced Cotton Production in Mozambique, 1938–1961', *International Journal of African Studies*, Vol. 13, No. 4.
Kartini, Raden Adjeng, 1964, *Letters of a Javanese Princess*, New York: Norton.
Kartodirdjo, Sartono, 1972, 'Agrarian Radicalism in Java', in Claire Holt (ed.), *Culture and Politics in Indonesia*, Ithaca, NY: Cornell University Press.
Kartoni, Margaret, 1976, 'Performance, Music and Meaning of Reyog Ponogoro', *Indonesia*, Vol. 22, No. 1.
Kumar, Ravindra, 1968, *Western India in the Nineteenth Century*, London: Routledge & Kegan Paul.
Last, Murray, 1970, 'Aspects of Administration and Dissent in Hausaland, 1800–1968', *Africa*, Vol. 40, No. 4.
Le Roy Ladurie, Emmanuel, 1974, *The Peasants of Languedoc*, Urbana: University of Illinois Press.
Liebermann, Victor, 1984, *Southeast Asian Administrative Cycles: The Burmese Pattern, c. 1590–1760*, Princeton: Princeton University Press.
Louw, Pieter and E.S. de Klerck, 1894, *De Java-Oorlog van 1825–1830*, The Hague: Nijhoff.
Mair, Lucy, 1966, *Primitive Government*, Baltimore: Penguin.
Meijer, D.H., 1949–50, 'Over het bendwezen op Java', *Indonesië*, Vol. 3, No. 2.
Mendelson, E. Michael, 1975, *State and Sangha in Burma*, Ithaca, NY: Cornell University Press.
Moertono, Soemarsaid, 1968, *State and Statecraft in Old Java*, Ithaca, NY: Cornell University Press.
Mullin, Gerald W., 1972, *Flight and Rebellion: Slave Resistance in Eighteenth-Century Virginia*, Oxford: Oxford University Press.
Ngo Vinh Long, 1973, *Before the Revolution: The Vietnamese Peasants under the French*, Cambridge, MA: MIT Press.
Onghokham, 1975, 'The Residency of Madium Pryayi and Peasant in the Nineteenth Century', Ph. D. dissertation, Yale University.
Pandey, Gyanendra, 1978, *The Ascendancy of the Congress in Uttar Pradesh, 1926–34*, New Delhi: Oxford University Press.
Peacock, James, 1967, 'Anti-Dutch, Anti-Muslim Drama among Surabaya Proletarians: A Description of Performances and Responses', *Indonesia*, Vol. 4, No. 1.
Perry, Elizabeth, 1980, *Rebels and Revolutionaries in North China, 1845–1945*, Palo Alto, CA: Stanford University Press.
Pierson, N.G., 1868, *Het Kultuurstelsel: Zes Voorlezingen*, Amsterdam: Van Kampen.
Price, Richard (ed.), 1979, *Maroon Societies: Rebel Slave Communities in the Americas*, Baltimore: Johns Hopkins University Press.
RAP, 1911, Government of Burma, *Revenue and Agriculture Proceedings*, India Office Records: London, England.
Rabibhadana, Akin, 1969, *The Organization of Thai Society in the Early Bangkok Period*, Ithaca, NY: Cornell University Press.
RPAB, 1911–1919, Government of Burma, *Report(s) on the Police Administration of Burma*, London: India Office Records.
Scott, James, 1972a, 'Patron–Client Politics and Political Change in Southeast Asia', *American Political Science Quarterly*, Vol. 66, No. 1.
Scott, James, 1972b, 'The Erosion of Patron–Client Bonds and Social Change in Southeast Asia', *The Journal of Asian Studies*, Vol. 22, No. 1.
Scott, James and Kerkvliet, Ben, 1973, 'The Politics of Survival: Peasant Responses to "Progress" in Southeast Asia', *Journal of Southeast Asian Studies*, Vol. 4, No. 2.
Soest, G.H. van, 1869, *Geschiedenis van het Kultuurstelsel*, Rotterdam: H. Nijgh.
Sturtevant, David R., 1976, *Popular Uprisings in the Philippines*, Ithaca, NY: Cornell Univer-

sity Press.

Tai, Hue-Tam Ho, 1983, *Millenarianism and Peasant Politics in Vietnam*, Cambridge, MA: Harvard University Press.

Than Tun, 1968, 'Administration of King Tha-lun (1629–48)', *Journal of the Burma Research Society*, Vol. 51, No. 2.

Thein Pe Myint, 1973, 'Her Husband or Her Money', in P.M. Milne (trans.), *Selected Short Stories of Thein Pe Myint*, Ithaca, NY: Cornell University Press.

Thompson, Edward, 1972, '"Rough Music": Le Charivari anglais', *Annales: économies sociétés civilisations*, Vol. 27, No. 3.

Tin Gyi, U., 1926, *Myaungmya Settlement Report, 1924–25*, Rangoon: Government of Burma.

Vitalis, L., 1851, *De invoering, werking en gebreken van het stelsel van Kultuurs op Java*, Zalt-Bommel: Norman en zoon.

III

"MORAL ECONOMY" OR "CONTEST STATE"?:
ELITE DEMANDS AND THE ORIGINS OF PEASANT PROTEST
IN SOUTHEAST ASIA

In an era of scholarship dominated by regional specialization and an awesome proliferation of studies on protest and revolution, it is rare for works to appear that contain such innovative and provocative theoretical contributions that one is forced to pause and reexamine his own analytical assumptions and interpretations. For scholars whose research focuses on the causes of social unrest and collective protest, the studies of E.P. Thompson and more recently James C. Scott should stimulate such an evaluation. The concept of the "moral economy," which Thompson suggests in *The Making of the English Working Class*[1] and develops more fully in his essay on "The Moral Economy of the English Crowd in the Eighteenth Century,"[2] provides a broad and compelling framework for the analysis of a wide variety of forms of popular protest. Thompson focuses on food riots during a period of profound social and economic transition. His central purpose is to demonstrate that crowd actions to lower food prices in times of dearth or to put an end to practices which violated customary marketing arrangements were not the spasmodic, wanton, and implicitly marginal outbursts of popular outrage that many earlier writers had pictured. Thompson argues that these disturbances represented a "highly-complex form of direct political action, disciplined and with clear objectives."[3] They were approved by "popular consensus" and often tolerated by local officials, unless they became unduly violent and destructive. In Thompson's view, food riots and efforts to prevent the abuses of marketing middlemen were attempts on the part of the laboring classes and the poor to uphold the ethical precepts of the moral economy, which he argues (and produces considerable evidence to demonstrate) existed in pre-industrial England at the level of royal policymaking, genteel philosophizing, and in the popular consciousness. Food riots (or as Thompson convincingly argues, the threat of food riots) were a means of defending paternalistic, consumer-oriented marketing patterns, which were regulated by custom and common law, against the advance of practices and institutions which reflected the laissez-faire doctrines of Adam Smith and the classical, capitalistic economists.

Although Thompson's ideas have stimulated considerable debate among European historians,[4] James C. Scott has made the fullest use of the concept of the moral economy to date in his comparative study of *The Moral Economy of the Peasant: Rebellion and Subsistence in Southeast Asia.*[5] Using evidence drawn primarily from Asian rather than European societies, Scott focuses on revenue and rental demands made by pre-colonial and colonial elite groups upon the peasantry rather than the marketing patterns which are Thompson's main concern. Although the pre-colonial source materials on popular protest in

Southeast Asia are far more meager and less informative about peasant conditions than the evidence used by Thompson to document widespread adherence to the precepts of the moral economy in pre-industrial England, Scott's application of the concept is more elaborate and more specific in its statement of the moral economy's attributes. Because my own research has dealt mainly with Southeast Asian societies, the following critique of the moral economy approach to the study of the causes of peasant protest is based upon reactions to Scott's study, rather than Thompson's earlier work. The alternative framework which I will offer is also derived primarily from evidence relating to Southeast Asia societies, especially Java and Burma which have been the focus of my own research.[6] I believe, however, that many of my findings are applicable beyond Southeast Asia, particularly to state systems in India and sub-Saharan Africa. Some of what I have to say may also be of use for European societies to those who are more familiar with the empirical data which form the basis for judging the value of this or any theoretical proposition.

Although this essay focuses upon Scott's application of the concept of the moral economy and an exploration of alternatives to it, it is important to note at the outset that the scope of *The Moral Economy of the Peasant* is much broader than the themes dealt with here. Taken as a whole the work is an insightful and intellectually exciting contribution to the study of Southeast Asian societies and the origins of social protest. Scott not only develops a cohesive and well-argued theoretical framework for the analysis of peasant rebellions, he argues persuasively for a fundamental reorientation of our approaches to peasant interaction with the elites whom they support. He asserts that abstract theories, which are very often based on elite-centric studies of the "Great Revolutions," are of little use in understanding peasant perceptions of their living conditions or evaluating the peasants' criteria for determining whether the demands of bureaucrats and landlords are just or exploitative. Scott argues that in order to understand the roots of peasant discontent and protest we must direct our attention to issues that are fundamental to the peasants themselves, rather than become enmeshed in complex sequences of grievances and supposed frustrations devised by scholars whose premises are all too often largely products of their own urban, bourgeois backgrounds. Implicitly, Scott asserts that the study of agrarian protest demands that the social scientist consciously strive to develop a sensitivity to peasant cultures and an ability to empathize with peasant concerns. In several brilliant sections of *The Moral Economy of the Peasant*, he demonstrates the way in which "unorthodox" sources, such as folk songs, peasant tales and traditions, and popular literature, can be used to gain insights into the peasants' perspective and world view. Though familiar to European social historians and anthropologists,[7] these sources have until recently been neglected by historians of Asia and Scott's study should do much to encourage their more extensive use in studies of collective protest.

As Scott is surely aware, his decision to concentrate on general theory, even though he develops two case studies in considerable depth, means that he is bound to arouse questions and objections on many fronts. Inevitably many of these will involve his selection and interpretation of evidence relating to the two case studies, the Saya San rebellion in Burma and the soviets of Nghe-An and Ha Tinh in Vietnam, which provide much of the empirical backing for his theoretical speculations. However, because the central thrust of Scott's work is theoretical and his main aim is to advance our conceptual understanding of peasant responses and peasant protest, the most critical debates concerning his work ought to concentrate upon his analytical concepts and the overall framework for the study of elite-peasant relations which he has so forcefully advanced. Though the theoretical issues raised by Scott in *The Moral Economy of the Peasant* are numerous and complex, my concern in this essay is the concept of the moral economy itself, which is central to Scott's whole analytical framework and worthy of rigorous evaluation in its own right.

The peasants' all-pervasive and unrelenting struggle for subsistence provides the starting point for James Scott's application of the theory of the moral economy. Although the criteria for distinguishing "subsistence" peasants from their more affluent counterparts are never precisely identified, Scott acknowledges that his findings apply in their "full force" only to peasants with "very low incomes, little land, large families, highly variable yields, and few outside opportunities."[8] He argues that peasants of this sort, which would include a clear majority of the populations of Africa, Asia, and Latin America, are understandably obsessed with the problems involved in growing and retaining enough food to guarantee their "minimum subsistence." This grim struggle for mere survival is in Scott's view the key to understanding the institutions, relationships, and thought systems of subsistence peasant societies. The knowledge that they live on the very margin of subsistence and that even temporary disruptions of the cropping cycle caused by either man or nature can mean starvation instills in the peasants a strong aversion to changes in crops or cultivation techniques that involve even a minimal degree of risk, however great the potential of these changes for increased production. Subsistence peasants, Scott argues, value stability and security above all else. They work for a "minimum guaranteed return," rather than surpluses to hoard or market. They are deeply attached to communally oriented villages, which strive to maximize autonomy and internal control. Social and economic relations within the village are regulated by the precepts of what Scott lables the "subsistence ethic," which places a heavy premium on reciprocity, mutual assistance, and the guarantee of minimum subsistence for all village members. To insure that the subsistence ethic is followed, the village community employs a wide range of devices from the periodic reassignment of village common lands and the maintainence of communal granaries to the use of fines, sorcery, and even violence to punish village members who defy established norms.[9]

In Scott's view the subsistence ethic also shapes the peasants' attitudes toward and responses to the demands of supra-village elite groups. The peasants judge the exactions of landlords, regional officials, or monarchs not according to how much rent or revenue these overlords take in absolute terms, but how much they leave relative to the peasants' output and their subsistence needs. Scott argues that the peasants' definition of a "just" lord is one who recognizes the peasants' right to subsistence and regulates the timing and size of his rent or revenue demands to insure that the cultivator will retain enough food to support himself and his household. A "moral" political economy is one in which elite demands fluctuate to take into account the impact of natural calamities and the depredations of marauding armies or bandit gangs on the level of agricultural production in any given year. In times of dearth, the lord, like the peasant, consumes less and grants remissions so that the cultivator can maintain a minimum level of subsistence. Thus, there is in Scott's view a critical ethical dimension to the peasants' perception of his relationship to landholding and governing elite groups. Lords who respect the precepts of the moral economy and

II

524

allow the cultivating classes to retain enough for subsistence may not be loved by
the peasantry, but their demands are viewed as legitimate and tolerable.
Conversely, elites whose demands are rigid and take no account of the peasants'
subsistence needs are considered exploitative and unjust. Because the latter elite
groups violate the subsistence ethic which is central to the peasants' vision of a
moral economic order, the cultivating classes believe that they are justified in
resisting these exactions and supporting protest movements aimed at the
overthrow of those who demand them.

Although the existence of precolonial societies where elite-peasant exchanges
were vitally influenced by the precepts of the moral economy is essential to Scott's
interpretations of the impact of colonialism in rural Southeast Asia, the latter
process forms his central concern and is the subject of all but the early chapters of
The Moral Economy of the Peasant. He argues that the European colonizers'
violation of the precepts of the moral economy, whether out of ignorance or
volition, was the underlying cause of unrest and rebellion among peasant groups
at the subsistence level. Alien, colonial officials, both because they were
insensitive to peasant needs and expectations and because they had to satisfy the
insatiable demands of politicians in the European metropolises to "make the
colonies pay," rigidly enforced revenue demands once they were established. In
years of good harvests these demands might appear to be low by precolonial
standards, but in times of scarcity they were impossible for the peasantry to meet.
European colonization also resulted in the extension of the global, capitalist
economic system to societies that had previously been oriented to susistence
production. Market mechanisms and contractual and impersonal relationships
proved beneficial to a small minority of able and ambitious indigenous
agriculturists, but for the vast majority of peasants, struggling for survival, these
innovations meant major challenges to their margin of subsistence. The security
and stability of the pre-colonial peasant community and household were
undermined by wildly fluctuating commodity prices, often determined by
international market conditions entirely beyond the peasants' control or even
comprehension. Moneylenders and large landholders, backed by the property-
oriented courts and constabulary of the colonizers, became the dominant forces in
village economies and extracted steadily increasing shares of what the cultivators
were able to produce.

All of these forces led to the disintegration of the subsistence- and communally-
oriented village. Emphasis on profit-making and competition exacerbated growing
divisions between landed and landless agriculturists. They also eroded the
peasants' sense of mutual assistance and their commitment to the subsistence
ethic. The penetration of bureaucratic control and the agents of the global market
system to the village level rendered internal regulation superfluous and village
sanctions impotent. They also exposed increasingly isolated peasant households
to the vagaries and bewildering transformations of the world beyond the village
walls. Whatever regional and local variations one might detect in peasant
grievances in the colonial era, Scott asserts that the movements of protest
supported by peasants living on the subsistence margin shared common origins
involving violations of the precepts of the moral economy by the forces of
European imperialism and capitalism. Outraged by the ever-increasing and
inflexible demands of their colonial overlords, the peasantry rose up to overthrow
the new order and replace it with an idealized, utopian world of communal
harmony, stability, and security. Whether rebellious peasants followed prophetic
leaders who promised magical-millenarian solutions, like Saya San who led the

1930-32 risings in Burma, or communist-nationalist leaders, such as those who organized the Nghe-An and Ha-Tinh soviets in roughly the same period, their underlying goals were the same — the restoration of institutions and elite-peasant relationships that were attuned to the dictates of the moral economy.

In contrast to E.P. Thompson who is concerned to demonstrate that early modern monarchs and the English gentry shared many of the assumptions held by peasants and laborers regarding the ethical constraints that governed England's pre-industrial market economy,[10] Scott focuses his discussion of the moral economy almost exclusively on peasant perceptions and responses. Scott alludes in a number of places to the organizational and technological limits on the capacity of pre-colonial regimes in Southeast Asia to extract produce and labor services from the peasantry.[11] He also argues, at least by inference from the strong contrast which he draws between elite behavior in the pre-colonial and colonial periods, that pre-colonial elite groups acknowleged the peasants' right to a subsistence minimum.[12] On the whole, however, Scott has surprisingly little to say about the elite side of the pre-colonial political economies of Southeast Asia. This omission itself is serious because it is difficult to build a convincing theory which focuses on the workings of revenue systems and peasant attitudes towards those who extract their surplus without a detailed understanding of the roles and attitudes of elite groups at various levels of the pre-colonial agro-bureaucratic hierarchy.

Without an elite dimension, the central argument in Scott's theory of the moral economy comes close to tautology: the primary concern of peasants who live on the subsistence margin is to subsist. When landlords or tax collectors attempt to extract so large a share of what the cultivators produce that they are not left enought to survive, they react with moral outrage, resistance, and under certain circumstances, open rebellion. As Scott demonstrates, there is a good deal of evidence from colonial and post-colonial sources to satisfy those who refuse to accept the importance of subsistence concerns on logical grounds alone. Many of the corollaries of the subsistence-centric thesis — peasant aversion to risk-taking, village institutions geared to mutual assistance, etc. — can also be well documented and are persuasively presented in *The Moral Economy of the Peasant.* Among the major contributions of Scott's work is his integration of these patterns into a cohesive and convincing typology, which he labels the subsistence ethic, and his magisterial marshalling of empirical evidence from many areas and disciplines to support his arguments.

Scott's determination to stress the overriding importance of these concerns is justified in view of the fact that they have often been neglected by social scientists based in urban, industrial societies where the process of food production is remote and the threat of starvation appears to be. His argument would be greatly enhanced, however, and its circular quality obviated if peasant behavior, responses, and expectations were viewed in the context of political, economic, and ethical-legal systems as a whole. This is in fact the approach Scott takes in dealing with the colonial period, where he discusses the policies and actions of the Europeans and their indigenous allies in great detail. The contrast that Scott argues existed between the pre-colonial and colonial elite demands suggests, at least implicitly and in places explicitly, a broader meaning of the concept of the moral economy. As in E.P. Thompson's original formulation, this wider definition of the concept involves constraints and controls that are acknowledged in principle, if not followed in practice, by both elite groups and peasant producers.

From the elite side, the notion of a subsistence guarantee also has something of a self-evident quality to it. Except for transistory and excessively rapacious tax farmers and psychotics who reveled in cruelty to others, administrators and local notables would have seen little point in extracting so much revenue from the peasantry under their control that their subjects were unable to survive. Because starving peasants meant less or no surplus production to support the elite, the latter sought to optimize in the long-term, rather than maximize in a single cropping season, the share of the peasants' output that they extracted. Though compassion cannot be ruled as a motive, elite groups were inclined to grant remissions and even share hoarded grain in times of scarcity because if they did not do so, they would lose the peasants who supported them through migration or starvation. Without relief measures, the elite also ran the risk of food riots and localized rebellions which their small numbers and limited military clout made difficult to repress.

Scott's concentration on subsistence concerns causes him to neglect or deny the importance of other issues which vitally affect the condition and responses of the peasantry. Many of the problems which arise in this regard can be traced to his failure clearly to distinguish between subsistence-oriented and other kinds of peasants. As a result, he frequently makes use of evidence relating to agrarian groups which clearly fall outside his subsistence-peasant category in order to develop and support his typology. His use of Burma, particularly Lower Burma, in the period of British rule dramatically illustrates the problems arising from his choice of sources for empirical verification of his theoretical assertions. For much of the colonial period Lower Burma was not only a frontier region with vast stretches of fertile, unclaimed land, low population densities, and relatively large landholdings, it was also a region where both indigenous and Indian cultivators voluntarily, and even enthusiastically, participated on a massive scale in the development of a major export economy based primarily on the production of rice.[13] Although aspects of Scott's subsistence typology may be useful for the study of some of the agrarian groups involved in Lower Burma's development, particularly in the decades of social and economic crisis in the 1920s and 1930s, the typology as a whole is inappropriate. The majority of the agrarian population in Lower Burma became deeply committed to production for the market and attached to consumer rewards. For over half a century the economy of Lower Burma was dominated by highly mobile smallholders who energetically acquired and cultivated vast tracts of open land which they themselves owned. In response to a steadily rising market demand for rice and an abundance of resources, they willingly took risks, competed with their countrymen and immigrants from overseas, and in numerous cases accumulated the capital necessary to launch careers as landlords, moneylenders, and rice brokers. Similar objections to the blanket application of the subsistence-ethic typology could be raised by specialists working in other areas of Africa, Asia, and Latin America.

Even if one confines his evaluation of Scott's subsistence-centric approach to more appropriate groups, like the majority of the peasants of north and central Vietnam, his assertions remain too constrictive. His implicit argument that subsistence-oriented peasants are satisfied to retain only enough of their produce to stay alive and plant their next crop is open to question. The evidence we have suggests that cultivating groups sought to maximize the amount of produce they retained, and to deny labor and military services to their overlords whenever possible. In addition, the whole thrust of Scott's argument, despite his ingenious amalgamation of moral philosophy, economics, and social history, is monocausal and overly materialistic. Even peasants on the margin of subsistence have deeply felt concerns beyond rice and taxes. Scott's decision to concentrate almost exclusively on these admittedly critical issues obscures other vitally important aspects of the peasants' life and outlook. These include their religious beliefs, personal attachments to particular leaders or groups, aspirations for higher social status and prestige, the threat of military conscription, and deeply felt prejudices towards different ethnic groups or immigrants. Subsistence peasants can and have joined rebellions to defend their religions, to support popular local leaders who have been demoted or displaced, or to settle ancient feuds with rival villages or neighboring peoples with different ethnic and cultural backgrounds.[14] The aspirations of peasant supporters of pre-colonial millenarian rebellions (which are the movements we have the most information about) extended far beyond the subsistence minimum to visions of material abundance, political stability and probity, and social harmony.[15]

Scott's approach to the subsistence ethic also overstates the degree to which communal harmony and cohesion dominated village life in the pre-colonial era.[16] Anthropological evidence drawn from many areas supports the contrasting paradigm of the peasant village developed by Mehmet Begiraj.[17] Begiraj argues that deep and bitter factional divisions have been a central feature of village life. These divisions have led not only to quarrels and periodic outbursts of violence within the village; they have rendered the peasant community vulnerable to exploitation by regional bureaucrats and the landed gentry. Scott's emphasis on communal homogeneity and solidarity also obscures significant differences in social and economic status that existed within the peasant village long before European colonizers arrived on the scene. The villages of central Java, for example, which have long been considered the epitome of subsistence- and communally-oriented social units,[18] were in fact highly stratified in the pre-colonial period. They were dominated by the chief "landowning"* families or *sikeps* who regulated village affairs through their control of economic resources and the community councils, and mediated the efforts of supra-village elite groups to extract produce or labor services. The *sikeps'* fields were cultivated by client-tenants and laborers called *numpangs*, who were divided into several grades according to the extent of their dependence on their *sikep* patrons. Apanage holders and regional officials designated certain *sikep* notables as *bekels*, who were responsible for the collection of taxes in their villages, as well as the organization of corvée labor and the conscription of peasants for military service. Taxes were assessed by individual households and little village land was held in common. The *sikeps*, or at least those who were descended from the foundling families of the village, also dominated the village council and monopolized the position of *lurah* or headman.[19] In direct contrast to the general patterns identified by Scott, distinctions between social strata within the village appear to have been greatly reduced in the colonial period due to the nature of Dutch demands for revenue and export production. Recent evidence indicates, however, that divisions have begun to reemerge in the post-colonial era.[20]

Scott's vision of subsistence peasants dedicated to intra-village reciprocity and the survival of all members of the community is at variance with the findings of George Foster and other writers who argue that the interaction of poor peasants is determined mainly by their "image of the limited good."[21] In this view peasant households are locked in a constant struggle to maximize for themselves the

*Technically all land was "owned" by the Javanese monarch.

largest possible share of what is perceived to be a limited supply of material goods, status rewards, and even religious benefits. The village world as a result is dominated by suspicion, rivalries, and petty squabbling. Competition, rather than cooperation and mutual aid, is the keynote of the peasants' struggle for survival in the face of natural disasters and manmade tribulations. Scott's analysis may provide valuable correctives for the "limited goods" typology, and perhaps indicates a need to distinguish different types of subsistence peasants, but the findings of Foster, Banfield, and other anthropologists need to be taken into account in any general assessment of the attitudes, interaction, and ethical norms of subsistence cultivators.

In the Southeast Asian context Scott's neglect of the roles of elite groups in pre-colonial political economies is especially problematical because the nature of the sources available for this period makes it very difficult to deal directly with peasant conditions and attitudes. Precise data relating to issues that are central to Scott's theoretical assertions, such as the peasants' standard of living or how much of their produce was extracted by indigenous elite groups, do not exist for most areas and time periods. Because virtually none of the sources available to contemporary scholars was written by peasants, it is impossible to know with any certainty about the less tangible aspects of Scott's thesis that involve peasant assumptions regarding legitimate revenue demands and their attitudes towards elite groups at different levels of the pre-colonial socio-political hierarchy. For information about the peasantry in pre-colonial Southeast Asia, we are dependent upon the monastic scribes or court chroniclers who authored the few indigenous historical works which we possess. Unfortunately, these works, which were devoted mainly to "des intrigues de cour, des faits de guerre, des évènements merveilleux,"[22] had little to say about peasants, rich or poor. Royal edicts, temple inscriptions, and surviving revenue records make it possible for us to know something about the condition of agriculturists in the pre-colonial era, and these sources have been used in imaginative and productive ways in recent decades.[23] At best, however, we can learn about population distribution, the sorts of goods and services cultivators were expected to provide for their overlords, and elite attitudes towards the peasantry. The available sources contain no evidence relating to peasant perceptions of the elite or peasant expectations, and little concrete information about peasant living standards or their reactions to the exactions of local, regional, or court-based elite groups.

The source problems outlined above are reflected in Scott's heavy reliance, in the pre-colonial chapters, on studies from areas outside Southeast Asia, especially Europe and China, or from colonial and post-colonial societies,[24] where there is better evidence on elite-peasant interactions and the underlying ethical assumptions which governed these exchanges. For the pre-colonial period in Southeast Asia, and for much of South Asia and sub-Saharan Africa, the kind of evidence needed to test Scott's assertions regarding peasant attitudes simply does not exist. Thus, evidence for an ethical dimension to the process of revenue gathering in the pre-colonial era must be gleaned from sources written by and about elite groups. As I shall argue, these sources indicate that ethical considerations did play a role in determining the nature of elite-peasant interaction, but the structure of the agrarian-based political economies of pre-colonial Southeast Asia rendered religious injunctions, legal restraints and the edicts of pious and well-meaning monarchs difficult to enforce. However much the peasants may have shared religiously based concepts regarding the behavior of a "just" king or the rulers' rightful share of the produce, cultivators relied less on these abstract principles than on competition among different elite groups, the organizational and technological limitations of their overlords, and their own time-honored devices for concealment and evasion in their efforts to retain as much as possible of what they produced.

The extant evidence relating to the nature of the political economies of pre-colonial Southeast Asia indicates that there was an ethical or moral dimension to the interaction between lord and peasant that was far more encompassing than the peasant responses that are central in Scott's approach. These ethical principles extended far beyond the state granaries and revenue remissions which Scott correctly argues were aimed at helping hard-pressed peasants survive periods of poor weather conditions and extensive crop losses, and equally critically, averting social unrest that might be caused by these conditions.[25] Moral restraints on elite demands on the peasantry were contained in the court chronicles, coronation oaths, and religious texts which defined, often in surprising detail, the monarch's obligations to his subjects. Elite-peasant interaction was also regulated at the local level by long-standing customs that included precedents for elite demands upon and responsibilities toward their peasant subjects.

Like their counterparts in India and China from which many precedents for political organization and thinking in Southeast Asia were derived, pre-colonial rulers in areas like Java and Burma were considered responsible for the prosperity and welfare of their subjects and the fertility of their domains. In most Southeast Asian kingdoms, these general obligations were supplemented by quite specific instructions concerning the policies and behavior of an ideal king. A ruler who strove to be a just or righteous sovereign was enjoined by the sacred texts and expected by his subjects to limit taxes to a specified portion of the peasants' output, restrain his officials from excessive demands on the common people, and provide tax remissions and relief from areas struck by famine.[26] Popular notions of the behavior of a just ruler were also embodied in apocalyptic prophecies, such as those relating to Jayabaya in Java, which indicate widespread adherence to some of the ethical principles stressed by Scott. In prophesied times of decay and chaos, when the ruler's administration of justice was arbitrary and uneven and his revenue demands fluctuated or increased, powerful men treated the lower orders badly, and at harvest time the crops failed and the fields were flooded.[27]

In periods of dynastic strength, when effective rulers committed to these ideals were on the throne, moral precepts appear to have had some impact on the conduct of government and a restraining influence on the revenue demands of at least those serving in the central administration. Under the strongest of monarchs, these ethical considerations may also have been taken into account in the formulation of measures designed to control regional lords and the local gentry. It is difficult to determine how great the impact of these ethical principles was, but it is doubtful that, even in the best of times, Southeast Asian rulers lived up to them to the extent that the court chroniclers claimed. In periods of dynastic weakness, moral injunctions were given little more than lip-service at all levels and ignored in day-to-day governance. In all periods, ethical constraints were difficult, if not impossible, to enforce beyond the walls of the capital city and the surrounding core regions of the kingdom.

From the peasants' perspective the belief that the intercession of a righteous sovereign with the forces of the cosmos was essential to an abundant harvest had little to do with their expectations as to how much of that harvest they would be allowed to retain. Scott's assertion that the peasants believed that they had a right to a particular share and that this right was acknowledged by their overlords lacks an empirical basis. It also runs counter to what we know about the actual functioning of pre-colonial political economies and the realities of the ongoing contest between peasants and elite groups for control of what the cultivators produced. In this context fluid and highly personalized patron-client ties and obligations, and local custom, were the main ethical or moral means of achieving restraint in elite demands and the adherence of the peasantry to the commands of their overlords. Moral precepts, however, were far less important determinants of the peasants' welfare than the administrative and technological deficiences of pre-colonial states and the defense mechanisms which these weaknesses allowed the peasantry to develop to buffer elite demands. Ethical principles did temper the incessant contest among monarchs, ministers, tax collectors, and peasant households for control of the available resources in pre-colonial societies, but the contest itself was the most important determinant of the nature of pre-colonial political economies. Elite exactions and peasant expectations can be best understood by focusing not on the ethical precepts which were supposed to govern the contest, but on the contest itself as it was manifested in inter-elite and elite-peasant interaction at a number of levels from the ruler and central administration to local notables and the cultivating classes.

It is doubtful that even the most benevolent and pious pre-colonial monarchs had much to say about the way in which their peasant subjects were treated. However essential to their kingdom's well-being their intercession with the forces of the cosmos might be thought to be, Southeast Asian rulers exercised only limited control over the regional and local elite groups who actually extracted the produce and labor services which supported king and noble alike. When a dynasty was strong, the effective control exerted by a monarch's chief ministers was confined mainly to the "core" areas of his kingdom that surrounded the capital city. These areas were dominated by lands held directly by the sovereign and administered by court appointees. The surplus from these areas was devoted mainly to the support of the ruler and his court. Interspersed with the royal domains were tracts of land which had been granted as apanage holdings to princes, powerful ministers, and other members of the nobility. In the best of times, the ruler exercised some control in these areas. When the court's power was on the wane, the apanage areas became increasingly autonomous. In some instances these areas emerged as the bases from which rival claimants to the throne launched their campaigns for succession.[28]

As one moved away from the capital and "core" areas of the kingdom, the ruler's effective control decreased markedly (though there were often regional variations) and the power of regional lords became more and more apparent. The *bupatis* of Mataram or the *bayin* and *wuns* of the Taung-Ngu or Kòn-baung kingdoms in Burma ruled the provinces placed in their charge as virtually autonomous and self-sufficient units. If a particular monarch was a strong ruler, which meant that he was an able warrior-statesman (with emphasis on the former), the revenue and ceremonial obligations of his regional administrators were fulfilled with some degree of regularity. When a weak ruler was on the throne, the regional lords frequently withdrew their military support, funneled the ruler's share of the taxes collected into their own coffers, and either sided with promising princely claimants to the throne or set out themselves to found new dynasties.[29]

The poor vertical integration of pre-colonial Southeast Asian states extended beyond the relationship between the court center and the provincial lords into the administrative hierarchies of the regions themselves. The regional lords divided the population placed under their control among their client-retainers who in turn delegated the task of extracting revenue and labor services from the villages allotted for their support to a motley host of middlemen, tax collectors, and overseers.[30] In the last resort, however, officials at all levels depended on local and village leaders, who were not part of the regular bureaucracy extending from the court, in their efforts to collect taxes or conscript peasants for corvée labor or military service. Because pre-colonial Southeast Asian state systems (with the possible exception of Vietnam in some periods) did not reach down to the village level, the cooperation of hereditary village or township leaders was essential to the success of transient revenue officials. The latter knew little or nothing about local conditions, and in the absence of assistance from local men of influence, they were reduced to brute force as a means of extracting labor or produce from the peasantry.[31]

The low degree of integration which characterized the polities of pre-colonial Southeast Asia meant that the kind of bureaucratic control and records keeping that were essential to determining the peasants' "fair share" and insuring that they retained enough for subsistence simply did not exist. Though revenue inquests were ordered by vigorous Javanese and Burmese monarchs and revenue ministers amassed and stored large quantities of data, the information available relating to population, land tenure, and village conditions was incomplete, uneven in coverage, and very dubious in accuracy. Full-scale and reasonably systematic revenue inquests were rare. The surveys ordered in the 1770s by the rulers of the fragment states that were carved out of the kingdom of Mataram in central Java formed the basis of revenue assessments in the princely states and in areas taken over directly by the Dutch until the 1860s. Inquests in pre-colonial Burma were somewhat more frequent, but there were nearly twenty year intervals between the three carried out under the Kòn-baung monarchs. The last, effective revenue and population survey was made in 1802, even though the dynasty continued to rule large portions of Burma until 1885.[32] The European colonial officials who tried to make use of these records as portions of Burma and Java came under their control were unanimous in their opinion that indigenous bookkeeping was in a sorry state. Records were not updated regularly; they were haphazardly filed and poorly stored; and they merely recorded "what a ruler expected to collect" from a particular area rather than its actual output.[33]

Because the administrators of Southeast Asian kingdoms, with the partial exception of Vietnam, were apanage holders and not salaried bureaucrats, it was in their interest to underreport the population (and hence the revenue due) under their control and to pocket the difference between what they actually collected and what they were required to pass on to the court. Numerous royal edicts enjoining administrators to keep accurate and up-to-date records amply testify to the courts' persistent anxieties regarding the deficiencies of existing accounts and the consequent loss of revenue to the sovereign. Officials at all levels, from village notable to the ministers in charge of the kings' storehouses, engaged in underreporting, a form of corruption that was instituionalized and hence universally accepted within customary limits. This practice meant, however, that population and resources were consistently undercounted, and that the regional lords, much less the ruler, had little idea what the productivity of their domains really was. In addition to deliberate undercounting, government revenues were lost and its efforts at bookkeeping frustrated by the fact that movements of population or acreage brought into cultivation after a cadastral survey was made often went unrecorded.[34] Thus, though the ruler or his vassals might claim the right to a certain portion of the peasants' output, it is unlikely that they ever actually collected this amount or even expected to do so. It was also impossible for them to insure that a "fair share" was left for the peasant producers, even if they had been so inclined.

Even if the state of indigenous bookkeeping had made it possible for the elite to determine with precision the "subsistence minimum" which their peasant subjects required, there is little evidence that they acknowledged any limits on what they demanded in accordance with abstract ethical principles, however pious and well-intentioned a given ruler might be. In fact, elite attitudes and behavior indicate that they were out to get all they possibly could, and that they expected the peasantry to do everything in their power to retain as much of what they produced as possible. It was by no means assumed that the lord had a right to all of the peasants' surplus or that the peasant had a right to keep all that fell below a hypothetical "minimum subsistence" level. Shares were determined by protracted annual contests, and the amount collected by the elite or retained by the peasantry could fluctuate substantially from one year to the next.

The great difference in life style and status which separated court and regional elite groups from the agrarian population, despite their participation in a common sociocultural tradition, render the very idea of "fair share" commitment on the part of the elite suspect. Though one does not have to accept Jan Myrdal's impression that pre-colonial Southeast Asian lords felt nothing but contempt for their peasant subjects,[35] there is little question that the ruling classes of Java, Burma, and other areas in Southeast Asia believed that they were privileged and superior beings, and sought to emphasize the gulf that separated them from the mass of the population. Detailed sumptuary laws regarding housing, dress, and even eating utensils; elaborate conventions to regulate encounters between superiors and inferiors; a widely-diffused aesthetic sensitivity to the contrast between ideas, actions, and objects that were refined (in Javanese *halus*) and those that were base and rough (*kasar*); and even differences in the language used depending upon the status of the person one was addressing, give ample testimony to the sense of hierarchy and sociocultural distinctiveness that permeated pre-colonial societies.[36]

If sociocultural differences made it unlikely that the lord would be overly sensitive to the expectations of his peasant subjects, his life style and the demands of his position as a man of status and power forced him to extract as much as possible in taxes and labor from the population he controlled. The needs and hence the revenue demands of the pre-colonial elite of Southeast Asia were perhaps even less flexible than those of the European colonial overlords, which Scott characterizes as rigid and relentless. A *bupati* in Java or a *wun* in Burma had numerous retainers, relatives, and domestic servants to support, and the numbers of his dependents invariably increased as his position improved or his tenure of office lengthened. In Southeast Asia, as in many pre-industrial societies, dependents were a visible sign of a man's power and status. If their numbers grew, so did the popular conviction that he was a man of worth and ability. If he lost clients or was unable to maintain them properly (in which case he was likely to lose them eventually), his status declined and his power was threatened. The mere possession of many dependents was one of the major signs that an individual had the capacity to assume positions of authority.[37]

Another indication of that capacity was the ability to collect large amounts of revenue and proffer splendid gifts to the ruler. A recent study of the Madiun region of Java, for example, reveals that the regional lords most revered in pre-colonial writings and popular traditions were those who were able to extract the greatest amounts of tribute from the peasantry and those whose orders were obeyed.[38] If the ruler or a powerful minister paid a visit to a regional lord or journeyed through his territory, the latter was forced to raise additional revenue to house and entertain his superiors and their retinues. The vassal himself was usually compelled to make periodic and costly visits to the capital. These expenses, in addition to those involved in the constant burden of maintaining a household that to some degree imitated and reflected the splendor and luxury of the sovereign's court, resulted in a wide variety of special revenue and service demands that were levied on the peasantry beyond formal land and household taxes. In some instances, these special cesses were so great that what appeared on the basis of formal payments to be a relatively mild system of taxation was in fact an onerous one.[39]

Although the existence of state granaries and government edicts proclaiming that remissions ought to be granted in years of poor harvests are indicative of the sort of elite concern for the peasants' welfare that was expected of a just and powerful ruler, there is abundant evidence that the demands of pre-colonial elite groups often rose in times of distress and dwindling resources. For example, the increase in tribute which the ruler of Yogyakarta, Hamengkubuwana II, demanded from his apanage holders in the early years of the nineteenth century meant additional burdens for the peasants of his kingdom, who were expected to provide more goods and services on the basis of stable or declining resources. As Dutch and British annexations reduced the areas controlled by the Javanese rulers in the following decades, increasing numbers of their apanage holders and their retainers sought to force a greatly diminished peasant population to support them at levels more appropriate to an earlier and more affluent age. *Bupatis*, who were pressed for funds, farmed out their apanage holdings to Chinese overseers, who promised to squeeze the maximum revenue from the hard-pressed peasantry. Aristocratic administrators and low-born farmers showed little hestitation in resorting to extortion, violence, and forcible dispossesion of the peasantry to achieve their revenue demands.[40]

In addition to pressures produced by political or economic crises, the very nature of pre-colonial political systems encouraged regional leaders and apanage holders to extract as much as they possible could from the peasantry. Strong rulers shifted their retainers' holdings or required their intermittent attendance at court in order to prevent them from building up local bases of power.[41] These devices of control encouraged office and apanage holders to squeeze all they could get from the districts under their control while their tenure of office lasted. They also made it unlikely that nobles or administrators would develop a strong sense of responsibility for the welfare of the populations alloted for their support.

Given these conditions, official edicts about remissions or the maintenance of storage granaries strike one as Kafkaesque. In the best of circumstances, these measures were promoted by tiny and vulnerable elite groups primarily to prevent social unrest in times of scarcity. This is not to argue that there were no pre-colonial lords who were concerned with the well-being of their peasant subjects or that there were no ethical principles that regulated elite-peasant interaction. There were indeed benevolent officials, and there were limits on what the elite could demand and what the peasantry had to concede in goods and services. However, benevolence was encouraged and limits established not on the basis of abstract ethical principles or idealized standards for the behavior of a just king. They were determined by the very structure of the pre-colonial economy and by time-honored customs which regulated specific and personalized exchanges between lords and their client-dependents.

Some of the most fundamental checks on the degree to which elite groups could control their peasant subjects resulted from the intense, and often lethal, inter-elite rivalries that were a dominant feature of pre-colonial Southeast Asian politics. Even under strong rulers, Southeast Asian courts were deeply divided between rival factions of the nobility, vying for key positions in the central administration and ultimately control of the throne. Like the peoples in the Islamic heartlands and the Indian subcontinent from whom they borrowed many of their courtly traditions and political institutions, Southeast Asians, whether their rulers claimed to be Hindu, Buddhist, or Muslim, never solved the problems related to dynastic succession. The numerous and prolific, official and unofficial wives of most Southeast Asian monarchs insured that there was usually a surfeit of princely contenders for succession. In a ruler's lifetime there was the ever present danger that one of his sons (or a brother or uncle) would become disgruntled or impatient and attempt to seize the throne by force or withdraw from the capital and raise the standard of revolt. Court factions tended to coalesce around these princely contenders. These groups varied in size according to the promise exhibited by a particular individual, either because he was an able leader or because he was a weak man who could be manipulated once he had been installed as sovereign. Courtiers and palace ministers devoted much of their time to the interminable plots, squabbles, and Machiavellian maneuvers which resulted from these factional divisions. It was by no means time idly spent, for the death of a monarch very often meant the beginning of violent civil strife and purges of great brutality. In these struggles the ill-prepared or those who attached themselves to the wrong princely claimant frequently lost their lives.[42]

In addition to deep divisions within the court and central administration, Southeast Asian rulers had to contend with actual or potential threats from religious leaders and the challenges of autonomy-minded regional lords. Buddhist monks and Muslim holymen often became embroiled in factional rivalries at court and played influential roles as advisors to powerful ministers or the rulers themselves. Monks, holymen, and religious teachers also became involved in the contest for power and resource control as the foci of rebellions against regional lords or the reigning monarch. The millenarian ideas often associated with these risings and their explicit challenges to the legitimacy of those in power gave these movements widespread popular appeal and made them especially dangerous threats to the tenuous authority of pre-colonial regimes.[43] In the Buddhist kingdoms of mainland Southeast Asia the very existence of monastic estates could pose a major problem for reigning monarchs. In times of heavy revenue exactions by the state, peasants and artisans came to regard monastic lands as refuge areas where they could avoid royal demands. The movement of population from royal domains to monastic areas in these circumstances sometimes became so substantial that it eroded the monarch's own base of power. Although the seriousness of this threat is best illustrated by its central role in the collapse of the Pagan dynasty in Burma, royal edicts, confiscations, and even bloody persecutions in other areas and time periods testify to its continuing importance.[44]

III

Devising ways to check the centrifugal pull of regional lords was a major preoccupation of all pre-colonial rulers and their advisors. Elaborate regulations and special institutional arrangements evolved that were designed to undercut attempts by the nobility or regional officials to build up local power bases and to insure the loyalty of these groups to the sovereign. In Java the apanage holdings of princely contenders and the most powerful nobles were confined mainly or wholly to the inner core of territory which surrounded the capital city. Visits to the capital to pay homage to the ruler, usually at times of religious festivities, were another major means by which sovereigns maintained control over appointed officials and noble apanage holders. Because their often sizable retinues had to be suitably clad and fed during the journey to and stay in the court city, the vassals fround these periodic visits a considerable financial burden. This was, of course, what the ruler intended. Regular audiences with the assembled notables of his realm not only gave the monarch a splendid opportunity to display his power, but they also forced his vassals to expend resources which might otherwise be used to build up their own power base.[45] Far from being the absolute despotisms that Karl Wittfogel and other writers have argued dominated the wet-rice areas of Asia,[46] pre-colonial Southeast Asian states were uneasy combinations of often diverse regions and rival principalities. The successful monarch ruled not by undisputed fiat, but rather by the skillful manipulation of rival factions and forces, by balancing one power center against another, and by alternatively cajoling and threatening unruly nobles and administrators.[47]

Though these devices were intended to constrict the independent action of the nobility and bind them firmly to the sovereign, they had the added effect of impairing the apanage holders' and regional administrators' capacity to govern the areas to which they were assigned. Lengthy stays in the capital, factional plotting and maneuvering, and disputes within his own extensive household consumed a good deal of time and energy, which an official might otherwise have devoted to controlling the population in his charge. Even a conscientious or ambitious administrator, who spent as much time as possible in the areas assigned to him, lacked a trained and professionally committed bureaucratic corps to assist him. The most capable leader was forced to depend upon relatives, client-retainers, and self-seeking and often rapacious tax farmers and overseers to staff the provincial government. They viewed their appointments as opportunities for personal profit and sought to extract as much tribute as they could from the villages assigned to them, while passing on as little as possible to their superiors. Their lack of knowledge regarding local affairs and the transitory nature of their positions meant that they were extremely dependent upon village notables and men of local influence in their efforts to collect taxes, recruit corveé laborers, or conscript peasants for military service. The contest which they waged with each other and the provincial officials who appointed them for control of the peasants' output was paralleled by a similar struggle with the village leaders who provided an essential link between the state and the peasantry.[48]

The village headman was the most secure and best informed person of authority in the pre-colonial Southeast Asian state. Courtiers and regional lords were fortunate to maintain their postions throughout the reign of a single sovereign, much less the transition to a new monarch or dynasty. The tenure of their appointees was even less durable. In contrast, the positions of village leaders and township notables were hereditary and long term. Local officials in both Java and Burma could normally trace their families' control of their posts back many generations, and in some cases, centuries.[49] Although the assumption of office by these leaders usually required approval by the king's ministers, more often than not this certification was merely a formality. In reality the basis of the local leaders' power rested in the village or villages which they represented in dealings with the government's functionaries. Their authority depended upon their control of substantial economic resources, principally land, within the village, their skillful management of village factions, and the support of kinsmen and client tenants and laborers.[50]

Because the regular administrative system did not reach down to the village level, village headmen and elders were indispensable links in the pre-colonial political hierarchy. They mediated between supra-village elite groups and the mass of the peasantry and made possible the surplus extraction that was the life blood of the state. Like officials at all levels above them, it was in the interest of village leaders to concede as little as possible in either taxes or labor services to the middlemen who descended periodically to collect their lord's due. Centuries of experience enabled village notables to outwit even the most vigilant tax collector by underreporting, temporarily settling part of the village population in a nearby forest, hiding harvested crops, or any number of other, time-tested devices. Very often bribes proved less troublesome than these time-consuming ruses, and middlemen normally found cooperation with village leaders in their best interest.[51]

The low level of integration and diffusion of power[52] in the contest state meant that force and military prowess played key roles at all levels. Their importance is amply attested by the fact that "strong" rulers were almost invariably able warriors, and by the high esteem in which the *jago* (lit. fighting cock) and *boh* (lit. the equivalent of a colonel in the Burman army) figures were held in Javanese and Burman societies respectively. Men of great courage and physical strength proudly bore these titles, and their deeds as warriors or bandits were enshrined in local legends and folk songs. Leaders at all levels sought to induce them to join their bands of retainers, for if *jagos* or *bohs* were allowed to retain their independence, they often became sources of disruption and, if provoked, formidable adversaries.[53]

Poor communications, the high degree of autonomy of regional and local leaders, and the low level of military technology in pre-colonial Southeast Asia also meant that force could easily be transformed from a buttress to a threat to reigning monarchs. Rulers simply did not possess the logistical systems necessary to maintain armies in distant provinces for long periods of time, and extensive campaigns against recalcitrant vassals could easily become major dynastic crises. Because the bulk of the manpower in Southeast Asian armies consisted of forcibly conscripted peasants, armies too long in the field had a tendency to melt away. These forces were armed mainly with slings, knives, and pikes which most villages possessed in abundance, and thus the basis of support for rebels or rival claimants to the throne was ever-present.[54] The very small advantages in military sophistication which the central government enjoyed vis-à-vis regional lords or even local dissidents limited the state's capacity to obtain compliance by force. Usually a monarch resorted to force only after threats, bribes, intrigues, and diplomacy had failed to reconcile malcontents or subdue groups in rebellion.

Though force was an important mainstay of Southeast Asian kingdoms, these were held together on a day-to-day basis primarily by the personal and reciprocal patron-client links that are a central feature of the type of political system which Max Weber has characterized as patrimonial.[55] Chains of patron-client clusters, like the kawula-gusti in Java or the nai-phrai in Siam, extended from the ruler and his courtiers to village notables and their dependent tenants and laborers. In kingdoms where there was a low population density and vast areas of unoccupied, fertile land, labor control was a major preoccupation of government officials and village landholders. Patron-client reciprocity (protection for suppport, land and implements for labor and produce, etc.) was one of the main ways a lord retained and controlled dependents. Comparable exchanges also bound together religious teachers and their students, sectarian leaders and their disciples, bandit chiefs and their gangs, and even trading magnates and their brokers and middlemen. If the status and authority of a political or religious leader was roughly proportional to the number of his clients, an individual's well-being depended on his ability to attach himself to a prosperous and powerful patron. If morality and customary norms, such as those contained in the Javanese *adat*, influenced the relationships between elite and peasant groups, they did so primarily within the context of patron-client clusters. The lord's concern for the peasants' well-being and ethical constraints on his demands were specific and personal, not generalized and abstract. The vertical hierarchy of patron-client clusters and not horizontal class distinctions provided the nexus for the interaction of lord and peasant in pre-colonial kingdoms.[56]

The "contest-state" structure of pre-colonial politics in Southeast Asia provided the peasantry with many buffers against oppressive demands on the part of the ruling elite. The pervasive struggles between factions at the court, between the court and regional administrators and apanage holders, and between regional lords and their subordinates diverted time and scarce resources from the task of controlling the village population. Chronic manpower shortages resulted in intense competition between neighboring lords and officials at different levels for peasants to work their lands. This rivalry, plus the availability of unoccupied land, made it possible for peasants to seek another patron or migrate to another territory if the demands of their overlord became too burdensome. It was common for clients whose patrons were losing power (and thus the ability to shield them from excessive demands) or growing tyrannical to shift their allegiance and services to other men of influence. Lords were happy to gain supporters at the expense of rivals, and, given the poor state of communications, there was very little that could be done to prevent such transfers.[57] In Java, the widespread acceptance of migration as a means of relief for dissatisfied cultivators is reflected in the existence of a customary procedure by which a tenant or laborer gave his landlord notice of his intention to move to another village, work another landlord's fields, or seek employment as a porter along the main roads that linked the inland towns with the coast.[58]

The existence in most areas of Southeast Asia of vast tracts of unoccupied land made avoidance migration another major means of peasant defense. Although highly-mobile, dry crop farmers more readily resorted to this way of escaping excessive elite demands, the flight of large numbers of hard-pressed peasant in irrigated, wet-rice areas was also recorded with surprising frequency. In fact, Southeast Asian rulers considered the flight of peasants into the forest or to monastery lands one of the main signs of maladministration and oppression. Reports of such population movements could result in an official's dismissal or even his execution.[59]

Vague and contested administrative boundries, poor communications, and open lands also made banditry a possible means of resistance to exorbitant demands. Though there is little evidence relating to other forms of peasant protest, it is likely that riots flared up periodically in response to food shortages or unreasonable revenue demands. Disgruntled peasants were also known to support princely pretenders, who promised to restore order and lower taxes, and prophetic leaders who promulgated millenarian visions of a just and harmonious social order and economic abundance.[60]

If the contest state view of pre-colonial political economies is correct, the search for the origins of peasant protest in the colonial era should focus upon the technological, organizational, and socio-economic transformations which altered the relationships between elite groups and peasant and weakened peasant defense mechanisms, rather than the violation of peasant assumptions about the functioning of a "moral" political and economic order that is stressed by James Scott. When peasants contrasted their position in the colonial era with the "good old days" before European conquest, they complained of grievances that were rooted in the greatly enhanced powers of bureaucrats and large landholders in their contest with the cultivating classes for control of labor and produce. Because European colonial officials shared neither the religious beliefs nor the cultural presuppositions of Southeast Asian peoples, they lacked the aura of sacral-religious legitmacy that in part justified the revenue demands of pre-colonial elites. In this sense the moral dimension of the contest state was also diminished to the disadvantge of the peasant in the colonial era. This does not mean, however, that the European colonizers disavowed all ethical responsibility for the welfare of the peasantry. Though the extent of the colonizers' commitment and their success in translating ethical principles into effective restraints on ambitious bureaucrats varied widely by time period and colonial regime, revenue remissions were granted, relief works were established, and attempts were made to transfer emergency food supplies from surplus to deficit areas. Like pre-colonial administrative systems, those established in the colonial era were often clumsy and oppressive, but European officials had no more reason than their Southeast Asian predecessors to intentionally deprive the peasantry of the minimum portion of their produce which they needed to survive. In some cases, contrary to Scott's general argument, European bureaucrats sought to establish flexible revenue systems that left the peasants with a good deal more than mere subsistence. Aside from a genuine concern for the peasants' welfare and improvement, which was felt by many of these officials, these measures were introduced to encourage the cultivating classes to increase their output (and thus tax revenues) and to participate actively in the market sector of the colonial economy. The fact that these systems were introduced in the name of paternalistic ideologies that are no longer in fashion, or that many of them failed to achieve their goals, should not cause the contemporary scholar to ignore their very real impact on the condition of the peasantry under many colonial regimes.

More and better-trained bureaucrats, superior techniques of organization and administration, and vastly improved communications and military technology made it possible for colonial regimes to exert, for the first time, effective control over local elites and the peasant population as a whole. The transition from pre-colonial to colonial conditions, especially at the village level, was far less abrupt than many writers have assumed, and local leaders and cultivators alike continued the age-old struggle to maintain their high degree of autonomy and to maximize the resources they retained at the expense of the colonial state. Collusion and corruption were rampant in the early decades of the European colonizers' advance into conquered areas and remained endemic throughout the colonial era.[61] In most colonial societies, however, local notables and village headmen were gradually transformed from exponents of local interests into agents of centralized bureaucracies.[62] This process greatly reduced the opportunities for collusion and evasion that had provided such an effective buffer against elite exactions in the pre-colonial era. Detailed and increasingly accurate censuses and cadastral surveys conducted by trained bureaucrats, whose loyalties were directed to the administrative corps and colonial system as a whole rather than a local patron or powerful minister, made it possible for the government to collect that share of the produce which it claimed as its due.

This momentous shift from the pre-colonial norms of under-reporting and under-collecting is vividly described by British settlement officers working in Upper Burma in the late nineteenth century. They noted that local officials in the core regions of the Konbaung kingdom were "very discomfited" when the new government actually collected the 1/5 or 1/6 of the peasants' output that it determined after careful surveys and enquiries was a just revenue demand. Though this amount was considerably less than the 1/4 or better claimed by pre-colonial regimes, they had never collected anything approaching this amount. In the absence of trained surveyors and accurate cadastral records, pre-colonial lords were forced to settle for a "customary share" that fell far below the hypothetical amount which the sovereign demanded as the symbolic owner of all land. Thus, what the British or other colonizers viewed as a low assessment compared to pre-colonial exactions, often represented a considerable increase in revenue actually taken and hence a greater burden on the peasantry.[63]

As the market sector of Southeast Asian economies expanded in the colonial period, village autonomy and self-sufficiency were further reduced. Merchants, moneylenders, and export-oriented landlords gained increasing control over what rural workers, tenants, and even small landholders produced, and how the product of their labors were distributed. Demands for loan repayments and enhanced rents were backed by contract and property-oriented courts, staffed by European or Western-trained judges and lawyers. Landlords and moneylenders could also best afford the heavy expenses of litigation and smooth over shady transactions and improprieties with timely bribes or appeals to prominent officials. As the reach of the bureaucracy and the influence of the market grew, the effectiveness of intra-village mechanisms for social control declined. Patron-client reciprocity very often degenerated into patron dominance and exploitation and client oppresion or rebellion.[64] As competition between individuals and peasant households increased and became more and more linked to extra-village agents and institutions, class divisions hardened and class identities began to play a major role in protest mobilization in many areas.

Improved communications and bureaucratic control, as well as accelerated population growth which resulted in the settlement of frontier areas, reduced the possibilty of flight as a solution to the problems of the peasantry. Well-integrated, highly centralized administrative systems eliminated the option of transferring one's allegiance to another lord in defiance of a master whose demands were excessive. Though the deficiences of pre-colonial sources relating to popular protest make it impossible to state with certainty that peasant movements increased in number in the colonial era, it is certain that peasant *confrontations* with elite groups did. No longer able to evade or dilute elite demands or abscond should these tactics fail, peasants were increasingly forced to join protest movements that involved direct, often violent, actions against landlords and bureaucrats. These movments frequently challenged the legitimacy and very existence of the colonial order. Tragically, because the military strength of the

540

colonial overlords was vastly superior to that of pre-colonial regimes, peasant-elite confrontrations were far more lethal for cultivating classes than they had been in the pre-colonial era.

The actual grievances that drove peasant groups to rise in protest in different colonial societies and time periods varied widely and must be evaluated on the evidence relating to each case of peasant dissidence. However, the underlying causes of peasant unrest are more likely to be found in the factors that turned their age-old struggle with the elite decisively in favor of the latter than in the colonizers' violation of the principles of the moral economy. If peasant expectations and responses were actually shaped by widespread agreement over what as their "just share" and a belief that they had the "right" to a "subsistence minimum," one would expect them to rise *en masse* when these norms were ignored or intentionally violated in the colonial period. In fact, the great majority of peasants did not rise in protest against their colonial overlords. In addition, the studies on peasant protest in the colonial period which have appeared to date indicate that when peasant groups did join protest movements, they often did so for reasons that extended beyond or had little to do with taxes or threats to their subsistence. In many instances peasants rose in protest because they felt that they deserved more than a "minimum subsistence" share of the crops they produced; because their alien rulers lacked ritual and religio-political legitimacy; or because they believed their religious beliefs and customary ways were threatened. Peasants rallied to prophetic saviors or nationalist leaders not to restore hypothetical moral economies, but to alleviate specific socio-economic grievances, to reestablish effective and truly reciprocal networks of dependence, and to restore meaningful social relationships and viable village communities. As their contest with elite groups for control of the crops they produced turned increasingly in favor of the bureaucrats and landlords, the peasants of Africa and Asia demonstrated a strong desire for a return to the weak state systems and semi-autonomous villages of the past. This desire was reflected in the ideologies of peasant-supported movements from those which promised millenarian transformations to Gandhi's quasi-anarchistic vision of a village-centric and self-sufficient Indian nation.

Although violations of the precepts of the moral economy centering upon marketing practices and food prices may well have moved farm laborers and miners to riot in eighteenth century England, in colonial Southeast Asia (and India and Afiica) the disregard of ethical limits on elite demands for taxes and labor services was a far less important source of agrarian unrest than shifts in elite-peasant power relationships and socio-economic changes that weakened the peasants' defenses and bargaining position. One must allow that a pattern identified in one society and historical period may not be transferable, at least not without major modifications, to others that are fundamentally different. Unless better proof of the acceptance and actual impact of the principles of the moral economy is advanced, we must turn to other aspects of elite-peasant relationships and exchanges for explanations of the origins of peasant protest in Southeast Asia.

FOOTNOTES

1. London, 1963, chapter six, *passim.* As Thompson readily acknowledges, his formulation of the moral economy concept has been strongly influenced by the writings of R.B. Rose, George Rudé, and R.C. Cobb.

2. *Past and Present* 50 (1971), pp. 76-136.

3. *Ibid.*, p. 78.

4. See, for examples, A.W. Coats, "Contrary Moralities: Plebs, Paternalists and Political Economists," *Past and Present* 54 (1972), pp. 130-33; and Elizabeth Fox Genovese, "The Many Faces of Moral Economy: A Contribution to a Debate," *Past and Present* 58 (1973), pp. 161-8.

5. New Haven, Connecticut, 1976.

6. I would like to thank Peter Carey, Merle Ricklefs, Samuel Baily, Peter Vayda, John Bastin and Patricia Herbert for their valuable comments on early drafts of this essay. I am also grateful to Victor Lieberman and William Koenig for making available their excellent, but as yet unpublished, dissertation manuscripts on pre-colonial political systems in Burma.

7. For historical studies in which masterful use is made of this sort of source material, see Eugen Weber, *Peasants into Frenchmen* (Stanford, 1976) and Jacques Berque, *Egypt: Imperialism and Revolution* (New York, 1972). The works of anthropologists like Melford Spiro, S.J. Tambiah, Clifford Geertz, Lucien Hanks and E. Michael Mendelson have amply demonstrated both the availability and the richness of "popular" sources relating to Southeast Asia.

8. *Moral Economy*, pp. 25 (quoted portions), 44, 49-50.

9. *Ibid.*, chapters one and two.

10. "Moral Economy of the English Crowd," pp. 79-94.

11. *Moral Economy*, pp. 6, 52-5, 93-4, fn. 6.

12. See especially, *ibid.*, pp. 28-9, 52-3, 180-183, 186, and chapter four.

13. For discussion of this process from varying perspectives see, J.S. Furnivall, *An Introduction to the Political Economy of Burma* (Rangoon, 1931); Cheng Siok-Hwa, *The Rice Industry of Burma, 1852-1940* (Kuala Lumpur, 1968); and Michael Adas, *The Burma Delta: Economic Development and Social Change on an Asian Rice Frontier, 1852-1941* (Madison, 1974).

14. For examples see the fine studies of Sartono Kartodirdjo, especially *The Peasants' Revolt of Banten in 1888* (The Hague, 1966) and *Protest Movements in Rural Java* (Singapore, 1973); Stephen Fuchs, *Rebellious Prophets* (Bombay, 1965); David Strutevant, *Popular Uprisings in the Philippines, 1840-1940* (Ithaca, N.Y., 1976); Charles Tilly, *The Vendée* (Cambridge, Mass., 1964) and the case studies in Wilhelm E. Mühlmann, *Chiliasmus und Nativismus* (Berlin, 1961).

15. For discussions of these themes see, J.A.B. Wiselius, "Djaja Baja: Zijn Leven en Profetieen," *Bijdragen tot Taal-, Land-, en Volkenkunde* 7 (1872), pp. 186-9; Gerardus W.J. Drewes, *Drie Javaansche Goeroe's* (Leiden, 1925), especially part three; and Emanuel Sarkisyanz, *Buddhist Backgrounds of the Burmese Revolution* (The Hague, 1965), chapters seven to ten.

16. Interestingly, Scott idealizes the very sort of peasant community that Karl Marx denounced over a century ago as the "solid foundation of Oriental Despotism," and as a preserve of "superstition," "barbarian egotism," and "undignified, stagnatory and vegetative life." See, *The First Indian War of Independence* (Moscow, n.d.), p. 20.

III

17. In his essay on *Peasantry in Revolution* (Ithaca, 1966), especially pp. 1-2, 10-12, 15-18, 38-60. For supporting evidence see, Oscar Lewis, *Village Life in Northern India* (New York, 1965), chapter four; H. Dillon, *Leadership and Groups in a South Indian Village* (New Delhi, 1955); Bernard Siegel and Alan Beals, "Pervasive Factionalism," *American Anthropologist* 62/3 (1960), pp. 394-417; Elizabeth Colson and Max Gluckman, eds., *Seven Tribes of British Central Africa* (Manchester, 1959), esp. pp. 68-9, 210, 283-5, 317-24; and Ralph Smith, *Vietnam and the West* (Ithaca, 1971), pp. 60-64.

18. The writings of J.H. Boeke and D.H. Burger have perhaps been the most influential in establishing this view. See, (Boeke) *The Structure of the Netherlands Indian Economy* (New York, 1942) and *The Evolution of the Netherlands Indies Economy* (New York, 1946) and (Burger) "Structuur Veranderingen in de Javaanse Samenleving," *Indonesie* 1-3 (1947-1950), *passim.* The first part of the Burger essay has been translated by Leslie Palmier as *Structural Changes in Javanese Society: The Village Sphere* (Ithaca, 1956).

19. M.J.H. Kollman, "Bagelen onder het bestuur van Soerkarta en Djokjokarata," *Tijdschrift voor Indische Taal-, Land-, en Volkenkunde* (hereafter *TBG*) 14 (1864), pp. 362-4, 368. For examples from other areas see, John Larkin, *The Pampangans: Colonial Society in a Philippine Province* (Berkeley, 1972), pp. 20-22; Robert Tignor, *The Colonial Transformation of Kenya* (Princeton, 1976), pp. 11-12, 14, 21-2, 45, 66; and André Béteille, *Caste, Class and Power in a Tanjore Village* (Berkeley, 1965), chapters four and five.

20. On changes in the colonial period see, Onghokham, "The Residency of Madiun Pryayi and Peasant in the Nineteenth Century," Ph.D. dissertation, Yale University, 1975, pp. 209-11. For post-colonial patterns see, Margo Lyons, *Bases of Conflict in Rural Java* (Berkeley, 1970); and W.F. Wertheim, "From Aliran towards Class Struggle in the Countryside of Java," *Pacific Viewpoint* 10 (1969), pp. 1-17.

21. "Peasant Society and the Image of Limited Good," *American Anthropologist* 67 (1965), pp. 293-314. Edward C. Banfield has identified a comparable pattern which he labels "amoral familism." See, *The Moral Basis of a Backward Society* (New York, 1958).

22. Pierre Gourou, *Les Paysans du delta Tonkinois: étude de géographie humaine* (paris, 1936), p. 112.

23. See, for examples, the studies by Victor Lieberman, Akin Rabibhadana, Soemarsaid Moertono, Peter Carey, William Koenig, and Onghokham cited throughout this article.

24. *Moral Economy*, chapters one and two.

25. *Moral Economy*, pp. 28, 52-5.

26. For China and India see respectively, Michael Loewe, *Imperial China* (New York, 1965), especially chapter three and John Spellman, *Political Theory of Ancient India* (Oxford, 1964), chapter eight. For different areas in Southeast Asia see, Soemarsaid Moertono, *State and Statecraft in Old Java* (Ithaca, 1968), pp. 35ff.; Thaung, "Burmese Kingship in Theory and Practice under the Reign of King Mindon," *Journal of the Burma Research Society* (hereafter *JBRS*) 42 (1959), pp. 178-83; Le Thanh Khoi, *Le Vietnam: histoire et civilisation* (Paris, 1955), pp. 147-8; Akin Rabibhadana, *The Organization of Thai Society in the Early Bangkok Period 1782-1873* (Ithaca, 1969), pp 40-53; and the relevant portions of the studies by William Koenig and Victor Lieberman cited below.

27. J. Wiselius, "Djaja Baja," pp. 185-6.

28. The standard description of these patterns in pre-colonial Java remains G.P. Rouffaer's essay on the "Vorstenlanden," in the *Encyclopedia van Nederlandsch-Indië* (The Hague,

1905), vol. 4, pp. 588-93. The best documented and most detailed accounts for Burma have unfortunately not yet been published. See, Victor Lieberman, "The Burmese Dynastic Pattern, circa 1590-1760, An Administrative and Political Study of the Taung-ngu Dynasty and the Reign of Alaùng-Hpayà," Ph.D. dissertation, University of London, 1976; and William Koenig, "The Early Kòn-baung Polity, 1752-1819: A Study of Politics, Administration, and Social Organization in Burma," Ph.D. dissertation, University of London, 1978.

29. S. Moertono, *Statecraft in Java*, pp. 88ff, 104-5, 107, 134; H.J. de Graaf, *De Regering van Sultan Agung, vorst van Mataram, 1613-1645* (The Hague, 1958), pp. 118-21 and *Geschiedenis van Indonesië* (The Hague, 1949), pp. 101-5, 207, 210; Onghokham, "Madiun Pryayi," pp. 39, 60-61; Lieberman, *ibid.*, pp. 36, 39-40, 45, 120ff, 127ff; and Koenig, *ibid.*, pp. 35-6, 41ff, 246-51. Koenig argues that there was a partially successful attempt to reverse these patterns in the early Kon-baung period. See also, the excellent introduction by Kenneth Hall in Hall and John K. Whitmore, eds., *Explorations in Early Southeast Asian History: The Origins of Southeast Asian Statecraft* (Ann Arbor, 1976).

30. These positions survived well into the colonial period in their variety and complexity, as evidenced by W.A.J. van Davelaar's article on "Middenpersonen tusschen de districts-beambten en desa-hoofden op Java," *TGB* 34 (1891), pp. 365-72.

31. J.L.V., "Bijdrage tot de kennis der residentie Madioen," *Tijdschrift voor Nederlansch Indië* (hereafter TNI) 17/2 (1855), pp. 5-6; and Daw Mya Sein, *Administration of Burma* (Rangoon, 1938), pp. 46, 62-3. For discussions of the administrator's somewhat stronger position in Vietnam, see, Alexander Woodside, *Vietnam and the China Model* (Cambridge, Mass., 1971), pp. 145, 154-58, 163-65.

32. Information on the Javanese inquests was provided in a personal communication from Peter Carey. See also his forthcoming study on "Pangeran Dipanagara and the Origins of the Java War," *Verhandelingen van het Koninklijk Instituut* (Leiden, 1980), chapter one. For Konbaung Burma see, J.S. Furnivall, "Notes on the History of Hanthawaddy," *JBRS* 4 (1914), p. 210.

33. S. Moertono, *Statecraft in Java*, pp. 134, 137-8 (quoted portion), 143-4; J.L.V., "Kennis der Madioen," p. 6; James G. Scott & John P. Hardiman, *Gazetteer of Upper Burma and the Shan States* (Rangoon, 1900) vol. 1, pp. 413, 417-8; Government of Burma, *Report on the Settlement Operations in the Mandalay District, 1892-93* (Rangoon, 1894), p. 24; and H.G. Q. Wales, *Ancient Siamese Government and Administration* (New York, 1965), pp. 218-19.

34. For discussions of these different patterns, see Onghokham, "Madiun Pryayi," pp. 95-6, 167-8, 199-200; Anonymous, "De Toestand van Bagelan in 1830," *TNI* 20 (1858), pp. 76-81; Mya Sein, *Administration of Burma*, pp. 40, 52, 63-5, 67-8; U Kin Maung Kyi and Daw Tin Tin, *Administrative Patterns of Burma* (Singapore, 1973), pp. 37, 43-4; Scott & Hardiman, *ibid.*, p. 416; and C.M. Wilson, "State and Society in the Reign of Mongkut, 1851-68," Ph.D. dissertation, Cornell University, 1970, pp. 593-5, 601, 649-58, 661-2.

35. *Angkor: An Essay on Art and Imperialism* (New York, 1970), pp. 76-7, 92.

36. Clifford Geertz's, *Religion of Java* (New York, 1960), remains the fullest and most sensitive discussion of the historical and contemporary distinctions between *pryayi* elite and *abangan* peasants in Java. For the impressions of nineteenth century writers, see T.S. Raffles, *The History of Java* (London, 1817), vol. 1, pp. 252-4; H. Graaf van Hodgendorp, *Willem van Hogendorp in Nederlandsch-Indië* (The Hague, 1913), p. 154; and for Burma, see Michael Symes, *An Account of an Embassy to the Kingdom of Ava . . . in 1795* (London, 1800), vol. 1, pp. 353-4, vol. 2, pp. 60-62, 189-90.

37. J.F. Walraven van Nes, "Verhandeling over de waarschijnlijke oorzaaken, die aanleiding tot de onlusten van 1825 . . . ," *TNI* 6 (1844), pp. 137-9. For superb discussions of these patterns in other areas, see Lucien M. Hanks, "Merit and Power in the Thai Social Order," *American Anthropologist* 64/6 (1962), pp. 1247-62; and John Beattie, *The Nyoro State* (Oxford, 1971), pp. 137, 141-2.

38. Ongohokham, "Madiun Pryayi," pp. 42, 84, 107, 144-5. See also, Beattie, *ibid.*, pp. 142-4.

39. J.L.V., "Kennis der Madioen," pp. 2-3, 7-9; Anon., "Toestand van Bagelen," pp. 76, 79-81; Kin Maung Kyi & Daw Tin Tin, *Administrative Patterns*, p. 37; J. Scott & J. Hardiman, *Upper Burma Gazetteer*, p. 430; and C. Wilson, "State and Society," pp. 581-5.

40. G. Rouffaer, "Vorstenlanden," pp. 624-5; P. Carey, "The Origins of the Java War (1825-30)," *English Historical Review* 91 (1976), pp. 63-5; J. van Nes, "Waarschijnlijke oorzaaken," pp. 136-41; Anon., *ibid.*, pp. 76, 82; and T. Raffles, *History of Java*, pp. 144-49, 273-4.

41. For more detailed discussion of these patterns see below, pp. 534-5.

42. The best accounts of court intrigues and dynastic struggles in Java may be found in Peter Carey's fortcoming work on "Dipanagara and the Origins of the Java War," esp. chapter two; M.C. Ricklefs, *Jogjakarta under Sultan Mangkubumi, 1749-1792* (Oxford, 1974); and the relevant sections in M. van Deventer's narrative *Geschiedenis der Nederlanders op Java* (Haarlem, 1886-7), 2 vols. For Burma see, Yi Yi "The Last Days of the Nyaungyan Dynasty," *The Guardian* (1968), pp. 46-7; V. Lieberman, "Burmese Dynastic Pattern," *passim*; W. Koenig, "Early Kön-baung Polity," esp. chapter 7, or the narrative accounts by G.E. Harvey and Arthur Phayre.

43. M. Ricklefs, *ibid.*, pp. 16-18; B. Schrieke, *Indonesian Sociological Studies* (The Hague, 1957), vol. 2, pp. 79-86; and E. Sarkisyanz, *Buddhist Backgrounds*, especially chapter twelve.

44. For Pagan, see Michael Aung Thwin, "Kingship, the *Sangha*, and Society in Pagan," in K. Hall & J. Whitmore, *Explorations*, pp. 205-56. For examples from other areas and time periods see, Than Thun, "Administration under King Thalun," *JBRS* 51 (1968), pp. 181-87; Le Thanh Khoi, *Le Viêt-nam*, pp. 198-200, 219; and Akin, *Thai Society*, pp. 35, 87, 123.

45. For a general discussion of these control devices, see Max Weber, *Economy and Society: An Outline of Interpretive Sociology* (ed. by G. Roth & C. Wittich, New York, 1968), vol. 3, pp. 1042-44. For examples of different patterns in Java, see G. Rouffaer, "Vorstenlanden," pp. 588-90; Onghokham, "Madiun Pryayi," pp. 15, 35-6, 40-43, & 61ff; and J.L.V., "Kennis der Madioen," p. 2. Very often, of course, they concentrated disgruntled lords in the capital city. See M. van Deventer, *Nederlanders op Java*, vol. 1, pp. 222-3, 264.

46. *Oriental Despotism* (New Haven, 1957). Although Wittfogel's ideas have been strongly challenged by Wolfram Eberhard and other scholars of China, they have not been rigorously tested by scholars of pre-colonial Southeast Asian states where hydraulic systems abounded. Studies of comparable societies in Ceylon and Oceania, however, have found the Wittfogel model inappropriate in many respects. See E.R. Leach, "Hydraulic Society in Ceylon," *Past and Present* 15 (1959), pp. 2-26; and H.J.M. Claessen, "Despotism and Irrigation," *Bijdragen tot Taal-, Land-, en Volkenkunde* (hereafter *BKI*) 129 (1973), pp. 70-85.

47. For a superb discussion of the importance of these skills, see M. Ricklef's, *Sultan Mangkubumi*, esp. chapter one.

48. J.L.V., "Kennis der Madioen," pp. 2-3, 7-10; Anon., "Toestand van Bagelen," pp. 80-82; S. Moertono, *Statecraft in Java*, pp. 144-51; W. van Davelaar, "Districts-beambten," pp. 365-72; Peter Carey, "Dipanagara and the Origins of the Java War," chapter one; and W. Koenig, "Early Kon-baung Polity," pp. 226-34, 237-51.

49. Maung Tha Aung and Maung Mya Din, "The Pacification of Upper Burma: A Vernacular History," *JBRS* 31 (1941), pp. 131ff; and J. Furnivall, "Notes on Hanthawaddy," p. 210. In Java positions of leadership in the village were usually circulated among the landowning families descended from the village founders. Thus, continuity was maintained by groups of families rather than individual households.

50. Than Tun, "Administration under Thalun," p. 183; Mya Sein, *Administration of Burma*, pp. 47, 67, 69, 72; Ma Kyan, "Village Administration in Upper Burma," *JBRS* 52 (1969), p. 68; Onghokham, "Madiun Pryayi," pp. 63-8; and T. Raffles, *History of Java*, vol. 1, pp. 285-6.

51. J. Scott & J. Hardiman, *Upper Burma Gazetteer*, pp. 415-6; Mya Sein, *ibid.*, pp. 52, 67-8; Government of Burma, *Pakokku District Gazetteer* (Rangoon, 1914), p. 14; and P. Carey, "Dipanagara and the Origins of the Java War," chapter one. For a detailed analysis of the continuation of this collusion into the colonial period, see Robert F. Frykenberg, "Traditional Process of Power in South India: An Historical Analysis of Local Influence," *Indian Social and Economic History Review* 1 (1963), pp. 1-21.

52. The reality of competing foci of power ran counter to the ideal of total power concentration in the sovereign which Benedict Anderson argues was the goal of Javanese monarchs. See, "The Idea of Power in Javanese Culture," in Claire Holt, ed., *Culture and Politics in Indonesia* (Ithaca, 1972), pp. 1-70.

53. Onghokham, "Madiun Pryay," pp. 63ff; and Government of Burma, *Report on the Prevention of Crime and the Treatment of Criminals in the Province of Burma* (Rangoon, 1926), pp. 18-20.

54. Shway Yoe (James G. Scott), *The Burman: His Life and Notions* (New York, 1963), chapter 54; and P.F.J. Louw and F.S. de Klerck, *De Java-Oorlog van 1825-1830* (Batavia-The Hague, 1894-1900), vol. 1, pp. 203-8.

55. *Economy and Society*, vol. 3, chapter twelve. Southeast Asia states also contained prebendal elements, but offices tended to become hereditary despite the efforts of successive rulers to prevent this from occurring.

56. Onghokham, "Madiun Pryayi," pp. 15ff, 169-70; S. Moertono, *Statecraft in Java*, pp. 104ff; W. Koenig, "Early Kon-baung Polity," pp. 128-32; Victor B. Lieberman, "Ethnic Politics in Eighteenth-Century Burma," *Modern Asian Studies* 12/3 (1978), pp. 459, 470; and Akin, *Thai Society*, pp. 82-9. In his earlier writings on peasant protest, James Scott emphasized the importance of these patron-client links, and he has contributed a number of excellent essays on the subject, most notably, "Patron-client Politics and Political Change in Southeast Asia," *American Political Science Quarterly* 66 (1972), pp. 91-113.

57. S. Moertono, *Statecraft in Java*, p. 76; Onghokham, "Madiun Pryayi," pp. 43-4; Yi Yi, "Last Days," p. 47; V. Lieberman, "Burmese Dynastic Pattern," pp. 196-7, 205-6, 221-2; and Akin, *Thai Society*, pp. 89, 110-112, 181-2.

58. P. Carey, "Dipanagara and the Origins of the Java War," chapter one.

59. B. Schrieke, *Sociological Studies*, vol. 2, pp. 300-301; S. Moertono, *Statecraft in Java*, pp. 5-6, 75-6; Than Tun, "King Thalun," pp. 177-8; M. Kollman, "Bagelen Bestuur," p. 354; and Akin, *Thai Society*, pp. 73-4.

III

60. For sample descriptions of these different forms of protest, see D.H. Meijer, "Over het bendewezen op Java," *Indonesië* 3 (1949-50), pp. 178-84; Moertono, *ibid.*, pp. 85-6; Yi Yi, "Last Days," p. 47; Charles Crosthwaite, *The Pacification of Burma* (London, 1912), pp. 6-7; W. Koenig, "The Early Kòn-baung Dynasty," pp. 88-9, 131-2; and the sources cited in footnote 43.

61. The now classic description of these patterns is Robert E. Frykenberg's *Guntur District, 1788-1848* (Oxford, 1965). For Java, see Adelante, "De ontwikkeling van de inlandsche hoofden op Java," *De Indische Gids* 14 (1892), pp. 683-4; and for Burma, see Government of India, *Political and Foreign Proceedings*, Range 201, vol. 63, 8 August 1856, no. 160.

62. J.S. Furnivall, *Colonial Policy and Practice* (New York, 1956), pp. 70-1, 241-3; Mya Sein, *Administration of Burma*, pp. 81-115, 157, 161, 165-75; and Onghokham, "Madiun Pryayi," pp. 154ff.

63. Government of Burma, *Mandalay Settlement Report*, p. 24. See also J. Scott & J. Hardiman, *Upper Burma Gazetteer*, p. 416; Onghokham, *ibid.*, pp. 167-8; J. Larkin, *Pampangians*, pp. 244-5; and T.H. Beaglehole, *Thomas Monroe and the Development of Administrative Policy in Madras, 1792-1818* (Cambridge, 1966).

64. For superb studies of the breakdown of these ties, see James C. Scott, "The Erosion of Patron-Client Bonds and Social Change in Southeast Asia," *Journal of Southeast Asian Studies* 22 (1972), pp. 5-38; and Benjamin J. Kerkvliet, "Peasant Unrest Prior to the Huk Revolution in the Philippines," *Asian Studies* (Manila) 9 (1971), pp. 164-213. For a more general discussion of the multi-faceted "opening-up" of peasant villages in recent centuries, see Joel S. Migdal, *Peasants, Politics and Revolution: The Socioeconomic Basis of Political Change* (Princeton, 1974).

IV

Tactics versus Strategies in Peasant Protest Response

The attention given in recent years to "everyday resistance" and "avoidance protest" has developed into a fundamental reassessment of the approach to peasant societies and rural protest that dominated the work of social scientists through much of the 1960s and 1970s. The then-prevailing view of the peasantry was very much a product of a post-World War II era that had seen rural revolutionary movements, both successful and failed, throughout much of the Third World. A somewhat romanticized vision—the peasantry as a class prone to confrontational protest and highly susceptible to mobilization in the revolutionary movements that resulted—overcorrected for an earlier consensus that peasants were passive, hopelessly divided by "amoral familialism," and resigned to oppression due to their acceptance of a "limited good" view of the world. Emphasis on nonconfrontational and quotidian modes of peasant response has provided an important middle ground between the passive and revolutionary extremes of conceptualizing peasant societies and responses. It also offers a way around the stalemate that had developed in the late 1970s as a result of the often heated debate over the false dichotomy between the peasant as a "moral"—primarily ideological—or a "rational"—overwhelmingly pragmatic—actor. The everyday or avoidance approach redirects our attention to the larger context in which peasant communities operate and to their ongoing struggle to scale back the demands of the state and elite groups and, thereby, retain enough of what they produce to build decent lives for themselves. It also results in an understanding of confrontational protest that is very different than that of the protest as an aberration or abnormality that prevailed before and just after the war, and different than the "building to the big event" (peasant riots or rebellion) approach that dominated work on agrarian protest, including my own, in the 1960s and 1970s.

Reprinted from Nicholas B. Dirks, *Colonialism and Culture,* Copyright © by the University of Michigan Press, 1992.

Like all reassessments, the reorientation of our approaches to peasant societies suggested by the literature on everyday and avoidance protest creates new problems in methodology and conceptualization and resurrects issues that were never fully resolved in earlier debates. A major source of the former has resulted from the tendency to conflate modes of avoidance protest, which was the focus of the 1981 *CSSH* essay reprinted here, with forms of everyday resistance like foot-dragging, pilfering, and grousing behind the back of the local landlord. As I argue implicitly in this article and have done so explicitly elsewhere, the two are quite different phenomena in a number of important respects.[1] To begin with, everyday forms of peasant response are much more limited in time span and the numbers involved *in any given occurrence,* as well as in the degree to which they challenge or disrupt the existing order. The fact that everyday protest involves acts that are meant to be hidden—in fact, must be hidden if they are to be successful—from the dominant groups at whom they are directed, means that a record of them is unlikely to be preserved in the sorts of sources used by historians. As studies such as James Scott's *Weapons of the Weak* have so ably shown, the members of peasant communities at all class levels are well aware that subordinate groups are engaging in these defensive and retributive activities.[2] But the sorts of oral documentation for these responses that Scott and others have painstakingly recorded and insightfully analyzed in recent years rarely, if ever, exist for the precolonial or colonial periods, which are the subject of my *CSSH* essay. Official sources and written memoirs rarely, if ever, tell us much about everyday resistance in times past. In contrast, protest migrations, the spread of banditry, sectarian withdrawal, and other forms of avoidance protest are often treated in official sources, both those of central administrations and local functionaries, though rarely in the detail that the historian would like.

By interpolation from contemporary studies, we may surmise that, in former times, peasant groups widely resorted to everyday forms of resistance—perhaps even more commonly than today, given the more modest means at the disposal of the state and landed groups to control them. But the clandestine nature of everyday responses meant that they were unlikely to be recorded in village records, much less the reports of princely or colonial officials. A major exception to this general rule involved practices such as the concealment of produce and able-bodied laborers and the collusion of villagers with local officials to underreport crop yields or *corvée* labor quotas. These tactics, which are treated as peasant defenses rather than protest in the 1981 essay, can, I think, be included among everyday forms of peasant resistance. Interestingly, they were recorded because they were forms of everyday resistance that were primarily aimed at the state. On the whole, however, modes of everyday resistance tend to be employed to redress imbalances in the terms of exchange with landlords, moneylenders, and other local power brokers or in efforts to defame these individuals for their perceived injustices. The primacy of the local arena in the quotidian contests between the peasant underclasses and those who dominate them, contrasts with the centrality of the state's role in most occurrences of avoidance protest. As I try to show in this essay, the latter cannot be understood apart from the context provided by the state. On the other hand, the relatively minor presence of the state, aside from discussions of efforts to cheat on the *zakat* or religious tithe, in Scott's description in *Weapons of the Weak* of everyday resistance in a Malaysian village suggests the rather different targets typically associated with each type of nonconfrontational protest.

The existence of written documents dealing with various modes of avoidance protest in both the precolonial and colonial periods makes it possible to explore the significant continuities between systems of dominance and dependence and peasant responses in the two eras, as well as to assess the major shifts that occurred in each. The arguments advanced in the *CSSH* essay were intended to call into question the extent to which European conquest marked a significant break with the precolonial past for the majority of the peoples who came under colonial rule. For this reason, I have much regretted titling and organizing the essay in such a way that many have seen the precolonial/colonial division as central to shifts in the patterns of peasant response I have tried to identify. As I have argued here and elsewhere, the assumption of political power by the European colonizers often had little immediate effect on peasants and other subordinate groups.[3] In most instances, the continuities between political economies existing under indigenous rulers and those that emerged under colonial rule were far more striking than the changes under way. Though the incidence of confrontation in the early stages of European rule was often increased by the colonizers' suspicion, at times bordering on paranoia, of indigenous sectarian movements, whenever possible the colonizers retained the indigenous lords and employed indigenous symbols and rituals (which were often religious in origin) of political authority. In most instances, it was decades after the

European takeover before the forces that reduced, or eliminated altogether, the effectiveness of longstanding modes of avoidance protest began to take hold.

Without question, the aims and policies pursued by the colonizers and their new military and communications technology unleashed these forces. But the shift from avoidance protest techniques to increasingly confrontational forms of agitation was a gradual and uneven process that differed considerably from one colony—or even from one district—to the next. The extent to which it occurred depended on the mix of forces found in a particular area. Among other factors, the viability of different modes of avoidance protest tended to be undermined by the spread of the market economy and the consequent erosion of patron-client ties and community cohesion; demographic shifts, which altered population-to-land ratios and eliminated remaining frontier areas; and the communications revolution, which greatly increased the reach of the ruling elites. Virtually all peasant groups continued to rely on modes of avoidance protest well into the colonial era, and often this attachment continued long after they had ceased to be effective. It is also fair to assume that everyday forms of protest that are so prevalent in the present day have been inherited from the distant past. Indeed, if one can generalize from the evidence provided by Scott, this type of peasant resistance has fared better than most forms of avoidance response in the late- and postcolonial eras. On the other hand, as Gandhi's nonviolent approach to mass nationalist agitation or even revolutionary guerrilla warfare demonstrate, the principles of avoidance protest, and in some cases specific modes of avoidance response like flight and sabotage, have exerted considerable influence on movements designed to promote confrontations with, and eventually overthrow, the existing political order.

In contrast to clandestine acts of everyday retribution, avoidance protest involves open challenges to dominant elite groups and, at times, to the state itself. Because modes of avoidance protest are likely to be more open, more collective, and more threatening (while minimizing direct confrontation) to those in power, they also involve far greater risk for those who resort to them. In fact, challenge and risk are key attributes of the protest dimension of this type of response on the part of peasants and other subordinate groups. Transferring one's loyalties and services from one patron to another, for which, in societies such as in central Java, there was an accepted procedure to be observed, involved the explicit expression of the client's dissatisfaction with the patron he was abandoning. Mass migrations of village communities or a considerable portion of the population of entire districts was a potent way for peasants to draw attention to the oppression of local notables or the maladministration of state officials in their region. There are numerous instances of the dismissal and punishment of officials whose misdeeds were publicized in this manner. At times, the movement of populations across territorial boundaries or into unsettled frontier areas was so extensive that the continued viability of the state itself was put at risk. In fact, the spread of vagabondage and retributive forms of avoidance protest, such as banditry, have traditionally been associated in many societies with the decline of dynastic houses.

The indirect and nonviolent, but very real and well recognized, challenges that avoidance protest poses for the existing order contrast with the hidden, nondisruptive occurrence of everyday resistance. Although Scott argues that the cumulative effect of everyday protest actions on the part of the peasant classes of a given polity over a period of time can undermine the polity's viability, this is a proposition that has yet to be tested.[4] In fact, the evidence we have to date suggests that the reverse is the case, that as rulers begin to lose control and state systems go into decline, the need and opportunities for both everyday and avoidance types of protest increase dramatically. On the face of it, mass migrations and banditry are more likely to play major roles in a state's continuing decline and collapse than shoddy work, illegally gleaning the spilled seeds in the local headman's fields, and "accidents" that damage a landlord's equipment or disable his or her livestock.

It is also important to keep in mind that neither everyday nor avoidance protest responses are intended to destroy, or even radically alter, the political system or the social structure in which peasants or other subordinate groups operate. They have developed both types of response to defend themselves against the excessive demands of dominant groups in the first instance, and, when the defenses fail, to provide ways of protesting their exploitation without directly confronting their oppressors. In terms of the latter, modes of the avoidance type tend to be a good deal more effective than the everyday tactics that are the focus of much recent work. But both types of response are designed to work within the existing system. As the terms *everyday* and *avoidance* suggest, these modes of response to oppression by subordinate groups are built into the ongoing interaction between dominant and subordinate classes. Many forms of everyday resistance are, in effect, routinized. Though more sporadic, avoidance responses become predictable in particular circumstances—the peasantry will fall back on them; their overlords must anticipate them and find ways of containing or fending them off. When peasants or other subordinate groups turn to responses that involve open confrontation with those whom they identify as the source of their suffering, they do so because everyday and avoidance tactics are ineffective. Riots and rebellions signal the breakdown of the uneasy and ever-shifting networks of dominance and dependency that provide the essential contexts for everyday and avoidance protest.

Both everyday resistance and avoidance protest give a degree of agency and voice to peasants and other subordinate groups, but we should be cautious about overestimating either the extent of the autonomy or the level of ideological sophistication that underclass groups can attain by employing them. Both are responsive: they are aimed at winning relief or some degree of retribution within a system that is taken as a given. The very modes of expression associated with either type of protest are dependent on the existing order, as recent studies of ritual protest through role reversals at carnival time and in other sorts of religious festivals dramatically illustrate.[5] Social roles are symbolically—and temporarily— exchanged, and members of the underclass are permitted to act in ways normally prohibited. But the reversals and outrageous behavior of the subordinate take the established order and elite classes as their referents. When carnival rowdiness leads to rioting or role reversals are proclaimed by millennarian rebels who hold out the promise of a world turned upside down, we have moved to a different type of protest response on the part of subordinate groups.

This is not to deny that subordinate groups play far more active roles than many writers have allowed in the making of the existing order, and that, through devices such as everyday resistance and avoidance protest, they are able to bring pressure on dominant groups to reformulate aspects of that order. But, despite small and usually temporary victories, they continue to accept their subordination; they remain victims of political economies designed to further the interests of elites, whether they be local landlords or the functionaries of princely or colonial regimes. In fact, both types of peasant response reinforce the existing order in a number of ways. If effective, they render the hard lot of the cultivators who resort to them bearable by ameliorating the oppressive demands of state and landlord. At the same time, they force necessary, but often temporary, concessions from dominant groups. Though varying in importance, the cumulative effect of these adjustments may well have proved critical to the persistence of systems based on exploitation and injustice. In addition, everyday resistance and avoidance protest provide outlets for peasants and other subordinate groups to vent their anger and, in a limited way, to strike back against those who use and humiliate them. Though we lack the evidence to determine this sort of thing with any precision, it is possible that activities like flight to the frontier, banditry, and sectarian retreat draw off the boldest, most politically conscious members of peasant communities and other subordinate groups. If this is the case, they cannot help but weaken whatever impetus there is for fundamentally restructuring the existing order, either through lasting reforms or revolutionary action.

The stress in my *CSSH* essay on the limits of both types of protest should not be taken as an implicit argument that members of subordinate social groups are incapable of doubting, indeed rejecting, the hegemonic ideas and structures designed to keep them in their place. Skillfully using oral testimony of a sort rarely available to the historian, Scott demonstrates just how pervasive and sophisticated this sort of demystification can be. The alternative "transcript" that he uncovers by listening to villagers from the underclasses leads him to doubt the utility of the concept of hegemony itself, at least as it was intended by Gramsci and has been frequently applied by social scientists in recent years. If the concept is used in the elite-centric, uncontested, and static formulation found in Gramsci's admittedly fragmentary writings on the subject, and so effectively demolished by Scott, it is indeed of questionable utility. But Scott's comparisons of the current situation of disarray with an apparently effective hegemonic system that existed in the Malaysian villagers' past and his admission that the peasants with whom he worked had just experienced a decade of unprecedented change, both point to the need to revise rather than outright reject Gramsci's formulation of hegemony. If hegemony is viewed as ideological and institutional dominance that is continually being tested and challenged (both openly and behind the scenes) by subordinate groups at a variety of levels and being reworked by elite groups to respond to these challenges and changing conditions more generally,[6] it becomes a far more useful analytical tool.

A dyachronic approach, which assumes that dominant and subordinate social groups are locked in an ongoing contest over the terms by which hegemony is imposed and accepted, gives the peasantry agency without attributing to them a capacity, which they have rarely possessed, to master

IV

fully the intricacies of the political or social systems in which they live and to act collectively to right the injustices they perceive in those arrangements. Both tactics of everyday resistance and modes of avoidance protest are key ways by which peasants and other subordinate groups test and challenge, and sometimes force changes in, hegemonic systems. But the limitations of these responses and the draconian repression they have frequently brought upon those who resort to them caution against a new sort of romanticization of peasant consciousness and overestimating the capacity of subordinate groups in rural or urban settings to right the wrongs inflicted upon them by those who monopolize power and control the resources of the societies in which they live.

NOTES

1. See Michael Adas, "From Foot-dragging to Flight: The Evasive History of Peasant Avoidance Protest in South and Southeast Asia," *Journal of Peasant Studies* 13, no. 2 (1986): 64–86.

2. James Scott, *Weapons of the Weak* (New Haven: Yale University Press, 1985), esp. chaps. 5 and 6. See also the essays in James Scott and Benedict J. Tria Kerkvliet, eds., *Everyday Forms of Peasant Resistance in Southeast Asia* (London: Frank Cass, 1986); and the contributions to *Contesting Power: Everyday Resistance in South Asian Society and History,* ed. Douglas Haynes and Gyan Prakash (Delhi: Oxford University Press, 1991).

3. See Michael Adas, "Bandits, Monks, and Pretender Kings: Patterns of Peasant Resistance and Protest in Colonial Burma, 1826–1941," in *Power and Protest in the Countryside,* ed. Robert P. Weller and Scott E. Guggenheim (Durham, N.C.: Duke University Press, 1982), 75–105.

4. See Scott, *Weapons,* 35–37, 348–50.

5. Perhaps the fullest exploration of these patterns can be found in Emmanuel LeRoy Ladurie, *Carnival in Romans* (New York: Braziller, 1979). For further examples in a variety of contexts, see Peter Burke, *Popular Culture in Early Modern Europe* (New York: Harper and Row, 1978); Barbara A. Babcock, ed., *The Reversible World: Symbolic Inversion in Art and Society* (Ithaca, N.Y.: Cornell University Press, 1978).

6. As Williams argued (over a decade ago) that it must be. See Raymond Williams, *Marxism and Literature* (London: Oxford University Press, 1977), esp. 111–14.

V

Bandits, Monks, and Pretender Kings: Patterns of Peasant Resistance and Protest in Colonial Burma, 1826–1941

One of the greatest advances in our understanding of the meaning of the era of European imperialist dominance for the peoples of Africa and Asia has resulted from recent studies which have forced a blurring of the distinction between the precolonial and colonial periods. Battle dates charting campaigns of European conquest, the overthrow of indigenous dynasties, or official proclamations of new modes of administrative organization have diminished in importance as numerous studies, focused on conditions at the local level, have documented the persistence of precolonial institutions, the tenacity of entrenched elite groups, and the limitations of the European colonizers in manpower, material resources, and knowledge of the areas and peoples that came under their control. The combination of these factors greatly restricted the colonizers' ability to exert effective political control, particularly over local elite groups and beneath them the mass of the cultivators at the village level. This meant in turn that European policies and initiatives from revenue collection to public works and social reforms were considerably transformed, steadily undermined, and at times completely ignored by the colonized peoples for whom they were intended (Washbrook, 1976; Baker, 1976; Ranger, 1969; van Velsen, 1964). Indigenous elite groups learned to turn the military might and legal apparatus of the alien colonizers to their own advantage, thereby establishing or enhancing their own power over the mass of the cultivators. In areas like South India, which has been the focus of extensive research in recent years, after decades of European rule, indigenous factions and local leaders were in some ways more autonomous and influential, and indigenous institutions, especially caste, more entrenched than they had been in the precolonial era. Ambitious British schemes for remaking the Indian sociopolitical order had been frustrated by the surprising resilience and strength of institutions and arrangements that had once appeared vulnerable and in need of reform.

Although our growing awareness of the limited usefulness of chronological compartmentalization, the checks on European power, and the persistence of indigenous elites and institutions has forced reassessments of many aspects of the colonial experience, perhaps none merits reexamination more than our approach to resistance and protest on the part of colonized peoples. Clearcut distinctions between primary resistance, postconquest risings, "archaic" or primitive protest, and "real" nationalist movements that were never very convincing, have been blurred, if not obliterated, by recent research. Writers like T. O. Ranger (1968), Sartono Kartodirdjo (1973), and Reyaldo Ileto (1979) have amply demonstrated that there are not only fundamental ideological and organizational links between movements grouped in each of these categories, but that forms of protest like millenarianism or banditry, once associated with primary resistance or the archaic phase, persist in the so-called nationalistic era and beyond into the independence period. As the studies of Washbrook and Baker cited above also reveal, an understanding of precolonial social and political institutions and the ways in which these persisted, despite European conquest and rule, is essential to any attempt to explain outbursts of social protest or, as important, the absence of them in the colonial era. Nationalist leaders, for example, did not suddenly appear, but emerged gradually as the result of shifts in the orientation and organization of longstanding elite groups and factions. Thus, the large-scale rebellions and nation-alist party struggles that hitherto have been the focus of most research cannot be isolated from modes of thinking and organization or from broader traditions of protest whose roots lay in the precolonial past.

The historiography of the area that presently makes up the nation of Burma provides a striking illustration of the distortions that result from placing too much emphasis on discontinuity and differences between phases of anticolonial resist-ance and protest. It is difficult to think of an example of imperialist expansion where the contrast between pre- and postconquest conditions has been more sharply drawn. In the established view, shared even by the critics of British expansion in Burma (Furnivall, 1957; Adas, 1972), a poor, backward and isolated enclave ruled by despotic, often cruel monarchs was, as the result of British conquest, abruptly opened to the forces of the world economy and brought under the administration of one of the most effective bureaucracies of the nineteenth century, the Indian Civil Service. Though Burma was conquered in stages between 1824 and 1886 and most writers clearly recognized that the colonial impact was greater in some regions than in others, the rapid expansion of cultivated acreage, steadily rising revenue and export figures, the ready participation of the Burmese in the market economy, and their addiction to the consumer rewards that resulted, all appeared to confirm the official assessment—at least until the late 1920s—that Burma was a model province, a superb example of the good government and economic benefits that could result from colonial rule.[1] This view also appeared to be supported by the long periods of internal peace and stability that followed each colonial conquest. According to this interpretation, after the xenophobic and misguided defenders of inept rulers had been defeated and criminal elements put down in the 1850s and 1880s, the province enjoyed decades of prosperity and tranquility until nationalist agitators, often posing as Buddhist monks, sought to stir up the peasant masses in the years after World War I.

Though some writers, most notably J. S. Furnivall, dissented from the view that change benefitted the great majority of the Burmese, all stressed the depth and abruptness of the transformations resulting from European conquest and rule. Both defenders and critics of colonization have seen discontinuity—political, economic, social, and intellectual—and the decline of "traditional" ideas and institutions as the central features of the British period in Burmese history. In fact, discontinuity and the decline of tradition came to be viewed as the underlying causes of the succession of popular upheavals that shattered the facade of colonial peace and prosperity in the 1920s and 1930s, and they have also been considered responsible for Burma's return to a position of isolation and limited development in the postindependence era.

It cannot be disputed that colonialism brought fundamental changes to Burma. These changes, however, were neither as abrupt nor often as pervasive and lasting as they have generally been pictured. Even in Lower Burma, where the spread of the market economy and the introduction of new land tenure systems were concentrated, precolonial attitudes, institutions, and modes of organization and interaction persisted decades after the formal British takeover, and in some cases outlasted the colonizers into the independence era. A close examination of the responses of Burmese peasants and local elite groups in both Upper and Lower Burma to British conquest and rule reveals much continuity with the precolonial period amid the far reaching changes that have been emphasized in most works on British Burma. Despite grand British schemes for administrative reorganization and claims of centralized bureaucratic control, large portions of conquered areas remained beyond the effective control of the colonizers for decades after they were formally annexed, and some regions were never governed by the British at all in any meaningful way. Even in the more accessible riverine and coastal lowland areas where the British most actively pursued their political and economic designs for the province, the peasants' centuries-old hostility toward government officials and their struggle to retain the maximum degree of local autonomy continued. Local elite groups, who had succeeded in attaching themselves to the new rulers and in winning administrative posts on the lower rungs of the colonial hierarchy, employed the same techniques of concealment, deception, and tactics of bribery and embezzlement that their ancestors had used to blunt the revenue demands of Burmese monarchs.

Despite the deep involvement of large numbers of peasants, especially in Lower Burma, in the export economy that developed in the late nineteenth century, my investigation through revenue records, police reports, and special enquiries into economic conditions and incidents of social unrest, reveals that large numbers of the cultivating classes were never reconciled to British rule. They retained a deep longing for the return of their own monarchs and a fierce attachment to the beliefs, rituals, and symbols—both religious *and* political—of Theravada Buddhism as it was practiced in Burma. The British tendency to link rising crime rates and other social disorders to the breakdown of Buddhist education and to the weakening hold of Buddhist ethics on an increasingly market-oriented and consumer-minded peasant population not only diverts attention from causes of unrest rooted in the disruptions and injustices of the colonial political economy, but also seriously distorts the relationship between the peasantry and Buddhism. Despite decreases in the proportion of youths receiving a formal Buddhist education, especially in areas

V

like Lower Burma, and a decline in discipline within the Buddhist Sangha, Buddhism remained central to the identity of the vast majority of lowland Burmese. As in precolonial times, Buddhist ethics played a vital role in the regulation of social and economic relations and in judging the performance of those who governed. From the earliest risings against the British colonizers in the 1820s, through the rebellions and communal clashes of the 1930s, and the final struggles for independence, the defense of Buddhism was used by princely pretenders, prophets, and nationalist leaders alike to rally peasant supporters to their cause.

The persistence of this theme was paralleled by a broader continuity of ideological appeals, leadership styles, and symbols employed by all Burmese leaders who were able to build a popular base for their movements, with the partial exception of the *Thakins* who emerged in the late 1920s. In addition, the main modes of popular protest—banditry, cult withdrawal, risings led by princely pretenders, flight, and communal clashes—remained constant throughout the colonial era, though the causes that gave rise to individual outbreaks or movements varied somewhat as new grievances were spawned by political and economic change. For example, economic hardship and nationalism, in the European sense of the term, contributed to the depression rebellions of the 1930s, usually associated with the prophet-pretender, Saya San. The causes for which most cultivators rose in these rebellions, however, and especially the forms their dissidence took were strikingly similar to those of the local lords, *pongyis* (Buddhist monks), and peasants who so stubbornly resisted the advance of the British conquerors in the 1850s or in the 1880s and 1890s.

Relying primarily on the abundant archival and published evidence available for British Burma, I will attempt in this essay to demonstrate the persistence of traditions of peasant resistance and protest. I will also seek to show why and how these traditions changed in response to broader political and socioeconomic transformations. Central to my approach is the assumption that individual instances of collective protest are shaped not just by the conditions and specific causes that consciously motivate their participants, but also by longstanding and well-tested traditions of protest, which shape the ways in which aggrieved groups respond to those whom they view as their oppressors. According to this approach, movements that are normally treated as single "great rebellions," such as the Saya San risings of the 1930s, can often be found upon examination to be loosely-linked conglomerations of local risings and disturbances involving very different modes of collective protest. This approach results in an emphasis on the continuity between protest movements of different types and widely varying sizes, and the ways in which these movements are rooted in traditions of resistance and protest that predated the period of colonization and that persist into the independence era.

Excepting the temporary setbacks which the British suffered at the hands of the able Burman commander,[2] Maha Bandula, in the First Anglo-Burmese War, the resistance offered by the Konbaung rulers to the advance of British armies in the wars of 1824–1826, 1852, and 1885, was at best feeble, and increasingly so in each encounter (Hall, 1964; Woodman, 1962; Htin Aung, 1965). This poor showing on the part of the Burman defenders was surprising to contemporaries given the Burmans' reputation for military prowess and bellicosity, and their impressive victories in the late eighteenth century over their bitter rivals, the Siamese, and invaders from Ch'ing China. The ease of the British conquest has normally been attributed to the inept leadership of the later Konbaung rulers and their officials and military commanders (excepting Bandula), and especially to the overwhelming technological and organizational superiority which the British possessed in armed conflict with a backward and inward-looking kingdom. As the century progressed, the weaknesses of the Burman rulers became more and more apparent and the British military edge ever more awesome.

Whatever the merits of these arguments, they obscure more fundamental reasons for the failure of Burman resistance, reasons centered on the monarch and state. Resistance at this level was ineffectual not only because conventional armies and battles played to the strengths of the British, who could draw upon the technology and resources of an industrializing society and a global empire, but also because the center of the Konbaung state was perhaps its most fragile and vulnerable component. This was especially true by the first decades of the nineteenth century when that state was clearly in decline. Thus, the British confronted a dynasty whose court was riven by the struggles of rival claimants to the throne, factional intrigues, and the plots of disgruntled princes and nobles (Koenig, 1978; Htin Aung, 1967). The debilitating effects of these struggles, which were characteristic of the contest-state (Adas, 1981) form of polity found in precolonial Burma, were exacerbated by the steady increase in the degree of autonomy enjoyed by regional lords and local leaders that was both a consequence and a symptom of dynastic decline (Lieberman, 1976: 39, 45, 105–6, 220, 227ff).

As the court's control of areas beyond the capital decreased, its ability to marshal the manpower and supplies needed to meet the British challenge diminished. In the first Anglo-Burman confrontation, the Konbaung state could still muster substantial armies and support these for fairly extended periods of time. Even in this phase, however, Burman forces were made up mainly of ill-trained, poorly armed, and unwilling conscripts recruited by the retainers of regional lords. These troops repeatedly failed to hold, and often to man at all, superb defensive positions, and only stood their ground when led by able and charismatic commanders like Bandula. The feebleness of state-led resistance at its strongest in the first war is most strikingly revealed by British and Indian casualty figures. Deaths by disease (malaria, cholera, dysentery) greatly exceeded those due to battle wounds (Majumdar, 1963: 110). At the time of the second war in 1852, the control of the court had grown so weak that Burman armies offered only token resistance to the rapid advance of the British up the deltas of the Irrawaddy and Sittang rivers. In the final clash in 1885, the capital and the dynasty itself fell with virtually no armed struggle whatsoever.

The importance of the vulnerability of the Burman state structure in the failure of resistance to British conquest is evidenced by the greater success achieved by risings which broke out in the months just after different areas of the Konbaung kingdom had been formally annexed by the British. Though fugitive nobles and officials from the Konbaung court played some role in these risings, they were led for the most part by regional lords and local notables, or in some instances by *pongyis* and bandit chiefs. As the capacity of the Konbaung state to check the British advance declined with each successive confrontation, local resistance grew in scale and duration. After the annexation of Arakan and Tenasserim in 1826, only minor disturbances occurred (Furnivall, 1939: 15; *Akyab*: 36). By contrast, the annexation of the Irrawaddy delta region in 1852 was followed by nearly a decade of local risings and "bandit" attacks. After the 1886 annexation of the remaining portions of the Konbaung kingdom to the Indian Empire, British occupation forces struggled for over five years to put down widespread resistance, again spearheaded by local leaders, in both Upper and Lower Burma. Though the last Konbaung monarch, Thibaw, was easily toppled, the British were forced to call in reinforcements from India and expend considerable resources to put down repeated challenges to their rule at the regional and village level. Despite soaring exports in the following decades and frequent references on the part of British writers to the peace and good government that colonial rule had brought to Burma, rising crime rates—which were regularly the highest in Burma of any province in the Indian Empire (*Rangoon Gazette*, 1929: 22; RPAB, 1920: 12)— sporadic local risings, and communal clashes sustained a tradition of anticolonial resistance and peasant protest which peaked in the antitax campaigns, rebellions, and communal riots of the 1920s and 1930s.

The greater effectiveness of postconquest resistance was in part due to the fact that the gap between the British and local Burmese forces in manpower and armaments was so great that conventional assaults were suicidal. Therefore, regional lords or bandit chiefs resorted to hit-and-run attacks, ambushes, and raids that were characteristic of centuries-old techniques of guerrilla-style warfare. The British ignorance of the local terrain, which rebel bands exploited fully, and the dense forest cover that in many areas prevented the British from making effective use of their overwhelming advantage in firepower, rendered guerrilla resistance by far the most difficult for the British to suppress (Crosthwaite, 1912; Geary, 1886; Tha Aung and Mya Din, 1941). The more effective resistance provided by localized risings was also due to the greater strength of the ties that bound regional lords, village headmen, and bandit chiefs to their supporters—ties that were usually based on personalist and reciprocal patron-client exchanges. In contrast to the rather fragile and often short-lived power of the state center, the dominance of local elite groups was frequently maintained for generations and, in some instances, centuries (Tha Aung and Mya Din, 1941: 131; Lieberman, 1976: 202). In the precolonial era the authority and influence of headmen and regional lords peaked in periods of dynastic decline and breakdown as the already limited control of the state was more and more constricted, and these local leaders became the upholders of law and order in the locality. With each defeat and finally the collapse of the Konbaung dynasty in the face of foreign invasion, local notables rallied their followers to resist the imposition of British control over their lands and villages. If their proclamations to their followers are to be believed, some of these leaders themselves hoped to establish a new dynasty in place of the vanquished Konbaung overlords. These aspirations were by no means without foundation, for on a number of occasions in Burmese history local leaders had succeeded in winning the throne—in fact, Alaungpaya, the founder of the Konbaung dynasty had begun his rise to power as a village headman in the Shwebo district who had organized resistance against Mon invaders from Lower Burma (Htin Aung, 1967: 157ff).

Local Konbaung officials, especially *thugyis* (heads of clusters of tiny hamlets) and *myothugyis* (township heads), who were displaced by the British conquest and annexation, were the main leaders of the resistance struggles that followed the 1852 war. Resistance in a number of areas was led by *pongyis*, but they tended to support *thugyi*-led bands rather than assume control themselves. According to British accounts, the other major source of resistance in the post-1852 period came from bandit gangs that roamed the wilderness of the lower and western Irrawaddy delta region for decades after the formal conquest. As some British officials admitted (*Tharrawaddy*: 26), however, the bandit or *dacoit* label was applied rather indiscriminately to resisting ex-Konbaung officials and professional criminals alike. This meant that men like the ex-*thugyi*, Gaung Gyi, who fought to drive out the alien invaders and restore the rule of his Konbaung overlords, were hunted down like common criminals.

Whether ex-officials, *pongyis*, or professional bandits, all resistance leaders claimed to be commissioned by the Konbaung court, which in 1852 still ruled in Upper Burma, to carry on the struggle against the British. Leaders of the larger risings, like Gaung Gyi, wielded the ancient symbols of Burmese political authority: gilt umbrellas, royal elephants, and sacred gongs. Some rebel leaders claimed to be princes of the royal house. Widespread popular support for resistance groups, particularly in the form of food and shelter, demonstrates the strong hold these symbols and appeals continued to exercise over peasant communities despite the dynasty's setbacks. Some of this support was admittedly given out of fear of reprisal raids, but many villagers willingly allowed themselves to be treated as subjects by rebel leaders and refused information and supplies to British forces in pursuit of rebel bands. Any Burmese who cooperated with the invaders became targets of rebel assaults. Headmen and cultivators were slain and on a number of occasions whole villages were put to the torch, such as several settlements along the Irrawaddy that had supplied fuel for British steamboats moving up or down the river. Though robberies were carried out and a number of ambushes against British columns and raids on occupied towns were attempted, most rebel bands spent much of their time eluding British patrols or simply struggling to survive. When the hopelessness of their cause became apparent following the new king, Mindon's, refusal to continue the struggle, many rebels resorted to the time-tested peasant defense of flight and slipped into Upper Burma.[3]

After the overthrow of the Konbaung dynasty and the annexation to the Indian Empire of the remaining portions of the Burman kingdom in 1885–1886, the British were confronted by resistance in both Upper and Lower Burma that far exceeded in scale and ferocity that which had appeared so troublesome at mid-century. The modes of resistance adopted after 1886 were much the same as those employed earlier, but rebel bands were much larger and better organized, and rebel leaders made much more elaborate use of kingly rituals and royal symbols in their efforts to give legitimacy to their cause. Some forms of resistance were also more in evidence in this phase. Of these, an increase in flight or mass migration is the most notable. As British columns advanced into the Dry Zone, they found many villages deserted. Though in many cases the British argued that the inhabitants of these villages had fled to avoid dacoit depredations, they were also forced to admit that peasants had abandoned their homes in an effort to avoid submission to alien invaders. Most villagers sought at first to hide in nearby forests or distant hills, but many eventually joined the rebel bands and dacoit gangs that spearheaded resistance to the imposition of British rule (Geary, 1886: 49, 51; Crosthwaite, 1912: 34; Mya Khan, 1969: 68).

Because the court center itself was overthrown in 1885, Konbaung officials, princes, and princely pretenders played a much greater role in the disturbances following the third Anglo-Burman war than they had in earlier resistance efforts. In December of 1886, two princes, Teiktin Hmat and Teiktin Thein, raised the standard of revolt in Shwebo, the home district of the Konbaung dynasty's founder, Alaungpaya. Several "dacoit" leaders, their followers, and thousands of peasants armed with *dahs* (long knives), spears, and muskets rallied to the princes' cause, but after a series of defeats in skirmishes with British and Indian troops, in which one of the princes was killed, resistance in the district soon dissipated (Geary: 276–78; *Shwebo*: 34ff).

One of the exiled King Thibaw's stewards also left the palace to arouse the people to resist the British and he was joined by one of King Mindon's surviving sons,[4] who left his monastery refuge to fight against the British conquerors. In addition to genuine scions of the royal house, numerous pretenders appeared who claimed to be of royal blood and urged their followers to aid them in their efforts to restore Konbaung rule. Perhaps the most interesting of the would-be princes was a former actor who took the title of the Kyimyindaing Prince. His great skill at assuming the style and manipulating the symbols of Burman kingship in order to attract peasant followers is explained by the fact that he had often played the role of a senior prince in *pwe* (theatrical) performances at the palace. The pretender claimed that he had been carried away as an infant into the wilderness by one of the queens who feared for his life. Indigenous accounts also relate that he had led a rather feeble rebellion against King Thibaw and was on his way to the court in chains when war with the British broke out. Other royal pretenders—some claiming to be *Minlaungs* or imminent kings—emerged in areas as widely separated as the Myingyan district in the heart of the Dry Zone and the Ye–U township in Lower Burma (Tha Aung and Mya Din, 1941: 81–4, 93, 97, 103, 121–4; *Yamethin*: 37).

Both genuine princes and pretenders sought to rally support for their resistance efforts by building palace centers that were essential symbols of kingly authority in Burmese culture, and recreating, insofar as possible given their limited resources and constant challenges from British forces, the administrative hierarchy and procedures associated with the Burman monarchy (Heine-Geldern, 1942: 17, 19–26; Yi Yi, 1961; Ireland, 1907, 49). Mindon's son, who came to be known as the Myinzaing Prince, bestowed military commissions and official titles on the *Bohs* or commanders of the forces that fought in his name. He appointed counsellors and a "prime minister," and mobilized thousands of peasants in his struggle to restore the dynasty. After being driven from the Dry Zone, the Myinzaing Prince took refuge in the rugged Shan hills where he found time to direct the construction of a royal city and palace which was given the auspicious title of the "City of the White Elephant." Though he was later to die of malaria, a fugitive abandoned by his followers, in the weeks after his palace center was established his armies swelled to over twenty thousand men and proved a major challenge to the British conquerors (Tha Aung and Mya Din, 1941: 85–6, 107, 124).

As was the case with the post-1852 resistance in Lower Burma, most of the support for princely rebels—genuine or pretender—after the 1886 annexation in Upper Burma was recruited from the dependents and retainers of local lords and village notables. Though some court officials, like the steward mentioned above and the commander of the king's cavalry, threw in their lot with the rebels, township heads (*myothugyis*) and village headmen (*thugyis*) made up the great majority of the secondary leaders of the resistance (Tha Aung and Mya Din, 1941: 83–4, 91–6; 101, 105, 114, 117, 121; *Pakokku*: 18) with the exception of the so-called *dacoit* chiefs who will be discussed in greater detail below. As British observers pointed out, the decision of headmen or township leaders to resist normally meant that large numbers of villagers rallied to the rebel side. Thus, rebel forces were made up of uneasy alliances of distinct, and sometimes hostile, bands of untrained peasants, rather than well-integrated and drilled soldiers. When confronted by the well-armed and disciplined troops of the colonizers, rebel forces usually broke down into small groups whose continued resistance was dependent on the strength of the personalist, patron-client bonds that were the backbone of social and political relations in precolonial Burma. However cohesive and steadfast these bands proved to be, the British were able to hunt them down and defeat them piecemeal.

Other than pressures applied by local men of power, the main motives for joining rebel bands in Upper Burma were hostility towards the British invaders and a desire to restore rule by indigenous overlords. The British, who had long regarded Burman monarchs as cruel tyrants, were surprised by the extent and intensity of resistance to foreign conquest, particularly that on the part of ordinary villagers. As Grattan Geary, who wrote one of the most vivid and honest accounts

V

of the campaigns in Upper Burma, admitted, the conquerors were amazed to find good roads and a population that was well fed and housed, and generally content with their rulers. He noted that most of the former subjects of the Konbaung monarch, " . . . made no complaint of oppression and gave no evidence of rejoicing at our (the British) coming; on the contrary they took kindly to dacoity against us" (Geary, 1886: 292–3).

The resistance offered by regional lords and village leaders in Upper Burma in the name of the defeated Konbaung dynasty was also inspired by a less "patriotic", but perhaps more deeply felt desire to preserve the high degree of autonomy that regional and local elites and village dwellers generally had enjoyed in the precolonial era. The ancient struggle of these groups against state intervention into and control over their affairs, and especially their efforts to limit state tax and manpower demands, was now directed against the new British rulers. Some sense of the transformations that had occurred in Lower Burma since 1852, must have heightened fears for the erosion of local control and the patron-client exchanges on which it was based. More immediately threatening was the impressive display of mobility and military strength by which the British had so easily toppled the enfeebled Konbaung dynasty and moved to establish their control over the village population. Our post-World War II obsession with anticolonial resistance has often led us to lose sight of the importance of this age-old struggle for local autonomy against *any* overlord, whether European or indigenous.

Although some *pongyis* or Buddhist monks had joined in the resistance after the 1852 annexation of Lower Burma, in the late 1880s for the first time they assumed a major role in the struggle against the British. Their leadership of rebel bands was most apparent in Lower Burma which had been ruled by non-Buddhist foreigners for over three decades. It was also in this area, especially in the delta districts around Rangoon, that the challenges to Buddhism posed by the influx of a market, consumer-oriented economy, Christian missionaries, and Western courts and legal procedures had been felt the most strongly. *Pongyis*, most of whom claimed to be acting on orders from the king, led risings in Tenasserim, Toungoo, and Tharrawaddy in Lower Burma and in the Minbu district in the Dry Zone (Geary, 1886: 7, 225; Crosthwaite, 1912: 107ff; Sarkisyanz, 1965: 104–5; Plant, 1886: 1, 4–6). The most serious of these risings was that begun by a monk named U Thuriya in the Tharrawaddy district in July of 1888. This outbreak warrants detailed examination both because it exhibited patterns that were strikingly similar to the majority of postconquest rebellions that followed and because it illustrates some of the major differences between the causes that gave rise to resistance in Upper Burma, which had just been annexed, and Lower Burma, which had been under colonial rule for over thirty years.

The British advance into Upper Burma in 1885–86 touched off disturbances throughout the Tharrawaddy district in the upper delta region. Policemen and village leaders in many areas refused to continue to serve the colonial authorities and joined or formed rebel bands or dacoit gangs that roamed the district with impunity for several years. Tax collectors, loyal headmen, and police posts were the major targets of rebel assaults. Most leaders claimed to have been commissioned by the deposed king, but some like Nga Aung adopted regalia, including gilt umbrellas, that suggest that they themselves had dynastic ambitions. The causes of these disturbances were similar to those focusing on the defense of the monarchy and hostility to foreign conquest that motivated those who resisted in Upper Burma. The causes of U Thuriya's rebellion, however, which was by far the largest rising in Lower Burma in this period, went beyond patriotism and involved disaffection caused in part by changes that had occurred as a result of colonial rule.

A severe cholera epidemic, poor rainfall, and crop shortages fueled the discontent that gave rise to U Thuriya's rebellion. These conditions may also have lent credence to widespread rumors concerning dynastic decline that had long been associated with bad weather and that were now directed against the foreign overlords. Special taxes on peasant households, that the British levied to pay for extra manpower to police the troubled district, also contributed to widespread disaffection. Discontent was heightened by further rumors that an income tax would soon be imposed on all town dwellers in the district. These cesses—actual and imagined—were doubly resented because the policemen they supported were mainly recruited from the ethnic minority Karens, who were said to demand food and labor from the peasant population without payment. The recent confiscation of firearms held by villagers in the district also angered the peasants since it left them at the mercy of wandering gangs of dacoits for which the heavily forested district had been notorious for centuries. Crop shortages in conjunction with the gradual abandonment of communal village granaries in the face of the market-oriented, competitive political economy that had developed under colonial rule resulted in sharp increases in local food prices that the government did little or nothing to bring under control. The sale of children by peasant families to rich merchants and landowners for adoption was perhaps the most dramatic sign of the desperate condition of the poorest cultivators in the district.

The rising had apparently been prepared well in advance of the actual outbreak on 2 July 1888. Its leader, U Thuriya, a *pongyi* from a monastery near the town of Gyobingauk, administered an oath of loyalty to those who agreed to join him in rebellion. Many of his followers were also tattooed with magic letters that were intended to identify them as the *pongyi's* supporters and make them invulnerable to British bullets. Recruits were also given palm-leaf enlistment tickets, of which over seventeen hundred were prepared, and read proclamations that U Thuriya claimed had been issued by the Myingun prince. According to British accounts, all of the dacoit gangs in the district pledged their support for the rising. On the night of 2 July, which had been chosen by an astrologer as auspicious, attacks were launched on several towns, telegraph lines were cut, and the railway line between Gyobingauk and Zigon was badly damaged. After threatening a village records-keeper, the rebels headed south to attack the Prome mail train, or at least the British believed that this was what they intended to do. Before they reached their target, however, the special police and military had been alerted. No major clashes between government forces and the rebels occurred, but by the end of the following day the rising had been put down without any loss of life and eighty-four arrests. Once again resistance in the district reverted to sporadic raids by dacoit gangs (*Tharrawaddy*, 1920: 35–7; Dunn, 1920: 17–19).

Although the nature of resistance in Upper and Lower Burma differed in important ways, one mode of response was, according to British accounts, pervasive in both areas—dacoity or gang robbery. Most of the *Bohs*, whose followers swelled the ranks of the forces of princes and pretenders in Upper Burma and *pongyi* agitators in Lower Burma, were classified as bandits or common criminals by the British. In part the label represented an attempt, whether conscious or unconscious, on the part of the British to allay doubts about policies that had evoked such widespread and determined resistance by the Burmans. As it is used in official accounts of the disturbances after the 1852 and 1886 annexations, the term is meaningless. To begin with, though some leaders whom the British branded as dacoits had in fact been bandits in the precolonial period (Tha Aung and Mya Din, 1941: 129; *Pakokku*: 18), the label was also applied to resistance leaders whose prior occupations ranged from courtiers and Konbaung administrators to betel-leaf sellers, messengers, cultivators, and disbanded soldiers. So-called bandit gangs sometimes numbered in the thousands. They were often well armed and organized into regular fighting units with battle standards and battle orders which called for conventional encounters with advancing British forces (*Thayetmyo*: 13–14; Tha Aung and Mya Din, 1941: 119–20, 122; *Shwebo*: 35, 37, 41). As Grattan Geary candidly observed, it was usually difficult to distinguish between ordinary villagers and professional dacoits, especially in times of economic or political breakdown when community survival could depend on alliances with dacoit gangs and the forcible seizure of scarce food supplies (Geary, 1886: 46–7, 71, 232, 276).

It cannot be doubted that some dacoits were in fact professional criminals, but many of those whom the British routinely referred to as dacoits opposed the colonizers for political reasons and received widespread support, often long after their cause was clearly lost. So-called dacoit chiefs or *Bohs* often claimed control over specific areas, from which they collected revenue on a fairly regular basis, and respected the territory of allied rebel leaders. In some cases *Bohs* brandished gilt umbrellas or other royal regalia and one leader in Shwebo used some of the revenue he collected to build a pagoda that he managed to complete before he died (Crosthwaite, 1912: 14, 23, 27, 31, 53, 103–5; *Yamethin*: 38; *Shwebo*: 40). The *Bohs*' own sense of their genuine patriotism and the righteousness of their cause is perhaps best indicated by the papers found on a dacoit leader from the Minbu district who was killed in action in October 1877. In addition to oaths swearing loyalty to the throne and orders that all *Bohs* and their followers shall, "Obey (their) superiors as the cow obeys the cowherd," the papers contain repeated references to the British as "foreign rebels." It appears that both sides were capable of employing ad hominem labels to discredit their opponents (White, ms. IOR).

Though the degree to which villagers in different areas willingly submitted to the demands of rebel *Bohs* is difficult to determine, British writers reported widespread collusion between village leaders and alleged dacoit chiefs. British commanders complained that the peasants in areas where dacoit bands were active refused to provide supplies for government troops or information concerning the whereabouts of bandit gangs. The British also had great difficulty recruiting informers or scouts from peasant communities in the disturbed tracts. The British practice of supplying arms to villages in these areas to enable their inhabitants to defend themselves had to be abandoned because these arms soon found their way into rebel or (in official parlance) dacoit hands. Even the British commander, Sir Charles Crosthwaite, was forced to concede the widespread support which the so-called dacoits received from the village populace when he concluded that: "If the people would have given us information, the dacoit system could have been broken in a very short time. As they would not, the only course open was to make them fear us more than the dacoits (1912: 104)."

Two additional patterns emerge from accounts of the post-1886 disturbances that, though they are mentioned only in passing, ought to be noted because they take on great importance in later protest movements. Necromancers and charm sellers are for the first time mentioned as leaders of local risings, and though direct references to talismans are rare, Burmese cultural traditions and the evidence we have suggest that magic was a potent means by which rebel leaders attracted and held peasant support. U Thuriya used cabalistic tattooes. Bo Shwe, the dacoit leader from Minbu, was found with numerous charms on his body, including one designed to prevent bullet wounds, one to induce bouyancy and great speed, another to make one's enemies sleepy (*Tharrawaddy*: 36; White ms., 10R). Though millenarian ideas that would play a prominent role in many later rebellions are rarely mentioned in accounts of the postconquest resistance struggles, a pretender in the Kyaukse district in Upper Burma is referred to as a *Sektya* or embryo Buddha in a British police report (RPAB, 1888: 11). Little more is said about the use of the title by this rebel leader, but the term and its millenarian associations would come to be closely identified by the British with protest and sedition.

Though stubborn and costly, Burman resistance to conquest and colonial rule was ultimately crushed. British organizational and military superiority played critical roles, particularly since the forces which opposed them were generally poorly trained and coordinated. British success, however, often depended heavily on a number of age-old techniques of empire builders. They recruited police and special military forces from minority ethnic groups, like the Karens and Shans. The British also bought elite allies and Burman informers, one of whom played a critical role in the quick suppression of U Thuriya's rising (*Tharrawaddy*: 37). The British bribed rebel chiefs, including some whom they considered dacoits, into submission with the promise of positions under the new regime. The colonizers exploited rivalries between Burman nobles and local lords, between village headmen, and between neighboring villages whose inhabitants sometimes saw the breakdown of political order as an opportunity to settle old grudges. As the indigenous accounts of the post-1886 disturbances in Upper Burma amply illustrate, Burman officials who collaborated with the British played vital roles in defeating those who resisted and in enabling the colonizers to establish lasting control (Tha Aung and Mya Din, 1941: 81, 85–6, 88, 98, 102, 120, 123, 130). When these more subtle techniques failed to put an end to local resistance, the British resorted to more brutal measures, including village burning, and in at least one instance the destruction of forest cover within fifty feet of a roadway where British forces had been ambushed (Geary, 1886, 49, 52, 75–7; *Thayetmyo*: 13; *Shwebo*: 41).

In the standard accounts of Burmese history and according to the accepted categories for the analysis of resistance and protest, the risings described thus far can be grouped under the heading of primary resistance. Closer examination, however, reveals important differences, particularly between resistance in Upper and Lower Burma in the period after the 1886 annexation. Though the late nineteenth century is normally viewed as a time of prosperity and rapid economic growth in the delta regions of Lower Burma, some groups and whole areas were either left behind or adversely affected by the great transformations that accompanied British rule and Burma's integration into the global economy. Natural setbacks—drought and crop shortages—combined with adverse market conditions and colonial taxation to threaten considerable numbers of peasant households with starvation, at least in limited areas in the upper delta. Some peasants chose to barter their children for the means to survive; others followed leaders like the *pongyi*, U Thuriya, into rebellion. Like those who resisted the British thoughout Upper Burma, the rebels in Tharrawaddy also fought to save the Konbaung dynasty and protect Buddhism. In Upper Burma, however, patriotism and the defense of religion were largely unrivalled motives for resistance because the market economy had only marginally affected the Burman rump state that survived after 1852, and colonial bureaucracy and taxes were as yet only a future menace.

Both of these issues—the restoration of the monarchy and the protection of Buddhism—were to remain central to protest movements throughout the colonial period. As Grattan Geary perceptively noted in his account of the conquest, the British made a major error when they deposed King Thibaw and put an end to the Konbaung dynasty. After describing how grown men and women wept when the king and his queen were taken down the Irrawaddy river to be exiled, Geary argued that the conquerors might better have left a puppet Burman ruler on the throne, for in removing the king the British created among their Burman subjects a deep sense of injury and humiliation and a rallying cause for anticolonial protest that would cost the British dearly in subsequent decades (1886: 294). In overthrowing the dynasty and failing to preserve at least a facade of religious and political legitimacy, which had centered upon the king in precolonial Burma, the British forfeited any possibility that they might have had of gaining widespread acceptance of their rule and of mollifying Burman fears for their religion and distinctive cultural identity. These fears would fuel protest movements throughout the colonial era, just as they had motivated those who suported the postannexation resistance efforts.

The post-1886 resistance temporarily slowed the rapid expansion of rice cultivation for export, which was concentrated in the delta regions of Lower Burma. Rice exports, which had recovered from a fairly severe slump in 1884–85 and risen in 1885–86 to near record totals, dropped steadily from late 1886 until the end of 1889, when they again began to increase as the colonial economy entered a period of sustained growth that was to continue for nearly two decades. The amount of acreage under rice cultivation also declined in the troubled Pegu division of Lower Burma between late 1886 and 1889, though offsetting increases in less disturbed areas in Lower Burma sustained steady growth in rice production in the province as a whole (Cheng, 1968: 244, 257). Beginning in the 1890s, however, Burma entered a period of rapid growth that soon transformed it into the world's leading rice-exporting area. This growth was paralleled by dramatic increases in the population of the rice-producing districts; fed by a rising stream of migration from India and Upper Burma, and to a lesser extent by natural increase. It also meant deeper and deeper involvement in the market economy, as the British intended, by large numbers of Burman cultivators. In addition, the extension in the 1890s of export production into Upper Burma, on a more limited scale, and into crops like peanuts and sesame rather than rice, exposed the cultivators of large tracts who had formerly been subsistence-oriented to the opportunities and perils of involvement in an unstable world market system (Adas, 1974: chs. 2, 3, 4, 7).

The peasants' eagerness to claim new lands and cultivate cash crops and their avid pursuit of the consumer rewards—from kerosene lamps and watches to bicycles and Western furniture—that could be gained through the sale of surplus rice, concealed from all but the most perceptive observers the underlying weaknesses of the economy and the society that had developed under British rule. Ancient rivalries between ethnic groups within Burma itself were greatly intensified by competition in the laissez faire market arena and by the collaboration of minority groups like the Kachins and Chins with the colonizers. The Karens, who had once been concentrated in the highland areas to the west and east of the Irrawaddy delta region and who were largely isolated from contacts with the predominately Burman-Mon population of the lowlands, migrated in large numbers into the Sittang and Irrawaddy deltas to take up rice production for the export market. Large Karen villages that were established throughout Lower Burma were known for their prosperity and for their avoidance of contact with nearby Mon or Burman settlements. Burman suspicion of and antipathy toward Karen settlers, as well as toward Chin and Shan migrants, was also aroused by the willingness of these groups to serve in the colonial police and military forces where their numbers far exceeded the number of Burman-Mon recruits in proportion to the percentage each group made up in the indigenous population as a whole (Marshall, 1922; Tadaw, 1959; Furnivall, 1956: 178–84).

The great influx of Indian migrants into Burma, especially after 1852, added a new dimension to preexisting communal tensions and rivalries. Indian laborers, merchants, moneylenders, and civil servants were drawn primarily to Lower

Burma like internal migrants by the economic opportunities which the rapid development of the rice export economy provided. From several thousand in the early 1800s, the Indian population in Burma rose to nearly 300,000 by 1900. Indian administrators, soldiers, and policemen had been essential in the campaigns to conquer and to establish British rule in Burma. By the end of the nineteenth century, Indian landlords controlled large estates throughout the districts of the Irrawaddy delta region; Indian merchants, millers, and money-lenders played pivotal roles in the marketing and processing of rice for export; and a surfeit of Indian laborers vied with a growing class of Burmese landless cultivators for positions as tenants, rural laborers, and mill workers, and for jobs on the wharves of Rangoon and in other urban centers (Cheng, 1968: chs. 4–7; Adas, 1974: chs. 4, 5, 7).

As long as the export economy expanded steadily in step with rising overseas demand for Burma rice at ever higher prices, and cultivable but unclaimed land was available in the delta frontier area, inter-ethnic tensions and the discontent of the colonized remained at manageable levels. Resistance continued, however, and protest movements erupted even in the boom decades of the 1890s and early 1900s. Much of this resistance was led, as earlier, by local leaders and dacoit gangs struggling to maintain their autonomy in the face of British determination to extend effective control to the village level. In response to the poor showing of local leaders and the indigenous constabulary during the post-1886 disturbances, the British carried out far reaching changes in the nature of village and local administration in Lower Burma. They abolished the indigenous hamlet circle and replaced it with the forced creation of nucleated village settlements patterned after those the British had long known in India and had recently encountered in Upper Burma. Circle *thugyis*, whose authority had depended mainly upon their standing among the hamlet populations under their jurisdiction, were replaced with village headmen. The British strove to orient the headmen to the demands and needs of the colonial administration rather than to those of the village populace and to strengthen their position within the village community. Only headmen were allowed to keep firearms, and they were provided with recordskeepers and policemen to help them keep order, at least in the larger villages. Most critically, the headmen were placed in charge of revenue collection in the areas assigned to them—a move that simultaneously enhanced their power and ability to profit from the posts they occupied and transformed them into the most prominent, and often the most disliked, agents of the colonial regime (Mya Sein, 1938).[5]

Although intended to strengthen the position of the village headmen, the changes introduced by the British actually weakened their hold over the peasants in their charge, for the latter came to regard the headmen, often quite rightly, as mere pawns of the alien overlords. The severing of the paternalist and reciprocal patron-client ties that had linked village notables and ordinary villagers in the precolonial era was a major blow to the system of social control that had evolved over centuries at the local level. The disintegration of the *athin* and *ahmudan* systems of regimental organization that had been central to manpower control in precolonial Burman kingdoms,[6] but were discarded by the British conquerors, also undercut the webs of dependency that had traditionally bound together elite groups and the peasantry.

In Lower Burma in particular, the open land frontier and its concomitant high rates of geographical and social mobility among the cultivating classes meant that patron-client ties were generally weak and short-lived. The absence of a well-entrenched landlord class in Burma, similar to those which the British had encountered in most areas of India, was a key factor in the success of British efforts to encourage the growth of a peasant-proprietor-dominated economy. This initial advantage, however, ultimately proved a liability for the colonial rulers as market reverses, land shortages, indebtedness, and land alienation produced growing numbers of displaced landowners and disgruntled tenants and laborers whose ties to an emerging landlord class—a class that in many areas was made up of a large percentage of immigrant Indians—were transient and purely contractual, rather than long-term, personalist, patron-client bonds. This meant that in contrast to most areas in India (Low, 1977: 2–3), the British could not base their strategy of rural social control on landlords and well-to-do peasants who were able to dominate a large portion of the cultivating classes through dependencies rooted in patron-client exchanges. Also in contrast to India,[7] landlord groups in Burma, though active in different nationalist organizations, were able to do little to check the mounting unrest in rural Burma in the 1920s and 1930s. Violent protest was rarely led by rural notables. It was, on the other hand, often directed against landlord groups, especially Indian estate owners and moneylenders who were so prominent in many areas of Lower Burma. The communal rather than class thrust of most rural protest tended to shield Burmese landlords and moneylenders who strove to deflect the dissatisfaction of the cultivating classes against the British overlords.

In addition to village reorganization and administrative reform, the British sought to gain effective control over the rural populace through an acceleration of the land-revenue inquests and settlements that had begun in the late 1870s. New areas brought under cultivation were quickly surveyed, mapped, and recorded with a thoroughness that was inconceivable in the precolonial era. Periodic revisions were carried out in areas where settlement operations had previously been conducted, and settlement operations were extended to the Dry Zone districts of Upper Burma. As a consequence of these efforts and related census work, the British knew a good deal more about the numbers and composition of the cultivating classes under their control, and the quality and productivity of the land they worked, than had even the strongest of Burman monarchs.

British control, however, was not gained without a struggle and was never fully complete, even in those areas that appeared to be the most secure. The rapid expansion of cultivated acreage and the highly mobile character of the peasant population, especially in Lower Burma, had posed great difficulties for census takers and revenue collectors from the first years after the 1826 and 1852 annexations (*RAP*, 1854–55: para. 26). As long as large tracts of open land remained, cultivators could and did evade taxes or debts they could not pay by migrating—just as they had migrated to escape what they considered to be intolerable demands by indigenous overlords in the precolonial era (*R & A Proc.*, 1904: 84; Bridges, 1881: 10; Nisbet, 1901: 1, 296–7). The existence of unclaimed, but arable land, provided opportunities for landless peasants and laborers to become small landholders; it also offered a second chance for peasants to succeed who had once held land and lost it through debts in the unfamiliar and unstable market arena. Until the late 1890s, opportunities for horizontal and, in many instances, vertical mobility deflected confrontations and potential clashes between the cultivators and the moneylenders, merchants and large landowners, Indian and Burmese. Peasant mobility and sustained economic growth also reduced tension between different ethnic groups which, like the British rulers themselves, continued to believe that there were enough places for all long after this was in fact the case.

Though losses in the post-1886 risings and systematic removals in the years of reform that followed did much to deplete the ranks of heriditary *thugyis*, there is evidence of continued resistance to colonial control at the village level. As in the years after the 1852 annexation (*RAB*, 1865-6: 10), remnants of rebel bands, which often turned to crime to survive and thus truly merited the title of dacoits applied by the British, were sheltered by or in collusion with local headmen. In the Akyab district, which had been relatively quiet in the years after 1886, a peasant named Paw Aung proclaimed himself the Minlaung, or imminent prince, and joined with his father, who had been a *thugyi* under the British, in forming a gang that attacked other headmen and military police stations. Paw Aung's band refrained from attacking local villages and was in turn supported by them in the belief that the gang was fighting to free Burma from foreign rule. Similar support given by villagers in other areas and the widespread refusal of peasants to assist the British in their efforts to hunt down dacoit bands suggests continued local resistance to the imposition of British control (*RPAB*, 1891: 10; 1894: 64; 1899: 4–5; 1900: v; 1901: iv, 10). In some instances popular support for dacoit gangs was so great that bandit leaders had the audacity to offer large rewards for the heads of the British officers charged with hunting the outlaws down (*Amherst*: 56). Despite heavy fines levied on uncooperative villages and sustained military and police campaigns, some bandit groups survived due to peasant support and protection, for over a decade after 1886. The fragmentary evidence we have suggests that many of these gangs were social bandits in Eric Hobsbawm's sense, viz. disgruntled peasants who resort to crime to strike back at the state and its allies when other avenues of protest fail and who are perceived by other agriculturists as avengers or proponents of causes they deem themselves helpless to advance.

In addition to collusion with dacoit bands, village headmen and lower level Burman officials sought to thwart British efforts to gain control at the local level through time-tested techniques of corruption and evasion that had served them so well in the precolonial era. In the years after the 1852 annexation, underreporting on census rolls and revenue inquests was rampant, and as late as 1889 investigations by British settlement officers revealed that the *thugyis* in some districts had reported as little as 25 percent of the area actually cultivated in the villages placed in their charge (Mya Sein, 1938: 111; *SPC*, 1856: para. 179; Matthews, 1890: 23). Local officials also supported the efforts of large landowners to amass great estates, often at the expense of peasant settlers and in direct opposition to the government's policy of fostering a smallholder-based market economy. One of the key signs of the power and quasi-autonomy enjoyed by local land magnates and their administrative allies was the presence of what amounted to private armies in many areas on the delta frontier. Bands of retainers, sometimes numbering in the hundreds, were used to collect the landowner's or moneylender's full due from recalcitrant tenants, to bully smallholders into abandoning their holdings so they could be claimed by large landlords, and even at times to do battle with the forces of rival landlord families (Adas, 1974: 73, 142, 172–3).

Even though the resistance of local notables to effective British control was mainly self-serving rather than patriotic, its widespread and sustained occurrence indicates that the social and economic changes brought about by colonization may not have been as pervasive and radical at the grass roots level as the British believed and as subsequent historians have argued. It also suggests that there were ample opportunities for disaffected cultivators to protest against specific grievances or even to plot the overthrow of the colonial regime.

From 1886 until the 1920s, protest in British Burma took three main forms: localized and usually short-lived rebellions; violent assaults on government officials and men of property, which the British viewed as common crimes; and communal rioting. Between the 1890s and the late 1920s, the tradition of resistance established in the post-1852 and 1886 annexation disturbances periodically burst forth in small-scale risings that, though they were easily suppressed, kept alive challenges to the legitimacy of British rule and the dream of restoring the Burman monarchy. Little is reported in the available sources about the social or economic conditions that gave rise to these disturbances, but, unlike the other major forms of protest in this period, their timing, location, and goals appear to have been little influenced by market fluctuations or the social conflicts that developed as the export economy began to unravel in the first decades of the twentieth century.[8] The risings in Pakkoku (1894), Mandalay (1897), Toungoo (1906), Shwebo and Sagaing (1910), and Henzada (1912), as well as risings in Meiktila, Pegu, and Tavoy which broke out in the early and mid-1920s, all occurred in periods of growth and prosperity in Burma as a whole and in areas that were not economically distressed at that time. In fact, the rising in Toungoo came just a year *before* the post-1907 slump that was touched off by a worldwide credit squeeze; the Myoka rebellion in Henzada broke out on the eve of the period of economic contraction and hardship brought on by shipping shortages in World War I, and perhaps the largest of these rebellions, U Bandaka's in Shwebo in 1928, occurred just before the Great Depression began to ravage the export-oriented economy of the province. A survey of the followers of U Bandaka, one of the few such enquiries extant, found that though many were laborers whose families existed barely above subsistence, many others were well-to-do landowners and local leaders (Langham-Carter, 1939: 28).

Rather than economic grievances, political and religious concerns appear to have motivated those who supported these risings. Like U Oktama, who led the 1906 Toungoo rebellion, and Maung Tun Hla (alias U Bandalaka), who instigated the Shwebo outbreak nearly two decades later, the leaders of these movements claimed to be Konbaung princes, Minlaungs, or in some cases *Sekhya Mins* or embryo Buddhas. Some leaders like Tun Hla and Nga Po Mya, who organized the 1912 rising in Henzada, were *se sayas* or practitioners of traditional Burmese medicine; others like U Oktama and Nga Hmun, the leader of the Pakokku rising in 1894, were *pongyis*. In all of the rebellions where detailed information is available, *pongyis* played key roles as advisors and organizers, reflecting an early and sustained concern for the decline of Buddhist influence under colonial rule. Whether *pongyis* or healers, rebel leaders proclaimed themselves invulnerable to the weapons of the colonizers and distributed protective talismans to their followers. Many leaders attempted to bolster their claims to royal descent by establishing court centers and assuming the trappings of Burman monarchs. U Bandalaka made the fullest use of these key symbols of Burman rulers in the decade after he established his pilgrimage center at Bishu in the Shwebo district. He issued a biography in which he claimed to be invulnerable, built a palace patterned after those found in Ava and Mandalay, erected a victory pagoda, contributed to the repair of existing shrines in the vicinity of his capitol, and claimed to be a Minlaung with great magical powers.

In virtually all respects—including its outcome—U Bandalaka's movement and rebellion closely resembled U Thuriya's nearly a half century earlier. After the failure of police attempts to arrest Bandalaka and assaults by his followers on local headmen and police posts in retribution, Bandalaka's adherents were routed by a large police expedition in February 1927. Similar patterns can be discerned in all of the risings in the decades between U Thuriya's and U Bandalaka's which appear to have transcended causes associated with the great economic and social changes brought about by colonization. As in the post-1852 and 1886 resistance, the risings that periodically erupted in the 1890s and the first decades of the twentieth century arose mainly from a desire to put an end to foreign rule and to restore the Burman monarchy and the vital roles of the Buddhist *Sangha* in the Burman polity.

Because it took the form of acts which were regarded as common crimes by the colonial authorities, the second major form of protest in the post-1886 period is also the most difficult to identify clearly and to analyze in detail. The highly biased and often abbreviated summaries of dacoit raids, petty thefts, or violent assaults recorded in the police records or special government enquiries into crime, make it extremely difficult to distinguish between acts that were genuine expressions of protest and those that were in fact common crimes. The predisposition of many contemporary scholars to turn virtually all evidence of social unrest in colonial societies into patriotic outbursts of resistance compounds this difficulty and underscores the need for even greater caution. It is probable that the great majority of criminal acts dutifully recorded by colonial officials, and perhaps an even larger number that did not come to their attention, were in fact crimes pure and simple perpetrated out of the desire for illegal, personal gain at the expense of others. In some instances, however, what the colonizers labelled criminal acts were something more than that; they were expressions of anger, retribution, or desperation by dispossessed smallholders or laborers without work.

Though some administrators and government reports insisted that Burma's excessive crime rates relative to other provinces in the Indian empire were due to the greater number of wealthy targets in Burma, to the declining morality which was linked to problems in the Buddhist *Sangha*, or to Burmese personality traits such as a love for adventure or a need to prove manly virtue (*BCR*, 1926: 7–10; *RPAB*, 1904: 12; 1918: 8, 10; 1921: 16ff.), numerous government observers admitted that criminal acts were often tied to economic distress and tensions between well-to-do landowners and moneylenders and hard-pressed tenants and landless laborers. Criminal acts that were linked to adverse social and economic conditions were in fact much better gauges of the magnitude of the disruptions and inequities associated with the market economy and property-oriented legal system established under the British than the sporadic risings led by *pongyis* and pretenders aimed at restoring an imagined golden age of the past.

Assaults by large dacoit gangs, which had been one of the main forms of postconquest resistance, remained a major problem for government officials throughout the British period. As late as the 1920s, British officials admitted that the major obstacles to the suppression of dacoit bands operating in many areas remained the support and protection they received from local headmen and villagers generally, despite heavy fines that the British levied on all communities suspected of aiding the gangs. Headmen not only enjoyed a sizable cut of the earnings of bandit gangs, whose members often resided in their villages, they sometimes organized and led the gangs themselves. The fact that village communities as a whole gained from *dacoit* raids is suggested by the lavish, community-wide *ahlus* (feasts) that were reported to be held periodically even in villages of modest means—feasts that were financed, or so the British suspected but could not prove, by bandit operations. Popular support for at least some dacoit groups may also have been reflected in the encouragement and active support they were given by Buddhist *pongyis*.[9]

The targets of dacoit raids and violent crimes in general reflect the social tensions and economic distress that were generated by the uneven impact of the market economy. Rich landlords, merchants, and moneylenders—Burmese, Chinese and especially Indian—were the most frequently cited targets due to their wealth, but the available sources suggest a protest dimension to many of the recorded assaults, namely, laborers and tenants squaring accounts with exploitative landowners and indebted smallholders seeking to forcibly break the hold of local and foreign moneylenders. The struggle of marketing middlemen and land-lords with the cultivating classes is also indicated by widespread efforts by tenants and laborers to conceal part of the rice they harvested, thus depriving the landlords of the large and growing share they claimed as their due. Concealment became so pervasive after 1900, expecially on the tenant-cultivated estates that developed in many areas in the lower Irrawaddy delta region, that landlords were forced to hire *durwans* or watchmen to oversee cultivation, to guard warehouses, and to monitor the transportation of harvested paddy to the landlord's granaries. Watchmen also proved necessary in many areas to guard large landlords' holdings against poach-ing by the landlord's laborers or against arson and vandalism by disgruntled ex-owners or tenants, or mistreated workers seeking revenge (Adas, 1974: 149–50; Thein Pe, 1973: 25, 28).

Because of considerable variations between and within different regions in mar-ket and cropping conditions, it is difficult to plot clear connections between over-all indices of provincial prosperity or economic crisis—rice prices, export totals, etc.—and the rise or fall of crime rates. Many British officials, however, argued that there was a direct connection between socioeconomic conditions and fluctua-tions in crime rates.[10] As early as 1895, a sharp increase in crime in the districts of the lower Irrawaddy Delta was attributed to general poverty resulting from a sharp fall in the price of rice. In subsequent police reports, British administrators repeat-edly cited poor harvests and high rice prices, which made it difficult for the families of landless laborers to make ends meet, or market slumps, which hit tenants and smallholders especially hard, as the root causes of increases in criminal activities. More than any other, these contrasting effects of market shifts illustrate a funda-mental contradiction in the Delta economy that grew in importance as open land ran out and competition for employment grew. In a situation where a sizable pro-portion of the cultivating classes were smallholders dependent on stable or rising rice prices for their well being, while a large and growing number of cultivators were landless laborers who had to purchase their staple foods, whichever way the market turned some group was bound to be adversely affected.

The crimes which were linked in police reports to economic shifts ranged from cattle thefts to gang raids on the homes of moneylenders and rich landlords. Government observers frequently noted that the highest crime rates were found in the most progressive districts, that is, in those where the market economy was most firmly entrenched. In these areas greater discrepancies in incomes, the large sums of money amassed by moneylenders and large landlords, and the weakness or a complete absence of paternal patron-client links between the landowning classes and landless cultivators all contributed to the tendency on the part of the poor and displaced to turn to crime in times of economic need. The weaker hold of Buddhist institutions and ethical standards on the heterogeneous and consumer-oriented populations of these districts was also frequently cited as a major source of higher crime rates.

As time passed, the connection between increasing criminality and socioeco-nomic distress was more and more explicitly admitted by police and revenue officials. After the failure of a handful of insightful government officials to win approval in the 1890s and early 1900s for legislation regulating agricultural loans and land alienation (Adas, 1977: 112ff.), the smallholder-based economy which the British had painstakingly fashioned in the late nineteenth century began to break down. Market reverses and the closing of the land frontier greatly accelerated the agrarian indebtedness, land alienation, and spread of landlordism that had been confined to limited areas through most of the late nineteenth century. As officials like H. L. Eales, the Commissioner of Pegu, had warned as early as 1911, these trends were bound to stir up social unrest and eventually political challenges to the British overlords (*R & A Proc.*, 1911: 403). Though widespread political disturbances were still over a decade in the future, the immediate impact of the decline of the smallholder-based economy can be seen in the sharply rising incidence of crime in the first decades of the twentieth century. In districts in both Upper and Lower Burma, administrators reported that in addition to poor harvests and market fluctuations, unemployment and the loss of opportunities for social and economic mobility for the laboring classes were responsible for increases in crime rates (*RPAB*, 1918: 11).

The most detailed discussion of the relationship between worsening economic conditions and increased crime is provided by Thomas Couper, who carried out a special enquiry into the living standards and working patterns of tenants and agricultural laborers in Burma in 1924. Couper argued that there was a direct connection between the soaring increase in crime and the steady empoverishment of the laboring classes. He dated the marked rise in dacoity, theft, and other crimes against property in Burma from the 1905–1910 period, when a credit crisis forced widespread mortgage foreclosures, thus depriving many cultivators of land that they had transformed from wilderness into productive paddy fields after years of arduous labor. Reduced to the status of landless laborers at a time when the available cultivable land had all but run out, large numbers of cultivators found steady employment difficult to obtain and only at low wages when it was available. Couper argued that the great impact of the landless laborers' conditions on crime rates was clearly illustrated by the higher incidence of crime in the slack seasons after the planting and harvest when large numbers of laborers were unemployed and hard-pressed to feed themselves and their families (Couper, 1924: 10, 51).

Until the late 1920s, the other major form of agrarian protest in colonial Burma, communal violence, was often difficult to separate from actions which were classified as criminal. With the exception of Hindu-Muslim communal riots in the 1890s and the early 1900s, which arose from conflicts rooted in India proper rather than from conditions in Burma, there were few clashes between Burmans and immigrant groups until after the credit crisis of 1907–1908 (*RPAB*, 1907: 10; 1908: 16–17). The first anti-Indian assaults, as yet small and localized affairs, occurred in these years. In the next decade, Indian landlords, moneylenders (especially the ubiquitous Chettiers) and even poor and defenseless laborers became frequent targets of attacks by Burman dacoits (*RPAB*, 1913: 18; 1914: 21; 1915: 15; 1918: 17, 19). On several occasions, full-scale skirmishes between gangs of Burman and

Indian laborers occurred. By the early 1920s, the pressure of an ever-growing population, fed by virtually unrestricted immigration from East and South India, resulted in widespread communal tension and hostility (*RPAB*, 1919: 16–21; 1920: 15–6, 19; 1921: 16, 25). The Burman fears that, under the aegis of colonial rule, Indian and Chinese immigrants were steadily taking over their homeland— fears that appeared to be substantiated by the growth of an Indian landlord class and the vital roles played by Indian merchants, millers, moneylenders, and laborers in the export economy—would result in the early 1930s in an orgy of anti-Indian riots and assaults.

In addition to attacks on Indians, and occasionally on Chinese merchants and moneylenders in this period, there were also signs of growing tension between Burmans and other ethnic groups, especially the Karens. Karen villages were attacked, wealthy Karen homes looted, and Karen and Chin officials were murdered. Though clashes between indigenous ethnic groups would never attain the magnitude nor the intensity of Burman-Indian conflict in the 1930s, Burman assaults on members of indigenous minority groups were further signs of intensifying social tensions, as group rivalries mounted in an economy whose growth could no longer keep pace with rapid population increase.

The basic forms of Burmese protest and resistance to British rule that had emerged in the days of conquest—local risings led by *pongyis*, prophets, or pretenders, and banditry—persisted into the 1930s, and in some areas into the period of independence. Changing social and economic conditions led to the rise of·a new form of protest beginning in the early 1900s—communal rioting and Burman assaults on members of immigrant and ethnic minority groups. In the mid- and late 1920s, additional forms of protest were adopted by disgruntled cultivators and urban laborers as economic dislocations gave way to a full-scale collapse of the smallholder-based economy and Western-educated nationalist leaders sought to build a mass base for their challenges to British rule. In this period, growing numbers of *pongyis* also became involved in political agitation. Those who supported these movements of protest continued to rally to calls for the restoration of the Burman monarchy, the removal of the illegitimate and alien colonial overlords, and the defense of Buddhism and Burman culture. The breakdown of the smallholder-based export economy, however, and the class and communal tensions that it produced, gave added impetus to social and economic grievances that were felt by some groups in the late nineteenth century, but had not begun to play a major role as sources of protest until after 1900.

For well after a decade after they began to form political associations to lobby for the advancement of their interests in British official circles, Western-educated Burmese leaders had few contacts with, and in fact showed little concern for the condition of, the agrarian classes. Though many future nationalist leaders grew up in households whose prosperity and social prominence owed a good deal to sizable landholdings and successful participation in various sectors of the rice-export economy, the Western-educated Burmese were overwhelmingly urban-oriented and to a large degree isolated from the great majority of the colonized population. Caught up in endless factional struggles, quarrels with the British overlords, and hard-fought campaigns to increase opportunities for more and better education and jobs for themselves, until well into the 1920s most Western-educated Burmese gave little serious thought to organizing rural cultivators or the urban poor.

By the early 1920s, worsening economic conditions and the spread of agrarian and urban unrest, combined with a growing desire to recruit mass support for their struggles with the British overlords, led many Western-educated politicians and political factions to seek ways to involve the cultivating classes in the nationalist struggle. Though the definitive account of these efforts has yet to be completed,[11] the available evidence suggests that despite some organizational and ideological innovations, the nationalist-inspired peasant movements of the 1920s and 1930s strongly resembled earlier protest and resistance efforts in leadership, goals, and often the forms of protest adopted.

One of the strongest links to earlier protest movements was provided by Buddhist *pongyis* who played vital roles in nationalist-inspired village associations or *athins* and in arousing dissidence in rural areas. In 1921, those *pongyis* who were committed to political agitation established the General Council of the *Sangha Samettgyi* (GCSS) within the umbrella nationalist organization, the General Council of Burmese Associations (GCBA). The GCSS was to become the major vehicle of *pongyi* involvement in political action and one of the key links between the tiny minority of urban-based, Western-educated nationalist leaders and the cultivating classes (Maung, 1980: 23–6). Many of the so-called political *pongyis*, who, as Mendelson has argued, were often not *pongyis* at all (1975: 173ff.), were from rural origins and thus attuned to the grievances and outlook of the cultivating classes. The overriding concern of the *pongyi* organizers, however, was the decline of discipline within the Buddhist *Sangha* (which ironically had in part made their political activities possible under a religious cover), and especially the threat to Buddhist monastic education which the spread of Western education and the growth of a market-oriented, consumer-minded society clearly posed (Mendelson, 1975: chs. 3, 4; Brohm, 1957: 303–20; Smith, 1965: chs. 2, 3).

Pongyi orators, like U Ottama and U Wisara, who toured the rural areas of Lower Burma in 1924 and 1926 respectively, told the large crowds that turned out to cheer them, that foreign domination was the root cause of the decline of Buddhism in Burma and a vital threat to the survival of Burman culture. Reflecting their ties to Western-educated politicians in both Burma and India, *pongyi* agitators called for tax boycotts and civil disobedience campaigns to undermine the authority of the colonial regime. In some cases, their rousing speeches, whose seditious content guaranteed eventual arrest and imprisonment, touched off local riots, antitax campaigns, or the widespread posting of "no admittance" signs on village gates. More frequently, however, they inspired widespread tatooing with cabalistic designs, the manufacture of charms intended to confer invulnerability, and most ominously the collection of *dahs*, long knives, and arms for anticipated risings against the British overlords (Maung, 1980: 14–16, 51–4; Morris, 1930: 2–7; *Rangoon*, 18 Feb., 1929: 13).

Whether initiated by *pongyis* and the GCSS or by Western-educated nationalists from radical factions of the GCBA, like the So Thein group, the basic units of rural nationalist organization were village associations called *wunthanu athins*. Through these locally recruited and loosely coordinated associations, nationalist leaders of rival factions sought to arouse support for their stands in various political controversies that arose in the 1920s. With some exceptions, peasant interests were only peripherally involved in most of these constitutional and factional struggles. The most important of these exceptions was the antitax campaigns that spread to many areas in rural Burma in the mid- and late 1920s.

Because it was levied equally on all households regardless of income and collected at the worst possible time of the year for the cultivating classes, the capitation tax proved an ideal issue around which to rally widespread rural protest against colonial rule. Not only had landless laborers and deeply indebted tenants to pay the same amount as rich landlords and merchants, but also the tax was collected beginning in August before the harvest, which was precisely the time when the cultivator was the most pressed for food money and other essentials. In order to pay the tax, cultivators were often forced to borrow money at high rates of interest from Burmese and Indian moneylenders and were thus driven ever deeper into debt (Couper, 1924: 53; Saw, 1931: 7). The appeal of the capitation tax as a focus of protest was also enhanced by the fact that its payment had long been viewed by the Burmans as tantamount to an admission of the legitimacy of the overlord who demanded it. After the British conquest of Lower Burma, for example, Burman officials in many areas refused to collect the tax on the grounds that to do so would amount to a repudiation of the Konbaung monarch who still ruled in Upper Burma and to an acceptance of British rule which they vainly hoped would be temporary (*PFP*, 1853: no. 60).

The fact that the tax in the late nineteenth century was collected by village headmen gave it an additional potency as a cause for arousing rural protest. From the late 1880s, when the *thugyis* had been fully integrated into the colonial administrative machinery, they had become in most instances ever more alienated from the village populations whose interests they had once served. Saddled with onerous and unpopular tasks, such as tax collection, and granted little real power, *thugyis* became by the first decade of the twentieth century one of the major targets of rural unrest. In the 1880s and 1890s, headmen who cooperated with the government, often in marked contrast to the sullen refusal of assistance by the villagers in their charge, were condemned to death by dacoit leaders, and on some occasions executed for their collaboration with the colonizers. As economic conditions worsened after 1900, *thugyis* increasingly became the objects of dacoit attacks and growing numbers of headmen were murdered while attempting to collect taxes or quell local disturbances. As much as the capitation tax itself, the collaboration of Burman headmen was at issue in the anticapitation tax campaigns that periodically disturbed the uneasy colonial peace during the 1920s.[12]

In 1923–24, *pongyi* orators like U Ottama and Western-educated politicians like U Chit Hlaing toured the rural delta districts exhorting Burmese cultivators to refuse British capitation tax demands. In many areas of Lower Burma from Prome to Tavoy, villagers, usually led by *wunthanu athin* agitators, refused to pay the tax when the *thugyis* came to collect. In some regions, villagers responded to government measures to compel payment, with passive resistance campaigns patterned after those which had been so successfully employed by Gandhi and Indian nationalist agitators in the preceding years. In other areas, *athin* leaders used threats and violent measures, such as arson and livestock maiming, to insure widespread support for the antitax campaign. The government responded to this direct challenge to its authority by arrests of key leaders and confiscation of village and household grain supplies. In some cases villages supporting the campaign were occupied by punitive policemen. In all cases, the antitax campaign was defeated, but local outbreaks of this form of resistance flared up in 1927 and 1928, and again in 1929, on the eve of the Great Depression rebellions (*Rangoon*, 2 Feb. 1929: 11; Morris, 1930: 7; Saw, 1931: 7–8).

Saya San, who was the central figure in the series of peasant rebellions that raged in the Burmese countryside from 1930 to 1932, as a rebel leader combined both the long standing tradition of protest that had dominated Burman resistance through most of the colonial period and the new causes for unrest and nationalist innovations in protest organization that had emerged in the 1920s.[13] As a *se saya* or Burmese medical practitioner, sometime *pongyi*, and peddler of lottery tickets, Saya San had gained familiarity with conditions in many parts of Burma and a knowledge of the esoteric magical skills and modes of cult organization that were to provide much of his appeal to large numbers of cultivators. In raising the standard of rebellion, he promised to restore the Burman monarchy (in the person of himself), to defend Buddhism, to purify the *Sangha*, and to drive the "infidel" British from the land. His stress on the need to restore the monarchy was given added power by the belief held by many of his followers that Saya San was a *Mettaya* or embryo Buddha, a belief that Saya San himself appears to have shared. He prophesied that the victory of his *galon* (serpent) armies over the British would usher in a utopian age of social harmony and religious bliss. All of these key themes had persisted through the decades of colonial rule and their powerful hold over the peasantry was amply demonstrated by the number and size of the rebellions that were initiated by Saya San or led by his disciples.

Saya San was, however, more than a prophet-pretender in the traditional Burman mode. He was a leader with extensive links to the radical So Thein wing of the GCBA and widespread contacts with *wunthanu athin* leaders throughout the Irrawaddy delta region. In the years before the outbreak of the depression risings, he frequently spoke to *athin* gatherings, carried out a special enquiry for the So Thein GCBA into alleged police brutality involved in the suppression of the antitax campaigns, and made fiery speeches demanding full independence for

Burma. In recruiting support for the rebellion that he plotted for nearly two years, Saya San made frequent references to peasant distress arising out of the indebtedness, land alienation, and rack renting that had led in the 1920s to the final disintegration of the smallholder economy of colonial Burma and had culminated in the Great Depression. Displaced landholders, disgruntled tenants, and unemployed laborers—many of whom had previously joined *wunthanu athin* associations—responded to his call to drive the British and their Indian allies from Burma and to restore indigenous rule.

Although the causes which gave rise to the 1930–32 disturbances were a mix of appeals for monarchical and religious restoration, and grievances arising from the breakdown of the export economy, the forms which agrarian protest took in the turbulent decade of the 1930s were the same as those which had been dominant since the first decades of resistance to British conquest. Localized rebellions led by *pongyis* or princely pretenders like Saya San received the most attention in government enquiries and the contemporary press. More widespread, however, and more difficult for the British to suppress was the resistance offered by dacoit bands that were often formed after attempts at open rebellion had failed. During the 1930–32 disturbances, assaults on Indian moneylenders, landowners, and laborers were also widespread and indiscriminant with regard to victims within the Indian community, as had been the communal riots in Rangoon in May of 1930. Though bloody communal riots would again erupt in the towns, especially in Lower Burma in 1938, Indian-Burman conflict in the rural areas peaked during the 1930–32 rebellions. These clashes were paralleled by Burman assaults on minority ethnic groups like the Karens and Chins.

Perhaps no incident in this period of unrest better epitomized the persistence of traditional protest forms than the petition that was presented to the acting Governor of Burma, Joseph Maung Gyi, on the eve of the first Saya San rising. The complaints set forth in the petition focused on the problems of debts to foreign moneylenders, especially the Chettiars, and the spread of land alienation. The petitioners demanded government relief through the establishment of a land mortgage bank and official measures to check land alienation (Saw, 1931: 1–2). Though Maung Gyi curtly rejected the petition, those who offered it were acting in accordance with well-established Burman traditions. The peasants' right to petition the throne or high officials for tax reductions or to draw attention to the excesses of state officials was well established in precolonial Burma and there is evidence that in some instances such petitions brought relief to the groups involved (Scott and Hardiman, 1900: 432; Mya Sein, 1938: 67). The petition presented to Maung Gyi in December of 1930 may have been in part a device to rally wavering peasants to the rebels' cause, but its use demonstrates the strong hold ancient forms of peasant action and the peasants' sense of political legitimacy still had over the cultivating classes. It also illustrates the way in which peasants attempted to deal with grievances arising from new forms of social and economic organization with longstanding modes of protest expression.

Not only the forms taken by peasant protest in the depression era, but the causes espoused by those who supported it, indicate that the major approaches developed thus far for the study of anticolonial protest on the part of peasant groups may not be appropriate for Burma. At the very least, the great emphasis in the literature on colonial societies on the role of Western-educated nationalist leaders in arousing the colonized to rise against their alien overlords is misplaced, with the possible exception of the late 1930s when the *Thakin* movement gained widespread support in rural Burma. After over a hundred years of British rule in some areas and from fifty to eighty years in others, peasant rebels fought to restore Buddhism and the Burman monarchy, rather than to win independence and gain government by parliaments and Western-educated lawyers and journalists. They rallied to monks and princely pretenders, rather than to nationalist agitators. They also strove to put an end to the stifling control that railways, telegraphs, and European bureaucratic organization had given the colonizers over their once quasi-autonomous village communities.[14] Though rebel organizers made use of nationalist-inspired village associations, many of these had come under the influence of *pongyis*, and during the 1930–32 rebellions the *athins* functioned more like sectarian or *gaing* organizations than branches of nationalist parties. The peasants' adherence to millenarian prophecies and their pervasive reliance on magical talismans (with disasterous results) further distanced them from the urban-based nationalists who would have had little place in the new society which rebel leaders like Saya San envisioned.

The deep attachment felt by those who rose in rebellion for religious leaders, whether *pongyis* or royal pretenders, the heterogeneous composition of rebel bands in terms of the social strata from which they were recruited, and the targets of rebel assaults—all these indicate that a class-based, much less a Marxist, analysis of rural protest in colonial Burma would distort rather than advance our understanding of the meaning of rural unrest. Though tensions between landlord groups, and tenants and laborers had been on the rise since the first years of the twentieth century, government officials, policemen, and migrant Indians (*both* moneylender-landlords and poverty-stricken laborers), were the major targets of rural protest in the 1920s and 1930s. Insofar as group clashes were involved, communal not class divisions were decisive. Except for the urban laborers, who also vented their hostility primarily through communal rioting, there was little sense of class identity among the landless laborers or tenants whose ranks swelled as the smallholder economy declined in the early twentieth century. Members of these social groups worked in small bands, identified primarily with kin and household, and dealt with landlords and estate managers or moneylenders as individuals rather than as representatives of hostile classes. As in precolonial Burma, cultivators tended to be vertically, not horizontally, oriented, and in search of meaningful hierarchies of dependence rather than peasant-dominated utopias based on equality and communal sharing. Thus, though many of Eric Wolf's arguments concerning the impact of capitalism and colonialism on non-

V

Western peasant societies work well for Burma, neither "middle peasants" nor any other single agrarian social group dominated the ranks of those who rose in protest (1969a: 278–302).

Despite the fact that Burma provides a prime example of the sort of export economy identified by Jeffrey Paige, those who supported movements of protest were a mix of tenants, landless laborers, and smallholders, rather than a homogenous force representing one social strata as is suggested by Paige's theoretical formulations (Paige, 1975: ch. 1). These groups rose in protest neither against the rigid oppression of a landlord class locked into the agrarian sector nor against more diversified entrepreneurial groups with investments in the rural sector, but primarily against alien and illegitimate colonial overlords and their immigrant and indigenous allies. The protest options of the cultivating classes were not limited to strikes or full-scale rebellion, but displayed a wide range of longstanding modes of response from arson and flight to banditry and sect formation.

When they rose in rebellion, laborers joined tenants and indebted smallholders, and they all turned to *pongyis* or dacoit chiefs for leadership. Though the expulsion of the British, the end of taxation, or the cancellation of all debts re-occur as the goals of peasant risings, I have found no rebel references to the destruction of the landlord class, the redistribution of land, or even to the elimination of the market economy that one might expect if class considerations were in fact central to peasant protest in rural Burma.

Insofar as it was generated by economic grievances, protest in rural Burma in the colonial period arose primarily from frustrations resulting from market disfunctions and slumps, rather than from peasant concerns for subsistence or survival that have been stressed in James Scott's recent study on *The Moral Economy of the Peasant* (1976). Because the vast majority of cultivators of all kinds in Burma grew rice, the staple food, the threat of starvation was rarely an issue, except for the small percentage of landless laborers who could not find employment. For landowner peasants, market slumps and not colonial taxes (which were on the whole quite low in relation to the productivity of the cultivated lands) were the major source of discontent. Smallholders and tenants were not faced with starvation. On the contrary, they had too much rice to eat because they could not sell it at a decent price or at all. The vast majority of peasants in Lower Burma, where most rural protest and the Saya San rebellions were centered, were market, not subsistence, oriented. Market slumps and a shortage of open land, and not government taxation, were the key causes of the indebtedness, land alienation, and the declining wages and profits that undermined the cultivators' ability to purchase the consumer amenities and maintain the high standard of living (relative to other peasant societies) to which they had become accustomed in the late nineteenth century. For landless laborers, declining wages and unemployment and not land revenue payments were the major threat to survival.

The anger of the cultivating classes came to be focused on the colonial state not because the British overlords had violated the moral or ethical precepts which

Scott argues regulated state-peasant relations in the precolonial era, but because without the compensation of consumer rewards and economic well being, the peasants came to view the British as illegitimate and infidel rulers whose presence was a vital threat to Burman culture and traditions. The fact that protesting groups focused their economic complaints on capitation taxes, rather than on land taxes which were much higher, indicates that legitimacy rather than economic survival was the major issue employed by those who sought to recruit peasant supporters for rebellion. The importance of political and closely-related religious concerns for rural dissidents was also reflected in the repeated references by those who took part in rural protest to the restoration of the Burman monarchy and to the restoration of Buddhism as the state religion. To the extent that the dissidents' grievances were economically based, debts to Indian moneylenders and competition from Indian laborers were far more important sources of rural unrest than the allegedly rigid land revenue policies of the colonial government—which in fact were quite flexible and remarkably sensitive to local variations—or the colonial regime's hardhearted refusal to grant remissions in times of crisis—which in fact it did, in addition to providing rural relief works.[15]

The persistence of precolonial modes of protest in colonial Burma, the limited impact of nationalist leaders and ideas on agrarian movements, and the problems involved in applying recent general theories on the origins of agrarian rebellion to the Burmese experience—all indicate a need for a reappraisal of some of our basic assumptions about the character of anticolonial resistance on the part of peasant groups. Admittedly, it can be argued that this caution may need only be applied to Burma which in the degree of its precolonial isolation, the intensity of its xenophobia, the far reaching impact of its colonial change, and the extent of its postcolonial retreat back into isolation, is atypical. Recent work on local conditions and rural movements in India, Africa, and other areas in Southeast Asia, [16] however, indicate that many of the patterns discussed in this essay can be found beyond Burma. These studies also represent a much-needed shift in our approaches to and vision of the impact of colonial rule on the cultivating classes of Africa and Asia and the roles of different strata of the peasantry in the process of decolonization.

1. J. S. Furnivall was one of the few writers to challenge these assumptions.

2. Following contemporary usage, Burman in this essay refers to the majority ethnic group of present-day Burma who speak Burmese and whose original home was in the Dry Zone of Upper Burma. Burmese refers to all of the ethnic groups (Burman, Mon, Karen, Kachin, etc.) which have come to make up the population of independent Burma. Because inter-ethnic clashes were often involved in protest movements in colonial Burma, the distinction is important in the context of this paper.

3. The best accounts of the post-1852 resistance can be found in the District gazetteers for Lower Burma, especially *Maubin*, 1931: 12; *Thayetmyo*, 1911: 12–13; *Toungoo*, 1914: 12; *Bassein*, 1916: 16–18; *Tharrawaddy*, 1920: 25–34; *Henzada*, 1915: 22–4; and *Syriam*, 1914: 17. See also Dunn, 1920: 16.

4. The prince had been saved from the purge of male members of the royal house after Thibaw's accession to the throne by the intercession of the Thathanabaing or head of the Buddhist Sangha in precolonial Burma.

5. The process of local reorganization and the replacement of hereditary *thugyis* had actually begun shortly before the 1886 disturbances. See Browne (1873: 63ff).

6. In precolonial Burma peasants and artisans were organized into military-style groupings that were divided between those who provided taxes (*athins*) and those who proffered labor services (*ahmudan*).

7. For excellent illustrations of these patterns see the articles by Max Harcourt, Gyanendra Pandey and Brian Stoddart in Low, 1977.

8. This discussion of the predepression rebellions is based upon relevant sections of the Bassein, Henzada, Akyab, Pakokky and Toungoo gazetteers; Collis, 1953; Heine-Geldern, 1942; Langham-Carter, 1939; Sarkisyanz, 1965; Cary, 1930; White, 1913; and *Report(s) on the Police Administration of Burma*, 1894: 60, 68; 1901: 10; 1909: iv; 1912: 14; 1914: 20–21.

9. References to bandit activities abound in British police and judicial reports. The patterns discussed here are based primarily upon evidence drawn from the following: *Report(s) on the Police Administration of Burma*, 1899: iv; 1901: iv, 10; 1902: 18; 1903: 9; 1906: 17; 1910: 3, 15; 1913: 22, 23; 1915: 7; 1917: 111 1918: 19, 25.

10. Unless otherwise noted, this discussion of the links between crime rates and socioeconomic conditions is based upon: *Report(s) on the Police Administration of Burma* 1895: 64; 1897: 25; 1899: iv; 1903: 7–8; 1904: ii; 1916: iii–viii, 2–3; 1917: iii, vii; 1919: 9–11; 1920: iv, 9–11; 1921: iii, 11, 13, 16.

11. The one person who has had access to the Burmese archival sources in Rangoon that are essential to a full understanding of this critical period, Patricia Herbert, is presently at work on her Ph.D. dissertation.

12. Because headmen were allowed to keep firearms for self-protection, their houses were often key targets of groups seeking to arouse popular risings. For sample references to attacks on headmen throughout this period see: Moscotti, 1951: 38–41. For earlier attacks on headmen see *Report(s) on the Police Administration of Burma*, 1908: 16; 1909: 17, 18; 1910: 16, 17, 18; 1915: 20; 1917: 10; 1918: 11; 1921: 18; 1922: 15–19.

13. Because I have discussed the 1930 risings in detail in other works, my major purpose here is to identify themes linked to the long-term patterns of protest under consideration and explore the ways in which the depression risings can help us in evaluating the usefulness of some of the main theories that have been set forth to explain the origins of anticolonial protest.

14. The concern to weaken or destroy bureaucratic control is amply attested by the choice in most rebellions, including the Saya San, of telegraph and railway lines and the houses of village headmen as prime targets for assault. Though these measures were aimed at stunting the repressive capacity of the regime, the destruction of railway lines and telegraph stations and the atrocities often associated with attacks on headmen went far beyond the extent of damage or injury needed to deprive the colonizers of these critical means of social and political control.

15. For Scott's position on these issues see 1976: 92ff. For counter evidence and a different view see Adas, 1979: 201–2.

16. See, for example, the essays on peasant protest in Low, 1977; and the studies by Baker, 1976; Washbrook, 1976; Ranger, 1968, 1969; Ileto, 1979; and Kartodirdjo, 1973 cited in the text.

References

Abbreviations for Archival Sources and Periodicals

BCR — Government of Burma, *Report on the Prevention of Crime and the Treatment of Criminals in the Province of Burma*, 1926.

PFP — Government of India, Political and Foreign Proceedings, Range 200, vol. 47, 30 December 1853, no. 60, India Office Records, London, England (1OR).

RAB — *Report(s) on the Administration of the Province of Burma*, Rangoon, 1888-1930.

RAP — *Report(s) on the Administration of the Province of Pegu*, Rangoon, 1853-1961.

RPAB — *Report(s) on the Police Administration of Burma*, Rangoon, 1888-1930.

R & A Proc. — Government of Burma, Revenue and Agriculture Proceedings, vol. 8633, Nov. 1911 (1OR).

SPC — Government of India, Secret and Political Correspondence, vol. 30, no. 83, 22 August 1856, paragraph 179.

Publications Cited

Adas, Michael (1972). "Imperialist Rhetoric and Modern Historiography: The Case of lower Burma before and after Conquest," *Journal of Southeast Asian Studies* 3: 175-92.

_____ (1974). *The Burma Delta: Economic Development and Social Change on an Asian Rice Frontier, 1852-1941.* Madison: University of Wisconsin Press.

_____ (1979). *Prophets of Rebellion: Millenarian Protest Movements Against the European Colonial Order.* Chapel Hill: University of North Carolina Press.

Akyab District Gazetteer (1917). Rangoon: Government of Burma.

Amherst District Gazetteer (1913). Rangoon: Government of Burma.

Baker, Christopher (1976). *The Politics of South India, 1920-1937.* Cambridge: Cambridge University Press.

Bassein District Gazetteer (1916). Rangoon: Government of Burma.

Bridges, J. E. (1881). *Report on Settlement Operations in the Bassein District, 1880-81.* Rangoon: Government of Burma.

Brohm, John (1957). "Burmese Religion and the Burmese Religious Revival." Unpublished Ph.D. dissertation. Ann Arbor: University Microfilms.

Browne, Horace A. (1873). *Statistical and Historical Account of the District of Thayetmyo, Pegu Division of British Burma.* Rangoon: Government of Burma.

Cary, B. S. (1930). "Hints for the Guidance of Civil Officers in the Event of the Outbreak of Disturbances in Burma," Government of India, *Political and Judicial Correspondence*, File 7347, India Office Records, London.

Cheng, Siok-Hwa (1968). *The Rice Industry of Burma, 1852-1940.* Kuala Lumpur-Singapore: Oxford University Press.

Collis, Maurice (1953). *Into Hidden Burma.* London: Faber & Faber.

Couper, Thomas (1924). *Report of Inquiry into the Condition of Agricultural Tenants and Labourers.* Rangoon: Government of Burma.

Crosthwaite, Charles (1912). *The Pacification of Burma.* London: Macmillan.

Dunn, Charles S. (1920). *Studies in the History of Tharrawaddy.* Cambridge: Cambridge University Press.

Furnivall, J. S. (1939). The Fashioning of Leviathan: the Beginnings of British Rule in Burma," *Journal of the Burma Research Society* 29: 1-37.

_____ (1956). *Colonial Policy and Practice.* New York: New York University Press.

_____ (1957). *An Introduction to the Political Economy of Burma.* Third edition. Rangoon: Peoples' Literature Committee and House.

Geary, Grattan (1886). *Burma after the Conquest.* London: Sampson, Low & Co.

Hall, D. G. E. (1964 [1955]). *A History of South-East Asia.* London: Macmillan.

Heine-Geldern, Robert (1942). "Conceptions of State and Kingship in Southeast Asia," *Far Eastern Quarterly* 2: 15-30.

Henzada District Gazetteer (1915). Rangoon: Government of Burma.

Hobsbawm, Eric J. (1959). *Primitive Rebels.* New York: Norton.

_____ (1969). *Bandits.* New York: Delacorte Press.

Htin Aung, Maung (1965). *The Stricken Peacock: Anglo-Burmese Relations 1752-1948.* The Hague: Nijhoff.

_____ (1967). *A History of Burma.* New York: Columbia University Press.

Ileto, Reyaldo (1979). *Pasyon and Revolution.* Quezon City: Ateneo de Manila University Press.

Ireland, A. (1907). *The Province of Burma.* Cambridge: Harvard University Press.

Kartodirdjo, Sartono (1973). *Protest Movements in Rural Java.* Singapore: Oxford University Press.

Koenig, William (1978). "The Early Kon-baung Polity, 1752-1819: A Study in Politics, Administration and Social Organization in Burma." Unpublished Ph.D. dissertation. Ann Arbor: University microfilms.

Langham-Carter, R. R. (1939). "A Rebellion in Upper Burma," *The Burman Police Journal* 2: 15-29.

Lieberman, Victor (1976). "The Burmese Dynastic Pattern, Circa 1590-1760: An Administrative and Political Study of the Taung-Ngu Dynasty and the Reign of Alaunghpaya." Unpublished Ph.D. dissertation. Ann Arbor: University Microfilms.

Low, D. A. (1977). *The Congress and the Raj.* London: Heineman.

Majumdar, R. C. (1963). "Burma and Assam," in R. C. Majumdar et al. eds. *British Paramountcy and the Indian Renaissance*, partr 1. Bombay: Bharatiya Vidya Bhavan.

Marshall, H. I. (1922). *The Karen People of Burma.* Columbus: Ohio State University Press.

Matthews, H. M. S. (1890). *Report on Settlement Operations in the Bassein and Thongwa Districts, 1888-89.* Rangoon: Government of Burma.

Maubin District Gazetteer (1931). Rangoon: Government of Burma.

Maung, U Maung (1980). *From Sangha to Laity: Nationalist Movements of Burma, 1920-1940.* New Delhi: Hind Kitab.

Mendelson, E. M. (1975). *State and Sangha in Burma: A Study of Monastic Sectarianism and Leadership.* Ithaca: Cornell University Press.

Mooney, J. (1896). *The Ghost Dance Religion. Fourteenth Annual Report of the Bureau of American Ethnology,* vol. 2. Washington: Government Printing Office.

Moscotti, Albert (1951). "British Policy in Burma, 1917-1937." Unpublished Ph.D. dissertation. Ann Arbor: University Microfilms.

Mya Khan (1969). "Village Administration in Upper Burma," *Journal of the Burma Research Society* 52: 58-77.

Mya Sein, Daw (1938). *Sir Charles Crosthwaite and the Consolidation of Burma.* Rangoon: Zabu Meitswe Pitaka Press.

Nisbet, John (1901). *Burma under British Rule and Before.* London: Archibald Constable.

Pakokku District Gazetteer (1913). Rangoon: Government of Burma.

Plant, Colonel (1886). *Narrative of the Insurrection in the Tenasserim Division during 1885-86.* Rangoon: Baptist Mission Press.

Ranger, T. O. (1968). "Connections between 'Primary Resistance' Movements and Modern Mass nationalism in East and Central Africa," *Journal of African History* 9: 437-53, 631-41.

_____ (1969). "African Reactions to the Imposition of Colonial Rule in East and Central Africa," in L. H. Gann and Peter Duignan, eds., *Colonialism in Africa, 1870-1960.* Cambridge: Cambridge University Press.

Rangoon Gazette (Weekly Budget) (1828-30). Rangoon.

Sarkisyanz, Emanuel (1965). *Buddhist Backgrounds of the Burmese Revolution.* The Hague: Nijhoff.

Saw, U (1931). *The Burmese Situation, 1930-1931.* Rangoon.

Scott, James C. (1976). *The Moral Economy of the Peasant: Rebellion and Subsistence in Southeast Asia.* New Haven: Yale University Press.

Scott, James G. and John P. Hardiman (1900). *Gazetteer of Upper Burma and the Shan States.* Rangoon: Government of Burma.

Shwebo District Gazetteer (1929). Rangoon: Government of Burma.

Smith, Donald E. (1965). *Religion and Politics in Burma.* Princeton: Princeton University Press.

Syriam District Gazetteer (1914). Rangoon: Government of Burma.

Tadaw, Saw Hanson (1959). "The Karens of Burma," *Journal of the Burma Research*

Society 42: 31-40.

Tha Aung, Maung and Maung Mya Din (1941). "The pacification of Upper Burma: A Vernacula History," *Journal of the Burma Research Society* 31: 80-136.

Tharrawaddy District Gazetteer (1920). Rangoon: Government of Burma.

Thayetmyo District Gazetteer (1911). Rangoon: Government of Burma.

Thein Pe, Maung (1973). "Her Husband or Her Money," in P. M. Milne, trans., *Selected Short Stories of Thein Pe Myint*. Ithaca: Cornell University Press.

Toungoo District Gazetteer (1914). Rangoon: Government of Burma.

Velsen, J. van (1964). *The Politics of Kinship; A Study in Social Manipulation among the Lakeside Tonga of Malawi.* Manchester: University of Manchester Press.

Washbrook, D. A. (1976). *The Emergence of Provincial Politics in the Madras Presidency, 1870-1920.* Cambridge: Cambridge University Press.

White, Herbert T. *Herbert Thirkell White Collection,* India Office Records, London. European Mss.E. 254.

_____ (1913). *A Civil Servant in Burma.* London: Edward Arnold.

Wolf, Eric (1969). *Peasant Wars of the Twentieth Century.* New York: Harper & Row.

Woodman, Dorothy (1962). *The Making of Burma.* London: Crescent Press.

Woodside, Alexander B. (1976). *Community and Revolution in Modern Vietnam.* Boston: Houghton Mifflin.

Worsley, P. (1957). *The Trumpet Shall Sound.* London: MacGibbon and Kee.

Yamethin District Gazetteer (1922). Rangoon: Government of Burma.

Yi Yi (1961). "Life at the Burmese Court under the Konbaung Kings," *Journal of the Burma Research Society* 44: 85-129.

VI

Concepts of the Moral Economy and the Study of Commercialization in South Asia

The application of the concept of the "Moral Economy" to the analysis of commercialization in South Asia is problematic for a number of reasons. Except in its original formulation by E. P. Thompson (1963), discussion of the concept has focused primarily on peasant producers and their interaction with pre-colonial and colonial state systems. In the two major approaches to the moral economy, developed by Eric Wolf (1969) and James C. Scott (1976), which are based heavily upon Asian — but not Indian — case studies, the impact of the market and increased commercialization on peasant communities is dealt with in only the broadest of terms. The effects of these forces are assumed to be great, but detailed, empirical investigation of market influences and peasant responses to these forces is lacking. Even though it concerns a non-Asian society — England in the eighteenth century — Thompson's is the only approach to the moral economy in which marketing systems and the consumer, rather than the peasant villager and producer, are the focus. For South Asianists interested in the impact of commercialization in various time periods, the usefulness of Thompson's approach is also enhanced by the fact that he studies shifts within an *existing* market system that occur in the eighteenth century, rather than assuming, as do Scott's and Wolf's versions of the moral economy, that these sorts of ethical ideas are characteristic of subsistence-oriented, agrarian societies with a high degree of local autonomy and only peripheral commercialization. As I shall argue, the latter formulations are sharply at variance with the actual conditions in South Asia in the centuries

VI

2   CONCEPTS OF MORAL ECONOMY

before British dominance and the spread of capitalism.

Based heavily on a vision of the impact of the global extension of capitalism devised by Karl Polanyi (1957), Eric Wolf's rather vague notion of the moral economy rests on a series of assumptions that render it a conceptual tool of dubious utility for most areas in South Asia. Wolf's vision of a pre-colonial village world that is communally and subsistence oriented, largely autonomous and regulated by social customs and sanctions that assure all members a "minimal livelihood" (1969: 280), except in situations of extreme crisis, bears little relation to the reality of stratified, factionalized, notable dominated and often commercially involved villages that were typical of the most populous regions of pre-colonial India (Habib, 1963: esp. 81ff), and, as Popkin has argued, 1979), much of the rest of Asia. Thus, the dichotomy that is central to Wolf's thesis between a "moral" pre-capitalist order where the market is peripheral and peasants are shielded by a "protective covering of cultural institutions" (1963: 182, quoting Polayni), and a colonial-capitalist age when peasants (and the land they work) are reduced to mere commodities and their welfare becomes dependent on the inexorable and amoral workings of the market economy, distorts rather than informs when applied to the Indian context. Though Wolf is sensitive to social stratification and intra-community divisions in the pre-capitalist period, they are subordinated to sanctions and ethical norms that make for an implicit quasi-utopian order of communal cooperation and shared poverty. Ethical considerations — in the form of entrenched customs and village sanctions—were undoubtedly at work in South Asian peasant communities within the *jajman-kamin,* patron-client networks of dependency that formed the core of the local caste order. Contrary to Wolf's vision, however, a high price was paid for security by dependents, particularly landless laborers and tenants drawn from low-caste or untouchable groups, in terms of postures of deference, grinding poverty, and, if the recent work by Paul Greenough on Bengal (1980, 1982, 1983) is correct, extreme vulnerability in times of natural disorder and dearth.

Equally critically, peasant communities in many parts of South Asia, or at least the land controlling notable families within them, were a good deal more involved in production for the market than the Wolf schema allows, not only in the sale of foodstuffs and crops like cotton, indigo and tobacco, but also as moneylenders and organizers of handicraft production. Through *jajman* patrons, large numbers of *kamin* dependents would also have participated in market production. Thus, commercial opportunities and possibilities for the enrichment of individual families, if not the reduction of land and labor to mere commodities, existed in many regions long before colonialism and capitalism became dominant forces in South Asia.

One aspect of Wolf's handling of the links between capitalist commercialization and the origins of peasant protest that deserves special attention is his concept of the "middle peasant." Wolf argues that peasant rebellion in the age of global commercialization has tended to originate among communally-oriented peasant groups which consist of small to middling landholders, engaged primarily or exclusively in subsistence production, and who are deeply committed to the "moral" political economy of the pre-colonial, pre-capitalist era (1969, 1983). Though Wolf's middle peasant thesis has met with a mixed response from those who have tested it in specific areas (Paige, 1975; Skocpol, 1983: 158-67), it does not appear to work well for India. Much of the evidence, for example, that the fine regional studies undertaken in the last decade or so has produced, indicates that agrarian disturbances in the troubled early decades of the twentieth century were centered among peasant groups — both landholders and small-scale tenants — who were deeply involved in market production. Peasant agitation arose primarily from the convergence of the spread of urban-based nationalist aspirations, increased taxes, and market reverses that angered cash crop producing peasants who were deprived of the modest consumer amenities and higher standard of living they had come to enjoy. (For sample cases see Hardimann, 1977; Charlesworth, 1979; Pouchepadass, 1974).

James Scott's version of the moral economy is a good deal more specific and focused than Eric Wolf's, and it is based on case studies from societies that are in many ways more similar to those found in South Asia than those selected by Wolf. Scott's approach to the moral economy, however, is much less market-centric, and more vague about the impact of commercialization in both the pre-colonial and colonial eras. Because I have critiqued Scott's handling of state-peasant relations in both periods at some length in earlier studies (1979; 1980), I shall focus my comments here on his treatment of the commercial dimensions of the moral economy with reference to South Asia. Like Wolf, Scott greatly understates the extent of commercialization and overstates the subsistence orientation of the peasantry in the pre-colonial period. He also sees only the negative aspects of the spread of cash cropping and growth of market networks under the aegis of colonial rule. Scott's concept of the moral economy, which is developed in much

VI

greater detail than Wolf's, is rooted in the notion that a Lockeian sort of "social contract" prevailed in precolonial societies. In Scott's view, peasants who were preoccupied with subsistence concerns asserted their *right* to a minimum share of their production that was equivalent to that necessary for survival — a right to which elite groups, Scott implicitly argues, acquiesced. Beyond the churlishly Hobbesian objections to this view in light of what we know about the dynamics of precolonial political economies (Adas, 1980; 1981), a number of problems arise in attempting to apply Scott's thesis to the process of commercialization in South or Southeast Asia which are often related to the rather reductionist nature of Scott's approach to the moral economy.

Scott's focus on peasant groups who, he argues, subordinate all other concerns to an omnipresent obsession with subsistence is at variance with much of the evidence we have relating to cultivators in South Asia. Aside from the equally fundamental ritual and status concerns of even the poorest untouchable groups (see, for example, Moffat, 1979), it may be inappropriate, as Greenough has recently suggested (1983), to view subsistence as the thing most *valued* by even the poorest cultivator. Greenough asserts that, rather than subsistence, what is most valued by Bengali peasants is prosperity *(lakšmi)* or abundance. Good patrons are those who indulge their clients rather than merely guaranteeing their minimum survival. In contrast to Scott's view that peasants — including landed, patron groups — traditionally pooled their resources and reduced their demands on dependent classes in times of shortage, Greenough argues that in Bengal at least, the weak (children, landless laborers, etc.) were left to starve, while everything possible was done to ensure the survival of patrons and household heads who were seen as essential for reconstruction efforts after the crisis had passed.

Related to the problems arising from the subsistence emphasis of Scott's version of the moral economy are questions regarding the degree to which peasants are "risk averse," hostile to innovation or taking the sorts of chances that are usually associated with entree into the market sector. Landless laborers and impoverished tenants, whom Scott makes the focus of his study, are understandably risk averse due to the fact that their margin of error is slight and potential for meaningful gains from market participation virtually non-existent. However, peasants from diverse areas and social strata from all areas of South Asia have eagerly shifted from subsistence to market crop production in situations where real profits could be made and material and status rewards would result. The growth in the proportion of the peasantry who are market-oriented farmers in areas as disparate as the Punjab, Gujarat and the Deccan indicates a widespread willingness on the part of cultivating groups to risk market uncertainties and adopt new production techniques and technologies. In fact, as David Feeny has pointed out (1983: 783), involvement in market production can be seen as just one aspect of broader peasant survival strategies — "another tool in their self-insurance plans."

Scott's (often implicit) view of the effects of the spread of commercialization in the colonial period as almost wholly negative for peasants below the level of large landholders is at odds with much we have learned about South Asian peasants in recent years. Michelle McAlpin's investigations indicate, for example, that large numbers of peasants derived real benefits from the increase in market demand and the establishment of new market links. Improved transportation and communication systems, which were closely linked to the spread of commercialization, greatly enhanced the peasants' chances of survival in times of drought or flood in a given region by virtue of the possibility of transfer of crops from other areas. In this way the subsistence guarantees that are so critical for Scott were actually reinforced by changes related to the spread of the market economy. Though colonial officials were at times slow to realize the extent of natural dislocations and inefficient in their attempts at relief, they acted to make food from other areas available, establish soup kitchens and promote work projects. Improved transportation also made it possible for cultivators in stricken areas to migrate in search of work or famine relief projects. In addition, improved transportation lessened dependence on locally grown foodstuffs, thereby permitting peasants to specialize increasingly in market production. It reduced the need for local granaries, whose decline Scott views as a key indicator of the demise of moral economic arrangements. Better communications and transportation also meant more stable prices, though both short- and long-term slumps remained very real problems for peasant market producers. In some ways then, commercialization meant fewer risks for peasant groups, and very real gains in productivity and income for a not inconsiderable percentage of the cultivating classes in many areas. Because he tends to overstate the degree of control achieved by the colonial state (see, for example, Dewey, 1979) in South Asia and other areas, Scott also fails to recognize the extent to which — whatever their intentions — the British colonizers themselves were unable to control market fluctuations and buffer the effects of market downturns.

Although E. P. Thompson's formulation of the concept of the moral economy (in many ways the original and most convincing) was intended to explain the causes of social unrest in a specific, non-Asiatic society — eighteenth-century England — it raises perhaps the most useful questions with reference to ethics, commerce and peasant responses in the South Asian context. To begin with, Thompson's approach to the moral economy is focused on consumers and the workings and social impact of the market, rather than peasant producers who are the chief concerns of Scott and Wolf. Thompson is able to demonstrate a commitment to moral economic norms on the part of *both* elite groups and artisan/farmer consumers in contrast to Wolf and Scott whose formulations *imply* elite acquiescence which is never really documented. Thompson's approach to the moral economy focuses on the state not as a tax collector or guarantor of subsistence through remissions in times of dearth, but as the over-arching regulator of the market system. His vision of a society with extensive commercialization *before* the era of full capitalist development is well-suited to the South Asian environment where, as I have argued, market networks and cash crop production had been established long before the penetration of global capitalism. Thompson's thesis that English rulers in pre-capitalist times were expected to intervene in the market arena, not only to control the prices of staple foods, but also to regulate avaricious merchants and moneylenders and prevent adulteration of foods and other middleman abuses, could be profitably tested in a variety of South Asian historical contexts. Hindu, Buddhist or Islamic texts on statecraft and social mores provide key sources that can be explored to test these patterns, but injunctions and idealized stereotypes must be compared to the reality of pre-colonial political economies.

For the period of transition from pre-capitalist, pre-colonial commerce to market production for the global capitalist system under the aegis of British rule, Thompson's essay provides a wide range of potentially fruitful questions. To what extent and in what ways do the practices and behavior of merchants, moneylenders and other middlemen change from one epoch to the next? Were, for example, the peasant risings in western India, analyzed by Ravinder Kumar (1968), in part a response to what were perceived to be *new* moneylender tactics and treatment of indebted cultivators or simply the result of the intensification of age-old patterns of exploitation? To what extent were the *banias* of Sind, recently examined by David Cheeseman (1982), following time-tested patterns of credit extension and land accumulation or evolving new techniques fostered by the property-oriented, capitalist colonial milieu? Do peasant groups in fact hold the colonial state responsible for price slumps or sharp increases in the price of staple foods? If so, are these expectations shaped by pre-colonial norms? Do peasants expect the state to regulate credit transactions and the activities of middleman groups? Are middlemen less trusted and more likely to be the targets of peasant outbursts in the colonial era than they were in the pre-colonial period? Are they more immune to community sanctions and peasant reprisals, and more buttressed by extra-village courts and the constabulary established by the British? Do Indian peasants, like Thompson's eighteenth-century artisans, expect food to be consumed in the regions in which it is grown, particularly in time of shortage, or have railroads and regional specialization by radically altering production patterns in the nineteenth century rendered these concerns irrelevant?

These questions indicate that the moral economy perspective — in its broadest sense — may be a useful way of examining aspects of commercialization and the links between commerce and peasant protest in both pre-colonial and colonial South Asia. Norms of behavior, ethical values and ideas about justice and fair play, however amorphous, are clearly at work in both epochs and the moral economy debate has forced us to takes these issues as seriously as the analysis of social structures and increases in indebtedness, tenancy rates and landlordism. As James Polachek has shown, however, in his fine analysis of the workings of the political economy of the Kiangsi Province in China, rather than an overarching concept of a moral economy that functions much the same way regardless of socio-cultural context, we will be further ahead if we focus on specific, culturally-determined values, economic exchanges and social institutions that make up diverse kinds of moral economies in different historical and social settings. Patron-client ties; caste, clan and community sanctions and support systems; and religious injunctions intended to regulate the behavior of rulers who aspire to righteousness are interconnected, yet discrete, pieces of complex ethical systems that are situation specific and highly variable from one culture or even region to the next.

CONCEPTS OF MORAL ECONOMY

Bibliography

Adas, Michael. 1979. *Prophets of Rebellion: Millenarian Protest against the European Colonial Order.* Chapel Hill, U. of North Carolina Press.

1980. "'Moral Economy' or 'Contest State': The Origins of Peasant Protest in Southeast Asia," *Journal of Social History* 13/4, 521-46.

1981. "From Avoidance to Confrontation: Peasant Protest in Precolonial and Colonial Southeast Asia," *Comparative Studies in Society and History* 23/2, 217-47.

Charlesworth, Neil. 1979. "Rich Peasants and Poor Peasants in Late Nineteenth Century Maharashtra," in Clive Dewey and A. G. Hopkins, *Imperial Impact.*

Cheeseman, David. 1982. "The Omnipresent Bania: Merchants and Moneylenders in Colonial Sind," *Modern Asian Studies* 16/3, 445-62.

Dewey, Clive. 1979. "*Patwari* and *Chaukidar*: Subordinate Officials and the Reliability of India's Agricultural Statistics." In Clive Dewey and A. G. Hopkins, eds. *The Imperial Impact in Africa and South Asia.* London, Institute of Commonwealth Studies.

Feeny, David. 1983. "The Moral or the Rational Peasant? Competing Hypotheses of Collective Action," *Journal of Asian Studies* 42/4, 769-87.

Greenough, Paul R. 1980. "Indian Famines and Peasant Victims: The Case of Bengal in 1943-44," *Modern Asian Studies* 14/2, 205-35.

1982. *Prosperity and Misery in Modern Bengal: The Famine of 1943-44.* London, Oxford U. Press.

1983. "Indulgence and Abundance as Asian Peasant Values: A Bengali Case in Point," *Journal of Asian Studies* 42/4, 831-50.

Habib, Irfan. 1963. *The Agrarian System of Mughal India.* Bombay, Asia Publishing House.

Hardiman, David. 1977. "The Crisis of the Lesser patidars: peasant agitations in Kheda District, Gujarat, 1971-34," in D. A. Low, ed., *Congress and the Raj,* London, Heinemann.

Kumar, Ravinder. 1968. *Western India in the Nineteenth Century.* London, Routledge & Kegan Paul.

McAlpin, Michelle B. 1974. "Railroads, Prices and Peasant Rationality: India 1860-1900," *Journal of Economic History* 34/3, 667-84.

1979. "Death, Famine and Risk: the Changing Impact of Crop Failures in Western India, 1870-1920," *Journal of Economic History* 39/1, 143-57.

1980. "The Impact of Trade on Agricultural Development:

Bombay Presidency, 1855-1920," *Explorations in Economic History* 17/1, 26-47.

Moffat, Michael. 1979. *An Untouchable Community in South India.* Princeton, Princeton U. Press.

Paige, Jeffrey. 1975. *Agrarian Revolution: Social Movements and Export Agriculture in the Underdeveloped World.* New York, The Free Press.

Polachek, James A. 1983. "The Moral Economy of the Kiangsi Soviet (1828-1934)," *Journal of Asian Studies* 42/4, 805-29.

Polanyi, Karl. 1957. *The Great Transformation: The Political and Economic Origins of Our Time.* Boston, Beacon Press.

Popkin, Samuel. 1979. *The Rational Peasant: the Political Economy of Rural Society in Vietnam.* Berkeley, U. of California.

Pouchepadass, Jacques. 1974. "Local leaders and the Intelligensia in the Champaran Satyagraha (1917): A Study in Peasant Mobilization," *Contributions to Indian Sociology 8/1, 67-87.*

Scott, James C. *The Moral Economy of the Peasant: Rebellion and Subsistence in Southeast Asia.* New Haven, Yale U. Press.

Skocpol, Theda. 1982. "What Makes Peasants Revolutionary?" in S. Guggenheim and R. Weller, eds., *Power and Protest in the Countryside.* Durham, N.C., Duke U. Press.

Thompson, E. P. 1963. "The Moral Economy of the English Crowd in the Eighteenth Century," *Past and Present* 50/1, 76-136.

Wolf, Eric. 1969. *Peasant Wars of the Twentieth Century.* New York, Harper & Row.

VII

South Asian Resistance in Comparative Perspective

Given the time period when the study of protest and resistance in Third World societies first became a serious and sustained enterprise for social scientists with varying area studies orientations, it was inevitable that peasants and revolutions would dominate much of their research and scholarship. Depending upon perspective and political persuasion, the trauma or triumph of the Chinese revolution focused attention on hitherto largely neglected agrarian groups and their potential for violent, confrontational protest. Victorious and failed 'peoples' wars' in Latin America and South East Asia, and above all the protracted struggle of the peasant-based liberation movements in Vietnam, further intensified scholarly absorption with peasant issues. They also fixed in the academic mind, and in the popular imagination, a reified and romanticized image of the peasantry, downtrodden and exploited but conscious of its predicament and ready to strike back directly and violently at its oppressors whenever opportunities arose. Though there were important exceptions, the study of the conditions of the rural underclasses in a variety of Third World settings with an eye to identifying the causes that led to movements of overt protest, neglected elite groups and broader socio-economic contests or reduced them to caricatures that obscured key forms of material and symbolic interaction between elite groups and cultivators as well as between different social strata within the 'peasantry' itself.

In this intellectual climate, there appeared to be little place for the findings of South Asian specialists who had devoted their careers to unravelling the complexities of one of the world's largest and most diverse concentrations of peasants. The decidedly non-revolutionary path that the peoples of South Asia had taken to independence and the mistaken but remarkably durable view of Gandhi, who accounted for much of what those who were not area specialists knew about India, as a leader of 'passive'—hence non-confrontational—resistance, rendered India of little interest to those in search of peasants in revolution. Non-Indianists dismissed the South Asian peasantry as atypical; the more thoughtful among social scientists specializing in area studies regarded it as a troubling exception to the defiant and confrontational peasant norm. Stereotypes of the South Asian village and its caste-ridden inhabitants, which generations of paternalistic British administrators and the writings of Karl Marx had done so much to establish as stagnant, inert, passive and apolitical,[1] appeared to confirm the impression that evidence drawn from South Asian examples would do little to advance our understanding of the 'real' peasant.

It is not surprising then that the South Asian peasantry was passed over by scholars in search of case examples for works on patterns of peasant protest and revolution. India is not mentioned in Eric Wolf's 1969 study of the major 'peasant wars' of the twentieth century, which remains one of the best examples of the comparative protest genre.[2] The main antagonists in the 'moral economy' debate had little to say about South Asia,[3] though some of those who have tested their arguments have made use of South Asian examples and illustrations.[4] Despite a listing of references to government reports from post-independence India, Jeffery Paige's broadly-based paradigm with case studies on 'social movements and agrarian agriculture in the underdeveloped world' makes almost no use of Indian evidence.[5] Paige's neglect of India is all the more telling because he is concerned with uncovering patterns in a wide variety of agrarian protest actions, not just revolutions, and he is one of the few scholars in this period to have given serious attention to the theoretical implications of the composition and responses of elite groups and systems of elite dominance in different settings.

Comparativists and generalists, working on peasant protest in the 1960s and 1970s, who did bother to mention the peasants of South Asia usually characterized them in ways that simply reinforced the image of the passive, docile and intensely conservative cultivators, an image that had much to do with their neglect by non-Indianist area specialists. In the 'prelude' to his study of *The Rebels*[6] in the post–Second World War era, for example, Brian Crozier implicitly justifies his neglect of India with the remark: 'Millions in India are passive in conditions that would indeed be intolerable if suddenly imposed on people used to greater comfort and a higher intake of calories.' Claude Welch, Jr., whose use of the Telengana rebellions in the late 1940s marked a major departure from the comparativist scholars' neglect or dismissal of examples of Indian protest, did much to amplify the suggestions made by Crozier regarding the atypicality of the Indian rural classes in a world that appeared to be coming apart due to disruptions caused by recurring peasant risings. After noting that Indian peasants 'have not been *totally* passive' (italics mine) and citing the 'Mutiny', the Moplah rising and the Santhal disturbances to prove it,[7] Welch goes on to argue that the Telengana conflict was notable because it ran counter to the prevailing Indian trend of acquiescence in the face of poverty and exploitation. Predictably, Welch sees caste and karma as the keys to the Indian peasants' passivity:

... for most of its history, rural Telengana appears to have slumbered, its residents accepting what outsiders often perceived as injustices as the product of fate. Better, it seemed, to conform to present inequalities in the hope the next incarnation of one's soul would be less toilsome. The belief in karma justified conformity to one's situation, despite its vicissitudes, as part of the cosmic order.[8]

Apparently unaware that his underlying assumptions about the hegemonic functions of Hindu ideology were at variance with the work of many specialists who had done research on low-caste groups,[9] Welch goes on to argue that 'caste customs and regulations ... maintained a compartmentalized and essentially homeostatic society and crippled any attempts at joint action.'[10]

Given the widespread acceptance of these explanations for the supposedly atypical absence of resistance on the part of Indian peasants, it is little wonder that in his pioneering comparative study of the impact of differing agrarian systems in the *Social Origins of Dictatorship and Democracy*, Barrington Moore, Jr. returns again and again to issues relating to the 'apparent' or 'supposed' political docility of the Indian peasantry. As his hedging modifiers suggest, Moore questions the reliability of this stereotype and argues that 'There *is* revolutionary potential among the Indian peasants.' Moore also builds a much more sophisticated argument for the hegemonic functions of the caste system than the rather cursory dismissal of his work by South Asian specialists would lead one to expect, an argument that incorporates, with much caution, the karma/ acceptance of misery connection that so many authors take for granted. But as Moore points out, his inclusion of India among his cases of social upheaval was prompted by the exceptional nature of the course of development in the subcontinent. India provides him with a negative case, where the peasantry displays little of the rebelliousness that movements and regimes in other areas must harness or quell. Moore sees the Indian peasantry, past and present, as stasis-prone, inefficient, self-repressive and ultimately co-opted by Gandhi's non-violent and non-revolutionary approach to decolonization. He remarks on the low level of violent resistance on the part of the Indian peasantry, despite their 'appalling misery', and concludes that 'evidence of [the peasantry's] submissiveness' and 'willing acceptance of personal degradation' is 'overwhelming'. Moore finds the record of peasant risings in India 'unimpressive' when compared to China.[11] If a budding student of peasant protest were not already predisposed to do so, Moore's view of the South Asian peasantry as self-repressed, myopic, fatalistic and easily co-opted would most likely prod him or her to move on to other areas where peasant behaviour exhibited the resistance and rebellion that were widely (usually implicitly) accepted as the norm.

Admittedly, the near exclusion of South Asianists from the growth industry of peasant protest studies in the 1960s and 1970s was to some extent self-inflicted. In their writings and innumerable conference and seminar papers, South Asian specialists stressed the complexity and uniqueness of the type of society and culture system that had developed in the sub-continent. Most argued, ironically mirroring the assumptions of comparativists like Moore and Welch, that caste was the key variable behind a pattern of social organization and ritual performance that had no counterpart elsewhere. Both implicitly and explicitly, the comparability of Indian case examples to those drawn from areas beyond the South Asian cultural zone was questioned or its very possibility denied. At the same time, comparativists like Barrington Moore, Jr., who dared to venture into the Indianists' terrain, were almost invariably dismissed for their failure to appreciate the subtleties and inner workings of the caste-based Indian social order. With few exceptions, perhaps most notably Burton Stein who made extensive and imaginative use of the work of African anthropologists on segmentary societies in his own work on patterns of state and society building in South India,[12] South Asianists took little note of the analytical approaches developed by scholars working in other areas. References to Van Gennep, Turner or Lévi-Strauss, much less Braudel, Foucault or Geertz, are rare in their publications. Though these authors were presumably read by South Asianists, most assumed that the non-caste case evidence of scholars working in other culture areas was not comparable and their theoretical insights not applicable given the unique characteristics of South Asian social systems.

Beginning with the presupposition of South Asia's exceptionalism, a number of approaches developed either to account for the low level of social protest in the subcontinent or to explore the implications of its highly developed systems of social control for modes of human social organization more generally. One of the boldest of the latter was explored in the work of Louis Dumont and his disciples.[13] Though Dumont saw Indian caste organization as the most extreme and ritually-burdened of systems of human social division, he used it to advance comparative analysis by arguing that the rationalization and acceptance of hierarchy, which it had carried to the extreme, was in fact the norm in human social history. By contrast, the idealization of equality and the premium placed on mobility in Western societies in recent centuries was a new and aberrant development. Dumont's discussion of the structure and workings of the caste hierarchy not only offered an explanation of the high degree of social control he believed to be characteristic of

South Asian peoples, it implicitly accounted for the low level of protest among long subjugated and exploited groups like the untouchables and tribal peoples who were being incorporated into the caste order.

Another way of accounting for the apparently low level of social conflict in South Asia was pioneered by a succession of studies exploring the dynamics of caste factions and their ongoing contests for control over resources and local influence.[14] Though practitioners of this approach did not themselves relate their findings to the issues of the level and modes of peasant protest in South Asia, their emphasis on vertical rather than horizontal cleavages and social struggle between patron–client (jajman–kamin) systems, rather than class strata, suggested that social divisions were no less pronounced in rural India than in other peasant societies; they simply took different forms. The emphasis on factional contest over class conflict was in turn incorporated into the writings of some of the most prominent members of the 'Cambridge school' of South Asian historians.[15] Opportunism and rivalries between caste factions dominated by local notables are seen as the keys both to the consolidation of British power in the subcontinent and to the emergence of nationalist political alternatives. The Gandhian non-violence stressed by Moore and others recedes in importance as an explanation for the alleged passivity of the Indian peasantry. Though again explicit links to the literature of social protest are rarely made, the dynamics of the local power structure takes precedence and the frustrations and aspirations of the cultivating classes are channelled into inter-factional contests for social pre-eminence and political advantage.

A very different approach to the history of social protest in South Asia was pioneered by historians like S. B. Chaudhuri, who rejected the view that Indian peasants rarely rose up in rebellion. In two works, which surveyed incidents of confrontational or violent resistance to colonial rule in the nineteenth century,[16] Chaudhuri sought (again implicitly) to establish a place for Indianists in the rebellious peasant mainstream of area studies. After a hiatus of over two decades, Chaudhuri's efforts to demonstrate the high degree of class consciousness and active protest on the part of the South Asian peasantry were taken up in the vastly more sophisticated and more thoroughly researched studies of the group of social scientists identified with the *Subaltern Studies* series. Contributions to the volumes published thus far focus on case studies, as well as on theoretical overviews, involving incidents of confrontational, usually violent, protest in South Asia.[17] Much of the work of the subalternists raises important questions about the predominant view of the passive South Asian peasant.[18] But in countering one myth, the subalternists are in danger of creating another, that violence and confrontation were the dominant modes of response by exploited subordinate groups in South Asia. The relative paucity of the cases of confrontational protest, much less rebellion, that have so far been uncovered, the often small numbers of participants involved and the limited duration of the incidents studied, caution against the adoption of this view. As Gyan Prakash has argued,[19] the subaltern approach also isolates moments of confrontational or violent resistance from the more fundamental, ongoing struggles of subordinate groups to limit, indeed contest, the demands of dominant groups for deference and resources. The view underlying this argument that social systems are not equilibria that are periodically broken by violent assaults, but arenas in which different social groups continually vie for control over status, power and material goods, has been advanced by a number of scholars working on patterns of protest and elite response in recent years.[20]

It would be unfortunate if the confrontational approach to social dynamics in South Asia were embraced by specialists working on the history of the subcontinent at the very point when those studying protest in other areas are beginning to challenge the highly romanticized notion of the rebellious peasant. As the essays in this volume amply demonstrate, for a variety of reasons South Asianists have much to contribute to the very different approaches to protest and resistance that have been developed in recent decades, approaches that give serious attention to systems of social control and modes of contesting power and dominance beyond dramatic and rare instances of overt challenges or violent outbursts.

The avoidance or everyday resistance approach to peasant responses to elite domination owes much to studies of slave societies and those based on enserfed labour. In the early 1970s, the revisionist studies of scholars like Eugene Genovese and Gerald Mullin provided essential correctives to the earlier work of Herbert Aptheker, who had (much like Chaudhuri had done for Indian peasants) attempted to construct a tradition of slave revolution from scattered and slender evidence of risings spread over several centuries.[21] Instead of violent resistance, which, Genovese and Mullin stressed, had occurred but was invariably met with brutal repression, a whole range of non-confrontational slave responses including false deference, cheating, pilfering, and sloth, intentional clumsiness, arson, vandalism, and flight were shown to be the predominant modes of dealing with harsh and restrictive systems of labour control. The findings of scholars working on slave societies corresponded to those of earlier and contemporary studies on serf systems in western Europe and Russia. Rather than openly challenging the lord of the manor or the owner of the estate, serfs preferred to buffer the effects of their demands and gradually erode their exercise of control by smaller, everyday tactics of denial of deference and resources. In times of crisis, serfs, like slaves, preferred flight to violent confrontations, which generally proved as futile and as costly in lives as slave rebellions.[22] Research on modes of protest that did not involve direct confrontation was also prompted by the works of E. J. Hobsbawm on millenarian movements of withdrawal and banditry as a form of rural protest.[23]

Serious attention to alternatives to violent, confrontational protest has been a rather recent development in studies focused on African and Asian societies. Thus far, two related but organizationally and historically quite different configurations of response have been the focus of research and discussion. Anthropologists and political scientists working in contemporary societies have explored the forms of 'everyday resistance'—from mockery and sarcasm to pilfering and arson—that subordinate groups employ to combat the hegemonic claims of landholding or political elites and to counter what are viewed as exploitative demands for taxes or a share of the crop. The work of James Scott in particular has identified a whole range of these protective and retributive measures that raise important questions about the effectiveness of systems of social control and the degree to which underclass groups adhere to the hegemonic ideologies that are intended to justify them.[24] For scholars dealing with past situations, for which source materials on everyday forms of resistance are at best meagre, other, less ephemeral, modes of response, which have been characterized as 'avoidance protest', have been the focus of attention. Flight to sparsely settled frontier areas or the domains of rival patrons, banditry, formal petitions, 'sit-ins' before the residences of state officials, as well as clandestine retributive acts involving crop and implement destruction or arson and 'witchcraft', have been the focus of an increasing number of works in the past decade or so.[25] These modes of defence and protest are far more dramatic and dangerous than everyday acts of defiance and retribution and much more disruptive, even dangerous, for the social systems in which they occur.

Though everyday resistance received little notice from social scientists working on South Asia in the first decades after independence, modes of avoidance protest were treated in a number of early works, most notably and extensively in Irfan Habib's path-breaking study of the Indian peasantry under Mughal rule.[26] A heightened interest in patterns of social interaction and political organization at the local and regional level, in part inspired by the work of the Cambridge school, led in the late 1970s to important discoveries of the widespread resort to collusion between village notables and rural officials in the falsification of records, underreporting, and concealment as modes of resistance to the revenue demands of the British colonizers.[27] Works on agrarian conditions in different areas and on grass-roots support for nationalist organizations also dealt with incidents of peasant flight, banditry or clandestine reprisal.[28] In each of the instances cited, the study of peasant defences and non-violent modes of resistance to elite demands and techniques of political mobilization yielded valuable insights into the systems of social stratification and subordination that gave rise to these peasant responses.

As these examples suggest, important work has been done in recent years on non-confrontational protest in South Asia. But almost all the research and thinking on avoidance responses has been case specific, little concerned with the bearing of the events in question on broader theoretical problems relating to subordination and resistance, and oblivious to work on these patterns in other geographical areas. Like work done in other areas, studies of non-confrontational protest in South Asia have been focused almost exclusively upon contests between peasant groups of different social strata or between cultivators and the agents of the precolonial and colonial state.[29]

The nature of previous work on everyday resistance and avoidance protest in both South Asia and elsewhere underscores some of the most significant contributions of the essays in the present volume. These studies of everyday and avoidance resistance expand our approaches to these phenomena in numerous ways. Most obviously, they extend the scope of our investigations in many directions beyond the peasant groups which were the main concern of these who first explored non-confrontational forms of resistance.[30] Some of the essays explore hitherto neglected forms of everyday resistance and modes of avoidance response among non-peasant social groups, including women (O'Hanlon, Oldenburg), merchants (Haynes), and urban workers (Chandavarkar). It is noteworthy, I think, that half of the contributions to the collection are devoted to resistance and protest in urban settings. The essays that deal with everyday resistance or more extensive forms of protest in more familiar rural settings add new dimensions to our approach to issues in this sphere: Dirks emphasizes the importance of ritual rivalries in factional and inter-village contests; Prakash stresses the importance of ancestral myths and legends in defining subordinate and superordinate status; and Rogers shows the ways in which a pastime like gambling can become a vehicle for resistance by townsmen and rural cultivators to hegemonic ideas and the extension of state control. The studies of Haynes and Prakash reach into the precolonial past, painstakingly reconstructing, from sparse and difficult source materials, long-standing techniques employed by subordinate groups to contest the demands of dominant elites.

In encompassing new groups, extended time periods, and the ritual and ideological dimensions of everyday resistance and avoidance protest, the collection as a whole greatly expands the research agenda for all who are working on ongoing and non-confrontational responses of subordinate groups to their subjugation and exploitation. For South Asianists, it signals a shift which is clearly apparent in recent monographs on South

Asian history and anthropology: the extensive and fruitful application of theories and analytical approaches formulated by scholars working in other geographical areas. Though caution needs to be exercised in appropriating too readily paradigms or concepts worked out in response to very different social and cultural contexts, many of the studies in the present volume suggest that the isolation of South Asianists has given way to a heightened awareness of, and receptivity to, work in other areas. Coming at a time when we are beginning to realize the importance of cross-cultural and comparative analysis, these trends may well give South Asianists a central role in the testing and formulation of ideas relating to protest in its more typical non-confrontational guise. Not only are the sources available to the South Asianist on these patterns among the richest and best preserved on any non-Western area, but the study of everyday or avoidance protest necessarily places emphasis on symbolic and physical systems of social control and rituals of dominance and deference, which are found in South Asia in a variety, complexity and abundance unmatched by any other area. The realization that rebellions and revolutions are rare occurrences calls into question the assumptions that South Asia is atypical or unique. From a perspective which views resistance and protest as ongoing, constantly reworked, predominantly non-violent, and preferably non-confrontational components of evolving social systems, South Asian examples may well tell us a great deal about what the norm is.

Of the many ideas and insights contained in the essays in *Contesting Power*, several have a special bearing on the ways in which we approach the study of everyday resistance and avoidance protest. The often limited returns accruing to groups who resort to the modes of everyday resistance or avoidance protest discussed in these studies caution against another sort of romanticization, against overstating the extent to which these responses can ameliorate the plight of the exploited and permit them to punish their oppressors. Though the Bhuinyas may receive satisfaction from their bards' retelling of the mythical tales that chronicle the origins of their subjugations, they remain nonetheless the despised and unclean drudge labourers of high-caste groups. The 'matinée shows' of courtesans of Lucknow may mock and invert 'accepted' gender roles and sexual practices, but the women who find some escape in these entertainments continue to be commoditized and used by their clients. Tarabai Shinde, who dared publish a tract protesting the degradation of Hindu widows, lived the rest of her life in isolation, the butt of children's taunts and the censorious remarks of the self-appointed defenders of 'polite' society. As these examples indicate, the efficacy of everyday resistance and avoidance protest ought not to be overestimated. Though they may win temporary respite from oppressive demands or give those who resort to them a sense of being able to strike back at their exploiters, however feebly, in the long term they serve to perpetuate the systems of domination in which they are employed. They make the insufferable endurable, and channel into subterfuge and symbolic reprisal indignation and hostility that might otherwise be directed toward modes of protest which have the potential to force fundamental transformations in the relationships between subordinate and superordinate groups.

Taken together, the essays demonstrate that ongoing contests for power, material resources and deference occur at all social levels and sectors. They are as fundamental to gender relationships as to the interaction between different caste and class groups. As Gyan Prakash stresses (pp. 145–74), counter-myths and modes of resistance are integral parts of hegemonic ideologies and systems of social control. They arise and evolve with systems of domination, which are not imposed wholecloth from above, but constructed piecemeal through interaction over long periods of time—interaction involving demands and testing, claims and concessions on the part of both subordinate and superordinate groups. This ongoing process of negotiating the terms and recasting the rhetoric of domination and subordination is best illustrated by Douglas Haynes's survey of the responses of the merchants of Surat over several centuries to a succession of political overlords, regional officials and nationalist challengers to the British colonizers.[31] Haynes's studies, as well as the essay by Nicholas Dirks, also suggest that techniques of everyday resistance and avoidance defence are not the exclusive preserve of oppressed groups on the lowest rung of the social ladder. They can be employed by local notables and well-to-do townspeople to protest the excessive demands of the state or regional administrative officials, or to gain the upper hand in the factional struggles and inter-village and peer group rivalries that are dominant forces in local political life.

As virtually all the contributions to the volume remind us, subordinate groups play an active role in the construction and continuing reformulation of the systems of social control, rituals of deference, and hegemonic ideologies that do so much to define the conditions under which they live. Modes of resistance and (usually covert) defiance and counter-ideologies are inherent parts of that process of construction and refor- mulation. In this sense, the widely-employed approach to Gramsci's admittedly amorphous notion of hegemony distorts the realities of dominance and subordination. Social control is always contested; deference is always hedged; there are always myths and proverbs, legends and moral convictions, that chal- lenge the validity of ideologies of dominance.

From this perspective, violent protest can be seen not as an abrupt or episodic outburst of social conflict, but the result of the breakdown of the ongoing negotiations; the failure of the defensive and everyday retributive mechanisms developed by subordinate groups to contain the demands or respond to the excesses of the dominant. Revolutions occur in the relatively rare situations when these breakdowns are so severe and wide- spread that they undermine the very systems in which they occur. Metaphorically, they shatter the arenas in which the defences and modes of response have been devised to buffer the persistent contests between different social groups. Rebellion then is on the far end of a continuum of responses to oppression and exploitation that extends from everyday reactions like grumbling, work slowdowns, and cursing the overseer behind his back to more organized and disruptive measures such as flight and banditry. All are embedded in ongoing and mutable systems of domination and subordination that shape gestures of deference and modes of defiance, estimates of fair play, and myths explaining the origins of injustice.

NOTES

1. Marx's classic, and often quoted, formulation can be found in Marx and Engels, *On Colonialism* (Moscow: n.d.), pp. 36–7.
2. Nor is it mentioned, except in passing, in works like John Walton's, *Reluctant Rebels* (New York: 1984) or Gerard Chaliand's, *Revolution in the Third World* (New York: 1977).
3. Excluding Burma, one of James Scott's main cases, which historically lies outside the South Asian cultural zone. See Scott, *The Moral Economy of the Peasant* (New Haven: 1976) and Samuel Popkin, *The Rational Peasant: The Political Economy of Rural Society in Vietnam* (Berkeley: 1979).
4. See, for example, Paul R. Greenough, 'Indulgence and Abundance as Asian Peasant Values: A Bengali Case in Point', *Journal of Asian Studies*, 42/4 (1983), pp. 831–50; Arjun Appadurai, 'How Moral is South Asia's Economy—A Review Article', *JAS*, 43/3 (1984), pp. 481–98, and the studies reviewed therein, and Michael Adas, 'The Moral Economy and Peasant Responses to Commercialization in South Asia', *Proceedings of the Pennsylvania South Asia Seminar* (Philadelphia: 1987).
5. *Agrarian Revolution* (London: 1975).
6. Boston: 1960, p. 9.
7. *Anatomy of a Rebellion* (Albany, New York: 1980), p. 11.
8. Ibid., pp. 52–3.
9. See, for example, Kathleen Gough, 'Brahmin Kinship in a Tamil Village', *American Anthropologist*, 58/4 (1956), pp. 826–53; Gerald Berreman, 'The Brahminical View of Caste', *Contributions to Indian Sociology*, n.s., 5/1 (1971), pp. 16–23; and especially Joan Mencher, 'The Caste System Upside Down, or the Not-So-Mysterious East', *Current Anthropology*, 15/4 (1974), pp. 469–93. For case evidence that indicates that some of the ideas assumed by Welch to have been enlisted in the service of social control did permeate to the lowest castes, see Michael Moffat, *An Untouchable Community in South Asia* (Princeton: 1979).
10. Welch, *Anatomy*, p. 56.
11. *Social Origins of Dictatorship and Democracy: Lord and Peasant in the Making of the Modern World* (Boston: 1966), esp. pp. 334–40, 369, 379, 382–5.
12. See, for example, 'The Segmentary State in South Indian History', in Richard G. Fox (ed.), *Realm and Region in Traditional India* (Durham, North Carolina: 1977); and his seminal work, *Peasant State and Society in Medieval South India* (Delhi: 1980).
13. See especially Dumont, *Homo Hierarchicus: The Caste System and Its Implications* (London: 1970).
14. Two of the classics of this genre are Oscar Lewis, *Village Life in Northern India* (New York: 1965) and André Beteille, *Caste, Class, and Power: Changing Patterns of Stratification in a Tanjore Village* (Berkeley: 1971).
15. This process is particularly apparent in the earlier of the detailed regional studies by the proponents of this approach. See, for example, David Washbrook, *The Emergence of Provincial Politics: The Madras*

304

Presidency, 1870–1920 (Cambridge: 1976); and Christopher J. Baker, *The Politics of South India, 1920–1937* (Cambridge: 1976).

16. *Civil Disturbances during the British Rule in India* (Calcutta: 1955); and *Civil Rebellion in the Indian Mutinies, 1857–9* (Calcutta: 1957).

17. The series editor Ranajit Guha has, of course, in his own contributions and larger work on *Elementary Aspects of Peasant Insurgency in Colonial India* (Delhi: 1983), done much to set the agenda for the school as a whole.

18. However, the fact that many of Guha's case examples and his contributions to the series are drawn from incidents of conflict occurring in hill and forest or non-tribal areas, where the institutions and rituals of the caste hierarchy were weak or marginal, might be interpreted by the advocates of the passive South Asian peasant school as confirming some of their central arguments.

19. 'Empowered Resistance and Contested Power in South Asia: The State of Its Historiography', unpublished essay, pp. 3–6.

20. For a highly theoretical statement of this approach, see Charles Tilly, *From Mobilization to Revolution* (Reading, Mass: 1978). See also his application to specific French examples in 'Routine Conflicts and Peasant Rebellions in Seventeenth-Century France', in Robert P. Weller and Scott Guggenheim (eds), *Power and Protest in the Countryside* (Durham, N.C.: 1982) and *The Contentious French* (Glencoe, Illinois: 1988). For Asian examples, see Adas and Scott, discussed below.

21. Aptheker's perspective was argued in *American Negro Slave Revolts* (New York: 1943). For Genovese, see *Roll, Jordan, Roll* (New York: 1972), esp. book four; and Mullin, *Flight and Rebellion: Slave Resistance in Eighteenth-Century Virginia* (Oxford: 1972). For a superb recent work that represents a continuation of this corrective approach to the rebellious slave myth, see Michael Craton, *Testing the Chains: Resistance to Slavery in the British West Indies* (Ithaca, New York: 1982).

22. See, for example, Jerome Blum, *Lord and Peasant in Russia* (Princeton: 1961), esp. chapter fourteen; and Rodney Hilton, *Bond Men Made Free* (New York: 1973).

23. *Social Bandits and Primitive Rebels* (London: 1959) and *Bandits* (New York: 1969).

24. See especially *Weapons of the Weak* (New Haven, Conn.: 1985). For further examples drawn from contemporary Southeast Asia, see the contributions by Turton, White, Fegan and Kerkvliet in Scott and Kerkvliet (eds), *Everyday Forms of Peasant Resistance in South-east Asia* (London: 1986). For African examples of many of these patterns, see Allen Isaacman, Stephen Michael, et al., 'Cotton is the Mother of Poverty', *International Journal of African Studies*, 13/4 (1980).

25. For Asian examples see Michael Adas, 'From Avoidance to Confrontation: Peasant Protest in Precolonial and Colonial Southeast Asia', *Comparative Studies in Society and History*, 23/2 (1981); and 'From Foot-dragging to Flight: The Evasive History of Peasant Avoidance Protest in South and South-east Asia', in Scott and Kerkvliet, *Everyday Forms of Peasant Resistance*, pp. 64–86. For case studies from Africa, see Allen

Isaacman, *The Tradition of Resistance in Mozambique* (Berkeley: 1976) and Donald Crummey (ed.), *Banditry, Rebellion and Social Protest in Africa* (London: 1986).

26. *The Agrarian System of Mughal India* (Bombay: 1963). These patterns are also treated in Ravinder Kumar, 'The Rise of the Rich Peasants in Western India', in D. A. Low (ed.), *Soundings in South Asian History* (Berkeley: 1968), and Blair Kling, *The Blue Mutiny: The Indigo Disturbances in Bengal, 1859–62* (Philadelphia: 1966).

27. The work of Clive Dewey has been particularly important with regard to these avoidance measures. See, for example, '*Patwari* and *Chaukidar*: Subordinate Officials and the Reliability of India's Agricultural Statistics', in Clive Dewey and A. G. Hopkins (eds), *The Imperial Impact in Africa and South Asia* (London: 1979). See also P. Robb, 'Hierarchy and Resources: Peasant Stratification in Late-Nineteenth-Century Bihar', *Modern Asian Studies*, 13 (1979); and C. Baker, 'Tamilnad Estates in the Twentieth Century', *Indian Social and Economic History Review*, 13 (1976).

28. See, for example, David Hardiman, 'The Crisis of the Lesser Patidars: Peasant Agitations in Kheda District, Gujarat, 1917–34', in D. A. Low (ed.), *Congress and the Raj* (London: 1977); and Steven Henningham, 'Agrarian Relations in North Bihar', *Indian Economic and Social History Review*, 14 (1979).

29. In the past few years Africanists have given increasing attention to the key roles played by women, especially the so-called market women, in political agitation in the colonial period. In some instances, their activities represented interesting variants of non-violent resistance. See, for example, Judith van Allen, 'Aba Riots or the Igbo "Women's War"? ', in Nancy Hafkin and Edna Bay (eds), *Women in Africa: Studies in Social and Economic Change* (Stanford: 1976).

30. It is notable that most of those who have developed these patterns thus far have done so as a consequence of findings made while researching and writing on agrarian rebellions.

31. These themes are treated even more fully in his *Rhetoric and Ritual in Colonial India* (forthcoming from the University of California Press in the USA, and Oxford University Press in India).

PEASANT MOVEMENTS AND MILLENARIANISM

Tai, Hue-Tam Ho. *Millenarianism and Peasant Politics in Vietnam*. Harvard East Asian Series, no. 99. Cambridge, Massachusets: Harvard University Press, 1983. 220 pages

More than any other factor, scholarly interest in peasant protest has been responsible for the great profusion of studies on millenarianism in recent decades. Though works on millenarianism, like those by Bryan Wilson (1961), E. Michael Mendelson (1961, 1975), and Peter Worsley (1968), have appeared that deal with non-peasant groups or sects that are only peripherally involved in protest, most recent studies of millenarianism have been aimed at exploring the ways in which prophetic leaders and apocalyptic visions have focused peasant discontent and mobilized rural support for social protest movements. This trend represents a major shift from much of the earlier scholarship on millenarianism which tended towards an antiquarian interest in ancient eschatology or sensationalized accounts by Christian missionaries or ex-colonial officials of the manner in which faith healers and other charlatans manipulated the superstitions of the credulous "natives" in order to stir up anti-colonial unrest. Adopting an approach pioneered by writers like Katesa Schlosser (1949), Antony Wallace (1952, 1956), and Norman Cohn (1961), recent authors have greatly enhanced our understanding of the motives of those who are attracted to millenarianism, the organizational and ideological dynamics of these movements, and the reasons for their successes or, more commonly, their failures. This emphasis on millenarianism as an expression of social protest, however, has led most writers to concentrate on specific peasant riots or risings or movements that result in short-lived outbursts of peasant resistance. The sociocultural contexts of these incidents or movements are frequently analyzed in some depth, but they are almost always treated as the preludes to the "main event" — the peasant rising that is the focus of the study. In her well researched and beautifully written study of *Millenarianism and Peasant Politics in Vietnam*, Hue-Tam Ho Tai breaks from this tendency to concentrate on protest incidents or movements, opting instead for a thorough exploration of an entire millenarian *tradition* extending over a century, and its multifaceted impact on peasant responses to a difficult frontier environment, natural catastrophes, and elite oppression. Tai's study culminates in the fullest account to date of the important Hoa Hao sect that spread in the middle decades of this century through a number of the provinces in the western portions of the Mekong Delta region of Vietnam. In placing her analysis of that movement within a detailed examination of a much older millenarian tradition, Tai has written much more than the history of a single sect. She also provides a wide range of fine insights and well supported arguments about the nature of millenarianism and the complex relationships that exist between millenarian leaders and ideas and peasant behavior and organization with an emphasis on collective protest.

Theoretically oriented social scientists may find Professor Tai's study somewhat disappointing because she rarely explicitly tackles the many, often very controversial, issues regarding peasant protest and the role of religion in rebellion on which her materials have a direct bearing. It would be indeed unfortunate if Tai's decision to eschew direct involvement in current debates on various aspects of peasant protest obscured the major contributions her work makes to our understanding of many of the issues that these controversies have evoked. Without taking sides, resorting to jargon or applying labels, Tai moves with an ease and grace rare in studies on peasant societies from narrative based on the rich — but difficult to obtain and interpret — data she had gathered on a succession of millenarian movements in Vietnam to broader observations and conclusions that should prove instructive and provocative to all scholars with an interest in peasant societies or collective protest.

Above all, it is Professor Tai's long term perspective, her serious attempt to study an entire millenarian tradition, rather than a single outburst of protest, that makes this work more than just a fine monograph on sectarianism in Vietnam. Not only do specific incidents take on a different, often more significant, meaning when viewed as part of a larger tradition, the tradition itself becomes a potent force in shaping peasant attitudes and decisions *and* the responses of their adversaries, whether these be absentee landlords or nervous bureaucrats. This long term perspective underscores the erratic ebb and flow that characterizes millenarian traditions. As Tai shows, the Buu Son Ky Huong (literally: Strange Fragrance from the Precious Mountain) emerged in the mid–nineteenth century when the teachings of a prophetic figure who called himself the Buddha Master of Western Peace attracted a modest, but fervent, following made up largely of peasants who often joined *en bloc* as village communities. In the following decades the number of adherents to the Buu Son Ky Huong rose, usually in spurts, in response to natural catastrophes, social and political disturbances, and the periodic emergence of prophetic figures who reinvigorated the sectarian vision, often by reformulating it to meet changes in sociopolitical conditions or specific crises. Though the harsh frontier conditions in the Mekong Delta region were sufficient to sustain the Buu Son Ky Huong as part of the endemic sectarianism found in the area, the movement periodically grew so quiescent that it disappeared from view — at least from that of government officials who provide one of the main sources of information on the sect throughout its history. Repeatedly, however, worsening social and economic circumstances intensified nascent eschatological longings that led to new bursts of sectarian proselytization, rapid growth in membership, and short-lived rebellions. As Tai so skillfully argues, each spurt of growth, each rising — however ill-fated — served to propagate and implant more firmly the much modified message of the Buddha Master in the imaginations of the peasantry of Nam Bo or southern Vietnam. In this way, one rising reinforced the next and all were rooted in the Buu Son Ky Huong tradition, as well as in the larger sectarian undercurrent that pervaded society in the Mekong area.

Embedded in Tai's moving narrative of the ebb and flow of Buu Son Ky Huong strength is a good deal of speculation about the causes of sectarian transformations over time. She provides perhaps the fullest and most convincing example available for viewing frontier regions as particularly propitious environments for millenarian movements. Tai does not argue that millenarian sects cannot arise in long-settled and more heavily administered areas, as they indeed have, but she explores in considerable detail the connections between what Carl Brown (1970) had characterized as cultural "fringe" areas and the recurrence of millenarian fervor (See also Sartono, 1966 and Adas, 1979). The mobile, often vagrant, character of the population; the loose and unstable nature of village communities; the mixture of ethnic groups (in this case Vietnamese, Cambodians, and "tribals") and religious traditions; and the constant struggle of frontier dwellers, are all conducive to sectarain, if not millenarian, growth. In addition, Tai argues that the weakness of the state apparatus in frontier areas enables sects, even those which openly challenge the government's authority, to survive and spread.

Professor Tai does not extend her frontier thesis to embrace Norman Cohn's (1961) argument that millenarianism tends to arise among displaced and dispossessed groups which lack the protective ties and material security which are normally provided by community life. She in fact shows that this pattern may have been at work in the early stages of Buu Son Ky Huong growth when peasant settlers were attracted to sectarian communties where they found support from others in their difficult struggle for sheer survival. In this and later periods, however, Tai reveals that whole peasant communities often rallied to the Buu Son Ky Huong and Hoa Hao. This recruitment of members as parts of whole communities also indicates the need for caution in treating these movements as expressions of class conflict — even late in the colonial period. Tai, like Jayne Werner in her recent volume on the Cao Dai, a

VIII

rival sect of the Hoa Hao in Vietnam (1981), stresses the vertical orientation of sectarian mobilization in the Buu Son Ky Huong tradition. The conversion of landlords and other local notables to the sect often meant that their client tenants and laborers and, at times, whole village communities became members. The stated intention of prophet leaders like Huynh Pho So, who founded the Hoa Hao variant of the Buu Son Ky Huong, was to reestablish or shore up patron-client ties that had been eroded by landlord absenteeism and the competitive atmosphere of the rice-export, market oriented economy of French Cochinchina. Huynh Phu So exhorted his notable adherents to be good patrons and look after the welfare of the poorer members of the sect, especially in times of death. He sought to restore the Confucian hierarchy, not lead a class revolt. Though the Buu Son Ky Huong/Hoa Hao ideology found a ready response in many of the battered and impoverished communities of the western Mekong region, it had little appeal in urban areas to which Huynh Phu So was openly hostile. It also gained few adherents among plantation workers who were numerous and even more oppressed than tenants or laborers in Nam Bo in the French period. Estate workers knew little of Confucian hierarchies and had no patron–client bonds to restore or repair. These patterns, and similar ones identified in other studies of millenarian risings (Sartono, 1966; Adas, 1979), suggest that Jeffery Paige's useful paradigm of landlord–peasant interaction (1975) needs to be modified in order to accommodate situations where landed notables ally with tenants and laborers in protest, and agrarian unrest strengthens patron–client ties rather than provoking class conflict.

Throughout *Millenarianism and Peasant Politics in Vietnam*, Tai returns repeatedly to the theme of the frontier origins of millenarian expression in its various forms and phases. Because the fragmentary nature and poor quality of the extant sources often make it difficult for her to say much in depth about the social and economic background of specific risings, her strategy of grounding her discussion of causation in factors linked to the frontier environment serves her admirably. The frontier constant also reinforces her effort to analyze the Buu Son Ky Huong/Hoa Hao tradition as a whole. It permits her to distinguish between underlying, relatively constant conditions that produce an atmosphere conducive to sectarianism in general and those forces or events that tend to trigger the periodic fluctuations between apparent passivity and active proselytization, between inward-looking rituals and worship and overt hostility or aggression against outsiders that Tai delineates for this sectarian tradition. A number of interesting patterns emerge here. One is the shift over time from natural catastrophes, which Michael Barkun has argued are often associated with millenarianism (1974), to human oppression as the main precipitants of heightened sectarian activity and frequently of sectarian risings. In large part, this shift can be traced to the economic changes and enhanced state control over community affairs that resulted from French colonizers, to coopt sectarian leaders or at least to monitor the activities and restrain the fervor of their devotees.

Tai identifies the emergence of prophetic leaders as a second key determinant of major shifts in sectarian development. Just as the Buddha Master of Western Peace played an essential role in the genesis of the sect, later leaders like the Potato Seller Monk and the most eminent of the Buddha Master's successors, Huynh Pho So, acted as catalysts to renew apocalyptical hopes that hard pressed peasants had held in abeyance but not forgotten. Tai's treatment of the succession of prophets in the Buu Son Ky Huong/Hoa Hao tradition is as full as her sources allow and is especially good on Huynh Phu So, about whom the most has been written. Her detailed discussion of Huynh Phu So's background, personality and teachings provides further confirmation of a number of patterns related to prophetic leaders that emerge from comparisons of millenarian movements in a variety of cultural and historical contexts (Schlosser, 1950; Sartono, 1973; Adas, 1979). Huynh Phu So's comfortable family background, his opportunities for education, and his extensive contacts with Buddhist monks and folk healers have parallels in the lives of a surprising number of prophetic figures. Many other leaders of this type, like Huynh Phu So, are physically frail and experience serious illness accompanied by a deep spiritual crisis in the period when they begin to have the visions that launch their prophetic careers. Huynh Phu So's youthful mastery of the ideas of the Buu Son Ky Huong and related traditions and his exposure to a variety of thaumaturges proved vital to his ability to mix magical curing and predictive powers and millenarian visions. These skills were essential to his success in winning large numbers of peasant followers and holding their allegiance over time. As Tai's study repeatedly illustrates, prophetic leaders play perhaps a more pivotal role in determining the modes of expression that millenarianism takes at different points in time than do the leaders of any other form of collective behavior.

By approaching millenarianism from the perspective of an entire tradition, Tai is able to explore in depth the complex relationships between sectarianism and more "orthodox" forms of religious and political thinking, as well as alternative modes of peasant organization and protest. As Werner has for the Cao Dai, Tai shows the ways in selected elements of the *tam-giao*, the Vietnamese blend of Confucianism, Taoism and Buddhism, were combined by the Buddha Master to mold a persuasive apocalyptic ideology that was firmly rooted in Vietnamese folk culture. In the case of the Buu Son Ky Huong, this syncretism was heavily derived from Buddhism, particularly the eschatological beliefs that centered on the periodic appearance of Maitreya saviors who would cleanse the world of its wickedness and in so doing usher in a golden age of goodness and peace. Tai's narrative of the Buu Son Ky Huong tradition shows, however, the ways in which the relative importance of each strain of the *tam-giao* triad fluctuated over time, depending on the proclivities of a particular prophet or the concerns and aspirations of the sect's adherents. Huynh Phu So, for example, stressed Confucian paternalism, and both he and the Buddha Master drew heavily on Taoist traditions of healing and magic in the early phases of their prophetic careers.

In addition to the ideas of the *tam-giao*, the Buu Son Ky Huong/Hoa Hao tradition was shaped through interaction with other sectarian groups, like the Cao Dai, and secret societies, especially the Heaven and Earth Society. Bearing out the arguments of a number of recent authors (see, for example, Naquin, 1976), Tai stresses that it was often difficult to distinguish clearly between sect and secret society and that in fact individuals and whole communities could belong to both simultaneously. Tai argues that the secret societies of Nam Bo offered sectarian groups like those of the Buu Son Ky Huong/Hoa Hao an organizatonal model that was much superior to those which the sects themselves evolved. Often, however, the sects proved unwilling or unable to learn the lessons the secret societies might teach. Because the fortunes of both sects and secret societies fluctuated over time, the expansion of one might be influenced by the repression or temporary decline of another. Throughout its history, the Buu Son Ky Huong/Hoa Hao both enriched and borrowed from other movements at the same time it competed with them for followers and resources.

In viewing a millenarian tradition like that of the Buu Son Ky Huong/Hoa Hao across its alternating phases of relative quiescence, prophetic and proselytizing activity, and occasional outbursts of protest, its links to other forms of peasant protest tend to be accentuated. Sectarianism itself encompasses a number of forms of both confrontational and avoidance protest. The latter can be seen in instances where peasants renounce their ties to exploitative patrons in favor of membership in sectarian communities or flee state demands for taxes or corvee labor to join a prophet and his followers in a forest or wilderness refuge. In assessing various phases of Buu Son Ky Huong/Hoa Hao strength, Tai shows how strong specific, material incentives are in winning adherents for movements of this kind. Prophet and sect provide viable communities in situations where social bonds and structures are breaking down. These communities stress cooperation and sharing over competition and personal gain. Within this *Gemeinschaft* environment, converts are suppled with land to cultivate, housing, and even "health care" in the guise of herbal and folk medical techniques that are often blended with faith healing. Equally critical are the various ways in which sect members gain protection, through community assistance and magical talismans, from rapacious landlords, bullying tax collectors or soldiers, and natural scourges like floods and drought. Within the sect individuals of low birth who have ability and ambition have opportunities to assume positions of authority and responsibility. They and all members of the sect can also participate in often elaborate rituals and ceremonies which provide welcome relief from the tedium and hard work of everyday village life. The importance of these activities to sectarian members is difficult to gauge with precision, but their contribution to the appeal of millenarian movements should not be underestimated. These material gains and personal incentives can be seen as the major forces which sustain sectarian communities over time. They are the forces that dominate everyday life within the sect in the periods when it is not caught up in protest activities which, Tai intimates, are by far the longest over the whole course of the Buu Son Ky Huong/Hoa Hao tradition.

The contrast between day-to-day concerns and intervals of overt sectarian resistance highlights both the weaknesses of millenarianism as a form of collective protest and the variety of ways that it can be channeled into open confrontations with those whom sect members identify as adversaries. Tai describes riots, rebellions, assaults on minority ethnic groups, and bloody battles with sectarian and Communist rivals that all came within the Buu Son Ky Huong/Hoa Hao tradition. In contrast to the considerable strength of the millenarian community at peace, its weaknesses in situations of open conflict are repeatedly underscored. Early sectarian risings fail miserably, and even the strongest movement produced by the tradition, the Hoa Hao, cannot maintain itself in the face of hostility from the Diem regime and its successors and open warfare with the Viet Minh and later the Viet Cong. Situations of confrontation brutally expose the vulnerability of the prophet leader; the ineffectiveness of his magic and protective talismans; the virtual absence of a clear structure of command and overall organization; and the poor training and miserable weapons of the sect's adherents. These weaknesses are, of course, inherent in millenarianism where so much is left to the workings of the forces of the cosmos. They also explain the necessity for sectarian groups to resort to threats and physical force to recruit followers or discipline members, a need more often found in the confrontational phases of millenarian movements than in their periods of quiescence. Again and again challenges from the government or rival movements result in sectarian aggression and often bloody defeats that call into question the movement's millenarian legitimacy and its magical potency. These reverses lead — at least temporarily — to a decline in the sect's following and its appeal as an avenue of escape for hard pressed peasants.

Though Tai's long term perspective makes possible an extended discussion of sectarian-state relations under four regimes — Nguyen, French, Diem and successors, and Communist — these links are never fully examined. In fact, Tai's rather fragmentary and vague handling of the political contexts in which the Buu Son Ky Huong/Hoa Hao developed is, along with her equally patchy treatment of causal issues, the most disappointing aspect of the study. More successful are her attempts to analyze the struggle between the Hoa Hao and the Communists that has dominated the life of the Buu Son Ky Huong tradition from the late 1930s onward. When viewed in the context of the longer millenarian tradition, study of this rivalry suggests some interesting similarities between the sectarian Hoa Hao and the Indochinese Communist Party (ICP) — similarities that go a long way to explain the success of both in mobilizing peasant support. Both provided real material gains for their peasant adherents in terms of land and capital needed for cultivation; lower rents or better wages; medical care, however rudimentary; some schooling; and improved housing. The adherents to each of these movements gained a sense of community and purposefulness that comes of devotion to a cause that transcends personal advantage and short term gain. Membership in either the ICP or the Hoa Hao greatly enhanced the physical protection available to peasants whose vulnerability is a chronic source of suffering, particularly in regions like the Mekong Delta which are the focus of violent struggles over resources and state control. Participation in each movement also offered ordinary peasants opportunities for social mobility — which they at times converted into personal aggrandizement — and the means to strike back at hated rivals or oppressors. Beyond these mundane and rather immediate gains, there was the promise of victory and ultimate utopia enshrined in the ideology of each movement. The elect of the Hoa Hao could not fail because the forces of the cosmos, channeled through Huynh Phu So, were on their side, while the ultimate victory of the Communists was insured by the workings of the historical dialectic.

The parallels between the movements can be overstated and should not be allowed to obscure their very real differences. The Communists, for all of their early failures, were vastly better led and organized. Their political goals — including the intent to seize state power — were much more clearly defined, extensively propagated among their supporters, and persistently pursued. The rank and file of the ICP were generally better armed and invariably better trained that the paramilitary forces of the Hoa Hao. Rather than amulets and magical incantations, the Viet Minh offered cadre discipline and guerrilla tactics as means by which its recruits could strike at their adversaries and have some chance of survival. Though "charismatic" leaders like Ho Chi Minh were important to Communist success, Marxist ideology, the party, the larger struggles against imperialism, capitalism and feudalism, and not a prophet-figure, made up the core of the ICP movement. The Communists selectively adopted or rejected Western ideas, organizational models, and technology, rather than renouncing them totally as the anti-urban, anti- "modern" Huynh Phu So advocated, even to the point of writing a poem that mocked the unreliability of electric fans (Tai, p. 156). Though, like the Communists in China, the Viet Minh were forced to play down hositility towards the landlord classes in deference to "united front" struggles against outside adversaries, the Vietnamese Communist movement was built on an ideology of class struggle and the seizure of power by the propertyless and exploited that had no counterpart in the paternalistic patron-client oriented Hoa Hao. Above all, it was the broader vision of the Communists that distinguished them from sectarian groups like the Hoa Hao and Cao Dai. Their greater awareness of Vietnamese and international history and view of conditions throughout Indochina, not just the western Mekong area, drove them to struggle for the banner of nationalist legitimacy and build a base of support in all parts of Vietnam. The contrasts between the Hoa Hao and the Viet Minh in this respect are superbly illustrated by Tai's account of their differing responses to the famines that struck north and central Vietnam in the mid-1940s as a result of disruptions and crop shortages brought on by the Second World War. The Communists urged their supporters in Nam Bo to share their harvest with the peasants of the north and center, while the Hoa Hao knew little of the suffering and never considered aiding villagers who might as well have been those of a foreign land. Alexander Woodside (1976:232–3) has seen the famine relief efforts of the Communists in this period as one of the keys to their widespread support in the postwar era. In the decades of civil strife and warfare after 1945, the Viet Minh and later the Viet Cong could draw on men and resources throughout Vietnam to check, wear down and ultimately overwhelm foreign invaders and indigenous rivals like Hoa Hao.

The combination of detailed narrative and analytical insight found throughout *Millenarianism and Peasant Politics in Vietnam* make Tai's study one of the best I have read on millenarianism in any cultural setting. Like the recent work of Elizabeth Perry (1980), Tai's monograph convincingly demonstrates how much those who are interested in writing peasant history from a "grass roots" perspective (insofar as that is possible for bourgeois academics) can gain from the long term approach that takes into account factors ranging from the environment to the demands of the state and traces fluctuations in peasant conditions, behavior and aspirations over a substantial period of time. Two works may not be sufficient to proclaim a new trend, but one can hope that Tai and Perry will inspire more peasant studies adopting their approach and matching the high quality of their first books.

REFERENCES

Adas, Michael. 1979. *Prophets of Rebellion: Millenarian Protest Movements against the European Colonial Order*. Chapel Hill, University of North Carolina Press.

Barkun, Michael. 1974. *Disaster and the Millenium*. New Haven: Yale University Press.

Brown, L. Carl. 1970. "The Sudanese Mahdiya," in *Protest and Power in Black Africa*, edited by Robert Rotberg and Ali Mazrui. Oxford: Oxford University Press.

Cohn, Norman. 1961. *The Pursuit of the Millenium*. New York: Harper.

Mendelson, E. Michael. 1961. "A Messianic Buddhist Association in Upper Burma," *Bulletin of the School of Oriental and African Studies 24* (1961): 229-37.

——— 1975. *Sangha and State in Burma*. Ithaca: Cornell University Press.

Naquin, Susan. 1976. *Millenial Rebellion in China*. New Haven: Yale University Press.

Paige, Jeffery. 1975. *Agrarian Revolution: Social Movements and Export Agriculture in the Underdeveloped World*. Berkeley: University of California Press.

Perry, Elizabeth. 1980. *Rebels and Revolutionaries in North China, 1845–1945*. Stanford: Stanford University Press.

Sartono Kartodirdjo. 1966. *The Peasants' Revolt of Banten in 1888*. The Hague: Nijhoff.

⸻. 1973. *Peasant Protest in Rural Java*. Singapore-Kuala Lumpur: Oxford University Press.

Schlosser, Katesa. 1949. *Propheten in Afrika*. Braunschweig: Albert Limbach.

⸻. 1950. "Der Prophetismus in niederen Kulturen," *Zeitschrift für Ethnologie* 75 (1950): 60-72.

Wallace, Anthony. 1952. "Handsome Lake and the Great Revival in the West," *American Quarterly 4* (1952): 149-65.

⸻. 1956. "Revitalization Movements," *American Anthropologist 58*: 264–81.

Werner, Jayne Susan. 1981. *Peasant Politics and Religious Sectarianism: Peasant and Priest in the Cao Dai in Viet Nam*. New Haven: Yale University Press.

Wilson, Bryan. 1961. *Sects and Society*. London: Heinemann.

Woodside, Alexander B. 1976. *Community and Revolution in Modern Vietnam*. Boston: Houghton Mifflin.

Worsley, Peter. 1968. *The Trumpet Shall Sound: A Study of "Cargo" Cults in Melanesia*. New York: Schocken.

IX

Imperialist Rhetoric and Modern Historiography: The Case of Lower Burma before and after Conquest*

One of the most prevalent and influential themes in the literature on European imperialism has been the dichotomy between conditions in an area threatened by European conquest *prior to* and *following* the imposition of colonial rule. Even writers who have disapproved of the extension of European control normally have had little favourable to say about indigenous rulers or the state of kingdoms about to be annexed. Historians have generally pictured the pre-colonial history of these areas as periods of decadence and corruption, of administrative breakdown and social chaos, and of economic stagnation and popular unrest. In contrast, most writers have viewed the early colonial era as a time of recovery and progress.[1] In order to justify this view, they have attempted to show that the establishment of European rule brought peace and order, stable government, educational and legal reforms, public works projects and economic development. Most historians have implicitly assumed that the indigenous peoples accepted European overlords during the first decades after conquest because conditions were far better under alien rule than they had been under the traditional elites.

The belief in the decadence or barbarism of the indigenous regime provided both motive and justification for European writers and political leaders who advocated empire-building overseas. Colonial secretaries and leaders of imperialistic associations could argue that costly military expeditions had been necessitated not only by political and/or economic considerations but also by a more altruistic motive, the salvation of oppressed peoples living under cruel and rapacious monarchs. Joseph Chamberlain voiced this rationale in an 1896 speech explaining the necessity of a British expedition against the Kingdom of Ashanti in present-day Ghana:

> I think the duty of this country in regard to all these savage countries over which we are called upon to exercise some sort of dominion is to establish, at the earliest possible date, Pax Britannica, and force these people to keep the peace amongst themselves, and by doing so, whatever may be the destruction of life in an expedition which brings about this result, it will be nothing if weighed in the balance against the annual loss of life which goes on so long as we keep away.[2]

The views of Chamberlain and other leaders were shaped to a large extent by the reports, correspondence and published writings of European "men-on-the-spot"

* I would like to thank John Smail, Philip Curtin, Edwin Hirschmann, Joseph J. Brennig, and especially Allen Howard for their comments on portions of this article. The responsibility for the content is my own.

[1] Excepting anti-imperialist "Marxist" or "nationalist" historians and other revisionist scholars who will be considered below.

[2] As quoted in R. Koebner and H.D. Schmidt, *Imperialism: The Story and Significance of a Political Word, 1840–1960* (Cambridge 1964), p. 210. For similar beliefs expressed by Jules Ferry, see H. Brunschwig, *Mythes et Réalités de L'Imperialisme Colonial Francais, 1871–1914* (Paris, 1960), pp. 74–5.

in Asia and Africa. Numerous officials, missionaries and explorers, of whom Sir Richard Burton, David Livingstone and Sir John Kirk are the better known, wrote of the excesses and cruelties of "native" rulers and of the suffering and social dislocations caused by the slave trade, "tribal" warfare, and other abuses. Further evidence of the degraded state of the indigenous kingdoms was provided by the men who conquered and ruled the vast areas in Asia and Africa which came under European control in the last decades of the nineteenth century. Men like Lord Lugard, the Earl of Cromer and Francis Garnier firmly believed that they acted in the interest of the "native" peoples who had long been oppressed by corrupt or inept rulers.[3] A belief in the decadence or barbarism of the traditional regime was essential to those who saw imperial expansion as the God-given duty of a superior white or European "race."

Although the concepts of the *mission civilisatrice* and the "white man's burden" are normally associated with the period of high imperialism at the end of the nineteenth century, numerous advocates of European imperial expansion had expressed similar sentiments long before. Many British officers and civilian officials who directed the conquest and administration of the Indian Empire beginning in the last decades of the eighteenth century were convinced that the "native" kingdoms were degenerate and that British rule was beneficial. This "before and after" dichotomy underlay the beliefs that India was a "sacred trust" and that the British were duty-bound to improve the condition and "character" of the indigenous peoples.[4] These beliefs of the conquerors were taken up by the indigenous collaborators who served the new European overlords and reiterated by many first- and second-generation nationalist leaders.[5]

In the nineteenth and early twentieth centuries the accounts of travellers, missionaries and colonial administrators provided the main sources of information for European historians of Asia and Africa. In addition, many of the historical works produced in this period were written by European officials or missionaries themselves. Consequently, the "before and after" dichotomy became a standard theme in the early works on the modern history of colonized areas in Asia and Africa. The expressions of this theme ranged from James Mill's virulent denunciations of Hindu and Muslim civilization in India to milder assessments by historians like James Cunningham who, despite their admiration for the conquered peoples, concluded that European civilization and, by implication, European rule were superior and that their spread was inevitable.[6] John Kaye's assessment of the impact of *The Administration of the East India Company* was

---

[3] See, for example, Lugard, *The Dual Mandate in British Tropical Africa* (London, 1965; 1st ed. 1922), pp. 5–6, 612–19 *et passim*; Cromer as quoted in John Marlowe's *Cromer in Egypt*(New York, 1970), pp. 279–85; and Garnier as quoted in M. Osborne, *The French Presence in Cochinchina and Cambodia* (Ithaca, New York, 1969), p. 40.

[4] See P.E. Roberts, *India under Wellesley* (Gorakpur, 1961; 1st ed. 1929), pp. 131, 136 *et passim*; and G.D. Bearce, *British Attitudes Towards India, 1784–1858* (Oxford, 1961), pp. 34–78. Even administrators like Mountstuart Elphinstone and Thomas Munro, who displayed considerable ambivalence toward Indian elites and institutions, concluded that the populace as a whole was better off under British rule. See Kenneth Ballhatchet, *Social Policy and Social Change in Western India 1817–1830* (London, 1957), pp. 30–42, 248–51 *et passim*; and P. Griffiths, *The British Impact on India* (London, 1952), pp. 245–6.

[5] For examples, see Osborne, *French Presence*, pp. 93–8; K.C. Sen, *Lectures in India* (London, 1901), pp. 322–6; and selections from D. Naoroji's numerous *Essays, Speeches, Addresses, and Writings* . . . (Bombay, 1887).

[6] See especially volumes one and two of James Mill's multi-volumed *History of British India, 1756–83* (London, 1840); and James Cunningham, *A History of the Sikhs* (New Delhi, 1966; 1st ed. 1848), pp. 247–9 and his preface to the second edition, 1849.

based on the assumption of the "old story of misgovernment of Asiatic States,"[7] which permeates most of the historical literature of the colonial period. Kaye asserted that government by even the most "indolent and selfish" of British Governor-Generals was vastly superior to that of the Mughal "despots." He claimed that the "luxurious selfishness" of the Mughal nobility had "depressed and enfeebled" the general populace and that over a century after the break-up of their empire India was "... still prostrated by that great curse of Mughal tyranny."[8]

The first major challenges to the interpretations of the proponents of the "imperial" school have come from anti-imperialist, Marxist or leftist, and "nationalist" historians. Although much of the work of these writers was poorly researched and highly polemical, significant contributions have been made by scholars like T.O. Ranger, J.F.A. Ajayi and A.A. Boahen in African, R.C. Dutt in Indian and Le Thanh Khoi in Southeast Asian history. In many cases, however, these scholars have had little sympathy for the traditional elite and social order.[9] More important, most of the historians of the Marxist or "nationalist" persuasion have adopted the same perspective and concentrated on the same issues as the policy-makers and scholars they oppose.[10] As a result, they have neglected evidence which might be used to determine the validity of the assumed decadence or barbarism of the pre-European state and society.

The "before and after" dichotomy has survived the decades of "decolonization" and remains a basic premise in the works of many historians in the post-colonial era. In most cases the decadence or barbarism of the previous kingdom and the belief in the beneficial impact of colonial rule is tacitly accepted by contemporary authors of general histories and monographs without reassessment of the available sources relating to the area in question.[11] In some works, particularly in widely read texts and general histories, the contrast between pre- and post-annexation conditions is vividly drawn.[12] Often scholars who readily admit to the shortcomings of European empire-builders persist in uncritically reiterating the standard view of the depopulated and devastated state of vast areas about to be annexed.[13]

---

[7] Kimberley to Gladstone, 10 Sept. 1873, quoted by C.D. Cowan in *Nineteenth-Century Malaya* (London, 1961), p. 169.

[8] Allahabad, 1966 (1st ed. 1853), p. 50. For expressions of similar views with reference to other areas see J.S. Keltie, *The Partition of Africa*, Revised ed. (Philadelphia, 1906) pp. 47, 60–1, 68, 75, 126 *et passim*; and Camille Rousset, *La Conquete d'Alger* (Paris, 1880), pp. 1–3 *et passim*.

[9] See, for example, Le Thanh Khoi's treatment of the Nguyen nobility and bureaucracy in *Le Vietnam: histoire et civilisation* (Paris, 1955), pp. 322, 354–65 *et passim*.

[10] One of the best discussions of these unfortunate trends may be found in John R.W. Smail's article "On the Possibility of an Autonomous History of Indonesia," *Journal of Southeast Asian History* 2/2 (1961), pp. 80–82.

[11] This tendency was criticized as early as 1953 by L.J. Ragatz in his article, "Must We Rewrite the History of Imperialism?" *Historical Studies: Australia and New Zealand*, Vol. 6, pp. 90–8. M.D. Lewis noted a decade later that little serious attention had been given to the problem. See "One Hundred Million Frenchmen: The Assimilation Theory in French Colonial Policy," *Comparative Studies in Society and History* 4/2 (1962), p. 149. With the exceptions noted below, the problem remains much neglected.

[12] See, for examples, Z. Marsh and G.W. Kingsnorth, *An Introduction to the History of East Africa* 3rd. ed., (Cambridge, 1965), pp. 115–7, 131–4, 183 *et passim*; L.S.S. O'Malley (ed.), *Modern India and the West* (London, 1941), especially pp. 13–43 which set the tone on the "before and after" question for a whole generation of British, American and Indian historians; and H. Miller, *The Story of Malaysia* (London, 1965), pp. 99 and 125 *et passim*. The most recent and forceful restatement of the "before and after" theme may be found in L.H. Gann and Peter Duignan, *The Burden of Empire* (New York, 1967).

[13] Good examples of this pattern may be found in the texts and general surveys of Percival Spear. See *India: A Modern History* (Ann Arbon, Michigan, 1961), pp. 172–81.

Even scholars who are highly sympathetic to the sufferings of the colonized often accept the imperialist rhetoric of the European conquerors and early colonial historians. The following passage from Jacques Goutor's *Algeria and France 1830–1963*[14] strikingly illustrates how difficult it is for the historian to extricate himself from the "before and after" framework:

> Before the coming of the French, so the history books said, Algeria was a land of hunger and disease, of civil strife and banditry, subjected to the domination of conquerors who left the land bereft of any of the trappings of modern civilization. It was the French who brought Algeria from the dark ages to the modern world, who refurbished her economy, who rid the land of hunger and pestilence, and who made it possible for the population to increase from two to ten million in one hundred years. In many ways it is difficult to quarrel with the French on these points, since they did in fact fulfil a number of these claims.

In recent years a number of historians dealing mainly with areas in sub-Saharan Africa have presented substantial evidence to dispute the decadence and barbarism half of the "before and after" dichotomy. William Tordoff, M.S.M. Kiwanuka, Philip Igbafe, James Graham and others have attempted to show that pre-annexation conditions in various African kingdoms were not as grim as historians had previously asserted and/or that the causes of political fragmentation or social disruption in these areas differed from those normally cited.[15] In contrast to African historians, few scholars working on areas colonized in Asia have given serious attention to a re-examination of the evidence on which the assumption of the decadence of the pre-colonial kingdoms is based. Although the adverse effects of colonial rule have been considered in numerous studies, little has been done to improve our understanding of conditions in pre-conquest societies.[16]

Although the evidence and arguments of writers like Tordoff and Igbafe are extremely important, these writers have limited their reassessments mainly to the political and military aspects of the "before and after" dichotomy.[17] In order to test thoroughly the validity of this theme, the historian must make use of the information and techniques provided by other disciplines. He must take into account factors such as the level of technology, the impact of disease, the economic role of the government, the nature of economic incentives, the birth and mortality rates, and the market structure in the society with which he is dealing.

---

[14] (Muncie, Indiana, 1965), p. 2.

[15] Tordoff, *Ashanti under the Prempehs, 1888–1935* (London, 1965); Kiwanuka, "Bunyoro and the British: A Reappraisal of the causes for the Decline and Fall of an African Kingdom," *Journal of African History* 9/4 (1968), pp. 603–19; Igbafe, "The Fall of Benin: A Reassessment," *Journal of African History* 11/3(1970), pp. 385–400; and Graham, "The Slave Trade, Depopulation and Human Sacrifice in Benin History," *Cahiers D'etudes Africaines* 5/2(1965), pp. 317–34.

[16] A notable exception to this generalization is Ravinder Kumar's *Western India in the Nineteenth Century* (London, 1968).

[17] Important exceptions include Kumar, *ibid*; and Michael Mason, "Population Density and 'Slave Raiding' — the Case of the Middle Belt of Nigeria," *Journal of African History* 10/4(1969), pp. 551–64. See also the comment on Mason's article by M.B. Gleave and R.M. Prothero and a reply by Mason in the *Journal of African History* 12/2(1971), pp. 319–27. In studies of sub-Saharan Africa, trading patterns have also been given serious consideration. Non-historians have made perhaps the greatest contribution to our understanding of non-political aspects of the pre-colonial situation. See for example, T.R. DeGregori's *Technology and the Economic Development of the Tropical African Frontier* (London, 1969) especially pp. 83–181.

In many cases the sources employed by the historian in the examination of these factors will be more or less the same as those used by earlier scholars. Consequently new interpretations will depend primarily upon more careful appraisal and cross-checking of the available evidence, new criteria for selection, new questions posed and new methods of analysis based on those of related social sciences, particularly anthropology and epidemiology. Scholars should also make use, wherever possible, of oral sources of information that have been virtually ignored by earlier generations of historians.

The purpose of this essay is to demonstrate through a case study of Lower Burma how a thorough reappraisal of the existing evidence relating to conditions in an area prior to its conquest by a European power may yield a very different picture from that expressed in the standard sources by the "before and after" dichotomy. In this study I will focus upon the pre-colonial half of the dichotomy, but similar questions must also be applied to the post-colonial era. As the following examination will show, the decadence of the pre-colonial society cannot be assumed. More important, it will demonstrate that many of the previously accepted causes of the "underdeveloped" state of an area prior to European conquest may be false or misleading.

The historiography on modern Burma, particularly that which relates to the Irrawaddy-Sittang delta region or Lower Burma[18] which the British annexed to the Indian empire in 1852, provides one of the best illustrations of the continued adherence to the belief in the decadence of the previous kingdom. Historians have generally presented the century of Burman[19] rule which preceded the British conquest as an era of suffering and strife. Most writers mention conditions in Lower Burma in this period only by way of introduction to discussions of the rapid growth which occurred under British rule. It has become standard procedure to begin accounts of the Irrawaddy-Sittang delta's development in the late nineteenth century with descriptions of its desolate condition under the Konbaung monarchs.[20]

The origins of this view of pre-conquest conditions in Lower Burma can be traced to the attitudes of the British officials who negotiated with the Konbaung rulers and directed the piecemeal conquest of Burma in the nineteenth century. During the first Anglo-Burman war of 1824–6, the British issued proclamations calling upon the indigenous Mon inhabitants of the delta region to support the British war effort against the Burmans. The proclamations reminded the Mons of "the oppression and tyranny" and the "cruel and brutal conduct" of their Burman overlords, and urged them to compare their miserable conditions with the "comfort and happiness" of the inhabitants of nearby areas which had come under British rule.[21] In the year following the Burman defeat in the first Anglo-Burman war, John Crawfurd, an ambassador sent by the Governor-General of India to the Konbaung court, noted the underdeveloped state of the delta area. He concluded that since the region had good soil and a favourable climate, its

---

[18] References to Lower Burma in this article do not include Arakan and Tenasserim which are usually grouped with the Irrawaddy delta under that designation.

[19] Following current usage the term Burman refers specifically to the majority ethnic and linguistic group of Modern Burma. The term Burmese denotes all of the groups which presently comprise the population of Burma including the Burmans, Mons or Talaings, Chins, Shans, Karen and Kachins. The Burmans, whose traditional heartland was the Dry Zone of Upper Burma, conquered Lower Burma in the 1750's after defeating the Mons who comprised the dominant ethnic group in the region.

[20] The Konbaung dynasty (1752–1885) was the last and most powerful produced by the Burman people.

[21] As quoted in Dorothy Woodman, *The Making of Burma* (London, 1962), p. 75.

180

condition was "without a doubt" due to "bad government in a thousand shapes."[22] After Lower Burma had been annexed to the Indian Empire following the second Anglo-Burman war in 1852, Lord Dalhousie, then Governor-General of India, noted the "progress" that had been made under British rule and declared that it was proof of the "vast improvement which the introduction of British rule and the efficiency of the administration have effected ..."[23] Dalhousie's sentiments were also voiced by the British officials who administered the new province. These men made numerous references to their mission of assisting the "semi-civilized" indigenous peoples to raise themselves from the "Sloth of Ages," a development which had been impossible under the "extortionate" Burman regime.[24]

The views of Crawfurd, Dalhousie and early British administrators regarding conditions in Lower Burma prior to 1852 have been accepted by virtually all historians of Burma from G.E. Harvey to John Cady. These views have been incorporated into the theme of the "devastated delta" which is based on three main assumptions regarding the history of the pre-British era: (1) that Lower Burma was widely cultivated and well-populated prior to the Burman-Mon wars of the mid-eighteenth century; (2) that continued warfare and Burman misrule laid waste to large tracts of fertile and productive land; and (3) that these conditions led to the de-population of many areas of the delta. A small and highly selective set of stock quotations taken from the travel accounts of several British officials who visited Lower Burma in the Konbaung period furnished most of the evidence on which these assumptions were based. They have never been verified by a detailed examination of the available sources.

A vision of Lower Burma once "teeming with population"[25] and extensively cultivated is implicit in the standard view that it was depopulated and devastated in the Konbaung period. Assertions by scholars like John Cady and J.S. Furnivall that "many previously cultivated areas of Lower Burma ... reverted to jungle" and that intermittent warfare "laid waste to vast areas"[26] imply that the land in question was once cultivated and settled. This belief is based on the evidence provided by travellers who visited the Delta in Burman times and by the Burman officials who compiled the *Hanthawaddy Sittans* (Burman revenue rolls). These observers recorded that many areas of Lower Burma were covered with dense jungle and great plains of *kaing* or elephant grass. Although these writers seldom indicated that the areas which they were describing had previously been inhabited and productive, most historians have assumed that they were. This position is explicitly stated in the following passage by Cheng Siok-hwa:

> The Irrawaddy-Sittang delta region, once well-populated and prosperous and later to become the most important paddy-growing region in Burma, was devastated and greatly depopulated in the middle years of the eighteenth century following a series of unsuccessful uprisings of the Mons against oppressive Burman conquerors.[27]

---

[22] *Journal of an Embassy from the Governor-General of India to the Court of Ava in the Year 1827* (London, 1928), pp. 11–12.

[23] Letter from Dalhousie to Arthur Phayre, the first Chief Commissioner of the Province of Burma, 4 December, 1857, Govt. of India, *Political and Foreign Proceedings*, Range 203, Vol. 13, No. 255.

[24] See the Govt. of India, *Political and Foreign Proceedings*, Range 201, Vol. 21, No. 165 and Vol. 63, No. 160; *Foreign Proceedings (Revenue)*, Range 205, Vol. 39, No. 12; and the *Report on the Administration of the Province of Pegu* (hereafter *RAP*) for 1855–6, paragraph 267.

[25] H.R. Spearman, *The British Burma Gazetteer* (Rangoon, 1880), I, 443.

[26] Cady, *A History of Modern Burma* (Ithaca, 1958), 69; and Furnivall, *An Introduction to the Political Economy of Burma* (Rangoon, 1957), p. 41.

[27] *The Rice Industry of Burma 1852–1940* (Singapore, 1968), p. 3.

The available evidence demonstrates, however, that most of the desolate tracts mentioned in the accounts of travellers and Burman officials had not been developed prior to the Konbaung period. If this is the case, terms like "devastation," "depopulation" and "relapsed" cannot accurately be applied to them.

A survey of potentially productive regions in the delta during the Konbaung period reveals that most areas were in much the same state as they had been in pre-Konbaung times. The area around Rangoon and north of the city along the Hlaing river was probably less inhabited and cultivated in pre-Konbaung times than travellers like Francis Buchanan and John Crawfurd found it in the 1790's and 1820's[28] Prior to the Burman conquest, Rangoon or Dagon as it was then called, was a minor village whose chief attraction was its pagoda.[29] There is no evidence to indicate any sizable concentration of population near the town or along the Hlaing river to the northwest. The plains lying along both banks of the Irrawaddy south of the town of Henzada could not have been occupied prior to the mid-eighteenth century for the same reason they were reported to be unoccupied throughout the Konbaung period.[30] The area was inundated annually by the flooding of the Irrawaddy which turned it into a vast swamp unfit for habitation.[31]

None of the travellers who passed through Lower Burma in the Konbaung period visited the town of Bassein in the western delta area. However, Gasparo Balbi spent several days in this area in the sixteenth century when the Mon culture of Lower Burma was at its height. He reported that the country along the Bassein river and around Bassein, or Cosmin as it was then called, was covered with jungle and swamp which was "frequented with Parrots, Tigres, wilde Boores, Apes, and such like creatures."[32] The region was not extensively developed until Burman migrants from the north arrived in the last decades of the eighteenth century. Except for occasional references to towns like Myaungmya, little is known of the south-central portion of Lower Burma in pre-Konbaung times. It is probable that the area was as sparsely populated and cultivated as the British found it when they first surveyed the delta in the 1860's.

Passages in which travellers or Burman officials not only describe the desolation of an area but also indicate that it was once prosperous,[33] are exceptions in accounts written in the Konbaung period. Most observers merely stated that an apparently fertile tract of land was not cultivated. Later writers have inferred that it once had been.

Prior to the Burman conquest of Lower Burma in the 1750's, most of the region's population was concentrated in the valley of the Sittang river in the vicinity of the Mon capital of Pegu, along the river route from Cosmin (Bassein) to Pegu, and on the plain that runs along the Martaban littoral between Thaton

---

[28] Francis Buchanan, *Extracts and Observations Respecting the Dominions of Ava ...*, India Office Archives, MSS European, D. 106, p. 31; and Crawfurd, *Journal*, pp. 5–6.

[29] B.R. Pearn, *History of Rangoon* (Rangoon, 1939), pp. 30 & 37.

[30] Michael Symes, *An Account of an Embassy to the Kingdom of Ava ... in 1795* (London, Debrett, ed., 1800), II, 157–9; and Crawfurd, *Journal*, pp. 11–12.

[31] *Henzada District Gazetteer* (Rangoon, 1915), p. 58.

[32] Gasparo Balbi, "His Voyage to Pegu, and Observations There, Gathered out of His Italian Relation," in Samuel Purchas, *Haklytus Posthumus or Purchas His Pilgrims* (Glasgow, 1905), X, 151–2.

[33] Symes, *Account of Ava*, II, 15–16; V. Sangermano *The Burmese Empire* (London, 1893), p. 101; and J.S. Furnivall, "Some Historical Documents" in the *Journal of the Burma Research Society* 8/1(1918), pp. 43 & 47 and 9/1(1919), p. 41.

and Martaban.[34] These were the core areas of the Mon kingdom of Pegu which reached the peak of its power and prosperity in the early sixteenth century. Because many of the Mon chronicles were lost in the wars of the late sixteenth and later centuries, our main sources of information regarding Pegu are the travel accounts and letters of European merchants and missionaries who visited Lower Burma in the sixteenth and early seventeenth centuries. The picture of Pegu that emerges from these sources is not one of an agrarian-based state paralleling the wet-rice complex which centred on Ava in the Dry Zone, but rather of a kingdom based on a combination of trade and agriculture with emphasis on the former. The only notices of extensive rice cultivation came in references to the plains around the city of Pegu and along the coast of Martaban.[35] Since Tome Pires reported that the entrepot of Malacca was dependent upon Pegu for part of its grain supply in the early sixteenth century,[36] it is clear that these areas produced a surplus, part of which was exported. The rest of the surplus was used to support the populations of the urban trading centres which dominated the political, social and economic life of the kingdom of Pegu.

The urban centres of Pegu carried on extensive trade with Malacca, the commercial states of the Indonesian archipelago, Bengal, the Coromandel Coast and with ports as far distant as Gujerat and the Red Sea. The extent of the kingdom's trade can be gauged from W.H. Moreland's estimate that over eight per cent (5,000 tons) of the total volume of exports from Mughal India were carried to Pegu.[37] Although Tome Pires stated that Malacca's chief import from Pegu was rice,[38] most of the kingdom's exports were minerals, manufactured goods, precious stones and luxury items, rather than agricultural products. In identical summaries of the exports of the kingdom in the sixteenth century, Cesar Frederick and Ralph Fitch mentioned rice and sugar last after a list of precious gems and metals, minerals and exotic goods like musk and benjamin.[39] Pegu was best known commercially for these latter items, as well as its martaban jars, lac and sizable shipbuilding industry.[40] Until the end of the sixteenth century, the Mon population of Lower Burma was predominantly urban, primarily engaged in commerce and oriented toward the highly developed Asian trading network.

The flourishing Mon culture of Lower Burma came under Burman rule in the

[34] The regions around the towns of Prome and Toungoo, which were independent kingdoms in this period, were also fairly densely populated. Unlike the lower delta, however, the population of these areas was predominantly Burman.

[35] Duarte Barbosa, who wrote in the second decade of the sixteenth century, claimed on the basis of second hand evidence that the area around Pegu was well cultivated. See M.L. Dames, *The Book of Duarte Barbosa* (London, 1921), II, 153. Andrew Boves related that Martaban had been well cultivated prior to the last decades of the sixteenth century. See "Indian Observations Gathered out of the Letters of Nicholas Pimenta, Visitor of the Jesuites in India, and many others of that Societies" in Purchas, *Pilgrims*, Vol. X, pp. 215–16. Ludvico de Varthema also reported that there was a "great abundance" of grain in the region around Pegu. See R.C. Temple, *The Itinerary of Ludvico de Varthema of Bologna from 1502 to 1508* (London, 1928), p. 81.

[36] *Suma Oriental* (London, 1944), I, 98.

[37] *India at the Death of Akbar* (London, 1920), pp. 235–7.

[38] *Suma Oriental, loc. cit.*

[39] Frederick, "Voyages and Travels in India" in Robert Keer, *A General History and Collection of Voyages and Travels* (Edinburgh, 1812), p. 197; and Fitch, "A Voyage Perform'd by Mr. Ralph Fitch, Merchant of London ..." in John Harris (ed.), *Navigantium Atque Itinerantium Bibliotheca* (London, 1705), p. 212.

[40] J.H. von Linschoten, *Voyage to the East Indies* (New York, n.d.), II, 88–9; and M.A.P. Meilink-Roelofsz, *Asian Trade and European Influence in the Indonesian Archipelago between 1500 and About 1650* (The Hague), 1962, pp. 69–71.

middle decades of the sixteenth century. However, aside from the city of Martaban which was sacked after a long siege, Mon cities like Pegu and Syriam continued to prosper under the Toungoo monarchs Tabinshwehti and Bayinnaung. A combination of unsuccessful campaigns against Siam, internal strife and invasions from Siam and Arakan in the last decades of the sixteenth century proved disastrous for the urban trading culture of the Mons. Armies from Ava, Prome and Arakan captured Mon cities and levelled them, or sacked them and turned them over to foreign mercenaries like Philip de Brito. Mon rebels and Siamese invaders ravaged Martaban and the Pegu-Sittang river valley. The situation in Lower Burma led to the first waves of Mon migration to Siam. The number of Mons who left or were carried off from Lower Burma cannot be determined, but it was sufficient to serve as the basis of the present-day community of Mons in Thailand.[41]

Over a century and a half before the armies of Alaungpaya, the founder of the Konbaung dynasty, entered Lower Burma, the Mon people had suffered reverses from which they never fully recovered.[42] Although some urban centres, including Pegu, were partially restored in the seventeenth and eighteenth centuries, the surviving Mon population was more dispersed and more agrarian than it had been in the sixteenth century. By the middle of the eighteenth century the Mons had recovered sufficiently to conquer the Burman Kingdom of Ava, then weak from prolonged warfare and internal divisions. However, the rapid rise of Alaungpaya and his successful campaign to expel the Mons from the Dry Zone demonstrated that the recovery was superficial. After the ravages of the late sixteenth century, the Mons had neither the numbers nor the wealth to withstand the Burmans, once the latter were united under an effective leader.

According to the established version of Burmese history in the Konbaung period, the delta homeland of the Mons was devastated during its conquest by the Burmans in the 1750's. In the following century, the area was impoverished and neglected. It was a land "mainly of swamp and jungle"[43] where agricultural production was carried on by only "a few scattered families" who grew rice "in small clearings in the forest."[44] Careful examination of the evidence provided by contemporary travellers and the *Sittans*, however, reveals considerable disagreement as to conditions in various regions and Lower Burma generally. The contrast between the descriptions of the Rangoon-Hlaing river area made by various European travellers provides an excellent illustration of the contradictions found in eighteenth and early nineteenth century accounts. Michael Symes wrote in 1795, that the country along the Rangoon river and surrounding the town of Rangoon was covered with forest and sparsely inhabited, while his companion Buchanan found the Hlaing river region "a succession of grassy plains as far as the eye can see."[45] Hiram Cox, who passed through the Delta in the following year, observed an "extensive plain of paddy grounds" southwest of Rangoon, and found the country along the Hlaing river "well-cultivated."[46] Both Henry Gouger and John Crawfurd, who journeyed through the Rangoon-Hlaing region in the mid-

---

[41] H.G. Wales, *Ancient Siamese Government and Administration*, (London, 1934), p. 64. For an account of the Mon migrations see R. Halliday, *The Talaings* (Rangoon, 1917), pp. 1 & 14–15.

[42] D.G.E. Hall has also seen the late sixteenth century and not the Konbaung period as the time when Lower Burma was most seriously devastated and depopulated. See *A History of South-East Asia* (London, 1964), pp. 362 & 736.

[43] *Ibid.*, p. 736.

[44] Furnivall, *Political Economy*, p. 41.

[45] Symes, *Account of Ava*, I, 323 and II, 112–13; and Buchanan, *Extracts*, p. 31.

[46] *Journal of a Resident in the Burmhan Empire and More Particularly at the Court of Amorapoorah* (London, 1821), pp. 10–11 & 21.

1820's, found it poorly cultivated and thinly inhabited.[47] H.L. Maw who served in Lower Burma in 1824 reported that the area around Rangoon was well-cultivated, and Howard Malcolm who travelled along the Hlaing river in 1835 ,noted extensive cultivation and numerous villages.[48]

The estimates provided by European observers of conditions in the delta area as a whole also differed sharply. Maw claimed that Lower Burma was the granary of the Konbaung empire, while two years later Crawfurd complained that little commerce and agriculture was to be found in the region.[49] Contradictions sometimes appear within the same account. T.A. Trant claimed in one passage that with the exception of three or four towns the Delta had been given over to the "uncontrolled dominion of nature." In earlier portions of his account, however, he told of "innumerable granaries" of rice found in Rangoon and the "great quantities" of the grain which were sent annually to Upper Burma.[50]

A number of factors may account for the contradictory descriptions of conditions in Lower Burma provided by observers in the Konbaung period. Most travellers viewed the area from boats which followed a common route to Upper Burma (see map on p. 185). The accuracy of their impressions could have been impaired by the height of the Irrawaddy river, which fluctuates widely, and by the fact that mangrove swamps fringe most of the waterways in the lower Irrawaddy delta and often obscure extensive cultivation inland.[51] Since all of the travellers who recorded the dates of their passages were in Lower Burma during the monsoon season when cultivation was in progress, their differences cannot be attributed to the seasonal nature of agricultural production. They might have resulted, however, from the fact that shifting cultivation was widely practised in the lower delta during the Konbaung period.[52] This pattern may explain why an area found covered with *kaing* grass or jungle by one observer was said to be well-cultivated by another.

If the limitations of these eye-witness descriptions are taken into account and they are supplemented by the information provided by the *Sittans* and by British officials in the decade after 1852, it is possible to determine which areas of Lower Burma were cultivated in the Konbaung period. A topographical map of the Irrawaddy-Sittang delta region by Ferdinand Fitzroy dated 1862 is the chief source of information available in the early British records.[53] If corrections, based on Konbaung sources, are made to allow for the fact that the map was made ten years after the British annexation,[54] it serves as a fairly accurate gauge of the extent of

---

[47] Gouger, *A Personal Narrative of Two Years Imprisonment in Burma* (London, 1864), p. 17; and Crawfurd, *Journal*, pp. 5–6. Gouger passed through Lower Burma *before* and Crawfurd *after* the first Anglo-Burman war.

[48] Maw, *Memoir of Early Operations of the Burmese War* (London, 1832), p. 82; and Malcolm, *Travels in South-eastern Asia . . .and a Full Account of the Burman Empire* (Boston, 1840), I, 84. Maw arrived *after* the outbreak of the war.

[49] Maw, *Memoir*, pp. 82–5; and Crawfurd, *Journal*, pp. 11–12.

[50] *Two Years in Ava* (London, 1827), pp. 29 & 237.

[51] U Tin Gyi, *Report on the Original Settlement Operations in The Labutta Township of the Myaungmya District 1924–5* (Rangoon, 1926), p. 3; H. Maw, *Memoir*, p. 82; and a map appended to Henry Havelock's *Memoir of Three Campaigns . . . in Ava* (Serampore, 1828).

[52] Crawfurd, *Journal*, pp. 6, 421 & 448; Symes, *Account of Ava*, II, 15–16; and *RAP, 1854–5*, paragraph 26.

[53] India Office Records, Map Department, *Topographical Map of British Burma*, Pegu Division, April 1862.

[54] J.S. Furnivall points out in *Colonial Policy and Practice* (New York, 1956), p. 59, that there was little economic growth in Lower Burma until after 1861, when pacification was finally completed. Therefore, the ten year interval does not seriously affect the map's value as an indicator of conditions in Konbaung times.

Lower Burma in the Konbaung Period.

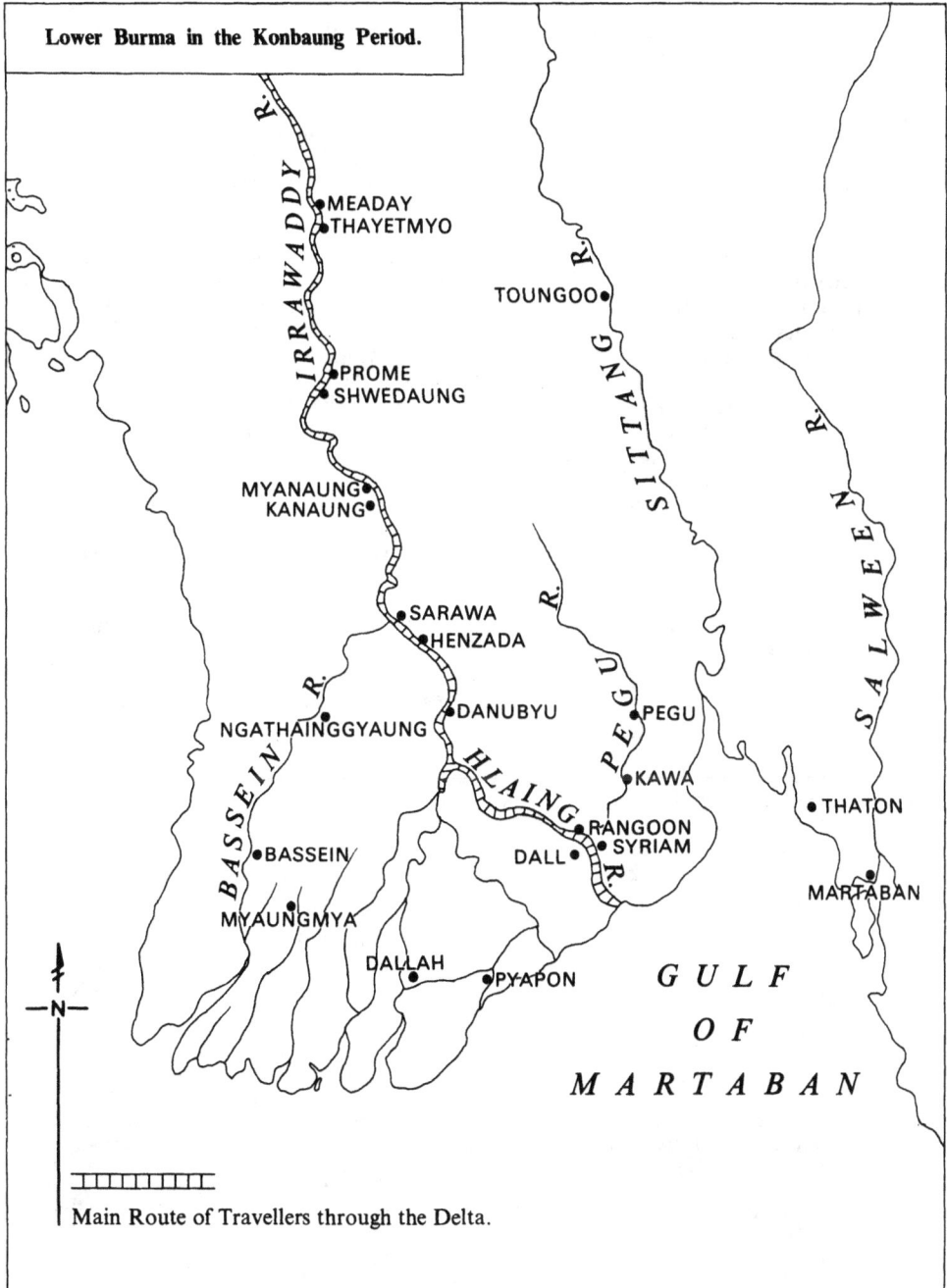

Main Route of Travellers through the Delta.

Source: Based upon H. Yule's Narrative ... (1858).

IX

cultivation in the Konbaung era. There were large concentrations of paddy cultivation around the towns of Bassein, Myaungmya and Ngathainggyaung in the
western portion of the Irrawaddy delta; near the town of Myaunaung, northwest
of Henzada and between Prome and Thayetmyo on the upper Irrawaddy; and
near Pyapon, Dallah, Danubyu and Toungoo in the central and east portions of
Lower Burma. As noted above, the extent of cultivation in the Rangoon and Pegu
areas is difficult to determine. It is probable that considerable numbers of shifting
cultivators were active in these regions, as well as in the lower central delta and in
the area between the Pegu and Hlaing rivers.[55]

A comparison of the Fitzroy Map and travel accounts from the Konbaung
era demonstrates that Lower Burma was more developed prior to 1852 than the
general statements of most writers would lead one to assume. Unfortunately, there
is no record of how extensively each of these tracts was cultivated, nor are there
estimates of how much land was occupied in Lower Burma as a whole. If one
assumes, however, that the area worked in the first years of British rule was roughly
equal to that cropped in the decades before 1852, the extent of cultivation in the
late Konbaung period can be estimated. The most reliable district figures of the
area occupied in the first years of British control were those compiled in 1856-7.
In that year over 662,000 acres of land in the Irrawaddy-Sittang delta region were
listed as cultivated of which 616,000 acres were planted in rice.[56] If corrections
are made for undercounting by indigenous officials,[57] land not yet reoccupied
following the 1852 warfare and land newly abandoned due to local resistance to
British rule, the total area under rice cultivation would have been at least 700,000
to 800,000 acres.

This amount of cultivated area was small compared to that occupied in later
decades. By 1872, 1,146,000 acres were cropped in Lower Burma, and by the mid-
1930's when the area occupied reached its greatest extent, over 8,700,000 acres were
under cultivation.[58] Vast tracts of fertile land on the Henzada-Tharrawaddy plain,
in the Pegu-Sittang river valley and in the lower Irrawaddy delta remained uncultivated in Konbaung times. Areas that were to be highly productive in the
British period were covered with *kaing* grass, scrub or swamp and dense forests
of mangrove and *kanazo*. Owing to the absence of embankments much of Lower
Burma, especially the lower delta, was flooded during the monsoon season and
unfit for habitation for several months of the year.[59]

Most historians, reflecting the attitudes of travellers like Father Sangermano
and John Crawfurd,[60] have asserted that Burman misrule was responsible for the

---

[55] See the Fitzroy Map and H. Cox, *Journal*, pp. 31 & 426–8; J. Crawford, *Journal*, pp. 7,
22, 31, 39 & 334; H. Malcolm, *Travels*, Vol. I, pp. 86 & 90; M. Symes, *Account of Ava*, Vol.
II, pp. 18–19, 27–9, 96–9, 154, 159, 165–6 & 168; and Vol. III, p. 250; H.L. Maw, *Memoir*,
p. 83; and *RAP (1860–1)*, p. 27; and *(1856–7)*, Appendix F.

[56] *RAP (1856–7)*, Appendix F.

[57] Although a far larger portion of the cultivated area was actually measured in 1856–7
than in earlier years, indigenous Burman and Mon officials did most of the counting for
revenue purposes. They felt little loyalty to the British, were unfamiliar with British revenue
concepts and methods, and profited greatly from underreporting and pocketing the difference
between revenue collected and that actually turned over to the new regime. See, for example,
Govt. of India, *Political and Foreign Proceedings*, Range 201, Vol. 63, 8 Aug. 1856, nu. 160;
and H. Matthews, *Report on Settlement Operations in the Bassein and Thongwa Districts
1888–9* (Rangoon, 1890), p. 23.

[58] *Report on the Administration of Burma 1871–2* (hereafter *RAB*), Appendix cix; and
Govt. of Burma, *Season and Crop Report, 1935–6*, Acreage Use Tables.

[59] Robert Gordon, *The Irrawaddy River* (1885), p. 5.

[60] Sangermano, *Burmese Empire*, p. 101; and Crawfurd, *Journal*, pp. 11–12.

underdeveloped state of Lower Burma prior to 1852. G.E. Harvey established this belief when he wrote in 1925, that it was an "indelible stain" on the Burman administration that the fertile region "should have been found by the English to be mainly an uncultivated waste . . ."[61] This explanation not only ignores evidence of Burman efforts to develop Lower Burma, it also obscures the fundamental reasons for the area's limited productivity. During his first visit, Michael Symes praised Bodawpaya's measures to conciliate the Mons, while a number of sources indicate that considerable numbers of Burmans moved into Lower Burma prior to 1852 and brought new lands under cultivation.[62] In the *Sittans*, local officers reported their attempts to develop tracts in the Pegu area and stated that they had been ordered to do so by high-ranking Burman officials.[63]

It can be argued that these positive measures were more than nullified by the frequent wars waged by Burman monarchs and by the Burmans' measures to suppress Mon resistance to their rule. The impact of these factors on Lower Burma's development, however, was minor compared to the dampening effect of a policy which the Konbaung monarchs probably viewed as humane and farsighted, the prohibition of the export of rice from the empire. Rather than export the surplus rice produced in Lower Burma, the Burmans stored it in granaries and used it to supply areas where there was a food shortage or where famine threatened. This store of rice, which comprised most of the revenue which the government received from the delta provinces, was carried annually to Upper Burma by great fleets of river vessels.[64] Although there was a foreign demand for the rice produced in Lower Burma, government restrictions ensured that exports of paddy were practically non-existent. In addition, the limited domestic market was regulated and stabilized by the great quantities held by the government. Consequently, the price of rice was very low in the Konbaung period.[65]

The low return which the cultivator received for the extra labour required to produce a surplus provided little incentive for him to harvest more than he needed for food, seed and taxes. There was no reason for him to bring new areas under cultivation. Even if he were able to harvest a sizable surplus for the market, the cultivator would have little to buy with the bullion he received for his produce. Consumer goods imported into Burma prior to 1852, were limited in quantity and quality and subject to heavy duties.[66] In addition, there were many sumptuary laws in Konbaung society. The type and size of a man's house, the domestic implements he was permitted to use, his clothing and jewelry were all rigidly regulated by his position and social standing.[67] The cultivator was low on the social scale and thus his options as a consumer were very limited.

The absence of market incentives to promote agrarian development was complemented by the obstacles and hazards facing the cultivator who sought to open new lands. Most of the available land in Lower Burma was covered with jungle and swamp. Considerable capital and labour were required to bring this land under cultivation. Because monetary and market systems were poorly developed,

---

[61] *History of Burma*, London, 1967, 236. See also J. Cady, *Modern Burma*, p. 69; and D.G.E. Hall, *Burma* (London, 1950), p. 156.

[62] For Symes, see the *Account of Ava*, II, 166–7. For Burman immigration see the District Gazetteers for Bassein, Henzada and Insein, pp. 25, 18 and 43 respectively.

[63] Furnivall, "Historical Documents" 6/3, pp. 218–9; 8/1, pp. 40, 43, 46 & 49; and 9/1, p. 41.

[64] M. Symes, *Account of Ava*, II, 166–7; and H. Gouger, *Narrative*, pp. 19–20.

[65] See the Comparative prices quoted by Howard Malcolm, *Travels*, I, 75. Wheat, for example, sold for eight times more than rice.

[66] B. Pearn, *Rangoon*, p. 67 and J. Crawford, *Journal*, pp. 428–9 & 439–41.

[67] M. Symes, *Account of Ava*, I, 353–4 and II, 60–2, 189–90 *et passim*.

188

there were few sources of credit in Konbaung times and the rates of interest were high.[68] There was virtually no labour available for hire. In addition, the malarial conditions which prevailed in newly cropped areas severely limited the productivity of the labour which the cultivator could generate from within his own household. Malaria was (and is) endemic to most of Lower Burma. It was particularly intense in those areas which were being settled for the first time. S. Grantham reported in 1920, that colonies attempting to open jungle tracts in the Myaungmya district were debilitated and even wiped out by malaria epidemics. He observed that after an area had been worked for some time the death rate and general malaise of the population declined. He attributed this drop to immunities developed by settlers who survived and a decrease in the number of mosquito vectors.[69] More recent research bears out Grantham's observations. It has been shown that the *Anopheles hyrcanus* mosquito, which is the principal vector in Lower Burma, becomes extremely prolific in areas where forest has recently been cleared. If such areas are in tropical climates, the species has been known to produce serious malarial epidemics.[70] British officers in many Lower Burma districts concurred with Grantham's claim that malarial conditions had greatly hindered efforts to bring fertile tracts into production.[71]

In the British period there was a large and growing demand for rice and an abundance of consumer rewards which could be purchased with the money earned through surplus production. These provided sufficient incentive for cultivators to brave the obstacles which invariably impeded attempts to open new lands. In the Konbaung period governmental economic policies, and not wars or calculated and cruel repression, were primarily responsible for the relatively low level of agrarian development. The ban on rice exports, sumptuary laws, and a low market demand for rice reduced the rewards and thus the incentive for cultivators in Lower Burma to increase their production. Consequently, expansion was limited to the periphery of established concentrations of rice culture, and vast tracts of fertile land remained uncultivated.

Most observers have pointed out that given the fertility of its soil and the reliability of its rainfall, Lower Burma was underpopulated prior to 1852.[72] In the last few decades historians have generally assumed that the Burman-Mon wars and Burman misrule were responsible for the low density of the Delta's population.[73] B.N. Kaul asserted nearly four decades ago, however, that the impact of warfare and Burman reprisals on the population of Lower Burma had been greatly overestimated. It is true that those Mons who were concentrated in the partially restored urban centres of Lower Burma suffered greatly in the Burman-Mon wars. But by the mid-eighteenth century most of the Delta's population lived away from the large towns in small and scattered settlements. Most of these were unaffected by the movements of the relatively small armies of the day whose

[68] U Tun Wai, *Currency and Credit in Burma* (Bombay, 1953), 1.

[69] *Report on Settlement Operations in the Myaungmya District 1916–19* (Rangoon, 1920), p. 19.

[70] M.F. Boyd, *Malariology* (Philadelphia, 1949), I, 316, 433 & 619, and II, p. 815.

[71] *Settlement Reports — Henzada (1900–01)*, p.2; *Pegu (1900–01)*, 2; *Tharrawaddy (1901–2)*, p. 3; and *Pegu (1911–13)*, p. 4.

[72] There were no systematic counts of the population in Lower Burma in the Konbaung period. A comparison of John Crawfurd's estimate in 1826 and British counts in the early 1850's, however, indicates that there were approximately nine hundred thousand to one million inhabitants in the decades prior to 1852. See Crawfurd, *Journal*, p. 464 and *RAP*, *1855–6*, paragraph 234.

[73] G. Harvey, *History*, pp. 235, 241 *et passim*; J.R. Andrus, *Burmese Economic Life* (Stanford, 1948), p. 13; and Cheng Siok-hwa, *Burma Rice Industry*, p. 3.

weapons were rather harmless by contemporary European standards. Since many of the inhabitants of Lower Burma practised shifting cultivation or were fishermen, they could move away from marauding troops or government "recruiting" parties. If these assumptions are correct, the impact of reprisal raids or recruiting campaigns would have been minimal.[74]

A careful examination of the available data also demonstrates that most historians of Burma have greatly exaggerated the numbers of indigenous Mons who migrated from Lower Burma to Siam or were carried off by Burman and Siamese armies in the Konbaung period. Although there are no reliable estimates of the exact numbers of Mons involved, careful scholars like Cheng Siok-hwa picture "mass emigration into Siam" and "vast numbers" being sold into slavery, while D.G.E. Hall refers to the "great exodus" of the Mons.[75] J.S. Furnivall has demonstrated that the earlier estimates, upon which these assertions are presumably based, are gross overstatements. He points out, for instance, that contemporary records list only 10,000 immigrants in Arakan and Tenasserim from Burman territories between 1826 and 1852. Earlier writers, he notes, had calculated that as many as 257,000 persons migrated in this period.[76] It is probable that much of the decrease in the Mon population can be attributed to the Burman policy to suppress the Mon language, rather than to an increase in the Mons' death rate or mass emigration. Since language was the major difference between the two groups,[77] many Mons would have been listed as Burmans once they spoke Burmese. The numbers of Mons who were Burmanized cannot be determined, but by the first decades of British rule the Rangoon district was the only area where Mons were still in the majority. The only other region where they comprised a sizable proportion of the population was in the vicinity of Henzada in the northern delta.[78] It is probable that any decreases in population that Mon migration from Lower Burma prior to 1852 may have caused were more than cancelled out by the influx of Burman immigrants from the Dry Zone.

Some British officials who served in Lower Burma in the first decades after 1852, rejected the notion that warfare and bad government were responsible for the low population density of the area.[79] Arthur Phayre, the first Chief Commissioner, and his subordinates singled out some of the fundamental causes of Lower Burma's underpopulation. Phayre concluded, presumably on the basis of a report made by a Lieutenant Williams in 1855, that high "child" mortality had been the major check to population growth.[80] Contemporary evidence supports this conclusion for Burma's infant mortality rate is currently one of the highest in the world,[81] and it was probably much higher in Konbaung times.

In a special report prepared for Phayre, a Dr. Stewart suggested another factor, malaria, which not only contributed to a high death rate in Konbaung Burma, but also influenced the distribution of population. Stewart referred to malaria as the "great scourge" of Lower Burma and claimed that it was the prime reason

---

[74] Discussion based on B.N. Kaul, *Some Aspects of the Population Problem in Burma* (Unpublished PhD Dissertation, University of London, 1930), pp. 24 & 34–9.

[75] Cheng, *Burma Rice Industry*, p. 3; and Hall, *South-East Asia*, p. 388.

[76] *Colonial Policy*, pp. 59–60.

[77] R. Halliday, *Talaings*, pp. 16–17; and *Burma Census, 1881*, Pt. 1, p. 64.

[78] *RAP, 1856–7*, Appendix W.

[79] Arthur Phayre, *Memorandum on the Sparseness of Population in British Burmah* (Rangoon, 1862), pp. 4–5.

[80] *RAP, 1855–6*, paragraph 236; and Govt. of India, *Political and Foreign Proceedings*, Range 201, Vol. 25, 13 July 1855, No. 95, "Report by Lt. Williams on the Survey of Pegu."

[81] Norton Ginsburg, *Atlas of Economic Development* (Chicago, 1961), p. 66.

190

for the low population of the area.[82] Malaria contributed to high mortality both because of the deaths it caused directly and because it debilitated its victims and weakened their resistance to other diseases.[83] The fever must have taken a particularly heavy toll of Burman migrants from the Dry Zone whose immunities would have been of little use against the plasmodium of the different vectors found in Lower Burma.[84] The inhabitants of Lower Burma tended to cluster in established concentrations where malaria was less likely to be epidemic. They avoided the swamps and forests where whole colonies had been known to be wiped out by disease. Malaria was a prime determinant of settlement patterns in Lower Burma, just as it had been on Java, in Vietnam and in other tropical areas.[85]

In addition to those factors which made for a higher death rate, there were a number of social customs which might have depressed the birth rate in Konbaung times. On the basis of anthropological and demographic research conducted in Upper Burma, June and Manning Nash have discerned three practices which hold down the Burman birth rate because "they delay or withdraw women from the breeding population." These are the late age of marriage, a high percentage of unmarried persons, and the fact that widows and widowers often choose not to remarry. Since illegitimacy is very low in rural Burma, these factors have a significant impact on population growth.[86] Although rural society in Burma has changed considerably since the Konbaung period, it is likely that these familial practices represent traditional norms rather than products of the modernizing process. In this respect the fact that they characterize familial patterns in Upper Burma is particularly significant because social and cultural institutions and practices in the Dry Zones were much less affected by outside influences in the British period than their counterparts in Lower Burma. Therefore, it is very likely that these practices which retard population growth in Burma today retarded it at least among the Burmans and Mons in the Konbaung era.

Because of its dramatic effect, the "before and after" approach to the history of areas colonized by the European powers is extremely attractive to the historian. Narratives of effete dynasties, cruel tyrants, internecine warfare and social unrest make for interesting reading and permit the historian to demonstrate his aptitude for creative writing.[87] They also provide compelling introductions to more mundane discussions of colonial administrative structures and policies, new economic developments and the beginnings of social change. But if uncritically adopted, these narratives which embody the themes of the decadence of the previous kingdom and implicity or explicitly the benefits of colonial rule (pax imperium, schools and hospitals, roads, railways and telegraph lines, etc.) can seriously distort the reality of the pre-conquest situation and in turn seriously impair our ability to understand the impact of European colonial rule.

Critical re-examination of the available sources could conceivably reveal that the pre-conquest situation in an Asian or African kingdom was far worse

---

[82] A. Phayre, *Memorandum*, pp. 7–8.

[83] Ronald Ross, *A Summary of Facts Regarding Malaria* (London, 1930), p. 5.

[84] M. Boyd, *Malariology*, II, 815.

[85] Clifford Geertz, *Agricultural Involution* (Berkeley, 1966), p. 45; and Pierre Gourou, *L'utilisation du Sol en Indochine Francaise* (Paris, 1940), pp. 140 & 165–77.

[86] June and Manning Nash, "Marriage, Family and Population Growth in Upper Burma," *Southwestern Journal of Anthropology* 19/3(1963), pp. 257–66.

[87] Often these narratives seem to serve as a vehicle by which would-be writers of fiction express themselves through historical scholarship. C.V. Wedgwood has been one of the few historians to admit to and analyze the latent literary drives that motivate many historians. See her delightful exchange with Ved Mehta in his *The Fly in the Fly Bottle* (Baltimore, 1965), pp. 164–8.

than historians have hitherto imagined. On the other hand, re-appraisal might uncover instances where the "before and after" dichotomy is completely misleading. Careful research may show that certain societies possessed viable polities, sound social arrangements and economies that were expanding prior to the imposition of colonial rule. It may further demonstrate that the policies of the new European rulers were highly detrimental to indigenous institutions and the welfare of the colonized peoples. It is most probable, however, that new research and re-evaluation will show that the "standard" view of pre-conquest conditions was a blend of error and accuracy. As in the case of Lower Burma, re-examination may reveal that in fact a given area was underdeveloped and sparsely populated compared to its state several decades after the imposition of colonial rule. At the same time, new research may demonstrate that the causes which colonial officials and historians have generally seen as responsible for a region's underdevelopment were only of secondary importance or completely irrelevant. Disease, the vagaries of climate, topography, the lack of market incentives and technological limitations, for example, may have been far more responsible for a region's underdeveloped state than corrupt dynasts or traditional warfare. In addition, the impact of pre-conquest European penetration into Africa and Asia may have been far less important or far different than historians have generally assumed.[88]

As this study of Lower Burma illustrates, the reports of European merchants and travellers, on whom the historian must rely for much of his information relating to pre-conquest conditions, should be carefully evaluated and compared. Attention should be given to the routes they travelled, to plotting the areas they *actually* observed, to the season of their journeys and to the nature of settlement and agricultural production in the areas they describe. The occupations, biases and motivations of these men should also be taken into account.

In assessing conditions in pre-colonial Asian or African kingdoms historians should be wary of imposing rather recently devised Western gauges of political or economic performance. The extent to which a state's economy is monetized or the volume of its exports may say very little about the general condition of its inhabitants. Quantitative measures, such as the rising volume of goods marketed, which are often used by historians to document the "progress" made after colonial conquest may be equally deceptive. To cite an obvious example, the increase in rubber and ivory exported from the Congo after King Leopold of Belgium claimed it as his personal fief in 1884 hardly reflected an increase in the standard of living of the Congolese peoples. Similarly, strong and efficient administration did not necessarily mean that a kingdom's subjects were well ruled. In fact, the general populace was often best off in states where the government's control was loose and intermittent. In Lower Burma, for example, the average villager was fairly well off if he managed to avoid military recruiting parties, avaricious tax collectors and the hungry *Anopheles hyrcanus*. Dynastic squabbles and bloody fratricidal struggles among the elite in the court centres that so dominate the literature on the Konbaung period had little effect on the great majority of the population.

In judging the condition of the general populace it is also misleading to assume that a secular social philosophy geared to progress, increased productivity and innovation is *prima facie* superior to a tradition-oriented *Weltanschauung* stressing

---

[88] On the beginnings of a re-evaluation of the European impact on African or Asian societies see the fine conclusion to Philip Curtin's *The Atlantic Slave Trade: A Census* (Madison, Wisconsin, 1970), pp. 265–73; J.D. Fage, "Slavery and the Slave Trade in the Context of West African History," *Journal of African History* 10/3(1969), pp. 393–404; Sadia Touval, "Treaties, Borders, and the Partition of Africa," *Journal of African History* 7/2(1966), pp. 279–92; Kiwanuka, *op. cit.*; and Mason, *op. cit.*

stasis and social custom. European travellers in the early nineteenth century did not make the sharp distinctions between traditional and modern, or developed and underdeveloped societies which so dominate contemporary thought. Only in this context can one understand the comment of John Crawfurd, who was no admirer of the Konbaung monarchs, that the state of their subjects "might bear a comparison with the peasantry of most European countries."[89] New research and re-appraisal may show that the same was true of the populace of much of the Afro-Asian world. Clearly the historian can no longer accept uncritically views propounded by European conquerors and colonial administrators.

---

[89] *Journal*, p. 469.

X

The Village and State
in Vietnam and Burma:
An Open and Shut Case?

Without question one of the great achievements of social scientists working on southeast Asia in the past three or four decades has been to bring peasant groups fully into history, in most cases for the first time. Important work on peasant societies had been done by colonial officials and ethnologists who were often linked to colonial bureaucracies.[1] But it has only been in the decades since the end of the Second World War that peasant ethnographies and surveys of peasant conditions in particular regions have given way to studies in which the experience of the peasantry has been meaningfully integrated into the analysis of the broader political and socioeconomic history of the peoples of Southeast Asia.[2] Curiously, however, though peasant institutions, beliefs and responses have become the focus of much recent work, at times at the risk of unduly diminishing the roles of supra-village groups and foreign colonizers, rural groups and their cultures have usually been treated as subordinate entities overwhelmed and largely at the mercy of vast and complex global forces. The combination of these forces is familiar. It has become standard fare in works on agrarian change and peasant resistance: bureaucratic centralization, the spread of modern communications networks, the incorporation of local and regional economies into the global market system and the concomitants of this process, intensified economic fluctuations, heightened competition, and the increasing substitution of contractual agreements and monetary transactions for

---

[1]   For an exploration of the nature of thee links see Gérard Leclerc, *Anthropologie et Colonialisme: essai sur l'histoire de l'africanisme* (Pris, 1972), esp. parts one & two. For case studies in Asia, see the essays in T. Asad, *Anthropology and the Colonial Encounter* (London, 1973).

[2]   There were, of course, important exceptions, the works of J. F. Furnivall, Paul Mus and Th. G. Pigeaud come readily to mind.

2 VILLAGE AND STATE IN VIETNAM AND BURMA

personalist, patron-client exchanges of goods and services. In addition to these common forces, peasant societies in Southeast Asia have been buffeted in varying degrees by campaigns of colonial conquest, indigenous resistance movements, global wars between the great powers both East and West, depressions and famines, and struggles for political supremacy that have frequently generated bitter and lengthy civil wars.

Though serious and often successful efforts have been made to understand the impact of these forces from the peasant perspective, agriculturists are invariably seen as caught up in processes that have been generated externally and that they have very little or no ability to control. Peasants respond to economic incentives, resist increased state and elite demands, and revolt when footdragging and avoidance measures no longer effectively shield them from oppression. They are reactive rather than proactive; victims rather than agents. Even when peasants rise in sustained protest, they respond to appeals for support from religious leaders or urban-based intellectuals and political organizers. With rare (and invariably localized) exceptions, they are mobilized, organized and led into battle by non-peasants. In defeat, peasants bear the brunt of repression campaigns; in rare moments of victory, they are squeezed to provide the means to build self-reliant, militarily-potent states in which industrialization and urban populations are given priority.[3] Though this approach reflects to varying degrees the reality of the peasants predicament, it also minimizes the extent to which the peasants are able to determine their own fate. It obscures the ways in which peasant culture and peasant institutions, as well as peasant initiatives, frustrate the designs of the most determined officials and revolutionary leaders, constrict or channel the impact of market forces, and tip the balance against or in favor of elite factions struggling to assert their ascendancy over rivals. Insofar as they have been able to do so, Southeast Asian peasants have influenced the course of the political and socioeconomic history of the societies in which they live not as individuals but as members of groups based upon village residence. Like urban workers and even members of the urban professional classes, ordinary peasants, acting on their own, have had little hope of altering the

---

[3] Perhaps the most striking instance of this outcome has occurred in China where the Communists were brought to power by a revolution based overwhelmingly on peasant support. See, for example, Maurice Meisner, *Mao's China* (New York, 1977), esp. chapter nine.

effects of bureaucratic initiatives or global economic forces. Perhaps even more than workers and certainly more than professionals, it has been rare for peasants to rise to positions of power that might permit them to make a difference as individuals. Though in some time periods and locales, non-cultivating notable families in Southeast Asia have been able to exert considerable influence on the direction of social or economic change at the regional level,[4] cultivators at any level from smallholders to landless laborers have rarely, if ever, exerted such an influence on an individual household or family basis. Thus, the extent to which cultivating groups have been able to modify or channel the economic and political forces that have so profoundly transformed southeast Asian societies in recent centuries has been determined by the nature of the village communities in which they have lived ,and the level of resources and degree of solidarity that village membership has provided in their ongoing struggles with supra-village elite groups.[5]

In view of many questions raised in recent years about the nature, in extreme cases even the existence, of the village community in various parts of Southeast Asia, this village-centric view of the peasants' role in shaping Southeast Asian history is likely to prove problematic to some. But I think that much of the controversy can be obviated, if we first set aside straw men like Marx's rather uninformed caricature of the *Indian* village and similar stereotypes of other village systems propounded by colonial officials with their own administrative agendas rather than actual conditions uppermost. Clive

---

[4]   For a study in which these patterns are explored in considerable depth over an extended time period, see John A. Larkin, *The* Pampangans (Berkeley, 1972).

[5]   As the works of Jeffrey Paige (*Agrarian Revolution*, Berkeley, 1975) and Ann Stoler (*Capitalism and Confrontation in Sumatra's* Plantation Belt, 1870-1979, New Haven, 1985) illustrate cultivators in estate areas have been able to organize and protest on the basis of class-occupational linkages. These movements are, however, extreme expressions of the reactive pattern outlined above. The plantation system sets the socioeconomic context and range of options available, and collective worker demands focus on improving conditions within the existing system. In cases where the workers turn revolutionary and thus pose a threat too the estate system itself, they do so as supporters of larger revolutionary movements, over which they have little control. In Vietnam and elsewhere, sectarian movements have also proven means by which cultivating groups acting collectively have been able to influence political and socioeconomic circumstances. These will be dealt with to some extent in discussion of the case examples below.

4   VILLAGE AND STATE IN VIETNAM AND BURMA

Dewey and more recently Jan Breman have performed this task quite ably.[6] Breman concludes with an observation that, if its implications are pursued, ought to spare us a round of arid exchanges over whether or not the village actually exists. Breman points out that there is no *Asian* village but rather many and very different kinds of rural communities whose organization and physical contours have been shaped by ecological and historical factors. Both of these points are central to my argument. Varying conditions in different parts of southeast Asia produced very different kinds of village communities and these in turn determined both the extent to which cultivating groups could actively influence the course of political and socioeconomic change in the areas they inhabited, and the ways in which peasant groups responded to supra-village forces at different points in time.

Perhaps the best way to both illustrate village differences between regions and analyze their impact on historical outcomes is to contrast two cases of agrarian transformation, Lower Burma and northern Vietnam. Each of these represents an extreme type in terms of village organization and reflects a very different historical experience from the precolonial period through the era dominated by the struggle for decolonization. The divergence between northern Vietnam and Lower Burma in these respects is in fact so stark that one is tempted to anchor comparisons of the two in the dichotomy between "closed corporate" and "open" peasant communities that Eric Wolf first proposed over three decades ago.[7] Though aspects of Wolf's typology inform the comparison that follows, I have attempted to work out a different analytical framework. Rather than the dichotomous contrast that is central to Wolf's formulation, I propose a continuum with the village systems of northern Vietnam and Lower Burma representing, in some periods at least, near polar opposites. Given the

---

[6]   Clive Dewey, "Images of the village community: a study in Anglo-Indian ideology," *Modern Asian Studies* 6/3 (1972), pp. 291-328; and Jan Breman, *The Village on Java and the Early Colonial State* (Rotterdam, 1980) and *The Shattered Image: Construction and Deconstruction of the Village in Colonial Asia* (Amsterdam, 1987).

[7]   In his essay on "Closed Corporate Peasant Communities in MesoAmerica and Central Java," *Southwestern Journal of Anthropology* 13/1 (1957), pp. 1-18. The basic features of Wolf's argument were actually presented in an earlier essay on "Types of Latin American Peasantry: A Preliminary Discussion," *American Anthropologist* 57/4 (1955), pp. 452-71.

great diversity of village systems in Southeast Asia,[8] a continuum of overlapping types not only more accurately reflects the reality of rural organization in the region, it reduces the likelihood that ideal types, in the Weberian sense, will be reified. Whatever Wolf's intentions, the latter is in fact what has often happened when his closed corporate and open village types have been applied to other areas. In addition, however accurately Wolf's types may have represented the reality of village life in the highlands of Mesoamerica or the cash-cropping communities of the lowlands,[9] the open-closed designations often fit poorly with the reality of the experience of the Southeast Asian peasantry. Few village systems in the region, for example, appear to correspond to the closed, corporate type as well as those of northern Vietnam. Yet long before the colonial period, these communities were far less closed to the outside world than their physical make-up would suggest. Their notables and resident scholar-teachers provided important links to the court and bureaucracy, and their household production and purchasing was linked in varying degrees to regional and in some cases international market systems. The village population of the region was also a good deal more geographically mobile than the closed image would suggest, and a good deal less corporate as evidence of social stratification, factional fights and notable machinations indicates. In Lower Burma the contrasting linear and dispersed settlement pattern that predominated in the Kon-baung period had little to do with a greater commitment to market production than was the case in Vietnam. There is in addition some evidence that the hamlets that made up the circles or *taiks* that were the basic administrative units in this era were often made up of kin-linked households that may have migrated together from the Dry Zone.

---

[8]   Here and throughout the essay Southeast Asia refers to lowland, sedentary-cropping areas. If the highland cultures and village patterns are added, the variety of village configurations increases greatly.

[9]   Wolf's inclusion of the village communities of central Java as an example of his closed, corporate type was, of course, based on the evidence then available that was provided mainly by colonial officials like Boeke. Much of what we have learned about the Javanese village in recent decades suggests that major modifications are necessary for the closed, corporate patterns that Boeke and after him Furnivall expounded. See especially the essays by Breman cited above, and Peter Carey, "Waiting for the 'Just King': The Agrarian World of South-Central Java from Giyanti (1755) to the Java War (1825-30)," *Modern Asian Studies* 20/1 (1986), pp. 59-137.

6 VILLAGE AND STATE IN VIETNAM AND BURMA

In the Southeast Asian context, G. W. Skinner's reworking of Wolf's closed and open village types[10] is unhelpful for several reasons. At the theoretical level it obliterates the structural differences that were central to Wolf's formulation and vital to its conceptual payoff. In attempting to apply Skinner's alternative, one finds that peasant communities in Southeast Asia, in contrast to those in China, if Skinner is correct, did not fluctuate on a cyclical basis from closed to open. At least they have not done so in recent centuries. Skinner's fluctuations are closely linked to shifts in dynastic strength, with Chinese villages "opening up" in times of stability and internal peace and closing in when the ruling house declines and social unrest is widespread. Though this pattern may work for short-term periods of crisis, like the last years of the Pacific War, the steady growth of the power and reach of the state, and a concomitant spread of market forces, in most of lowland Southeast Asia has meant that village communities have tended to move in a more linear progression from more "closed" to more "open". They have seldom, even in times of severe distress, had the means to reverse this process, though as I shall argue, communities that began with a stronger corporate sense were sometimes more able to act as a unit in fending off outside threats than villages that were largely the product of administrative initiatives.

As an alternative to the closed/open dichotomy, I propose a continuum of Southeast Asian village types that can be arranged according to the degree to which they exhibit genuine community cohesion and consciousness at one polar extreme and the extent to which they are merely administrative units, artificial constructions of the state at the other. Each pole represents an ideal type rather than an actual village system. But actual village types can be plotted on the continuum between the poles according to the mix of community and administrative characteristics that they exhibit. Except for isolated communities, which are rare in the lowland areas that are the focus of this paper, no village community, no matter how corporate, is likely to be free of state intervention in its affairs and state influence in defining its boundaries or determining resource allocation among its member households. In some of the more homogenous village units that the British colonial regime artificially created in Lower Burma . After 1852, on the other hand, a sense of

---

[10] In his essay on "Chinese Peasants and the Closed Community: An Open and Shut Case," *Comparative Studies in Society and History* 13/3 (1971), pp. 271-81.

community, however weak, did develop, which was most commonly evidenced on feast days or other ceremonial occasions, but was sometimes expressed in political organization and agitation.

After surveying the source materials and research findings that are available for the agrarian history of several regions in Southeast Asia, I have been able to identify a n umber of criteria that social scientists might use in determining where on the continuum suggested above specific village types might be located. Though the list set forth below is by no means exhaustive, in combination these criteria should provide a reasonably reliable gauge of the extent to which different villages are genuinely communal as opposed to administrative units.

Degree of Community Cohesion and Consciousness

1. Character of village leadership: Corporate/elective vs. individual/appointed
2. Strength of village means of providing community welfare/relief
3. Degree to which village member-ship is explicitly recognized and the extent to which the village deals with the state on a collective basis.
4. Strength of village sanctions

5. Strength of the village role in determining land tenure and distribution.

6. Nature and extent of ceremonial coherence and bonding.

Extent to which the Village is a Construction of the State

1. Extent to which village leaders are appointed and removed by the state
2. Degree to which village house-holds are oriented to supra-village patron-client hierarchies
3. The means by which the state collects revenue, administers justice and conscripts troops/ labor at the village level.

4. Degree to which official edicts and regulations are observed within the village
5. Extent to which the state can redistribute village land and impose a generalized system of land tenure
6. Degree to which villagers adhere to the ideologies and cults of

	state legitimization.
7. Extent to which the village is a unit of defense/protest	7. Extent to which supra-village elite groups can mobilize support through patron-client linkages to village households.

Insofar as possible, I have tried to pair each of the characteristics by which the strength of community cohesion versus state control might be tested with regard to village systems in different parts of Southeast Asia. Strength in various aspects of community cohesion tends to be correlated with the relative weakness of parallel forms of state intervention and vice versa, though the correspondence is not invariable. Depending upon the sources available, it may not be possible to gauge strength or weakness in every category, and in some cases alternative gauges may be more relevant than those suggested here. Because very little subjective evidence is available before the post-World War II period, when extensive research has been conducted at the village level, I have tried to avoid criteria that depend heavily upon peasant perceptions. We do, for example, have considerable evidence relating to the ways in which landless residents or outsiders were treated by villagers in central Java or Vietnam. But we cannot gauge with any accuracy the degree to which those same villagers felt a sense of commitment to their fellow villagers or a sense of security that was rooted in village solidarity. Although the gauges must necessarily be applied in a synchronic way to village communities as they existed at given points in time, the continuum can and ought to accommodate a diachronic dimension. As I hope to demonstrate in the case studies that follow, village systems in different regions may fluctuate significantly in degree of community cohesion and extent of state intervention from one time period to the next. Thus, the most useful village profile for purposes of typology and comparison would need to be plotted over several continua representing different stages of the political socioeconomic development of the region in question.

    Although different aspects of each of the criteria for gauging community strength and extent of state control will be explored in some detail in the comparison of Lower Burma and northern Vietnam that follows, a number of general observations may be useful, particularly since the evidence for the case examples selected does not always permit discussion of modes of community interaction and state intervention that have been documented for other areas. To begin with, I have excluded the physical layout of the village from my list of criteria. As Jeremy Kemp has observed in a recent essay,[11] the way a village is arranged physically does not necessarily tell us how its inhabitants interact. Though nucleated villages have often been associated with strong community cohesion, fierce factionalism may deeply divide the households clustered within bamboo or hedgerow walls and invite extensive intervention in village affairs by government agents or regional lords.[12] By contrast, historical evidence relating to the extent to which a village chooses its own leaders, controls its internal affairs, and deals collectively with supra-village elites (criteria 1, 3, 5, 7) is the most readily available and perhaps the surest gauge of village cohesion in the face of state demands. The presence of arrangements for the periodic redistribution of village lands, of lands that are shared and whose use is regulated by leaders representing the community, and intra-village modes of arbitrating land disputes have normally been associated with communities with a strong sense of identity and a considerable capacity to resist the imposition of new tenure arrangements from above. The ability to maintain collective, rather than household, responsibility for revenue payments and corvee obligations has often been associated with strong village solidarity in the face of external claimants. Community strength can also be gauged by the ability of the village to defend itself against the demands of the state through defensive measures ranging from concealment and bribery to collective petitions and demonstrations, as well as its capacity to become a miniature fortress in times of civil unrest and bandit assaults. In testing each of these criteria, however, village patterns have to be checked against the nature and strength of the state systems in which they operate. In some cases, states with considerable capacity to intervene in village affairs find it advantageous to permit a high degree of internal regulation and collusion at the village level.

Modes of community relief and other methods of resource distribution within the village are perhaps the most variable of the indices of village

---

[11]   *Seductive mirage: The Search for the Village Community in Southeast Asia* (Amsterdam, 1987), p. 10.

[12]   The classic study by Oscar Lewis on *Village Life in Northern India* (New York, 1965) provides superb illustrations of these patterns. See especially chapter four.

10   VILLAGE AND STATE IN VIETNAM AND BURMA

cohesion. Village granaries provide the most readily observable evidence of village solidarity, but mutual aid associations for funerals and other ceremonies, village funds for the support of orphans and widows, gleaning privileges granted to the village poor, and access to firewood, housing materials and game in forest reserves suggest the many ways in which villages with strong community identity seek to insure survival for all of their members Times of scarcity and famine often provide graphic tests of the strength of village dependency versus patron-client bonds that extend beyond the village limits.[13] Because until after world War II there were few anthropologists on hand to record which villagers attended what ceremonies, it is often difficult to determine ceremonial coherence in earlier periods with any degree of accuracy.   But the ethnographic accounts and some of the surviving administrative records provide evidence which gives us insights into the extent to which rites of passage and religious rituals were observed in village communities in most lowland areas in Southeast Asia. Protest petitions, millenarian visions, rebel proclamations and police records can help us to understand which legitimizing ideas and rituals were actually accepted by the peasantry. In contrast to European sources, descriptions of village community sanctions from slander and verbal abuse to shunning and witchcraft are surprisingly rare in Southeast Asian historical materials. We can make use of literary sources[14] or interpolate from current anthropological findings,[15] but this criteria for testing community strength is often difficult to apply convincingly for all but the most recent period. In the matter of village ties and regulations with agents of the state, using presentday patterns to establish past practice is a very risky enterprise indeed. The extensive political, communications and economic transformations that most Southeast Asian societies have undergone since the end of World War II render it likely that peasant attitudes towards the

---

[13]   Though as Paul Greenough's study of the 1943-44 famine in Bengal demonstrates in times of extreme crisis all forms of patronage, including family dependencies, can break down. See *Poverty and Misery in Modern Bengal* (Oxford, 1982), esp. Pp. 207-25.

[14]   As James peacock has done so skillfully for the lower classes of urban east Java in his essay on "Anti-Dutch, Anti-Muslim Drama among Surabaya proletarians," *Indonesia* 4/1 (1967), pp. 44-73.

[15]   James Scott's *Weapons of the Weak* (New Haven, 1985) provides the most detailed and sensitive exploration of these patterns we have to date.

village community have altered significantly from those held in the colonial or precolonial eras.

Testing the Typology: A Comparison of Lower Burma and Vietnam

The Precolonial Era

Virtually every account we have confirms that the villages of the lowland areas of northern Vietnam have historically been among the most cohesive peasant communities in Southeast Asia. As the pioneering ethnographies of Gourou and Robequain make clear however,[16] they did not necessarily conform physically to the compact, nucleated settlements that are commonly associated with the "corporate" village type.[17] Depending on the topography of the area in which a village was established, it might be dispersed, as was true of new settlements near the coast, or strung out along canals or creeks or on sandy ridges. Even though the settlements in the flatlands of the Tonkin delta and further south tended to be clustered, the *xà* or village was often made up of several hamlets (*thon*), which could be some distance from each other.[18] In the plains areas, the cluster pattern predominated both in villages that were founded as a result of state colonization efforts and those that developed due to private initiative. Again topography played a role, with households tending to be concentrated on high ground in areas that were liable to flooding, but the exposed nature of the terrain and resulting concerns for security against bandits, warring armies, and, in areas near the coast, pirate raids encouraged cluster settlement. These factors and the need for cooperative labor for diking and irrigation also contributed to the paucity of small clusters of from two to five households and the large proportion of villages with thirty to forty

---

[16] Gourou, *Les Paysans du delta tonkinois: étude de géographie humaine* (Paris, 1965 ed.), pp. 245ff & Plates XVII, XIX; and Robequain, *Le Than Hoá: étude géographique d'une province annamite* (Paris, 1929), vol. 2, pp. 292-3, 475-83.

[17] The image of the nucleated, northern Vietnamese village, contrasted with the linear villages of the southern areas, has been the most elaborately developed by Terry Rambo. See, for example, *A Comparison of Peasant Social Systems of Northern and Southern Vietnam* (Carbondale, Ill., 1973).

[18] Robequain, *Than Hoá*, p. 469.

12   VILLAGE AND STATE IN VIETNAM AND BURMA

households, and some well over one hundred.[19]   Security concerns also accounted for the enclosing bamboo hedges that virtually all observers have regarded as distinctive features of the village in northern Vietnam.   The thickly-planted and thorny hedges which can grow as high as fifteen to twenty feet, have not only protected the village from robbers and potential aggressors, but they have defined, symbolically if not literally, the boundaries of the village world.   Harsh penalties were meted out to villagers or outsiders who dared to cut down parts of the hedge barrier without the permission of the leaders of the community.   Villages involved in rebellious activities were sometimes forced by vengeful state officials to destroy their hedge walls — a measure that was intended to humiliate the community in question.[20]

Within the hedge walls, communities developed that had a strong sense of identity — even though they were socially stratified — and exercised a good deal of control over their internal affairs — but were not completely autonomous.[21]   Whether founded as a result of state colonization efforts or royal apanage grants or due to private initiative, villages in northern Vietnam were run by their own notables. A council, usually consisting of twelve men, was elected by limited suffrage enjoyed by the families with full membership in the village. The council in turn selected a spokesman who represented the village in dealings with outside officials as well as other communities.   The council played a central role in all aspects of village life. It acted as a tribunal to settle disputes between households and punish those who committed crimes or violated village custom. The council's power reached within the village's households in the form of intervention in situations where filial piety was

---

[19]   *Ibid.*, pp. 489-91; and Gourou, *Paysans tonkinois*, p. 226.

[20]   *Ibid.*, pp. 249-50.

[21]   This summary of political life in the Vietnamese village is based upon *ibid.*, pp. 352, 466-70; Gourou, *Paysans tonkinois,* pp. 226, 263-9; Samuel L. Popkin, *The Rational Peasant* (Berkeley, 1979), pp. 92-5, 106-17; Paul Mus, "The Role of the Village in Vietnamese Politics," *Pacific Affairs* 22 (1949), pp. 265-72; and especially the recent PhD thesis by Ngoc-Luu Nguyen, "Peasants, Party and Revolution: the Politics of Agrarian Transformation in northern Vietnam," University of Amsterdam, 1987. As I believe the following discussion will make clear, Ngoc-Luu Nguyen's work, which is heavily based on hitherto inaccessible Vietnamese-language sources, may force major reassessments of our ideas about the nature and workings of the village community in northern Vietnam.

flaunted or the relationship between spouses had become abusive and disruptive. The council was in charge of the periodic allotment of public paddy lands (*cong dien*) that the village controlled as a unit, the arbitration of boundary and water rights disputes between member households, and the maintenance of irrigation works, ponds and the *dinh* or communal meeting-place and ritual center of the village. The council, through its elected spokesman, collected taxes, which were paid on a village rather than household basis, and recruited corvee labor and young men to fill military quotas. Though far from autonomous, the village in northern Vietnam displayed a high degree of independence in political and fiscal matters. Its powerful council of notables, which both regulated village membership and represented the community (in varying degrees) as a whole, exemplified the corporate nature of the peasant community and reflected the minimal role played by the agents of the state in everyday life within the village hedgerows.

By all of the gauges I have suggested above, the northern Vietnamese village displayed a strong sense of community cohesion and identity. As Gourou noted, in the Tonkin delta peasants identified themselves primarily in terms of the village community to which they belonged, not as members of individual households.[22] The status of full membership in the community was recognized by the formal registration of eligible males at the age of eighteen. Registered residents were clearly distinguished from non-registered. The latter were migrants who had recently settled in the village. As outsiders they could not participate in village deliberations, serve on the village council or benefit from the distribution of the public lands. After years, at times generations, of residence, non-registered peasants could earn the right to participate in village councils and to cultivate public lands. But in gaining these rights they also incurred tax and corvee obligations that they were often unwilling or unable to assume.[23] Registered inhabitants not only had the right to claim a share of the public lands of the village that were periodically redistributed, but they were also permitted to participate in the cycle of village fetes and ceremonials that the notables bore the burden of organizing and financing.[24] The council of

---

[22]   *Ibid.,* p. 226.

[23]   Ngoc-Luu, Nguyen, "Agrarian Transformation," pp. 78-9.

[24]   Gourou, *Paysans tonkinois*, p. 270; Popkin, *Rational Peasant*, p. 93; and Neil L. Jamieson, "Multiple Models of Economics and Morality in Vietnam," Unpublished Paper, April, 1987, pp. 10-14.

14   VILLAGE AND STATE IN VIETNAM AND BURMA

notable also organized the cooperative labor that was essential for the maintenance of the dikes and irrigation systems on which agricultural production depended. Though a portion of the public paddy lands was set aside for the support of widows, orphans and the village poor,[25] most non-crisis, intra-village aid appears to have been on a mutual-assistance basis that was organized by sub-groups within the village.

The image of the village pulling together in times of severe crisis is commonly found in the literature on rural conditions in Vietnam. But there appears to be little hard evidence that in fact this happened. On the contrary, recent research suggests that rather pronounced social stratification within the village meant that its high degree of independence and self-regulation worked mainly to the advantage of the notable families who controlled the village council and the best of the village lands.[26] Notable households, which often included retired or active mandarins and soldiers and which usually maintained personal ties to local officials, were exempt from most taxes and corvee and military obligations. If they paid a capitation tax, they did so at a level equal to that of the other registered families in the village — families which normally had far less income. Notable families also laid claim to the use of the best of the village's public lands. In the decades before the French conquest, the expansion of market transactions had considerably increased the value of both public and privately-owned lands. These shifts had spurred the efforts of village notables to buy up land held by other village members and to appropriate and lease out tracts that had been considered part of the public lands. Thus, long before the French conquest, social stratification within the villages of northern Vietnam had intensified and substantial tenant and laboring classes, often including registered household, had developed.

---

[25]   Ngo Vinh Long, "Some Impacts of land Tenure on Social Changes in Vietnam during the French Period," Unpublished Essay, March 1973, p. 3; Ngoc-Luu Nguyen, "Agrarian Transformation," p. 81. Jamieson has argued that the village poor also had gleaning rights that were recognized by the village landowners. "Economics and Morality," pp. 14-15.

[26]   This line of argument has been advanced by a number of scholars. See, for examples, Le Thanh Khoi, Le Vietnam: histoire et civilization (Paris, 1955), esp. pp. 359-61 and Popkin, The Rational Peasant, pp. 98-105. It is supported by many of Ngoc-Luu-Nguyen's recent findings. My discussion is based heavily upon these sources, especially "Agrarian Transformation," pp. 80-89.

Although the villages of northern Vietnam enjoyed a high degree of independence, they were not autonomous in any meaningful sense. The state claimed formal control over all village lands and exercised actual control over portions of the public paddy lands, which could be distributed to local officials, ex-soldiers or court favorites. Officials chosen by the village had to be approved by the state, and the registration of village members was certified by government documents and records. Mandarins, who routinely retired to the village to teach and advise, established stronger links between the village community and the Vietnamese state than existed in China. The state regularly extracted resources from the village in the form of produce, corvee labor and military service. At the local level, village notables often colluded with nearby officials in under-reporting village populations and productivity. They also worked together in projects aimed at gaining control of public paddy lands and other village resources.[27]

The village community as a whole benefitted from measures aimed at depriving the state of revenue. But notable families and their official allies gained far more than ordinary villagers. Thus, the self-governing and cohesive nature of the village communities of pre-colonial Vietnam constricted the wealth and authority of the state in significant ways. But the resources and power that were thereby retained in the village went overwhelmingly to enhance the position of local notables rather than the peasantry as a whole. If as Ngo-Luu Nguyen argues,[28] the village not the state was the real locus of power in precolonial Vietnam, then the notables who controlled the village were the key to whatever influence the peasantry exerted over the direction of political and socioeconomic change in Vietnam. As we have seen, the influence that they exercised very often ran counter to the interests of the village populations as a whole. The limits of state power and the strength of the village notables were repeatedly demonstrated during the reign of the Nguyen dynasty that proved incapable of halting the advance of the French colonizers. Government efforts to compile accurate records on village populations and productivity were frustrated by the collusion of the notables, who were in charge of the census and cadastral survey efforts at the village level, and local officials, who were willing to underreport in return for a

---

[27]   Ngoc-Luu Nguyen, *ibid.*, pp. 83-5, 87-8; Popkin, *The Rational Peasant*, pp. 108-117; Robequain, *Than Hoá*, pp. 356-7.
[28]   *Ibid.*, p. 98.

portion of the resources thereby denied to the state. Nguyen decrees forbidding the sale or alienation of public paddy lands and insisting that they be divided among all registered households in the village community did little to check the landgrabbing alliances between local officials and village notables. Efforts by the court to curb excessive expenditures on ceremonial occasions and prevent the construction of new Buddhist temples, which again were aimed at the well-to-do, appear to have had little effect.[29]

Though the northern Vietnamese village community was certainly capable of closing ranks to defend itself against external threats, particularly in times of severe social unrest, the evidence uncovered thus far leaves open the question of the extent to which it provided the base for rural defense and protest. The growing power of the notables and their steady accumulation of village lands and appropriation of community resources suggests that village sanctions, which some authors have seen as key elements of moral suasion and social leveling at the village level,[30] were increasingly ineffective. The taunts of the *dầu bò* (lit. ox head) and the bad mouthing of village notables for their defiance of customary checks on familial avarice apparently did little to stem the tide of land alienation and income differentiation. Though peasant risings were frequent in the late-eighteenth and early-nineteenth centuries, the evidence available does not indicate the extent to which these were organized on the basis of village communities.[31] In fact, the recent findings of Ngo-Luu Nguyen indicate that hard-pressed peasants frequently resorted to flight in this period and that widespread desertions left numerous villages abandoned and fertile acreage uncultivated.[32] These patterns suggest that peasant communities could disintegrate in the face of growing internal divisions and external crises rather than fall back on their own resources to create miniature fortresses in a hostile world.

---

[29]   *Ibid.*, pp. 85-6, 94-5; Le Than Khoi, *Le Vietnam* (Paris, 1968), pp. 359-60; and Alexander Woodside, *Vietnam and the Chinese Model* (Cambridge, Mass., 1971), pp. 27-8.

[30]   Gourou, *Paysans tonkinois*, pp. 269-70; and Jamieson, "Economics and Morality," pp. 16-17.

[31]   See, for examples, Jean Chesneux, *Le Vietnam* (Paris, 1968), pp. 49ff; Le Thanh Khoi, *Le Vietnam*, pp. 258-2, 296ff; and Thomas Hodgkin, *Vietnam: The Revolutionary Path* (New York, 1981), chapter five & pp. 113-21.

[32]   "Agrarian Transformation," pp. 86-9.

At first glance the villages of Lower Burma in the precolonial era appear to be the very antithesis of the northern Vietnamese community.[33] Though Burmese households in the Irrawaddy delta could be arranged in clusters or dispersed, depending on local topography, they tended to be strung out along ridges and creeks or riverbanks and roadways. Like their Vietnamese counterparts, villages in Lower Burma were often made up of several hamlets or clusters of households. But in the Burmese case, these clusters tended to be widely dispersed and only bound together by their official inclusion in the *taiks* or circles of hamlets which made up the lowest unit of the government hierarchy. The *taiks*, which were administered by headmen called *thugyis*, were in turn grouped into large circles called *myos*, whose chief officials were called *myothugyis*. Though the *thugyis* were responsible for tax collection and corvee recruitment in their jurisdictions, these obligations were levied on a household rather than a community basis. As in Upper Burma, the *thugyis* exercised control only over the non-service or *athi* population in their *taiks*. The obligations of the service units or *ahmù-dàns* were administered by separate officials linked directly to the court by patron-client chains. But in Lower Burma the divisive effects of the mixture of *athi* and *ahmù-dàn* jurisdictions was minimized by the overwhelming preponderance of non-service peasants. There is evidence that the latter lived in kin-linked hamlets in some areas, but despite these ties and their tendency to ethnic homogeneity, the villages of Lower Burma displayed little of the cohesiveness found in northern Vietnam. Physically they were unimpressive. Village walls of any sort were rare, and houses tended to be flimsy structures that were easily abandoned in times of crisis. Shrines to the *nats* and other spirits and the Buddha were much less in evidence, and less imposing than those found in the larger and better integrated settlements in the Dry Zone.

We know little about the extent to which the residents of the hamlets were drawn together in this period by ceremonies and rituals, though Burman

---

[33]   This discussion of the village and its relationship to the state in Lower Burma in the centuries before the British conquest in 1852 is based primarily upon Victor Lieberman, *Burmese Administrative Cycles* (Princeton, 1984), esp. pp. 113-17, 127-30; Daw Mya Sein, *The Administration of Burma* (Rangoon, 1938), chapters 3-5; J. S. Furnivall, *The Political Economy of Burma* (Rangoon, 1957), esp. chapter three; and Michael Adas, *The Burma Delta* (Madison, Wisc., 1974), chapter one. Only additional sources and direct quotations will be cited below.

migrants may have sought to duplicate the cycle of religious celebrations and rites of passage fetes found in the Dry Zone.[34] Though membership in the *ahmù-dàn* units was officially recorded, the population of non-service villages fluctuated continuously and there was no status in Lower Burma comparable to the registered villagers in Vietnam. Though the ruler claimed ownership of all lands, the local hamlet actually regulated the division and use of the cultivated acreage in its vicinity. But because land was so abundant on the delta frontier, in effect tenure was determined by occupation and use. Land was not a market commodity in the pre-British period, but a "free gift of nature." Its use was granted by one household to another on the basis of verbal agreement and personal exchanges. There is no evidence that lands were set aside for community use or regular distribution, nor is there evidence of foundations for community welfare.[35] On the other hand, the abundance of fertile land relative to a sparse population and the ideal climatic conditions in the delta for the cultivation of rice and numerous other crops, meant that there were far fewer village poor to support. As numerous British travelers observed, these conditions also gave the delta region great potential for surplus production for the market. As the British also repeatedly pointed out, this potential was frustrated by measures that represented a rare instance of control exerted by successive Burman states over affairs in Lower Burma, the ban on rice exports overseas and the regular shipment of surplus grain collected in the delta to the Dry zone for storage or distribution to areas afflicted with crop shortages.

Despite the readily apparent differences between the villages of northern Vietnam and Lower Burma, there are at least two similarities that are striking and interrelated: the power of the local gentry and a corresponding weakness on the part of the state to intervene in village affairs. Though the *myothugyis* and *taikthugyis* of Lower Burma played a much less central role in regulating landholding and adjudicating intra-village disputes (though they

---

[34]   These are described in great detail in James G. Scott's (pseudonym Shway Yoe) classic account of *The Burman: his Life and Notions* (London, 1882), which has been revised and supplemented by the major anthropological studies of Melford Spiro, Manning Nash, and E. M. Mendelson.

[35]   The best study of land tenure arrangements in Lower Burma in the precolonial period remains J. S. Furnivall's, "Land as a Free Gift of Nature," in the *Economic Journal* 19 (1909), pp. 552-62.

were responsible for criminal justice in their jurisdictions) and in the everyday life of the peasant community, they enjoyed much the same autonomy vis-a-vis the Burman court and similar opportunities to turn their revenue collection functions into personal profit. *Taikthugyis* routinely underreported the number of households and cultivated acreage in their circles and pocketed as much of the difference as they are able to wrest from the hamlets in their charge. Though collusion among *taikthugyis* and between *taikthugyis* and *myóthugyis* was known, the gentry normally sought to tax and embezzle on an individual household and retainer basis. In Lower Burma where the *myóthugyis'* administrative apparatus was much more modest than in the Dry Zone, it was not difficult for the local gentry to conceal a great deal from their immediate superiors and operate on their own. Though various Burman kings sought to curb or break the power of the gentry, their reforms had as little effect as those of the court in Vietnam. The durability of gentry power in Burma is attested by the fact that families in both Lower Burma and the Dry Zone passed on *thugyi* positions from one generation to another. In some cases succession was maintained for centuries: a time period that was a good deal longer than the life of the dynasties that claimed to be the gentrys' overlords. There were no village walls to delineate symbolically the limits of state power in Lower Burma, and there was a low level of cooperation within the community. But the distance between the seat of state power in the Dry zone and the hamlets of the delta and the weakness of the state's means of administering the non-service elements of the population meant that the influence of the court over affairs in the hamlets was negligible, excepting rare settlements that housed *ahmù-dàn* regiments.

Residents of the non-service hamlets profited from gentry efforts to deprive the state of revenue and services. But they also strove to conceal paddy and household members from local officials. If a *thugyi's* demands became too oppressive, households or whole hamlets could move to the lands of a rival *thugyi*, who was happy to acquire the extra producers, particularly given the shortage of labor in the delta frontier areas. The lack of strong community ties and the rather modest investment in housing and family and village shrines and gravesites made flight to another *thugyi's* jurisdiction or sparsely settled areas beyond the reach of the state the preferred option of disgruntled settlers in the pre-British era. Though the state forbad these unauthorized movements of population, it could do little to prevent them given its very constricted bureaucratic reach and its own agents' stake in allowing such migrations to occur. Though peasant support for rebellions in Lower Burma is recorded, the risings in question almost invariably involved efforts by subjugated Mons or Karens to drive the Burmans from their homelands or by local leaders to extend their power at the expense of dynasties based in the Dry Zone. When peasants opted to confront the gentry or other agents of the state, they did so as members of bandit gangs or (less commonly) as adherents of sectarian movements which found ample refuge in the wilderness that covered much of the lower delta or the hills that fringed it on east and west.

Measured by the gauges for community cohesion versus state control suggested above, the village systems of Vietnam and Lower Burma fall on rather different points on the continuum of possible types. But they are not as far apart as their different physical structures and internal organization would suggest. The weakness of the Burman state, particularly with reference to the delta region, meant that despite their lack of strong community consciousness and cooperation, the hamlets of Lower Burma were far from creations or pawns of the government. Thus, the Vietnamese village would fall near the genuine community pole of the continuum, while the hamlets of Lower Burma could be plotted approximately equidistant from the poles.

In both cases the relative weakness of state intervention in the village was paralleled by the strength of local elite groups vis-a-vis the state. But the similarities shared by the two types are somewhat deceptive because they arose in part out of very different circumstances. A stronger state in Vietnam was thwarted by much more cohesive village communities that were run by notables who exerted far greater control over intra-village affairs than their gentry counterparts in Burma. The much weaker state in Lower Burma did not result in corresponding strength in the village community because of underlying demographic and ecological conditions that worked against strong village cohesion. The sparse population and abundance of open land int he Irrawaddy delta region provided refuge and potent protest options for disgruntled peasants. These made dense, clustered settlement and reliance on the village community for protection and support unnecessary. They also made it difficult for the Burman state to effectively control the non-service population which predominated among the peasantry in the delta. Community became vital to survival in the densely-populated plains of northern Vietnam and this in turn enhanced the power of the notables' families that were able to control the life and resources of the village. Their Burman counterparts were

X

able to get the upper hand in the struggle with the state, but had much less control over the mobile and self-reliant peasants in their charge. These differences constricted the options or opened up opportunities for the European colonizers who moved into each region in the second half of the nineteenth century. They go a long way to explaining the very different experiences of the agrarian classes in the two areas over the past century.

The Colonial Era

As in the precolonial era, a configuration of forces influenced changes in the village communities of northern Vietnam and Lower Burma, and in turn their relations with the more bureaucratized and market-oriented regimes that French and British conquests imposed on the peasantry of the two regions. In northern Vietnam, French options were severely restricted by dense concentrations of population and a corresponding scarcity of open land in most areas. Except on the highland periphery, estate agriculture was out of the question. On the heavily settled plains, the French were intimidated from the outset by the strength of the enclosed village communities. Though much research on local resistance patterns remains to be done,[36] some of the evidence we have suggests that large, hedged villages were often the focus of Vietnamese resistance to French conquest during the decades of the Can Voung movements. French expeditionary forces suffered heavy losses in efforts to capture these fortress-settlements, and French commanders found that the cost in time and labor of uprooting their bamboo hedges in retribution and to insure that they could no longer serve as foci of resistance was prohibitive. The French also tended to overestimate the cohesiveness of the Vietnamese "commune", which many officials viewed somewhat romantically as an autonomous, miniature republic.

Their preference for plantation agriculture and landlordism in the frontier regions of Western Cochinchina suggests that, in contrast to the British in Burma, the French were not inclined to push for an agrarian system based

---

[36]   The best account of this resistance can be found in David Marr, *Vietnamese Anticolonialism* (Berkeley, 1971), chapters two and three. On evidence of villages as centers of resistance, see pp. 55, 57. See also Charles Fourniau, "Les traditions de la lutte nationale au Vietnam: l'insurrection des lettrés (1885-1895)," in Jean Chesneaux et al., *Tradition et révolution au Vietnam* (Paris, 1971), pp. 91-4.

on smallholder proprietors, even if conditions favored it.[37] In northern Vietnam they decidedly did not. Well aware of the deeply entrenched power of the local notables and anxious to reconcile the regional scholar-gentry elite to their conquest, the French were content to allow the villagers to continue to regulate their own affairs. Thus, they made no attempt to reform or alter existing land tenure systems. Throughout the colonial era the council of notables, still elected by the well-to-do families of the village, went on collecting taxes and paying them to the new rulers on a collective basis. The notables also retained the power to administer intra-village justice, recruit corvee labor and distribute public paddy lands, even though the French claimed formal ownership of the latter. Though many writers assume that the tax burden on the peasantry increased sharply in the colonial era,[38] serious comparisons have been rare and rendered dubious by the poor quality of the statistics for both the Nguyen and early colonial periods. It may well be that the colonial regime claimed and believed that it received a good deal more in revenue than the Nguyen and preceding dynasties had been able to collect, but that, like the large, better trained and more thorough British administration in

---

[38]   The standard account of the overall economic impact of French colonialism on Vietnam remains Charles Robequain's *L'évolution économique de l'Indochine française* (Paris, 1939), which I have played off against the relevant sections in Le Thanh Khoi's *Le Vietnam*. Alexander Woodside's *Community and Revolution in Vietnam* (Boston, 1976) has superb sections on the peasantry under colonialism (see esp. chapter four), which I have supplemented with insights and information from Yves Henry's classic *Économie agricole de l'Indochine* (Paris, 1932); Ngoc-Luu Nguyen, "Agrarian Transformation," esp. pp. 98-123; Popkin, *Rational Peasant*, chapter four; and James Scott, *the Moral Economy of the Peasant* (New Haven, 19976). Only additional sources will be cited below.

[38]   See, for examples, Ngo Vinh Long, "Social Changes in Vietnam," *passim.*, pp. 3-4, 24; Popkin, *ibid.*, pp. 142-3. After commenting on the "crushing burden of French taxes on the peasantry, Popkin proceeds to discuss a whole range of factors that very much constricted the amount that the French actually collected. In this case, Scott's arguments about the increasing rigidity of the state's demands under colonialism may be critical to understanding peasant perceptions of exploitation. Nonetheless, we must be careful not to assume that the French, as opposed to their Vietnamese collaborateurs, got what they demanded.

India,[39] it was actually a good deal less efficient than we have assumed. The low degree of control which the French exercised over both regional and village officials until the 1920s suggests that this was the case, as does the fact that records on landholding, population, and productivity were compiled and stored by village and local officials. The fact that French efforts to alter the recruitment of the village headmen and councils in the early 1920s and to introduce village budgets and registration schemes were modified significantly before the decade was out, and abandoned altogether by 1941, also indicates that local elite groups were quite effective in their efforts to retain the considerable degree of autonomy and control over affairs within the village that they had traditionally enjoyed. All of these tendencies were, of course, intensified by growing nationalist challenges to the French, who had from the outset concluded that the cooptation of local elite groups and the low level of cooperation and social interaction between villages favored their efforts to pacify and rule on the cheap. Therefore, it may well be that the infamous array of cesses that the French levied on everything from "heads" and bicycles to salt and betel nuts may have in part arisen from a need to compensate for the incapacity to effectively draw land revenue from the villages of heavily populated areas of northern and central Vietnam.

As had been true in the precolonial era, revenue denied to the state seldom contributed to the improvement of the condition of the agrarian population as a whole. Before the 1920s, the French failure to check the power of the village notables meant that they continued to apportion collective revenue and labor burdens in ways that worked to their own advantage. Whatever gains the French made in tax yields over the Nguyen resulted largely from the notables cooperation with their tax collecting efforts. The notables also continued to buy up or extend their hold over the usage rights to public paddy lands that shrank steadily as a percentage of village-held arable land. Though the majority of the cultivators in most villages retained possession of some land, population growth and the slow demise of village patterns of redistribution left most households with tiny holdings that were not sufficient to support them. By contrast, notable families throughout the northern

---

[39]   For superb introductions to the Indian case, see Clive Dewey, "Patwari and Chaukidar: Subordinate officials and the Reliability of India's Agricultural Statistics," in Dewey and A. G. Hopkins, eds., *The Imperial Impact in Africa and South Asia* (London, 1979); and R. F. Frykenberg, *Guntur District, 1788-1848* (Oxford, 1965).

provinces came to control so much land and labor that their patriarchs could devote themselves to leisure activities like orchid cultivation and the composition of poetry, while their sons set off for the nearby provincial towns in search of intellectual stimulation and the pleasures of the flesh. Hired labor provided by males from households with little land who chose not to migrate to the mines or plantations, as well as women, increasingly tilled the village lands.

The decline of the notables' services to the village was paralleled by the breakdown of the Confucian system, which had undergirded their position in the precolonial era. The failure of the court and provincial scholar-gentry to halt the French advance and their acquiescence to puppet status under the colonizers discredited the old elite in the eyes of intellectuals and peasants alike. From the early twentieth-century onward, French courts, provincial schoolteachers and later revolutionary leaders moved into the countryside to challenge both the mandarin bureaucrats and the village notables.

French measures to reduce the control of the notables at the village level, which began to be introduced in the 1920s, did little to improve the position of poorer households. They worked mainly to the advantage of the provincial officials just above the village level. Many of these bureaucratic middlemen had already formed profitable alliances with the notables in the precolonial period. Taking advantage of French ignorance of or misinformation about local conditions and practices, these links were expanded and made even more lucrative in the period of French control. As the French demands on them increased, the notables became more and more reliant on provincial officials to both frustrate French efforts to compile accurate land and population registers, and to control the increasingly alienated and disgruntled villagers in their charge.

The decreasing effectiveness of village mechanisms for the redistribution of public paddy lands was symptomatic of a general decrease in cooperative support systems that had been so central to community cohesion in the precolonial period. Many poor villagers no longer had sufficient funds to make mutual-aid networks work, village and provincial granaries fell into disrepair, and though they continued to be observed,[40] village ceremonies and

---

[40]   As contemporary accounts by fieldworkers like Gourou and Robequain make clear.

X

celebrations often became sources of intra-village contention rather than group solidarity. The improvements to dikes and irrigation works that writers like Robequain describe at such great length, tended to benefit mainly the notables and officials who controlled much of the best land Production for the market and the export of cash crops increased, but the rice consumption and general nutrition levels of the peasantry as a whole declined alarmingly. For many households, both seasonal and longterm migration became essential to survival. The mines in the highlands, the plantations of Cochinchina and the Pacific, or the docks of port towns like Hanoi provided vital sources of cash. The movement of the rural population of northern Vietnam was extensive, but it was wholly geographical. In the absence of available credit, open lands, or plentiful skilled jobs, there was little chance that the migrants from impoverished rural households could move up the social ladder. They endured the unhealthy conditions and long hours of toil in the mines or on the plantations not out of any hope that they might rise in the world but because without their meager earnings their families in Tonkin or Annam might well go under.[41]

Court-led resistance in Burma at each stage of the British advance was more resolute and direct but just as futile as that in Vietnam. As in Vietnam, in both Upper and Lower Burma, localized resistance in the defense of the dynasty proved far more difficult for the British to put down.[42] Though circle and hamlet leaders played major roles in the resistance in Lower Burma in both the 1850s and 1880s, rebel bands operated from camps deep in the forest rather than attempting to defend the dispersed, open, and highly vulnerable villages of the delta region. Leaders emerging from the gentry may well have drawn their clients into the conflict, but there is no evidence to suggest that the latter were recruited or organized on a village basis. In the wake of the post-1886

[41]   Both Gourou (*Paysans tonkinois*, pp. 214-23) and Robequain (*Thanh Hoá*, pp. 503-9) provide rather detailed contemporary data on varying migration patterns.
[42]   On post-conquest resistance after the 1852 and 1886 annexations, see Michael Adas, "Bandits, Monks, and Pretender Kings: Patterns of Peasant Resistance and Protest in Colonial Burma, 1826-1941," in Robert P. Weller and Scott E. Guggenheim, eds., *Power and Protest in the C ountryside*)Durham, N.C., 1982), pp. 78-88.

disturbances, the British set about imposing their control at the local level.[43] They abolished the indigenous hamlet circle and replaced it with the forced creation of nucleated village settlements patterned after those they had long known in India and had recently encountered in the Dry Zone. They made circle *thugyis*, whose authority had depended largely on their standing with the populations of the hamlets in their charge, into headmen, who were artificial creations, mere functionaries of the state. The headmen were charged with tax collection and keeping the peace at the village level and provided with firearms, policemen and recordskeepers to carry out their assignments. The headmen, who very often used their positions of local power to enrich their own households, rapidly became from the ordinary villagers' point of view the most prominent and disliked agents of the colonial regime.

The rather weak sense of community that had existed in the villages of the delta before the British conquest was further diluted or dissolved altogether in the colonial era by administrative practice and far reaching social and economic change.[44] Taxes were levied and profits reckoned on a household not a village basis. The loose village structure and mobile nature of the population allowed the British to tap the productive potential of the vast tracts of open and fertile delta lands to the fullest. With the power of the notables broken and the absence of the landlord classes and the tight patron-client hierarchies that had frustrated similar schemes in India, the British were able to build an export economy in Lower Burma that was based on the surplus production of smallholder proprietors. Though British policy decisions, a strong market demand for paddy, and the abundance of open land were essential to the emergence of the delta region as the world's foremost exporter of rice, peasant responses to the potential of available lands and market incentives were critical to the success of the colonizers' schemes. Peasants

---

[43]   The best account of these changes can be found in Mya Sein, *Administration of Burma,* chapter seven.

[44]   There were, of course, exceptions, which included some of the large and long-established villages in the upper delta and the settlements of minority groups like the Karens and Shans. The latter were often singled out by revenue officers because of their reputations for community solidarity. This survey of agrarian change in the colonial period is based on Furnivall, *Political Economy;* Adas, *Burma Delta;* and Furnivall, *Colonial Policy and Practice* (New York, 1956 ed.), chapters 2-6; and Cheng Siok-Hwa, *The Rice Industry of Burma* (Kuala Lumpur, 1968).

from the more cohesive villages of the Dry Zone demonstrated a remarkable degree of mobility, independence and initiative after their arrival in Lower Burma. The already migration-prone peasants of the delta itself responded energetically to the potential for material advance that British trade and revenue policy and the frontier situation offered. Movement, by the tens and then hundreds of thousands of households, was both horizontal and vertical.[45] With moneylenders both from India and Burma, backed by British banks and Chettiar networks, providing ready capital for tools, seed, draft animals, and housing, enterprising cultivators (some of them Indian migrants from the crowded districts of Tamilnad and Telengana) were able to lay claim to their own holdings, profit from the steadily rising market demand and price for the sale of surplus paddy, and enjoy the consumer rewards that their labor made it possible to purchase.

Free of community constraints and elite domination and working in a resource abundant situation, where the perils of risk taking were much reduced, the migrant peasant base of the delta economy enjoyed a level of prosperity that is rare in agrarian history, colonial or otherwise. But this prosperity eventually exacted a high price. As long as the market was up and the cultivators' households filling with kerosene lamps, portraits of Queen Victoria and the Kaiser, bicycles and other consumer amenities, the weakness of community bonds did not seem a major issue. But from the early twentieth century, a succession of market slumps, the growing competition for increasingly scarce open land, and the failure of the British to control cultivator indebtedness or check the rise of landlordism brought an end to the economic boom and the perhaps unprecedented bout of peasant consumerism, however modest by bourgeois standards. Economic disappointments and mounting tensions between landlords and the landless laboring classes, whose numbers

---

[45]   Upon initially encountering these patterns, I, like Jan Breman ("Shattered Image," pp. 41-2), was suspicious of British claims about the social mobility of delta society. I too had been working with Indian agriculturists, and peasant mobility on this scale and to this extent struck me as implausible. Months of slogging through revenue and agricultural records convinced me that at least until the early twentieth century , the British had in fact been remarkably successful in creating a smallholder-based economy with great opportunities for "ordinary cultivators." This process also allowed me to discern the factors that made this situation possible. These are discussed at some length in *Burma Delta*, sections one and two.

X

28   VILLAGE AND STATE IN VIETNAM AND BURMA

increased rapidly in this era, drew attention to what the peasantry had given up or failed to develop in their pursuit of market rewards. Many longed for the community cohesion (inflated by nostalgia) that they or their parents had once enjoyed in the Dry Zone or highlands. They bemoaned the lack of community cooperation and mutual support in times of crisis, the fragmentation of villages along ethnic and religious lines, and the unyielding nature of the foreclosures served up by the colonial courts and the debt schedules of the Chettiars. Above all, the Burman majority lamented the decline of their culture that had been so marked in the delta in the decades of British rule. The relatively meager numbers of Buddhist monks and monastic schools and the decline of central religious rituals and festivals and traditional pastimes, such as the *pwes* or theatrical entertainments, in the districts of Lower Burma provided dramatic evidence of the extent to which colonialism was undermining Burmese culture and traditions.

In the colonial era, the majority of the villages of Lower Burma, already weak in community cohesion, were reduced to little more than units of administration. Their leaders were appointed by and served the interests of the state (and, of course, themselves). Households paid taxes separately, competed for agricultural land, loans and higher prices in the marketplace. Village populations were fluid and constantly in flux, especially in the lower delta districts where much of the development occurred in the last decades of the nineteenth century. The precolonial gentry, which had patron-client ties to many of the households of the hamlets in their charge, was supplanted by headmen who were creatures of the colonial state, and increasingly by Indian and Burmese landlords, whose links to their tenants and laborers were contractual and impersonal. In Vietnam, through most of the colonial period the degree of community cohesion was steadily eroded, while the extent of state control in village affairs increased modestly. The increase in the latter had more to do with the growing involvement of provincial scholar-gentry officials and the weakened position of the village notables, particularly after 1921, than more efficient administration on the part of the French overlords. Rivalries between new social groups, such as village schoolteachers and the notables, increasing social stratification in rural areas, and greatly increased migration to and from the villages of northern Vietnam also served to diminish community identity and solidarity. But the Vietnamese village remained far more than an administrative designation that had been imposed from above as was the case in Lower Burma. It was still taxed and governed on a collective basis, and it retained some of its public lands, cooperative projects (particularly in areas relating to irrigation), and systems of mutual-assistance in times of manmade and natural crisis. If the two types of village systems were replotted on the hypothetical continuum, the Vietnamese would fall closer to the center than it had in the precolonial era, largely because of the decline in community cohesion. The villages of Lower Burma would fall much nearer the artificial construction of the state pole than they had in the Kon-baung period.

The relative condition of the peasantry in the two areas suggests that community cohesion does not necessarily make for better living conditions. In terms of diet, access to consumer goods and social mobility, the peasants of Lower Burma were clearly a good deal better off than those in Vietnam, even in the Depression years of economic slump and social unrest. Differences in demography and resource availability had much to do with their higher standards of living, but these had also played critical roles in shaping the village communities in which they lived. Differences in colonial policy had in part been determined by the very different societies and village systems that the British and French conquerors encountered. It is much more difficult to compare the condition of the peasantry in the two regions in terms of cultural vitality and social relations, but in both Burma and Vietnam these declined markedly in the colonial period. Though their standard of living remained higher, Burmese peasants may have found the shocks of the decades of war and depression that began in 1929 more traumatic than the Vietnamese because most of them had few community ties to buffer the blows or compensate for their economic reverses.

As we have seen, the differing labor-land ratios and village structures in Lower Burma and northern Vietnam had resulted in the precolonial era in rather different defensive and protest strategies. If anything, these differences increased in the colonial period. Migration provided a means of alleviating poverty and escaping the harsh exactions of officials or landowners in both areas. But it was much more of an avenue of opportunity in Burma than in Vietnam, where it tended to be reluctantly undertaken in situations where survival was at issue. Few Burmans left their native land, where open lands and jobs were available through all but the last decade of the British era. Tens of thousands of Vietnamese emigrated to areas as distant as Tahiti and New Caledonia in search of a livelihood. Peasant movements *en masse* from villages in Burma were exceptional; in northern Vietnam they occurred with increasing frequency in the last years of Nguyen rule and throughout the French period. Group movements of this sort often indicated that the village or villages affected were disintegrating.[46]

In Burma, the village community rarely provided the basis for protest. With a headman who was an agent of the state rather than a member of the community and its dispersed and open structure, the village itself was not a viable locus of resistance. Though villagers sometimes petitioned regional and provincial officials passing through the areas where they lived, peasants in protest usually left their villages individually or in small groups to join bandit gangs or sectarian movements that were based in the wild hill and forest tracts that bordered on heavily settled areas.[47] In Vietnam, village communities throughout much of the north were still able to ward off the forces of warring contenders from behind their bamboo hedge barriers. Violent protest movements aimed at the overthrow of the colonial state were also often dependent on capturing the support of whole communities, though often this was made possible by assaults upon and the flight of notable families. The Nghe-Tinh soviets were organized on a village basis and the Viet Minh sought to establish their cadres in the villages of the northern plains and thereby supplant local leaders who had cooperated with the French. Once they had established their control over a particular region, the communists carried out their reforms within the existing village structure. Particularly in the early stages of the struggle against the French, many of their measures were designed to restore mutual-assistance schemes and public lands that had traditionally been central to community solidarity. Throughout their long struggles against the French and then the Americans, their base of power remained rooted in the villages of the northern rice plains.[48]

The community cohesion - state construction continuum not only provides an

---

[46]   See, for example, Ngoc-luu Nguyen, "Agrarian Transformation," pp. 84-6, which demonstrates that this pattern was already fairly widespread in the precolonial era.

[47]   Adas, "Resistance in Colonial Burma," pp. 93-105.

[48]   R. Bernard, "L'évolution des sociétés du Delta tonkinois sous l'influence de la guerre," *L'afrique et l'Asie* 27/3 (1954), pp. 42-8; Ngoc-Luu Nguyen, "Agrarian Transformation," chapters 3-5; Huynh Kim Khanh, *Vietnamese Communism 1925-1945* (Ithaca, 1982), esp. pp. 153-9; and Scott, *Moral Economy*, pp. 143-9.

analytical framework capable of encompassing the great variety of village types found in Southeast Asia, it makes it possible to trace changes in those types over time. It underscores the active role that peasants as members of village communities have played historically in determining the limits of state power, the nature and extent of economic transformations, and the success or failure of protest movements. This sort of approach might, for example, act as a corrective to the propensity on the part of historians of the state in Southeast Asia to focus on the strength or weakness of the court and bureaucracy in discussions of local control, rather than the composition and organization of the village communities, which might tell us a good deal about the limits of state power in both the precolonial and colonial eras. Vietnam, where the strongest precololnial state in Southeast Asia exercised only a low level of control and command of resources at the local level, provides a dramatic case in point. In the French period, the entrenched village system in combination with severe demographic and resource constraints, confronted the colonizers with very limited options. Consequently, the French left the system intact, tampered little and largely unsuccessfully with it, and eventually lost out to political rivals who were more successful at penetrating and capturing the village communities of northern Vietnam. In Lower Burma, the weakness of the village community in a situation where there was an abundance of untapped resources left the British far more openings to pursue political and socioeconomic initiatives that insured that the colony would be among the most prosperous and profitable in the empire. In both cases, the focus on the tradeoffs and tensions between the village as a community and the state striving for local control and resource appropriation fixes our attention on the notable or gentry households that appear to have been the main beneficiaries of "strong" village systems and major actors in the ongoing contest between the peasantry and the state.

XI

Colonization, Commercial Agriculture, and the Destruction of the Deltaic Rainforests of British Burma in the Late Nineteenth Century

The Forests of Burma and the Advance of British Imperial Control

Centuries before British merchants and timber entrepreneurs began to cast covetous eyes on the vast and highly variegated forests of the region that makes up the contemporary nation of Burma, the forest products of the area were renowned throughout much of the Southeast Asian segment of the great Asiatic trading network. As early as the fifteenth century, Asian and European travellers commented on the importance of the kingdom of Pegu, which then ruled the coastal areas of the Irrawaddy delta region, as a shipbuilding and ship-exporting center. As the Portuguese traveller, Tomé Pires, observed, this preeminence in ship construction and export was based on an abundance of woods suitable for shipbuilding, especially teak (*Tectona grandis*) and ironwood (*Xylia dolabriformis*), in the forests within and bordering on the kindgom of Pegu. In addition to ships and timber, Burma was known as a major producer of lac, cutch, sandlewood, and other forest products in high demand overseas.[1]

The importance of teak and other forest products in the precolonial era is also indicated by the fact that forests were traditionally declared the property and exclusive preserves of Burmese monarchs. The rulers of the last Burman dynasty, the Konbaungs, went beyond these general claims (that were, of course, difficult to enforce against peasants who lived on the edge of forest areas and shifting cultivators who lived within the forest zones) by reserving to themselves the monopoly over the cutting and sale of teak and other valuable hardwood trees. Because it was Burma's major export in the precolonial period, duties on teak proved a major source of government revenue in the early decades of Konbaung rule.[2] From the 1840s, the farming out of forest areas to British entrepreneurs became a lucrative, but increasingly troublesome, source of revenue both for Burman rulers like Mindon and ministers of state like the Yanaung Mintha who entered into contracts with British merchants mainly for personal gain.[3]

Interest in Burma's forest resources was also to prove one of the fatal links that contributed to a long series of confrontations between the British, based in their expanding Indian Empire to the west and north, and the Burmans, who grew more and more anxious to limit contacts with the assertive British and to restrict their activities within the Konbaung domains. Due to the depletion of the oak forests in England by the end of the eighteenth century, the British grew increasingly concerned to find new sources and kinds of hardwoods for the extensive ship construction that was essential to the maintainence of their global naval supremacy. After unregulated and often highly destructive exploitation of the teak forests of Malabar and other areas on the western coast of India had greatly diminished the already limited supplies of timber in these regions, the British turned to the fabled teak of Burma and Siam which proved ideal for the ship size and design of the day.[4] Though the British desire to harvest teak in the forests of Tenasserim and Martaban had little to do with the outbreak of the first Anglo-Burman war in 1824,[5] within a year after the British annexation of the Tenasserim province in 1826, the superintendent of the Calcutta Botanical Gardens, Dr. Wallich, was sent to study the forests of the area and estimate their potential for teak and hardwood production. After extensive travel in the newly acquired areas. Wallich concluded, "our ceded Provinces are second to no other part of the Honourable Company's possessions with which I am acquainted; in point of timber forests they stand altogether unrivalled."[6]

In the decades that followed, Wallich's hopes for strict government monopolies over and close regulation of the extraction of valuable timbers such as teak, ironwood, and *thengan* (*Hopea odorata*) went unrealized as the deciduous monsoon forests of eastern Tenasserim were opened to unchecked exploitation by private European contractors and their Burmese agents. In the absence of government supervision and in the pursuit of the highest possible profits, these speculators ravaged the Tenasserim forests—overcropping, cutting down young trees, and making no effort to replant the areas which they worked.[7] Having decimated the teak stands of Tenasserim in the 1830s and 1840s, the British timber merchants began to exploit the forests that fringed the Sittang and Salween river valleys, often employing Burmese agents to direct harvest operations in Burman controlled areas. The quarrels between British merchants at Moulmein and Konbaung officials that resulted from the extension of commercial cutting into the Burman domains contributed to the onset of the second Anglo-Burman war and the annexation of the Irrawaddy delta region (Lower Burma) to the Indian Empire in 1852.[8] After 1852, the forests of Lower Burma were thrown open to private companies, which soon sought to extend their operations into the rump Konbaung state in Upper Burma as well. Again in the 1880s, quarrels between Burman officials and British timber merchants, specifically the agents of the Bombay-Burma Trading Corporation, heightened the mounting tensions that led to the final Anglo-Burman War and the British annexation of the remaining portions of the Burman kingdom.[9]

From the 1840s onward, the efforts of concerned British officials to set aside forest reserves and regulate commercial cutting in Burma were concentrated almost exclusively on the evergreen rainforest and deciduous monsoon forest areas where European speculators had centered their activities and forest depletion had been the most severe. After several attempts by British officials assigned to Burma to establish effective safeguards to protect the invaluable forest tracts of the newly acquired province were overruled by their superiors in Calcutta or London or frustrated by the lobbying efforts of merchant groups based in India, major conservation efforts were mounted in Burma as a result of the 1855 memorandum issued by Lord Dalhousie, the Governor-General of India. The memorandum declared all of the teak trees and a number of other species the property of the Government of India and made it a criminal act to cut them without government permission. Dalhousie also called for the establishment of a Forest Department in Burma which began in the 1860s and 1870s to regulate leases to private timber firms, to demarcate permanent forest reserves, to limit the forest areas worked by shifting cultivators whose slash and burn methods of cultivation were viewed as extremely harmful to Burma's forests by British administrators, and to take the first steps necessary to conserve and replenish the province's forest resources. In 1894, as a result of a policy applied to India as a whole, special protected forest tracts were set aside from those that could be worked commercially under government supervision. After 1923 the Forest Department formed a separate ministry in the Government of Burma and employed over two thousand rangers and foresters.[10] The considerable success of British conservation efforts in the areas set aside as reserves is amply demonstrated by a 1956 Food and Agriculture Organization estimate of the United Nations that 39 million ha or nearly 58 percent of the total land area of the modern state of Burma was covered with forests.[11]

While British officials struggled to set aside large areas of the Burma highland and monsoon forests as protected reserves, they adopted a completely opposite policy with regard to the great evergreen monsoon forests of the Irrawaddy delta lowlands that had come under British rule in 1852. From the first months after the British annexation of the area to the Indian Empire, the colonizers pursued policies aimed at bringing this vast area under cultivation with little thought for the forests that covered much of the delta whose depletion was inevitable if their designs were to be realized.

The success of British efforts to transform the Irrawaddy delta wilderness into a productive agricultural zone, is evidenced by the fact that Lower Burma had become the world's greatest rice exporting area by the end of the nineteenth century. This enormous increase in agricultural productivity has diverted scholarly attention from the cost of this transformation in terms of the rain forest and wildlife resources that were lost as "jungles" were cleared to grow rice in great quantities for the market. No mention is made of the destruction of the lowland delta forests in recent studies of British conservation efforts in colonial Burma. Little, if anything, is said of this process in the many works which deal with the agrarian development of the region under British rule—including those that are highly critical of the policies followed by the colonial administration and their social and economic consequences.[12] Only the growing concern in recent decades over the effects of the depletion of the world's tropical rainforests renders an analysis of the deforestation of the Irrawaddy delta (hitherto regarded simply as a side effect of economic growth) a desirable, if not necessary, task. Central to that analysis of the process and consequences of deforestation in a specific region is a more general question relating to alternatives—to the choice between preserving valuable tropical forests or encouraging the spread of cultivation, whether for subsistence or market production.

The Forest Environment of the Irrawaddy Delta Region

Most of the 98,000 square kilometers that the British annexed to the Indian Empire after their victory in the second Anglo-Burman war in 1852 was well watered, lowland terrain that was ideal for agriculture. For millenia the mighty Irrawaddy river had carried rich alluvium from the highlands of south China and the Southeast Asian mainland interior down to the deltaic plains that had in part been formed in the Bay of Bengal by this massive transfer of fertile soil. From the flatlands that were innundated by as much as 330 cm of rainfall per annum in the lower reaches of the delta to the drier, but still well watered, districts of Henzada and Prome to the north, two major types of forest developed. Along the coast and the edges of the lower sections of the nine main branches of the Irrawaddy, as well as fringing the myriad small islands that were formed by *chaungs* or creeks fed by the tides, dense mangrove or *Rhizophora* forests formed. In the brackish waters of the mangrove belt, which played a vital role in the advance and consolidation of the alluvial delta, a wide variety of tree, vine, and plant species thrived. The mangrove forests, in which the dominant trees ranged from twelve to twenty-one meters in height, were a major source of timber for construction, firewood, and charcoal for the inhabitants of the lower delta. In addition, the various species of palm which had adapted to the swamp environment, particularly the *dhani* (*Nipa fruticans*), were used for thatch in house construction.[13]

Inland from the coastal swamps, in the low lying areas that formed the centers of the saucerlike islands of the lower delta and throughout the flat expanse of the upper Irrawaddy plains, evergreen rain forests covered the landscape in the pre-British period. Dominated by *kanazo* trees (*Heritiera fomes*) that sometimes reached a height of over forty-five meters in freshwater areas, these forests, like the mangrove swamps, displayed a wide variety of tree and plant species. Initially the *kanazo* forest areas had been occupied by lower-growing kambala (*Sonneratia dipetala*) trees which were the first major tree species to appear in the new lands formed by the silt deposits laid down by the Irrawaddy river. *Kanazo* forests displayed two main patterns of growth. In areas away from the coast, where tidal waters were less saline, *kanazo* trees grew to their greatest height, but the forest as a whole tended to be less dense. Here the *kanazo* was associated with a wide variety of other trees, ranging from the *pantagama* (*Amoora cuculata*) and khaya

(*Acantus ilicifolius*) to the towering *thabaw* (*Pandanus foetidus*) and the increasingly dominant *myinga* (*Cynametra ramiflora*) at higher elevations. Nearer the coast, where the tidal waters were brackish, the *kanazo* trees were shorter, but grew in thicker stands. Here they were associated with different and fewer tree species, particularly the kambala and mangrove, and a wide variety of palms and bamboo grasses.

These great forests were sources of timber for construction, firewood and charcoal, in addition to thatch and bamboo that were preferred by the Burmese over hardwoods for housebuilding over most of the delta. The forests also provided rattan for roping, bamboos for spears, arrows, and household utensils, resin, gums, camphor and lac, as well as important dietary staples and food supplements. The *kanazo* forests provided a suitable habitat for diverse forms of animal life, ranging from elephants, tigers, and wild buffalo, to snakes and wildfowl.[14]

Those delta areas that were not covered by rain forest or mangrove swamps and had not yet been brought under cultivation were overgrown with tall, thick *kaing* (*Saccharum spontaneum*) or elephant grass. Though it grew to a height of up to three meters, the grass was more easily cleared than *kanazo* forest, and thus *kaing* areas were normally the first to be cultivated in newly settled areas.

The poor quality of statistics available for the pre-British period make it difficult to determine with any degree of accuracy how much land was cultivated or covered with forest or *kaing* grass before the area was transformed into a booming rice export economy in the decades after 1852. The extent of the evergreen rainforests that once covered much of the region is thus unknown, and therefore the ecological consequences of their depletion are difficult to quantify with any precision. The best sources on the condition of the delta in the pre-British period are the accounts of European travelers who passed through Lower Burma on their way to the Konbaung court in Upper Burma in the late eighteenth and early nineteenth century, and a detailed topographical map of Lower Burma that was drawn by Ferdinand Fitzroy in 1862. When combined with information gleaned from the Burmese *sittans*, or revenue inquests, these sources allow us to locate the areas where cultivation was concentrated and make an approximate estimate as to how much land had been brought into agricultural production and how much remained in its wild state at the time of the British annexation. They also make it possible to locate the areas where rainforest growth was concentrated in the Konbaung era.

According to these sources, cultivation in Lower Burma in the decades before 1852 was confined for the most part to areas along the upper Irrawaddy river between and near major towns like Thayetmyo, Prome, and Henzada. Extensive tracts of cultivated land were also reported in the area around Bassein town and north along the Bassein river, in the areas surrounding the towns of Rangoon (though the sources give varying impressions of conditions in this area) and Myaungmya in the lower delta, and around Toungoo town in the Sittang river valley. On the basis of statistics compiled in 1856–57, it is possible to estimate that the total area cultivated in Lower Burma was over 264,000 ha. If cropped lands not listed due to underreporting by Burmese officials (which was widespread in this period) are included, the total cultivated area must have equalled at least 320,000 ha. The rest of the delta region was covered with forests or *kaing* grass plains, and large tracts, especially along the Irrawaddy river, were flooded during the monsoon season due to lack of embankments. These latter tracts were unfit for habitation for several months of the year.[15]

The area covered by evergreen rain forest or mangrove swamp when the British annexed the delta appears to have been a great deal larger than that which had been brought under cultivation. By comparing the Fitzroy map with travelers' accounts, the *Sittans*, and passages from land revenue settlement reports, which were compiled decades after 1852 but commented on the condition of the areas surveyed when they were first settled, the most heavily forested areas of Lower Burma can be identified. Such a comparison indicates that most of the Bassein, Myaungmya, Maubin, and Pyapon districts in the west and central portions of the lower delta were covered with *kanazo* forest inland and mangrove swamps near the coast, though low-lying areas prone to flooding were overgrown by *kaing* grass.[16] A series of special surveys carried out by British officials in 1855 revealed that the area north of Rangoon town along the Panlang creek was overgrown with *kaing* grass with scattered patches of forest. Some decades earlier John Crawfurd had reported that the land away from the river was covered with a "thick" and continuous forest.[17] The southern stretches of the Tharrawaddy district were also covered with thick forest which gave way in places to some cultivation. As one proceeded up the Irrawaddy, alternating stretches of *kaing* grass and thick "jungle" dominated the landscape. Between Rangoon and Pegu town to the northeast along the Pegu river similar conditions prevailed, with dense forests near Rangoon giving way to more cultivated tracts as one approached Pegu.[18]

According to surveys made in 1886–87, after three decades of feverish agrarian expansion, just over 22 percent of the land area of Lower Burma was cultivated or fallow, with the greatest concentration of cropped hectares in the upper delta and in the *kwins* or circles around Rangoon town. In the west and central delta the percentage of cultivated land had fallen to 10 percent. The area set aside for forest reserves, almost all of it deciduous monsoon woodland, equalled about 16 percent of the total land area of Lower Burma. The remainder of the land area of the delta region, some 62 percent, was *kaing* grass plains or *kanazo* and mangrove forest. Using a low estimate that at least one half of this area was covered by *kanazo* forest, or some 31 percent of the total land area of Lower Burma, excluding Toungoo and Thaton which were not listed, then the area that still remained under evergreen rain forest after decades of deforestation and new settlement was approximately three million hectares. If *kanazo* forest areas in Toungoo and Thaton are added and areas not cultivated but forested in the pre-British period are included, the area covered by deltic monsoon forests in the precolonial period would have equalled between 3.5 and four million hectares.[19]

Agrarian Expansion and the Deforestation of the Lowland Evergreen Forests of Burma

In contrast to the concern shown by British officials for the protection and replanting of the deciduous monsoon forests, particularly stands of teak and ironwood, colonial administrators regarded the *kanazo* forests of the Irrawaddy delta plains as impediments: barriers to economic development that must be removed. Parallelling a process that was occurring across the globe, the world market—in this instance a growing, and apparently insatiable, demand for rice—had become the arbiter of land values in colonial Burma. The following description of the area that had suddenly come under British control in 1852 is typical of official attitudes throughout the British period: "[Lower Burma] consist[s] of low lands covered with elephant grass, scrub and red[?] jungle which is waist deep for more than six months in the year, relieved by thicklier [sic] jungle nearer the sea parallel to which a belt of forest trees form a pleasant contrast to the apparently interminable and notorious waste lands."[20] In the British view the presence of so much wilderness or "wasteland" in an area that had long been occupied by Burmans, Mons, and other groups was proof of both the injurious effects of despotic "Asiatic" government, which numerous travellers had depicted at its lurid worst in Burma, and the "slothful" nature of the Burmese peoples who had shown so little initiative in bringing the area into production. As one official wrote in 1855–56: "The difficulty in raising the masses from the sloth of ages, would in any case have been considerable. . . . As the feeling of distrust among the people subsided, the country began to feel the benefit of the change of Government and the machinery having once been set in motion, the improvement has been rapid."[21]

British administrators had little doubt as to what needed to be done. Reflecting a sentiment that was widespread among European leaders and writers in the late-nineteenth century age of high imperialism,[22] they concluded that if the Burmese would not develop their own lands, it was the mission of the more progressive and energetic British to prod them into action and provide the necessary governmental structure, communications network, and market incentives that were seen as essential to economic growth. As Captain McMahon, an early settlement officer, wrote in the 1860s: "We are dealing with a semi-civilized race; we should assist them in advancing themselves; they cannot without our assistance; we should induce them—I go further, we should press them—to accept our system beneficial to advancement; our superiority as a nation warrants us to do this."[23]

Despite the allegedly "slothful" nature of their Burmese subjects, British officials were confident from the first years of their rule in Lower Burma that good government and the suitability of the delta region for the cultivation of a wide range of export crops would soon result in the clearing of forests and the planting of marketable and revenue-producing crops. By 1857, the Governor General of

India, Lord Dalhousie, who had played a major role in the annexation of the delta region to the Indian Empire, noted that the increasing revenues, internal peace (which was in fact far from established at this point), and rising migration into Lower Burma all "bear undeniable testimony to its prosperity and to the vast improvement which the introduction of British Rule, and the efficiency of the administration have effected."[24]

One would, of course, be guilty of the most blatant ex post facto reasoning if he were to judge British officials like Dalhousie and McMahon harshly for their complete disregard of the forests that their agrarian policies had doomed to destruction. Though, due to the benefit of hindsight and our better (but by no means complete) understanding of the social and ecological consequences of forest destruction, we can regret their oversight, it would be absurd to hold them accountable for it. This is all the more true in view of the fact that they were quite correct in seeing the forests as having been a major barrier to the settlement and development of the Irrawaddy delta area in the precolonial era. The great labor involved in clearing the rain forest and lack of incentives, either social or economic, to do so had been key factors discouraging migration to and settlement in Lower Burma before the British period.

The importance of these barriers was especially apparent in the Konbaung era when both the heavily populated and drought prone areas of the Dry Zone of Upper Burma and the sparsely inhabited delta were ruled by the same dynasty. Though the Konbaung monarchs sought to encourage the migration of cultivators to the delta,[25] until the British period the formidable hardships involved in migrating to what the Burmans considered a backward and uncivilized frontier area,[26] and the lack of incentives to do so, had resulted in only a very limited southward flow. In addition to the forests which had to be cleared if the land was to be permanently cultivated, new settlers faced a number of hazards: wild animals which thrived in the forest and *kaing* grass environment; periodic monsoon flooding over large tracts of the delta that were not protected by embankments; decimation by dysentery, malaria, and other diseases endemic to the area, and in the case of malaria epidemic in newly cleared districts; and the onslaughts of insects, wild pigs, deer, crabs, rats, and a multitude of wild birds that delighted in devouring the newly planted crops of migrant settlers.[27] Not only were credit sources, which were essential to agrarian expansion, extremely limited in precolonial Burma, but marketing outlets were stunted by a Konbaung ban on overseas exports and government monopoly control over surplus production, which was mainly shipped to Upper Burma for sale and storage in state granaries designed to relieve periodic crop shortages in the Dry Zone.[28] Konbaung sumptuary laws relating to dress and housing, which greatly restricted the consumer amenities that cultivators might purchase after the sale of their surplus production, also discouraged the extension of cultivation or efforts to improve the productivity of fields already cropped.[29]

To condemn the British for policies that would lead to the destruction of the deltaic rainforests would not only hold them accountable for consequences that the state of contemporary knowledge and awareness could not have allowed them to forsee, it would also obscure the very positive and benign (if paternalistic) thrust of the policies they actually pursued in Lower Burma. As I have argued, the British had long been aware of the ideal conditions the delta provided for agricultural production in terms of the fertility of its soil, the regularity and abundance of its rainfall and riverine water supply, and the quality of its climate. Though motivated in large part by the prospect of increased government revenues, the British also sought to encourage agrarian expansion in Lower Burma to benefit the great majority of their new Burmese subjects, as well as the Indians in the densely populated and famine-prone districts across the Bay of Bengal. Burma's potential as a rice granary that could serve to check famines in India proper was clearly recognized by British officials, as was the possibility of encouraging migration from overpopulated districts in India to the sparsely populated, but potentially highly productive province.[30] Equally important, British officials viewed the vast and rich, but scantily populated, delta region as something of a *tabula rasa*—a frontier zone in which decades of frustrated policies and attempts to create a viable peasant proprietor and market oriented agrarian system in India proper could at last be realized.

In pursuit of these ends, in the 1850s and 1860s British administrators concentrated on introducing systems of land tenure and taxation that would attract peasant migrants to Lower Burma, permit them to gain and hold title to the lands that they cleared from the "wilderness," and at the same time prevent the rise of the sort of landlord class that had so often blocked the effective implementation of their designs for social and economic reforms in rural India.[31] Contrary to our notions about the dominance of laissez-faire principles in government circles in the mid-nineteenth century, British administrators intervened directly and systematically to build a peasant proprietor based, export economy in Lower Burma. Immediately after 1852, they lifted the ban on the export of rice and other products imposed by the Konbaung monarchs, abrogated sumptuary laws, and negotiated an end to Konbaung restrictions on migration from Upper Burma. In the next decades the government financed the building of embankments to prevent flooding over large areas of the delta, and built roads, railways and canals to transport settlers to areas to be opened up to cultivation and carry to the mills and wharves of Rangoon and other port towns the products of these pioneering cultivators' labors. The colonial government also sought to improve port facilities and encourage private steamship lines to extend their services to Burma for both human migrants and export and import goods.[32]

Beyond these measures to build up the overall economic infrastructure of the delta region, the government gave direct assistance to specific groups of needy settlers, attempted to introduce better implements, such as the Malay plough, and supplied water buffalos to cultivators clearing new lands, which the latter contracted to pay for out of the proceeds from the sale of the surplus of their first harvests.[33] Equally remarkably, in the early years of British rule the colonial regime made efforts to avert the growth of a monocrop economy, which in

XI

retrospect has proven one of the greatest liabilities of the colonial era for the new nations of Asia and Africa. Through experimental stations and model farms, the British sought to encourage the cultivation by Burmese peasants of a variety of export crops, including cotton, tobacco, and sugar cane.[34] Unfortunately, their efforts met with little success because the Burmese showed virtually no interest in growing any market crop other than their staple, rice, which thrived in the delta climate and soil. In contrast to many other colonized areas where forced labor or special taxes were required to induce cultivators to produce for the market, in Burma the peasantry willingly and enthusiastically took up the cultivation of rice for the export market. A steadily increasing overseas demand and the influx of cheap consumer goods which the cultivator could purchase with the cash he earned for his surplus production led to the rapid extension of cultivation throughout Lower Burma in the last decades of the nineteenth century. Government land policies which strongly favored the smallholder meant that peasant producers were normally well rewarded for their labors at least in the early decades of British rule.[35]

British land policies and measures to stimulate commercial production in Lower Burma succeeded in attracting large numbers of migrants to the delta from both Upper Burma and India proper. The population of Lower Burma as a whole rose from less than 1,500,000 in 1852 to over 4,000,000 by 1900. This increase was fed by both a high rate of natural increase among the population resident in the delta and a steady flow of Burmese in-migrants and Indian immigrants. At the time of the 1901 census, over 400,000 Burmese migrants were living in the districts of the delta. Though Indian migration to Lower Burma peaked in the first decades of the twentieth century, by 1900 there were nearly 300,000 Indians in the delta region, compared to a few thousand in the Konbaung period. Delta towns, particularly Rangoon where rice milling and marketing and the colonial bureaucracy were centered, also grew rapidly. The land required to house and support this growing population itself meant the clearing and planting of tens of thousands of hectares of rainforest and *kaing* grass plains. As the British had hoped, however, migrants poured into the delta primarily to engage in the production of rice for the world market in order to share the profits that were to be made during the late nineteenth century boom in the rice trade.[36] Dramatic increases in surplus production for the rapidly expanding export market of Lower Burma resulted in deforestation on a much greater scale than subsistence production would have required. Market demand, much more than subsistence needs, doomed the *kanazo* rainforests of the Irrawaddy delta.

Colonial administrators, Indian migrants, and Burmese peasants all became so caught up in the rewarding process of clearing, cropping, marketing, milling, and exporting rice that no one, not even the sharpest critics of British policy in Burma like J. S. Furnivall, gave a thought to the destruction of the great rainforests that was a central consequence of the delta's development. As one administrator observed as early as 1856–57: "The whole population is intent upon increasing the production of their staple cereal—everywhere old neglected arable fields are being

XI

reclaimed and large tracts of virgin soil are for the first time being cleared of the primitive forest."[37] To participants at all levels the forest was seen only as an obstacle. To British officials it was a striking symbol of precolonial backwardness, ignorance, and neglect. Its tranformation into rice paddies was repeatedly cited by colonial administrators as clear proof of the superiority of European over indigenous rule: of the benefits of colonialism and participation in the capitalist, market oriented global economy.

The extension of cultivation proceeded unevenly, affecting different areas at different times, and gathered momentum in the last decades of the nineteenth century.[38] Before 1880, most of the new lands that were brought under cultivation were located in the northern districts of the delta (Prome, Henzada, and Tharrawaddy) and around the towns of Rangoon, Bassein and Pegu which were the most heavily settled areas in the precolonial era. A substantial percentage of the increase in cropped area in this period was due to the reclamation of fallow lands or those that had once been cultivated and were covered only by secondary forest growth rather than true rainforest. In addition, the areas where expansion was concentrated were those that precolonial accounts indicated were overgrown with *kaing* grass or seasonally flooded swamps. The available accounts from the early colonial period also indicate a preference on the part of pioneer settlers for areas other than those occupied by *kanazo* forest which was costly in terms of time and labor to clear.

In the 1880s, and especially the 1890s, there was a decisive shift in the areas where the extension of cultivation was concentrated to the heavily forested districts of the lower, central delta region. In this period the addition of over 1,200,000 hectares of cultivated land in Lower Burma was largely due to the clearing of virgin lands, predominately forest areas, and not to the reclamation of once occupied or fallow tracts. The process of settlement and forest clearance was so swift and complete that settlement officers in the first decades of the twentieth century wrote of the once heavily forested districts of the lower delta that "scarce a tree was to be seen", even on the water's edge where land hungry peasants had cleared the mangrove swamps to plant rice. Only in the southernmost tracts of the Myaungmya district, for example, did any forest remain, and there—as settlement officers recounted with no little satisfaction—"the sound of the pioneer's axe is heard daily as the forests are cleared to prepare for the rice crop."[39] By the first decades of the twentieth century, the *kanazo* forests of the Irrawaddy delta had virtually disappeared. No precise statistics relating to the forests that remained are available (in itself testimony to the lack of government concern for their fate), but an eminent British geographer estimated in the early 1920s that only "several hundreds" of square miles or several hundred thousand hectares were left standing in all of Lower Burma.[40]

Although they fell victim to agrarian expansion, the rainforests that once covered large portions of the delta proved the most resistant of all areas to settlement and required much greater investments of time and labor to bring under cultivation than *kaing* grass plains or formerly occupied areas covered with secondary growth. Normally, settlers opening up new areas, cleared and cultivated less densely vegetated higher ground and *kaing* areas first, even though they were well aware that the soil was much less fertile in these tracts than in the low lying areas that were covered with *kanazo* forest. The brush or *kaing* was burnt off and, in the early years of settlement, the paddy was often broadcast sown, rather than transplanted, because a high yield was not anticipated. When the *kanazo* areas were finally taken on, they were normally flooded for several seasons—in some cases the building of special bunds was required for this task—in order to kill the larger trees by suffocating the aerial roots and to induce root rotting. Trunks and large branches were used for construction or firewood, but roots had to be laboriously hacked out of the ground and hauled from the fields. Frequently, sugar cane rather than paddy was planted in the flooded fields during the first years of cropping. In the lower delta, rice was normally sown broadcast after the tree stumps and roots had been removed, which was at times as long as ten to fifteen years after the land was first cleared. Cultivators switched to transplanting only after the deterioration of the soil, due to the lack of manuring and constant cropping, had begun to seriously affect their output. *Kanazo* tracts did not normally reach full productivity until the seventh or eighth year of cropping in contrast to the *kaing* areas which did so in the third or fourth.[41]

The rather primitive and decidedly uninnovative techniques of forest and *kaing* clearing and paddy cultivation were typical of the process of agrarian development in Lower Burma as a whole. The dramatic growth of the rice-export economy in colonial Burma was based almost wholly on "horizontal" expansion or the extension of cultivation to new lands. Though production was geared to the market rather than subsistence, as it had been primarily oriented in the precolonial era, and paddy was transplanted rather than broadcast sown on a much higher proportion of cultivated area than had been the case in the Konbaung period, in-depth innovations in cropping techniques or agricultural technology were limited to very small numbers of cultivators who adopted new ploughs or introduced new varieties of seeds. When the "open" lands ran out in the early 1900s, all strata of the colonial society paid a heavy price for their failure to experiment and innovate and in most cases their refusal to replenish the soil with fertilizers.[42] The greatest price was paid, however, by the delta rainforests that were sacrificed to provide the new lands that were essential to the continued growth of an economy that was based on constant inputs of land and labor, rather than technological innovation. Assuming that well over three million hectares were covered with *kanazo* forest when the British annexed the delta in 1852, agrarian development in Lower Burma resulted in the deforestation of at least three million hectares of *kanazo* forest alone, plus uncounted hectares of mangrove swamp.

The Consequences of Deforestation in Burma

We have only begun to understand the long term consequences for Burma's ecosystem and that of the entire globe of the deforestation of regions such as the

XI

Irrawaddy delta area. Some of the short term effects, however, are clearly documented, while it is possible to suggest others that are not specifically recorded by colonial recordskeepers simply because they were oblivious to them.

Malarial epidemics were among the most immediate adverse effects of widespread deforestation in Lower Burma. Though malaria was (and is) endemic to most areas of deltaic Burma, it became epidemic in newly cleared areas. Settlement officers reported that entire families and at times whole villages were wiped out attempting to clear and cultivate forested tracts in the lower, central delta. Malaria often debilitated new settlers to the point where they could not work their lands and were thus forced to abandon areas cleared with great effort, or to borrow the money needed to hire laborers and see them through to the time when they had sufficiently recovered their strength to resume work in the fields. For many cultivators the latter option meant the beginning of ever increasing indebtedness and often the loss of their hard won lands to moneylenders or land grabbers. Settlement officers also observed that after an area had been worked for some time the death rate and general malaise of the population declined. They attributed this drop to immunities developed by settlers who survived the initial malarial attacks and a decrease in the number of mosquito vectors as stagnant ponds were drained and brought under cultivation. Recent research bears out their observations, for it has been shown that the *Anopheles hyrcanus* mosquito, which is the principal vector in Lower Burma, becomes extremely prolific in areas where forest has recently been cleared. If such areas are in tropical climates, the species has been known to produce serious malarial epidemics.[43]

The destruction of the delta's forests also meant a loss of the timber, bamboo, palm, and vine derived products that were essential to peasant households and had once been obtained free in the forest areas. Coupled with the government's closure of deciduous monsoon forest areas, the depletion of the *kanazo* woodlands forced cultivators to turn increasingly to market sources for building materials, wood for implements and even firewood. Though this market involvement may have been viewed favorably by colonial officials, it was certainly a factor in the decline in the standard of living of the great mass of Lower Burma's cultivators in the first decades of the twentieth century.[44] In fact, lack of access to the many products once gleaned in the forest was one of the causes of the agrarian unrest that signaled the breakdown of the peasant proprietor based economy in Burma in the last decades of British rule.[45] The destruction of the mangrove forests may also have contributed to the flooding that was recorded in many areas of the lower delta in the 1890s and early 1900s, to the decline of the fishing industry that once flourished in Lower Burma, and to the virtual extinction of thatch making and other handicraft industries (whose decline or disruption in the colonial era has been suggested but not yet fully studied).[46]

Because most of the forest land cleared in the Irrawaddy delta was immediately brought under wet rice cultivation, many of the negative effects of forest destruction that have occured in densely populated areas such as Java, China, and India or in the hilly tracts of monsoon Asia were not significant in Lower Burma. The cultivation of wet rice meant that most of the area cleared for agriculture was protected by water cover for much of the year. It also meant that nutrients carried by the Irrawaddy and Sittang rivers to the delta lowlands were supplied to cultivated areas on a regular basis,[47] except in areas where embankments designed to prevent flooding also blocked nutrient bearing river waters from reaching the fields. It can be argued that the sharp decline in soil fertility recorded after decades of cultivation in tracts not irrigated by river water was one of the most serious adverse effects of the manner in which Lower Burma was brought into agricultural production. Like forest clearing, poorly designed embankment and irrigation systems can lead to rapid soil deterioration in the tropics. Embankments and water cover, however, protected the areas cleared of forest from leaching and, ultimately, from the widespread laterization that has occurred in similar tropical lowland environments where extensive forest clearing and lack of water cover has forced the abandonment of densely populated centers of civilization.[48]

The uniformly flat nature of the delta plains and the continuous cultivation of most areas cleared of *kanazo* forests meant that soil erosion was not a serious consequence of woodland destruction in Lower Burma, as it has been in Java, India, and China. Though forest clearing in Lower Burma may have contributed to severe drought and famine which struck the Dry Zone in Upper Burma in the late 1890s[49], and over a larger period to the gradual expansion of the Dry Zone area, little definite evidence of a connection between these processes has been produced to date. The destruction of the *kanazo* forest, however, certainly had a devastating effect on the wildlife of Lower Burma since the habitat of large mammals—such as tigers and elephants—and smaller animals, as well as insects, was destroyed by fire and axe as the delta was brought under cultivation.

The consequences of forest clearing in terms of plant life were, if anything, even more devastating. As many writers have observed,[50] tropical rainforests are the richest and most complex of all ecological zones in terms of their plant life. Though the forests of Lower Burma contain fewer species than areas further to the south in Malaya and Indonesia, they still nurture a great variety of plant species, some of which are found in few other areas of the globe. For example, British botanists have estimated that the evergreen rainforests of Lower Burma contained as many as 300 to 350 tree species within 26 square kilometers.[51] As Longman and Jenik have argued, in terms of total organic matter or biomass generated and the net primary production of plant life, no type of vegetation system is superior to evergreen rainforests of the kind that were destroyed in the Irrawaddy delta.[52] As in other areas of Southeast Asia, Africa, and Latin America, the destruction of these great forests foreclosed important resource options that might have proven highly beneficial to man. The preservation and wise use of their rare and delicate plant life could contribute significantly to the development of new drugs and medicines, ecologically safe pesticides, and a wide range of chemical compounds useful to man.[53] The depletion of the forests also means a loss of valuable woods and timber that, if conserved and cropped judiciously, could provide vital materials for construction, paper, furnishings, and tools.[54] In addition, rainforests contain potential sources of human food and animal fodder—including leaf protein that may prove decisive in the struggle to support the exploding population that the global environment has been forced to carry as a result of demographic processes that have occurred within a rather restricted span of time.[55]

As P. W. Richards has so eloquently argued, the most far-reaching impact of the depletion of tropical forests such as those destroyed in Lower Burma will be upon the process of plant evolution itself. His conclusions merit lengthy citation:

> The rain-forest flora with its immense wealth of species belonging to thousands of genera and scores of families has acted in the past as a resevoir of genetical diversity and potential variability. During at least the more recent epochs in the earth's history it has been a centre of evolutionary activity from which the rest of the world's flora has been recruited.... The tropical forest has thus played a part different from that of the other plant formations.... This role, of a source of supply of genetical material for evolution and of new forms of plant life, the tropical rain forest will play no longer, or only in a much diminished degree. The area of the rain forest itself has been so much reduced and the adjacent formations which served as the path of plant migration from the wet tropics to other regions have been so much modified or destroyed, that the invasion of the subtropical and temperate regions by plant lineages evolved originally in the topics must, if it has not already ceased completely, become of small importance. It is therefore likely that the destruction of the Tropical Rain Forest accomplished during the past 100 years has changed fundamentally the future course of plant evolution and closed many avenues of evolutionary development.[56]

The other long term effects of deforestation in Lower Burma on the global environment in terms of shifts in rainfall, wind currents, temperature, and the oxygen-CO_2 cycle are more difficult to quantify, or even describe with precision, since virtually no records relating to these vital processes are available. It should be kept in mind, however, that the process of agrarian expansion and the development of a rice export economy that I have described for Lower Burma was also occurring in roughly the same time period in both the central valley of the Menam Chao Phraya river in Thailand and the Mekong delta region of Vietnam.[57] Though the evidence provided by Lucien Hanks and others[58] indicates that in Thailand, at least, rice cultivation was extended mainly at the expense of grassy plains rather than rain forests, the ecological consequences of forest clearing in Lower Burma must be multiplied to take into account the impact of agrarian expansion in mainland Southeast Asia as a whole.

In all three cases deforestation occurred so that food crops could be grown, and any discussion of the impact of forest clearing must be set against the gains in food production that resulted from the great expansion in cultivated area in this period. Forests were cut down, but hungry people in North Vietnam and Upper Burma, and as far away as India and China benefited from the bounty of the rice granaries that were created where the forests once stood. Burma then, and mainland Southeast Asia as a whole, provide cases of economic development that raise

XI

interesting ethical and environmental questions pitting food supplies against forest reserves—questions that need to be seriously considered. On the basis of hindsight one can wish that those who shaped colonial policy in Burma or in other forested areas might have developed ways to both preserve large portions of the forest and encourage rice cultivation. To expect them to have seen these options or to know how to handle them, however, would be, as I have argued, to resort to the worst sort of ex post facto judgement. This is especially the case because over a century later little of this sort of accommodation of forest and cropped areas has been successfully attained anywhere and the methods for doing so are still in the experimental stages.

Notes

1. Tomé Pires, *Suma Oriental* (London: 1944), vol. 1, pp. 17, 97–98, 195; vol. 2, p. 98. For a general discussion of the position of Pegu in Asian trade, see M. A. P. Meilink-Roelofsz, *Asian Trade and European Influence in the Indonesian Archipelago between 1500 and about 1630* (The Hague: 1962), pp. 69–70, 87–88, 103, 109.

2. E. P. Stebbing, *The Forests of British India* (London: 1922), pp. 65, 206, 244; William J. Koenig, "The Early Kòn-baung Dynasty, 1792–1819: A Study of Politics, Administration and Social Organization in Burma" (Ph.D. dissertation, University of London: 1978), p. 135.

3. Charles Lee Keeton III, *King Thebaw and the Ecological Rape of Burma* (Delhi: 1974), chapters 2, 3, 7.

4. E. Stebbing, *Forests of India*, pp. 62, 63, 65, 136, 160; and John Nisbet, *Burma under British Rule and Before* (London: 1901), vol. 2, p. 47. On the chronic problem of finding wood suitable for the ships of the Royal Navy see Robert G. Albion, *Forests and Sea Power: The Timber Problem of the Royal Navy, 1652–1862* (Cambridge, Mass: 1926), especially pp. 366–69 on India as a source of wood, and Ronald L. Pollitt, "Wooden Walls: English Seapower and the World's Forests," *Journal of Forest History* 15 (1971): 6–15.

5. On the origins of the war from different perspectives see, Maung Htin Aung, *The Stricken Peacock: Anglo-Burmese Relations, 1752–1948* (The Hague: 1965) and D. G. E. Hall, *A History of South-East Asia* (London: 1964), chapter 31.

6. Quoted in E. Stebbing, *Forests of India*, p. 135. See also R. Albion, *Forests and Sea Power*, pp. 35–36.

7. Ibid., pp. 66–67, 140ff.

8. Ibid., p. 244; and Oliver B. Pollack, *Empires in Collision: Anglo-Burmese Relations in the Mid-Nineteenth Century* (Westport, Conn.: 1979), chapters 2 and 3.

9. C. Keeton, *King Thebaw*, chapters 7 and 8.

10. E. Stebbing, *Forests of India*, chapters 13, 14, 20; J. Nisbet, *British Burma*, vol. 2, pp. 47–60; and J. R. Andrus, *Burmese Economic Life* (Stanford: 1947), pp. 98–102.

11. Food and Agriculture Organization of the United Nations, *Forest Resources in Asia and the Far Eastern Region* (Rome: 1976), pp. 40–41.

12. See, for example, J. S. Furnivall, *An Introduction to the Political Economy of Burma* (Rangoon: 1957); Cheng Siok-Hwa, *The Rice Industry of Burma, 1852–1940* (Kuala Lumpur-Singapore: 1968); or Michael Adas, *The Burma Delta: Economic Development and Social Change on an Asian Rice Frontier* (Madison: 1974).

13. Robert Gorden, *The Irrawaddy River* (London: 1885), p. 5; L. D. Stamp, "The Irrawaddy River," *Geographical Journal* 95 (1940): 34–35; K. E. Bruen, "The Agricultural Geography of the Irrawaddy River with Special Reference to Rice" (Ph.D. dissertation, University of London, 1939), pp. 1–4, 20–26, 33–38; Stebbing, *Forests of India*, p. 56; L. D. Stamp, "The Aerial Survey of the Irrawaddy Delta Forests," *Journal of Ecology* 13/2 (1925): 263, 265–67; and C. A. Fisher, *South-East Asia* (London: 1964), pp. 47–48.

14. Stebbing, *Forests of India*, pp. 42–43; Fisher, *South-East Asia*, pp. 45–46; P. W. Richards, *The Tropical Rain Forest: An Ecological Study* (Cambridge: 1952), pp. 329–31; and Stamp, "Survey", pp. 262, 266–69. The most complete accounts of forest life in Burma are included in L. D. Stamp, *Vegetation of Burma* (Calcutta: 1925), especially pp. 39–41 on the *kanazo* and mangrove forests; and S. Kurz, *Forest Flora of British Burma* (Calcutta; 1877), 2 vols., especially vol. 1, pp. 28–30.

15. The Fitzroy map is in the India Office Records map collection, no. A. 1. (4), Burma—India Office, London, England. See also R. Gordon, *Irrawaddy River*, p. 5; Michael Adas, "Agrarian Development and the Plural Society in Lower Burma, 1852–1941" (Ph.D. dissertation, University of Wisconsin, 1971), pp. 37–39; Government of Burma, "Report on the Administration of Pegu," India Office Records, *Secret and Political Correspondence*, 1858; and William J. Koenig and Frank N. Trager, eds., *Burmese Sit-tans, 1764–1826* (Tucson, Arizona: 1979).

16. B. N. Kaul, "Some Aspects of the Population Problem in Burma" (Ph.D. dissertation, University of London, 1930) p. 27; Government of Burma, *Insein District Gazetteer*, p. 60; T. A.

XI

194

Trant, *Two Years in Ava* (London: 1827), pp. 234–37; Michael Symes, *An Account of an Embassy to the Kingdom of Ava. . . .* (London, 1800), vol. 2, pp. 15–16, 77–79, 96–97, 113 et passim; H. L. Maw, *Memoir of the Early Operations of the Burmese War* (London, 1832), p. 82; Hiram Cox, *Journal of a Resident in the Burmhan Empire* (London, 1821), pp. 10–11, 427–28; 430; John Crawfurd, *Journal of an Embassy. . . .* (London: 1829), pp. 5, 10 et passim; Government of Burma, *Settlement Reports—Ma-ubin, 1925–8*, pp. 14–15; *Bassein-Thongwa, 1888–9*, p. 23.

17. J. Crawford, *Journal*, p. 10.

18. Government of India, *Political and Foreign Proceedings*, Range 201, vol. 25 (13 July 1855), nos. 96–100.

19. Government of Burma, *Revenue and Agriculture Proceedings*, vol. 2887 (April 1887), no. 5.

20. Government of India, *Foreign Proceedings (Revenue)*, Range 205, vol. 30 (October 1861), no. 19. A similar view was expressed over seventy years later. See, *Ma-ubin Settlement Report*, p. 15.

21. *Report on Pegu, 1855–6*, paragraph 267.

22. Arthur Girault, *Principes de colonisation et de législation coloniale* (Paris: 1895), pp. 29–31; and Benjamin Kidd, *The Control of the Tropics* (London: 1894), pp. 316, 324.

23. Government of India, *Foreign Proceedings (Revenue)*, Range 205, vol. 39 (January 1865), no. 12.

24. *Ibid., Political and Foreign Proceedings*, Range 203, vol. 13 (December 1857), no. 255.

25. Arthur Phayre, *History of Burma* (London: 1885), pp. 155–57; Government of Burma, *Syriam District Gazetteer* (Rangoon: 1914), p. 25; and *Bassein District Gazetteer* (Rangoon: 1916), p. 18.

26. For numerous expressions of these attitudes see Maung Htin Aung, *Epistles Written on the Eve of the Anglo-Burmese Wars* (The Hague, 1968).

27. R. Gordon, *Irrawaddy River*, p. 5; C. C. Ghosh, *Insect Pests of Burma* (Rangoon: 1940), pp. 53, 58, 59, 60, 67–68; and Government of Burma, *Settlement Reports—Myaungmya, 1916–19*, p. 26; *Thaton, 1897–98*, pp. 7–8; *Pegu, 1900–1901*, p. 5; and *Pyapon, 1921–22*, pp. 15, 18.

28. M. Symes, *Account*, vol. 2, pp. 166–67; and H. Maw, *Memoir*, pp. 83–84.

29. Symes, *ibid.*, vol. 1, pp. 353–54; vol. 2, pp. 60–62, 189–90.

30. Henry Bell, *An Account of the Burma Empire* (Calcutta: 1852), vol. 2, p. 57; and William Franklin, *Tracts, Political, Geographical, and Commercial on the Dominions of Ava. . . .* (London, 1911), p. 31.

31. For several excellent studies of this process see the essays on India in the British period in R. E. Frykenberg, ed., *Land Control and Social Structure in Indian History* (Madison: 1969). For British policy in Burma see Government of India, *Foreign Proceedings (General)*, Range 205, vol. 10, no. 59; and *Political and Foreign Proceedings*, Range 201, vol. 21, no. 165.

32. M. Adas, *Burma Delta*, pp. 28–38.

33. Government of Burma, *Secret and Political Correspondence*, Range 28, vol. 66, no. 642; Range 29, vol. 32, no. 297; Range 30, vol. 110, no. 537.

34. Government of India, *Political and Foreign Proceedings*, Range 200, vol. 1, nos. 119, 128–30; vol. 60, nos. 136–38; and *Report on Pegu, 1859–60*, p. 32; *1860–61*, p. 26.

35. *Report on the Administration of the Province of Burma, 1861–62* (Rangoon: 1863), pp. 15, 33.

36. For detailed discussions of these demographic and market trends see M. Adas, *Burma Delta*, chapters 1, 2, and 4; and Cheng Siok-hwa, *Rice Industry*, chapters 3 and 8.

37. *Report on Pegu, 1856–7*, paragraph 66.

38. This account of the expansion of cultivation in different periods is based on M. Adas, "Agrarian Development," pp. 145–53.

39. Government of Burma, *Settlement Reports—Myaungmya-Thongwa, 1902–3*, pp. 1–2; *Ma-ubin, 1925–8*, p. 15; K. Bruen, "Agricultural Geography," p. 37; and J. W. Grant, *The Rice Crop in Burma* (Rangoon: 1932), p. 3.

40. L. Stamp, *Vegetation of Burma*, p. 41.

41. Government of Burma, *Settlement Reports—Thongwa, 1890–91*, p. 5; *Myaungmya-Thongwa, 1902–3*, p. 5; *Pyapon, 1921–2*, p. 18; and *Myaungmya, 1924–5*, pp. 1–2.

42. M. Adas, *Burma Delta*, chapter 6 and conclusions.

43. Government of Burma, *Settlement Reports—Myaungmya, 1916–19*, p. 19; *Henzada, 1900–1901*, p. 2; *Pegu, 1900–1901*, p. 2; and M. F. Boyd, *Malariology* (Philadelphia, 1949), vol. 1, pp. 316, 433, 619; vol. 2, p. 815.

44. M. Adas, *Burma Delta*, chapter 6.

45. Government of Burma, *The Origin and Causes of the Burma Rebellion (1930–32)* (Rangoon, 1934), p. 16.

46. For preliminary observations on many of these critical themes see Aye Hlaing, "Trends of Economic Growth and Income Distribution in Burma, 1870–1940," *Journal of the Burma Research Society* 47/1 (June 1964): 89–148.

47. Pierre Gourou, *The Tropical World* (London: 1953), p. 100ff.

48. David Hendry, *Fertilizers for Paddy* (Rangoon: 1929), pp. 1–2, 11–12; and Government of Burma, *Revenue and Agriculture Proceedings*, vol. 8633 (November 1911), p. 501. For a detailed study of the effects of soil exposure in the tropics (with special reference to Nigeria) see R. K. Cunningham, "The effect of clearing a tropical forest soil," *Journal of Soil Science* 14 (1963): 334–45.

49. Government of Burma, *Report on the Famine in Burma, 1896–7* (Rangoon: 1898).

50. T. C. Whitmore, *Tropical Rain Forests of the Far East* (Oxford: 1975), pp. 3–11; P. Richards, *Rain Forests*, chapter 10.

51. P. Richards, *Rain Forest*, p. 329.

52. K. A. Longman and J. Jenik, *Tropical Forest and Its Environment* (London: 1974), pp. 121–23.

53. T. Whitmore, *Tropical Forests*, pp. 235–36.

54. Ibid., p. 234–35.

55. Ibid., p. 236; Longman and Jenik, *Forest Environment*, pp. 17–19.

56. P. Richards, *Rain Forest*, p. 405.

57. On Thailand, see D. Ingram, *Economic Change in Thailand since 1850* (Stanford 1955); and on Indochina, Charles Robequain, *The Economic Development of French Indochina* (Oxford: 1944).

58. Lucien M. Hanks, *Rice and Man* (Ithaca, N. Y.: 1972), p. 73ff.

XII

The Ryotwari in Lower Burma: The Establishment and Decline of a Peasant Proprietor System

DURING the past decade there have been a number of significant changes in the methodology of historians who are concerned with questions relating to Asian land tenure and land use.[1] Underlying these changes has been a decided shift away from studies focusing on government policy formation[2] toward an emphasis on the actual impact of land tenure policies and the ways in which abstract theory and official intentions are altered by the social and economic context into which they are introduced.[3] This emphasis on the actual workings of tenure systems has been expressed in two approaches which have dominated recent work on land tenure and land use. The first approach is characterized by detailed analysis of the workings of tenure systems at the local or micro-level. The historian's growing awareness of the importance of the use of anthropological data and techniques in the study of peasant societies has greatly influenced this shift to emphasis on the micro-level. The resulting fusion of anthropological methodology and historical perspective is perhaps best exemplified by Gananath Obeyesekere's pioneering study of *Land Tenure in Village Ceylon.*[4] A second approach to land tenure which has been increasingly adopted in recent years involves the rigorous examination of general social, economic, and demographic factors which have traditionally been considered important determinants of cropping patterns and systems of land rights. Ester Boserup's provocative essay on *The Conditions of Agricultural Growth,* which focuses on the relationships between population change and agricultural practices, is a superb example of this approach.[5]

Both of these approaches to land tenure systems and the factors which shape them have contributed much that is of great value to the social scientist. Micro-studies have yielded empirical data which can be used to test the assumptions of earlier historians who focused on economic theory or official decision-making. Local studies have also drawn attention to the influence of local conditions and institutions, such as kinship networks and village social hierarchies, which were much neglected in earlier works. Studies dealing with general determinants of tenure patterns have provided well-supported challenges to some of the most basic premises which shape our thinking on the workings of agrarian societies, such as that levelled by

Boserup in her assault on the Malthusian view that technological change
and resultant agrarian growth determine population increases.[6] Both
approaches have produced new insights and theories to be tested and new
models to be applied in future studies. They have also reaffirmed Dennis
FitzGerald's observation that land tenure involves more than land rights; it
also includes factors such as rents, taxation policies, and rural credit facilities,[7] and one could add land use and income.

Despite the important contributions made by scholars employing these
two approaches, both manifest a tendency to obscure the broader configurations of physical, technological, institutional, and ideological variables
which shape systems of land control and use. Obeyesekere, for example,
scarcely mentions the broader "factors of change" (such as government
ordinances and taxation policies and population trends) which influenced
landholding patterns in Ceylon until after he has discussed in elaborate
detail the traditional tenure system with reference to village structure and
kinship connections. He introduces pieces of the broader configuration to
explain changes in landholding at a specific point in time, rather than establishing the configuration as the context in which his local analysis is set
and examining its complex impact throughout all of the stages he identifies.[8]
Boserup stresses the impact of demographic trends to the near exclusion of
the influence of market factors on changes in land use and property rights,
despite the fact that the market has played a critical role in most areas in
the modern era.[9] Rawski's study of agricultural change in South China
reverses Boserup's stress by focusing on marketing and transportation
factors and neglecting the impact of demographic variables.[10]

As these examples illustrate, many recent studies represent an unfortunate
movement away from the approach of historians like Marc Bloch and Irfan
Habib who have analyzed land tenure and land use as parts of broader
configurations in the context of which they can best be treated. Bloch and
Habib clearly demonstrate that the complex webs of land rights and claims
to produce and services which characterized the feudal system in Medieval
Europe or the jagirdari system in Mughal India cannot be fully understood
unless they are related to the political and military needs, the ecological
and technological givens, the social and economic conditions, and the
historical precedents which gave rise to them.[11] The broader configuration
of variables not only determines the actual arrangement and functioning
of a land tenure system; it also shapes ideas relating to the meaning of land
itself, which as Walter Neale, Paul Bohannan and others have pointed out
may vary widely from one culture to another.[12] In addition, it is important
to note that the impact of a particular tenure system on social, economic,
or political development results not from the tenure system in and of itself,
but from the tenure system as it relates to the broader configuration of
variables.

The task of the social scientist who attempts to analyze the nature and
impact of land tenure in the Afro-Asian world is further complicated by the

XII

102

fact that he is almost invariably dealing with a composite system. He shares
with the European historian the need to take into account influences and
remnants of past configurations indigenous to his area of concern. Unlike the
European historian, however, he must come to terms with changes and
hybrid forms that have resulted from the imposition of elements and influences of an alien, western European configuration upon the configuration
indigenous to his area of interest. Although European influence in different
areas has varied widely, a number of common concepts and institutions
relating to land tenure have generally been introduced into Afro-Asian
cultures as a result of European commercial and political penetration.
These commonalities, which are largely a product of the commercial-
industrial revolutions in western Europe,[13] include: the concepts of land
as private property and a market commodity, emphasis on land rather
than population control, impersonal contractual relationships, and political
and legal systems oriented to regulating and preserving these forms.

The degree to which these concepts and practices have affected tenure
arrangements indigenous to Africa or Asia has varied in part according to
the extent of European political control or influence, the nature and intent
of European economic activity, and the degree to which European ideas,
institutions, and technology have resulted in the general transformation of
the society and culture of the peoples encountered. The nature of the changes
in landholding patterns which have resulted from the imposition of European
colonial rule in non-Western areas has also been determined by the revenue
needs of the European overlords, the availability of trained manpower for
the colonial bureaucracy,[14] and the cost of irrigation systems or other
improvements which have been essential prerequisites to agrarian development in many areas.[15] The impact of the introduction of elements of the
European configuration has also, and perhaps more importantly, been
determined by the strength and/or adaptability of the indigenous African or
Asian configuration. In this connection, the actual, as opposed to the intended, impact of the introduction of European land tenure concepts and
practices has often been proportional to the depth of the Europeans' understanding of the workings of the society they were attempting to influence.[16]

One could plot a continuum of the hybrids that have resulted from the
mixture of European and Afro-Asian configurations. At one pole would
stand the densely populated core areas which prior to the coming of the
Europeans possessed ancient and deeply rooted religious and legal codes
and customs, and complex socio-political arrangements relating to land
tenure. In these areas elements of the European configuration have normally
been substantially altered as a result of the strength and resilience of indigenous givens.[17] At the other end of the continuum would lie the sparsely
inhabited, shifting cultivation zones of Afro-Asia where the Europeans
established plantations which, in terms of the tenure patterns they displayed,
were fundamentally products of European commercial expansion and little
affected by the indigenous setting.[18]

The case examined in this essay, the development of the Irrawaddy Delta[19] region of Lower Burma during the period of British colonial rule, falls much closer to the plantation than to the core area pole of the continuum. For this reason, the changes resulting from the introduction of elements of the European configuration were extensive and profound. Lower Burma provides one of the best documented examples available of the rapid transformation of a subsistence-oriented, self-sufficient, natural economy into one that was market- and export-oriented and highly monetarized. This study will focus on the role of land tenure in that transformation, but considerable attention will also be given to the broader configurations which shaped tenure patterns in different periods. I will also deal in general terms with changes in social structure that resulted from configurational and tenurial transformations. Although for the purposes of analysis I will proceed from configuration to tenure patterns and then to social change, this should not be regarded as a causal sequence. The interplay between tenure and the broader configuration is complex and reciprocal with elements of the configuration determining tenure patterns and these in turn affecting broader economic, social, or political changes.[20]

As the result of the Burman victories in the Burman-Mon wars of the mid-eighteenth century, the Delta heartland of the Mon people was reduced to the status of a frontier area on the periphery of the slowly expanding Burman, wet-rice core located in the Dry Zone of Upper Burma. Although there was more development and less devastation in Lower Burma in the Konbaung period than historians have generally assumed, the region was sparsely populated and its great potential little exploited prior to its annexation by the British to their Indian Empire in 1852.[21] Among the central factors contributing to the area's low level of development were the Konbaung regime's ban on the export of rice, and its policy of using surplus rice to regulate and stabilize domestic grain prices. The low price paid for rice sold on the domestic market as a result of these policies, in combination with the elaborate sumptuary laws and restrictions on consumer imports enforced by the Konbaung regime, meant that there was little incentive for cultivators in the Delta to produce rice beyond that needed for subsistence, seed (wunsa), and taxes. This low level of incentive, coupled with the serious obstacles (such as malaria, flooding, wild animals, and insect crop pests) which faced cultivators who sought to bring virgin areas into production, greatly limited migration into and new settlement on the Delta frontier in the pre-British period.

In settled areas, which were concentrated along the Irrawaddy River, the peasant family was virtually a self-sufficient economic unit, which occasionally bartered surplus rice for salt or implements that it could not produce itself. If extra labor was required for planting or harvest, it was normally obtained on a mutual-assistance basis. Little capital was available, and it was almost exclusively invested in domestic trade.

Given the low ratio of population to land and the poor returns received for surplus agricultural production, land tenure arrangements in the pre-British Delta were extremely loose.[22] There were no concepts of private property or proprietary rights in the western European sense. Land rights were determined by personal relationships rather than by impersonal contracts. In Konbaung times, most of the Delta's inhabitants lived in small hamlets which were comprised of nuclear households often linked by kinship or ethnic ties. The land in the vicinity of the hamlet was held in common. Individual usufructuary rights (termed *dama-u-gya*) over a particular piece of land were established by the act of clearing and cultivating it. These rights were retained by the clearing household as long as the plot was cultivated.[23] If the land was abandoned or left fallow, it reverted to the common pool held by the hamlet unit. If another household chose to cultivate the land, it could do so with or without the permission of the original occupant, depending on local custom. Given the great abundance of cultivable land, elaborate formal mechanisms for land distribution proved unnecessary. Holdings were small, averaging less than ten acres. Competition for land was virtually nonexistent, and land sales were rare. Even in exceptional cases where sales transactions took place, the vendor had the right to repurchase the land should he decide to do so within ten years.[24] The buyer could not ordinarily resell the land without the original owner's permission.

In Lower Burma, as in many traditional societies where the population-to-land ratio was low, emphasis was placed on manpower control rather than the control of land. That portion of the Delta's population which was effectively regulated by the Konbaung administration was divided into regiments or orders called *athin*. Membership in a particular athin was normally determined by occupational, kinship, or ethnic ties, rather than by territorial considerations. Each athin unit of Delta society was linked to the elite hierarchy by officials known as *thugyis,* who were chosen from the ranks and considered the representatives of local athin groups. Officials above the thugyi level were appointed by the central government and normally recruited in the Dry Zone of Upper Burma. Given a low population density, the athin arrangement produced a society in which there was considerable geographical, but little vertical, mobility. Shifting, rather than wet-rice, cultivation was practiced over much of the lower Delta, and there are references to the migration of households and whole hamlets from areas where the exactions of Konbaung officials proved too burdensome.

Following the annexation of the Delta to the Indian Empire in 1852, the British colonial regime acted quickly to remove the impediments to growth which had existed under Konbaung rule and to promote economic development.[25] The ban on rice exports was lifted, and Burman sumptuary laws were no longer enforced. The British introduced legal and political institutions geared to a capitalistic economy, along with transportation improvements, embankments, and other public works. Private British investors built processing plants for rice, which was to become the Delta's predominant export, and European and Indian merchants furnished links with overseas market outlets. British and Indian merchants also imported consumer goods that were to prove an important stimulus to surplus production for export on the part of Burmese agriculturists.

These measures to promote economic development brought rapid and dramatic returns, for the British were acting upon a rich, but little developed frontier region. Most of Lower Burma was made up of a vast and fertile alluvial plain which had been formed, and was watered and nourished, by the Irrawaddy and Sittang rivers. In addition, abundant and reliable rainfall was provided annually by the Southwest monsoon. Prior to its annexation in 1852, numerous British merchants and diplomats had noted the favorable climate and fertility of the region and speculated about its potential as a source of a wide variety of export crops. After 1852, however, international market demands and the preference of the Burmese cultivator determined that the Delta would develop a monocrop economy dominated by rice for export. In the decades after 1852 there was a rising world demand, first centered in Europe and later India, for Burma's rice. This demand supported a steady rise in the price of rice on the Burma market which persisted into the first decades of the twentieth century.

Steadily rising prices in combination with an abundance of fertile unoccupied land, the spread of rural credit agencies, and the development of rural retail networks, which made available cheap consumer goods, provided both the means and incentives for Burmese agriculturists to bring the Delta wilderness under cultivation and engage in surplus production for the market. Many of the settlers on the Lower Burma frontier were migrants drawn from the Dry Zone or other regions within Burma. Some were Indians, though the Indian migrant stream tended to flow primarily to Rangoon and other urban centers. The ready response of the Burmese agriculturist to new market incentives was also facilitated by the British abrogation of many traditional restrictions and the very low level of risk involved in innovation, which consisted chiefly of the surplus production of their staple crop for the market.[26] For the Burmese cultivator the added labor input required to grow this surplus brought more than satisfactory returns. Consequently, the great majority of cultivators in Lower Burma made the shift from subsistence-oriented, self-sufficient peasants to full-time, market producers in a matter of decades. Their efforts made possible the Delta's rapid transformation into the world's premier rice-exporting region in the last decades of the nineteenth century.

The land tenure system which was introduced after 1852 was shaped by the needs and nature of the new political and economic framework which the British were working to establish in Lower Burma. The tenure system represented a blend of Indian precedents, contemporary British social and economic theory, and indigenous Burmese patterns.

In the years before the Indian Mutiny of 1857-58, the influence of the English Utilitarian philosophers on Indian revenue systems reached its

height. Writers like James Mill strongly opposed the Whig-oriented settlements through which the British had created a true landed aristocracy in
Bengal and other areas in the late eighteenth and early nineteenth centuries.
Mill and other Utilitarian thinkers argued that profits which accrued from
agricultural production in the form of rents should go to the state and not
landed intermediaries like the taluqdars of Oudh or the zamindars of Bengal.
Their works deeply influenced Indian administrators like Holt Mackenzie
and George Wingate, who worked for the introduction of land systems
under which the revenue was collected directly from the cultivator or the
communal village.[27] One such system, the ryotwari, had been established in
the first decades of the nineteenth century through large portions of the
Bombay and Madras Presidencies. After 1852, in keeping with the government's declared policy of protecting and promoting the interests of the
smallholder, the ryotwari system was introduced into Lower Burma.

Although Thomas Munro had not been the first to apply the ryotwari
system, he became its chief proponent in the first decades of the nineteenth
century. He was mainly responsible for the fact that it had become the
dominant land revenue arrangement in the Madras Presidency. Munro
believed that the ryotwari system would best promote the interests of the
small landholder and, in doing so, further the interests of the state. He
contended that the peasant proprietor was more likely to improve his holdings
than the large landholder. Munro reasoned that since the peasant proprietor
personally supervised the cultivation of his land, he would strive for maximum crop output, and thus in the long term prove the greatest source of
revenue for the state.[28] Munro also advocated the ryotwari system because
he believed that in furthering the interests of the bulk of agriculturists,
rather than a landed elite, the system would best promote the general social
welfare and social stability.[29] In addition, Munro believed that by granting
agriculturists proprietary rights over particular holdings, the ryotwari
system would render the cultivating classes more stationary. This aspect of
the system was particularly relevant to the British and Indian officials who
were struggling to establish order in the Delta after the second Anglo-
Burman war in 1852. Wartime dislocations combined with the shifting
cultivation which had traditionally been practiced over much of the region
made it difficult for colonial bureaucrats to count their new subjects accurately, much less to tax and administer them effectively.[30] Munro's arguments for the ryotwari system, especially those relating to the incentives it
would instill in the cultivator to innovate and produce more, have been
borne out by modern research. There is a general agreement in the literature
on agrarian development that tenure systems based on smallholder proprietorship are far more likely than landlord-based systems to generate
"dynamic responses to opportunities for commercial farming."[31]

Lower Burma seemed to provide ideal conditions for the successful
functioning of a tenure system based on the peasant proprietor. In fact,
the case of Lower Burma demonstrates the importance of focusing on local

conditions not only to discover the actual impact of tenure policies, but also in order to understand factors that play an important role in the formation of those policies. Relative to the heavy government expenditure on canals, irrigation, and related public works required to bring other frontier areas, like those in the United Provinces in India or in Cochin China,[32] into agricultural production, the sums which the British invested in Lower Burma were low. Bunds for water control and railway lines linking limited areas were the only major public works necessary. Thus, the new regime was not burdened with great debts which might have caused it to favor estate agriculture which in the short term would yield greater revenue returns than a small-landholder-based system. In addition, the abundance of cultivable land on the Delta frontier in the late nineteenth century meant that agriculturists could claim holdings of a size sufficient for them to produce a substantial surplus for the market and at the same time maintain a high level of home consumption. The presence of an open land frontier also permitted successful cultivators to increase the scale of their operation, and thus contribute to the further growth of the Delta's export economy.

Although Konbaung nobles and administrators had exercised prebendal domain[33] over certain Delta areas in the pre-British period, there was no true landlord class prior to 1852. Local leaders, like the thugyis or *ywa-oks* (local hamlet leaders), possessed none of the rights or means of control over the cultivating classes that were exercised by groups like the zamindars in pre-British India. The tenuous and indirect control of Konbaung officials and nobles was broken by the British conquest when most fled into Upper Burma (which was not brought under British control until 1886) or perished in futile resistance to the British advance. The absence of caste in Burmese society meant that there was no danger that high caste groups could frustrate the intent of the ryotwari system by acting as intermediaries between the government and the mass of the cultivators. In India high caste groups, like the mirasidars of the Bombay and Madras Presidencies, had gained considerable advantage from the ryotwari arrangement through collusion with indigenous revenue officials and by exercising their traditional control over lower caste cultivators and laborers.[34]

Buddhist inheritance laws were initially the only element in the indigenous society which posed a serious threat to the success of the ryotwari system in Lower Burma. According to Theravada Buddhist law as it was observed in Burma, all of the property of a deceased household head must be divided equally between his widow and both male and female children. If it had been strictly observed, this injunction would have rapidly resulted in the fragmentation of Delta holdings and undermined the cultivator's ability to produce for the market and ultimately to adequately support his own household. In some cases holdings were divided, and this process often led to quarrels among the heirs that were fought out in financially ruinous court suits and countersuits.[35] In most instances, however, Buddhist legal injunctions were not strictly applied or were circumvented. Since nuclear and neo-local households were prevalent in Lower Burma, a cultivator's children had normally married and moved away from their parental household long before the death of their parents. The abundance of open land on the frontier also meant that they were frequently well established on their own holdings before it came time to divide their parents' estate. Thus, the original family property could either be turned over to unmarried children who still lived in the parental home or to the least successful of the heirs. In either case, cash compensation was paid to the other heirs. Division of the parental estate was also obviated by a verbal agreement which stipulated that the heirs would work the holding on an annual rotation basis with a fixed portion of the harvest alloted to the noncultivating heirs for their support. More commonly, one heir would purchase the shares of the others, who would thereby gain the capital needed to go into trade or moneylending, or to move to another area on the Delta frontier and claim their own holdings.[36] In this way, Buddhist inheritance laws, at least in the early phase of development, resulted in most cases in a further extension of cultivation, rather than the financial ruin of the parties involved.

Through regulation of the means by which tenurial rights were acquired, the colonial regime sought to insure that a smallholder, rather than a large landlord, class would develop in the Delta. Several forms of land grants were experimented with, but two types proved dominant.[37] The government favored the patta system under which government officials allotted and to persons who could prove they were bonafide agriculturists an average of from fifteen to twenty acres of unoccupied land. The Burmese cultivator, however, preferred the "squatter" system, which closely resembled the pre-British dama-u-gya pattern of settlement. A cultivator established his claim to a particular holding by clearing and cultivating it. After 1876, his tenurial rights were recognized once he had occupied and paid revenue on the holding for twelve years. In that period he was prohibited from selling or mortgaging the land. At the end of the twelve years, the settler held a permanent and heritable title to the occupied land, which he could sell, mortgage, or transfer to another.

During the last decades of the nineteenth century the government sought to encourage Burmese cultivators to settle unoccupied lands or add to their existing holdings by granting revenue remissions during the first years of cultivation and temporary exemptions from the capitation tax, which was a carryover from the Konbaung period. Compared to the revenue rates established in the ryotwari areas in India in the first half of the nineteenth century, those charged in Lower Burma were low. The government normally took about 10 percent of the gross output, depending on the quality of the land assessed.[38] The moderate rates prevailing in Lower Burma were in part a product of the many errors and persistent overassessments which had characterized ryotwari settlements in both Bombay and Madras where the government had not infrequently taken 50 percent or more of the cultivator's net income.[39] In addition, in the years after 1852 the Government of Burma felt little need to raise large amounts of revenue from land taxes, a need which Dharma Kumar has argued led to assessments by the East India Company at "high, almost penal, rates" during the decades of the ryotwari's introduction into Madras.[40] By contrast, administrators in Burma were anxious to encourage the surplus production of rice for the export market, and peasant consumption of cheap manufactured goods imported from Great Britain and India. These ends could best be achieved by leaving the bulk of the cultivator's surplus in his own hands.[41]

Set in the context of a capitalist, export-oriented configuration, the introduction of the ryotwari system resulted in a radical transformation in the relationship between the Burmese agriculturist and the land. Rights to land use once regulated by the communal village gave way to proprietary rights vested in the individual. Traditional agreements regarding land control based on age-old customs, personal relationships, and informal verbal understandings were codified and impersonalized through legal contracts and property laws. Loosely demarcated boundaries were replaced with those carefully measured, marked, and registered at the local settlement office. Holdings once used to provide the mixed-crop, subsistence requirements of largely self-sufficient households were transformed into monocrop production units feeding a seemingly insatiable foreign demand for Burma's rice. Formerly a "free gift of nature," land became a market commodity and an object of competition to be sold, mortgaged, and inherited.[42] Birth and/or bureaucratic connections that had traditionally been the prime determinants of wealth, social status, and political power diminished in importance as land acquisition and Western education emerged as the chief means of achieving these ends. The sum of these transformations produced a profound change in the Burmese agriculturist's attitude toward the land he worked. This new attitude was succinctly summed up in the following passage by a British revenue official:

> The Burman in Lower Burma at least sits loosely on his holding, he has no sentimental attachment to it, he regards the land simply as the material with the aid of which paddy is produced, and therefore one field or holding is as good as another in his eyes if each yields the same amount of grain. In fact, the Burman prefers paddy to the land which yields it and if he could get paddy from the air or water alone, he would forsake the land altogether.[43]

The combination of extensive political and economic change and the new tenure arrangements introduced by the British resulted in a restructuring of rural Delta society. The vertical, highly stratified social system of the Konbaung period gave way to a more fluid, horizontally arranged social order in which four main strata can be distinguished for the purposes of analysis: landlords, cultivator-owners, tenants, and landless laborers. These groups were defined largely in terms of their relationship to the land. In the last half of the nineteenth century there was a high degree of mobility among the different strata, and the boundaries of the strata themselves were vague and highly mutable. It was possible for a cultivator who began as a landless laborer to work his way upward until he attained the status of a large landholder. The number of persons who began as laborers and rose to become landlords was small, but large numbers of agriculturists moved one or two notches up or down on the social scale. Although some owners became heavily indebted and fell to the status of tenants or laborers, movement was largely upward. Tenants and landless laborers generally regarded their positions as temporary, a phase in which they would acquire the means to clear and cultivate their own holdings.[44] There was also considerable differentiation within each social stratum. Some tenants, for example, owned small plots of land which they hoped to enlarge and thereby move up to full landonwer status. Other tenants worked part-time as wage laborers. Considerable numbers of tenants worked the same landlord's holdings for season after season, while many others moved about the Delta in search of more favorable rent rates or leasing conditions. With the population-to-land ratio on the Delta frontier running heavily in favor of the laboring classes and agriculturists at all levels retaining a substantial share of their production, the condition of the rural population was generally solvent, and in many cases prosperous until the first decades of the twentieth century.

The basic configuration, which had developed in Lower Burma in the decades after 1852 as the result of a blend of British and Indian innovations and indigenous givens, persisted throughout the British colonial period. In the last decades of the nineteenth century, however, there were major changes within this configuration, and, after 1910, new trends on the international rice market which gradually undermined the dominant position of the small landholder and the solvency of the great majority of Delta agriculturists. Although detailed examination of the factors which led to the deterioration of the Delta economy lies beyond the scope of this essay, some of the key factors can be indicated.[45] Perhaps the most critical development was the closing of the rice frontier, which greatly restricted the agriculturist's avenues of opportunity and in combination with rapid population growth turned the population-to-land ratio against the tenant and laboring classes. The growing scarcity of cultivable, unoccupied land was felt in some areas of Lower Burma as early as the 1890s, and prevailed throughout most of the Delta by the time of World War I. This shortage greatly impaired the ability of tenants and landless laborers to gain their own holdings or of cultivators, who had lost their original holdings through debt, to start again in a new area. It also resulted in a great increase in the sale price of land which made it difficult for the average cultivator to extend his holdings. Because there had been no in-depth transformation of agricultural techniques or technology in the late nineteenth century, the unavailability of additional inputs of land, which had been the basis of the early expansion of rice production, meant that the average cultivator's output stagnated and in some areas declined due to soil depletion.

These checks on the cultivator's capacity to increase his production came at a time when the claims of nonagricultural groups on his crop were growing, and when the market value of his surplus was fluctuating and often falling. As a consequence of his shift from self-sufficience and subsistence production to full-time production for the market, the Delta agriculturist became increasingly dependent on credit advances from professional money-lenders, rice brokers, local merchants, landlords, and other middlemen. These groups took ever greater shares of his harvest for payment on the interest and/or principal on loans. In addition, the great proliferation of marketing middlemen and the formation of marketing pools on the part of the milling interests meant that the cultivator received less for the sur-plus he was able to market. By the first decade of the twentieth century it was necessary for most cultivators to sell to brokers or rice merchants on the threshing floor at the peak of the harvest season when prices were the lowest. Recurring market slumps in the early twentieth century, which had severe effects on the Delta monocrop economy, further reduced the worth of the cultivator's surplus. His plight was compounded by a rather high rate of inflation in this period and was further exacerbated by the fact that in shifting to full-time market production, most Delta agriculturists had given up their self-sufficient base.

Worsening economic conditions exposed a number of serious weak-nesses in the seemingly ideal land tenure system which the British had intro-duced into Lower Burma. The most critical of these was the fact that under the ryotwari arrangement the cultivator-owner was permitted to offer mortgage liability for loans obtained from moneylenders, rice merchants, and other sources. From the earliest decades of the Delta's development, a high percentage of loans to agriculturists had been secured by mortgages on their holdings. As long as the majority of cultivators cleared sizable profits and were able to repay the interest and principal on their loans, mortgage security did not present a danger to the maintenance of a peasant-proprietor-dominated economy. However, when the average small land-holder found it increasingly difficult to meet his own expenses and repay his creditors, chronic indebtedness, widespread defaulting and foreclosures, and land alienation began to undermine the very foundations of the land tenure system which the British had originally established.

These problems and land alienation were, of course, not entirely new. Profligate landholders had lost their lands to moneylenders, merchants, urban speculators, and their more frugal neighbors in the early decades after 1852. Landgrabbers, both urban and rural based, had also found numerous ways of circumventing government safeguards and acquiring large estates long before land alienation became a serious problem in the last decades of the nineteenth century. For example, the government regulation which prohibited cultivators from mortgaging newly settled holdings until after twelve years of occupation was quite frequently violated through the use of "veiled" mortgages. These mortgages, which were almost certainly in use before the early 1900s when they are first mentioned in revenue reports, involved loans granted to settlers who offered their newly cleared holdings as security, but did not report the transaction to the government authorities. There was a clear understanding, however, between cultivator and creditor that should the former fail to meet his payments, his land would become the property of the latter. If a cultivator defaulted, his land would be "sold" to his creditor at the end of the twelve-year period. The lender-speculator, who was normally a Burmese merchant, moneylender, or landlord with considerable local influence (and often with a gang of client-ruffians on hand), felt little need to rely on the government to insure returns on his investment.[46]

As in many other agrarian societies, land speculators also relied on collusion with subordinate revenue officials to acquire large holdings. At times, they would direct their clients and retainers, who were often deeply in debt to them, to settle unoccupied tracts and register them in the client's name. The local revenue officer would, of course, be well paid for failing to discover and report these transactions. In other instances, the collusion between local officials and speculators was more direct. For a suitable bribe or a share of the profits, local revenue officials would register unoccupied tracts or the holdings of bonafide cultivators in the name of the land speculator. A popular tactic was for the revenue officer to under-report the output of his landlord partners' holdings, or to wipe sizeable portions of their estates off the revenue map with the comment that the area had relapsed into jungle.[47] In more remote areas of the Delta frontier, the land grabber did not bother with these costly and time-consuming subterfuges. He merely directed his retainers to harass and intimidate a cultivator who had just finished clearing a fertile holding. Violence was used if necessary to convince the settler to give up his hard-earned plot, after which one of the speculator's toughs became the new squatter in residence.

Although a number of large estates comprised mainly of noncontiguous holdings were pieced together through foreclosures and illegal tactics in the early decades of the Delta's development, land alienation was not a serious problem in most areas. As late as 1905, for example, only 18 percent of the occupied land in Lower Burma was controlled by nonagriculturists and of this amount 40 percent was held by resident owners who lived within three miles of their holdings.[48] Widespread alienation was also limited by the general solvency of the cultivating classes combined with the fact that most moneylenders, especially the South Indian Chettiars who had dominated rural credit provision since the 1880s, did not want the cultivator's land. Most lenders were content to collect the interest on their loans to cultivator-owners for season after season and leave the principal unpaid. As the general economic situation worsened, however, credit became more restricted and cultivators fell more and more deeply into debt. By the 1920s, many moneylenders, including some Chettiars, were increasingly forced to foreclose on mortgages due to defaulting on the part of their clients and/or

pressures for repayment of the working capital which the lenders had originally borrowed from rich merchants, banks, and other agencies. By 1930,
31 percent of the occupied land in Lower Burma was owned by nonagriculturists, of whom nearly 75 percent were nonresidents.[49]

As early as the 1880s government revenue officials in Lower Burma
began to voice concern regarding rising indebtedness and the spread of land
alienation and tenancy.[50] No measures were taken, however, until the 1890s
when a small group of British officials mounted a campaign to enact agrarian
relief measures. Tenancy and land alienation bills were submitted for
approval to the Government of India in 1896. Both bills were accompanied
by detailed opinions written by revenue and judicial officers, the memorials
of special interest groups like the Chettiars' and landlords' associations, and
surveys which had been conducted by the Government of Burma to test
the attitudes of landlords, cultivator-owners, moneylenders, and tenants
with regard to the measures. As this great mass of evidence demonstrated,
the main support for the relief measures came almost exclusively from the
small, but articulate, group of British revenue officials who had instigated
the legislative campaign. These officials were opposed by a powerful coalition
of Burmese and Indian landlord and moneylender associations, the Chambers
of Commerce of all of the main ethnic groups resident in Burma, Burmese
rice brokers, Indian and Chinese merchant groups, and the British and
Indian export-import and milling interests. Well attended public meetings
were held in Rangoon and other urban centers to protest against the proposed
bills, and special petitions were addressed to the Governor-General of
India.

Most disheartening for the sponsors of the bills was the fact that a
majority of the cultivators surveyed opposed the measures. A minority
of agriculturists favored the legislation with a vehemence that was best
expressed by a heavily indebted smallholder in the Hanthawaddy District
who declared that should the bills be passed he would "bend [his] head to
the Government three times a day."[51] However, most agriculturists, both
large and smallholders, opposed the measures, primarily because they feared
that the provisions for restricting mortgage liability would greatly impair
their ability to obtain credit from Chettiar, Burmese, and Chinese moneylenders. In the absence of large-scale or effective government credit agencies,
these private sources were essential to agricultural production in the Delta.

The Government of India refused to approve the bills drafted in the
1890s on the grounds that firmer statistical data were required regarding
tenant conditions and the extent of land alienation. The accelerating spread
of chronic indebtedness and land alienation and the worsening position of
the agrarian classes, however, generated renewed efforts to enact relief
measures in the first decade of the twentieth century. These efforts were
spearheaded by the then governor of Burma, Sir Herbert Thirkell White.
Once again, a small group of British officials waged a lonely campaign
against the forces which had opposed the earlier bills. Despite White's

fervent advocacy and his close association with the Governor-General of India, Lord Minto, the campaign again ended in defeat. In a revealing letter from Colonel Dunlap-Smith, the Secretary to the Governor-General, to White in December of 1907, Minto apologized to his friend for the embarassment caused by the Government of India's rejection of the proposed legislation. He argued that "hard figures" on the question were still lacking, but stressed the complications that the bills would have in view of circumstances in India. After explaining that there had been "serious objections" to similar legislation already enacted in the Panjab, Minto went on to explain that: *"Even if an Alienation Act is required in Burma,* its introduction would cause a certain amount of uneasiness in other provinces, where similar legislation has been threatened, and it is advisable to avoid anything of this sort at present."[52] White's successor as governor of Burma, Sir Harvey Adamson, shelved the legislation indefinitely in 1911. The campaign would not be renewed until the late 1930s when tenancy and land alienation bills were enacted only after the Great Depression, a major agrarian rebellion, and a series of bloody communal riots had made a shambles of the Delta economy and society.

In view of the government's failure to intervene to ameliorate the conditions that were steadily undermining the peasant-proprietor-based tenure system in the Delta, potential for effective adjustments rested mainly with the cultivating classes themselves. With rare exceptions, however, agriculturists in Lower Burma made few changes in their cultivating techniques or consumption patterns which would have allowed them to remain solvent in the face of less favorable economic circumstances and population growth. The revenue records and settlement reports for the early decades of the twentieth century indicate that there was very little intensification of cultivation, introduction of new crops, or adoption of new tools. New rice strains were used on only a small percentage of Delta holdings, and fertilizers continued to be used for nurseries and not on the main fields in most tracts. Broadcasting continued to be favored over transplanting in most of the lower Delta, despite the higher yields obtained by transplanting. The use of familial labor, as opposed to hired wage workers, actually declined as the landless laboring class grew steadily, fed by an increased influx of Indian migrant laborers. Multiple cropping remained confined to a limited area. Most agriculturists eschewed the introduction of alternate crops, and persisted in the monocrop production of rice despite adverse trends in the internal and international market. In the absence of these changes, the productivity of holdings in most areas of Lower Burma declined, in part due to the spread of embankments which prevented nutrients carried by the Delta's rivers from reaching the soil. There is also little evidence that cultivators in Lower Burma cut back on their consumption, at least not until the 1930s. Purchase of cheap consumer goods remained at high levels, and perhaps expanded as bicycles, watches and other tempting items became available. Expenditure on traditional pastimes, such as initiation ceremonies, monastery festivals, bullock racing, and gambling also showed few signs of tapering off.

The failure of the Delta agriculturist to alter significantly his cultivation and consumption patterns was determined by a complex combination of economic and social variables. In view of adjustments made by cultivators in other areas, the most important of these variables should be indicated. Unlike his counterparts in India or China, the Burmese agriculturist had traditionally functioned in a setting where Malthusian pressures rooted in high population density were low. Although there were occasional droughts and food shortages in the Dry Zone, these were not so severe as elsewhere in Asia and they were virtually unknown in the Delta region.[53] Even in the depression period of the early 1930s, when the crisis of the Delta economy was the most severe, few, if any, cultivators starved, though some may have been forced to cut back on food consumption. In addition, in the last half of the nineteenth century the cultivator in Lower Burma had come to expect steady rises in the market demand and the price paid for rice. Price slumps had for the most part been mild and temporary until World War I. Thus, the cultivator understandably calculated his production costs and possibilities for consumption on the assumption that rice prices would rise, or at least remain roughly equal, in the coming season. Decades of living at a high level of income, relative to peasants in most other areas, had also ingrained spending habits and a strong preference for the use of hired labor that most cultivators were reluctant to give up.

The spread of credit agencies in Lower Burma, which accelerated after the entry of the Chettiars into rural moneylending on a large scale after 1880, made it possible for the average cultivator-owner to maintain his high standard of living. Possessing little understanding of the intricacies of money-lending or mortgage liability, the cultivator freely offered his land for credit. The ease with which large amounts of cash could be obtained from money-lenders by landowning cultivators encouraged both small and large owners to run up sizable debts. Much of the money so easily obtained was squandered on village celebrations and consumer goods. The tendency to become deeply indebted was reinforced by the Burmese and Chettiar moneylenders' policy of leaving the principal on loans outstanding as long as the interest was paid.

Chronic indebtedness, widespread defaulting, and land alienation which eroded the smallholder base of the Delta economy also limited the capacity of Burmese agriculturists to innovate in response to changing conditions. Most landlords in Lower Burma closely resembled those whom Gunnar Myrdal has seen as typical in South Asia. They "managed to enjoy the prerogatives of a capitalist landlord without giving up the privileges of a feudal chief," while simultaneously avoiding "nearly all the obligations of both." With rare exceptions, they did not improve their holdings, nor did they encourage their tenants or laborers to do so.[54] Tenants had little in-centive or spare capital to improve holdings they worked on a temporary basis. Increased productivity merely meant higher rents, and often jeopardized the tenant's position because the landlord would be tempted to evict him and find a replacement at higher rental rates.[55] As more and more Delta land was alienated to nonagriculturists and worked by tenants, the potential for creative responses to new economic pressures diminished steadily.

Agrarian indebtedness, land alienation, rising rent rates, and declining real wages became the dominant themes of the Delta economy in the first decades of the twentieth century. The depression of the 1930s merely accelerated and intensified these well-established trends. By the mid-1930s over half of the cultivated land in Lower Burma was claimed outright by nonagriculturists, a sizable percentage of whom were absentee owners. In addition, a large percentage of the land that still remained in the hands of smallholders was heavily mortgaged to moneylenders, local shopkeepers, landlords, and urban speculators. The lines dividing the different social strata increasingly rigidified, and the upward mobility that had characterized rural Delta society in the early period of growth was largely a thing of the past. For all but members of the large landlord class, movement was largely downward from cultivator-owner to tenant or landless laborer. In the first decades of the twentieth century living conditions for all but the landlord class deteriorated markedly. In combination with the breakdown of the institutions of traditional Burman society, the erosion of the social and economic position of the agrarian classes in the Delta had important consequences in the last decades of British rule when agrarian unrest and urban strife attested to the manifold failures of the colonial system that had begun with such promise.

The decline of the smallholder, export economy of Lower Burma clearly demonstrates the need for ongoing government regulation of land tenure systems set in the unstable context of export-oriented, capitalistic configurations. When, beginning in the 1890s, the favorable market conditions and low population-to-land ratio that had made possible the successful application of the ryotwari system changed, the government failed to introduce countermeasures to control lending practices and marketing agencies and to protect the smallholder's ownership rights. The government's poorly financed and half-hearted attempts to provide agricultural loans, develop cooperative societies, or stimulate change in agricultural technology fell far short of the measures required to preserve the smallholder economy that remained its professed ideal. The repeated attempts of a number of British officials in the 1890s and early 1900s to enact legislation which would check land alienation and regulate tenancy conditions ended in failure. As a result, the Delta agriculturists who had responded with great alacrity to the incentives provided by an alien system, which they never fully understood, were forced to cope with that system when factors which for the most part they could not control had radically altered it to their disadvantage. Without extensive government assistance, most cultivators proved unable to adjust successfully to changing conditions. By the 1930s the smallholder economy of the late nineteenth century had largely given way to a system of extraction dominated by large landlords, moneylenders, millers, and wholesale merchants.

The failure of the ryotwari in Burma also calls into question the notion that full ownership rights vested in individual small landholders represent *ipso facto* the ideal form of land tenure. In the early stages of the introduction of a market-oriented, cash-nexus economy into societies that have tradition-ally been natural- and subsistence-oriented, certain governmental checks on the rights of cultivator-owners to alienate their land through sale or mortgage would seem necessary.[56] As the resistance of many cultivator-owners in Lower Burma to land alienation legislation in the 1890s and early 1900s indicates, however, the government must at the same time provide sufficient sources of agricultural credit at reasonable rates, and make available at a low cost tools, fertilizers, and seeds. Most critically, land tenure arrangements must be geared to the configuration into which they are introduced, and altered to meet changes within that configuration.

NOTES

1. A preliminary draft of this essay was read for a panel on land tenure and social change at the Association of Asian Studies Convention in Chicago, March 1973. I would like to thank Edgar Wickberg, Clark E. Cunningham, Karl Pelzer, Traian Stoianovich, and Karl von Loewe for their comments on and criticisms of the original draft, though I am solely responsible for the content of this subsequent essay.
2. B.H. Baden-Powell's multi-volumed study of *The Land Systems of British India* (London, 1892) provides a classic example of the policy approach. The fact that studies of this nature are not currently in vogue does not mean, of course, that they are without value. In fact, Eric Stokes' *English Utilitarians in India* (Oxford, 1959), which deals with land tenure questions mainly at the level of political and economic theory and policy-making, is one of the finest studies to date on the British period in India.
3. For examples see Dharma Kumar, *Land and Caste in South India* (Cambridge, 1965); Ravinder Kumar, *Western India in the Nineteenth Century* (London, 1968); or the chapters by Bernard Cohn, Thomas Metcalf, Tapan Raychaudhuri, Burton Stein, and Nilmani Mukherjee and Robert Frykenberg, in Robert Eric Frykenberg, ed., *Land Control and Social Structure in Indian History* (Madison, Wis., 1969).
4. Cambridge, 1967. See also W.T. Chambliss, *Chiaraijima Village: Land Tenure, Taxation, and Local Trade, 1818-1884* (Tuscon, Ariz., 1965). The influence of anthro-pology on the historiography of agrarian Asia has been paralleled by a growing tendency for anthropologists to give serious attention to the historical dimensions of the social and cultural systems under analysis. See, for examples, L.M. Hanks, *Rice and Man: Agricultural Ecology in Southeast Asia* (Chicago, 1972), and H.T. Lewis, *Ilocano Rice Farmers: A Comparative Study of Two Philippine Barrios* (Honolulu, 1971).
5. Chicago, 1965. For other examples of this approach with reference to specific geographical areas see Evelyn Sakakida Rawski, *Agricultural Change and the Peasant Economy of South China* (Cambridge, Mass., 1972), or Clifford Geertz, *Agricultural Involution* (Berkeley, 1966).
6. See *Conditions of Growth*, especially pp. 11-14, 116-18.
7. As cited by K.H. Parsons in "Land Reform and Agricultural Development," in Parsons, et al., eds., *Land Tenure* (Madison, Wis., 1956), p. 44.
8. *Tenure in Village Ceylon*, esp. pp. 98-143.
9. *Conditions of Growth*, passim. She deals briefly with market factors in Chapter 7.
10. This approach is somewhat puzzling in view of her admission at the outset that population trends are of "obvious importance" to changes in the agrarian sector. See *Change and the Peasant Economy of South China*, p. 9.
11. Bloch, *Feudal Society*, 2 vols (Chicago, 1964); and Habib, *The Agrarian System of Mughal India, 1556-1707* (Bombay, 1963).
12. Neale, "Land is to Rule," in Frykenberg, ed., *Land Control in Indian History*, pp. 3-15; and Bohannan, " 'Land,' 'Tenure' and Land Tenure," in Daniel Biebuyck, ed., *African Agrarian Systems* (Oxford, 1963), pp. 101-115.

XII

118

13. Although their ideological and institutional origins may in part be traced back to ancient Greece, see Richard Schlatter, *Private Property* (London, 1951).

14. The importance of adequate manpower is strikingly demonstrated by Thomas Beaglehole's observation that Cornwallis' decision to make a permanent settlement with the zamindars in Bengal was in part determined by the limited numbers of able administrators at his disposal. See *Thomas Munro and the Development of Administrative Policy in Madras 1792-1818* (Cambridge, Eng., 1966), p. 5.

15. As Ammar Siamwalla has argued, the great costs involved in canal building and the desalinization of the soil in the Transbassac area of Cochin China were important causes of the rise of a large-landlord-based tenure system in the area. The small-scale cultivator could not raise the capital or afford the considerable delay in returns on investment required to make the land cultivable. See "Land, Labour and Capital in Three Rice-Growing Deltas of Southeast Asia 1800-1940." Yale University, Discussion Paper no. 150 of the Economic Growth Center, Mimeo, p. 39.

16. As Boserup has pointed out, European errors with regard to tenure matters were often also due to the inconsistencies and imprecise nature of European tenure concepts themselves. *Conditions of Growth*, p. 87.

17. For examples see the fine case studies in Frykenberg, *Land Control*, or Geertz's *Agricultural Involution*, especially chapters 2-4. In some cases, the process of colonization led to the virtual elimination of long-standing land tenure arrangements in conjuction with the general collapse of the institutional framework of the indigenous society. See, for example, Andre Nouschi, *Enquete sur le niveau de vie des populations rurales Constantinoises de la conquete jusqu'en 1919: Essai d'histoire, economic et sociale* (Paris, 1961).

18. Although in some cases there was considerable adaptation to local givens. For an extreme example, see Karl Peltzer, "Western Impact on East Sumatra and North Tapanuli: The Roles of the Planter and Missionary," *Journal of Southeast Asian History* 2 (July 1961): 66-71.

19. For the purposes of this essay, the Delta or Lower Burma comprises the thirteen principal rice-growing districts of British Burma: Prome, Tharrawaddy, Henzada, Bassein, Myaungmya, Pyapon, Maubin, Hanthawaddy, Insein, Pegu, Toungoo, Thaton, and Amherst. With the exception of the portions of Amherst which lie east of the Salween River, all of this region was annexed by the British to the Indian Empire in 1852.

20. The importance of stressing the reciprocity and interrelatedness of economic, social, and political change was suggested by the writings of Hans-Ulrich Wehler who deals with these factors in industrializing societies. See *Bismarck und der Imperialismus* (Koln, 1969), pp. 19-20 et passim.

21. For a detailed discussion of social and economic conditions in Lower Burma prior to 1852, see Michael Adas, *The Burma Delta: Economic Development and Social Change on an Asian Rice Frontier* (Madison, Wis., 1974), Chapter 1, pt. 1.

22. There is considerable disagreement both in the primary and secondary sources as to the nature of these arrangements. The following discussion is based largely upon the information provided by government reports which related the findings of special inquiries conducted in the first decade of British rule. Some of this material is cited by J.S. Furnivall in his early article on "Land as a Free Gift of Nature," *Economic Journal* (Dec. 1909), pp. 552-62.

23. As V. Liversage has shown, tenure rights of this nature were quite common in traditional societies. See *Land Tenure in the Colonies* (Cambridge, Eng., 1945), pp. 4-5 et passim.

24. This pattern of redeemable purchase was also quite common in traditional African and Asian societies. See ibid., p. 15 et passim.

25. On early British measures to develop the Delta and early economic growth in the region see Adas, *Burma Delta*, Chapter 1, pt. 2, and Chapters 2 and 3.

26. For a fine discussion of the risk factor in agricultural change, see C.M. Elliot, "Agriculture and Economic Development in Africa: Theory and Experience, 1880-1914," in E.L. Jones and S.J. Woolf, eds., *Agrarian Change and Economic Development: The Historical Problems* (London, 1969), pp. 123-50.

27. Stokes, *Utilitarians in India*, pp. 76-78, 87-99, 104-9, 122-28.

28. Beaglehole, *Thomas Munro*, pp. 8, 18, 28-29, 80-81; and D. Kumar, *Land and Caste*, pp. 81-82.

29. Beaglehole, *Thomas Munro*, pp. 28-29, 80.

30. Ibid., p. 81; and Government of India, *Foreign Proceedings (Revenue)*, Range 205, vol. 31 (November, 1862), nos. 7, 10, 11.

31. Gunnar Myrdal, *Asian Drama: An Inquiry into the Poverty of Nations*, 3 vols. (New York, 1968), 1:442. See also John W. Mellor, *The Economics of Agricultural Development* (Ithaca, N.Y., 1966), p. 249.

32. For detailed discussions of the magnitude of government expenditure in these areas and some of their implications see Elizabeth Whitcombe, *Agrarian Conditions in Northern India* (Berkeley, 1972), especially pp. 61-119; and Charles Robequain; *L'evolution economique de l'Indochine Francaise* (Paris, 1939), pp. 122-27, 243-47. The fact that large government investment on public works need not necessarily lead to the rise of large

landlord or estate agriculture is demonstrated by the case of the canal colonies in the Panjab. See Malcolm Darling, *The Panjab Peasant in Prosperity and Debt* (Bombay, 1947, 4th ed.), pp. 111–31.

33. As the term is defined by Eric Wolf as noninheritable rights to command services and collect a share of the cultivator's produce granted by the ruler to compensate government officials. See *Peasants* (Englewood Cliffs, N.J., 1966), pp. 50–53.

34. Nilmani Mukherjee and Robert Eric Frykenberg, "The Ryotwari System and Social Organization in the Madras Presidency," in Frykenberg, ed., *Land Control in Indian History*, pp. 217–26; R. Kumar, *Western India*, pp. 94, 101–11, 121–22 et passim.

35. Baden-Powell, *Land Systems*, 3:491–92; and O.H.K. Spate, "The Beginnings of Industrialization in Burma," *Economic Geography* 17 (1941): 90–91.

36. Ibid. In Burma, the frontier and a rapidly expanding economy provided the alternate means of support that Liversage has viewed as critical for the avoidance of fragmented holdings (see *Land Tenure*, p. 65). When the frontier closed and economic growth slowed after 1900, it is probable that fragmented estates became more common. This trend is impossible to trace statistically, however, due to the spread of land alienation and large estates in this period.

37. The best discussion of land grants in the printed literature may be found in Government of Burma, *Report of the Land and Agriculture Committee* (Rangoon, 1938), pt. 2, pp. 39–43.

38. Compare the sections on output and land revenue in the district settlement reports for this period; or see John Nisbet, *Burma under British Rule and Before*, 2 vols. (London, 1901), 2:342.

39. In this connection, it is important to note than in 1853–54, when settlement policy was being shaped in Lower Burma, there was a farreaching enquiry into the problem of overassessment in Madras. See D. Kumar, *Land and Caste*, pp. 77, 82–89, 95.

40. Ibid., p. 77.

41. As it functioned for roughly the first half century of British rule in Lower Burma, the ryotwari system not only left the cultivator with the bulk of his surplus produce, but also met all of the basic criteria which have been set forth by R.F. Carroll as a means of "Appraising the Adequacy of Land Tenure Systems for Agricultural Production" in Parsons, ed., *Land Tenure*, pp. 583–89.

42. Like many other colonial situations, the case of Lower Burma provides an important exception to Ester Boserup's generalization that "there is never a direct transition from a state where land is free to everybody to one of private property in land." See *Conditions of Growth*, p. 79.

43. Government of Burma, *Revenue and Agriculture Proceedings*, vol. 8633 (November 1911), p. 651.

44. This high degree of upward mobility indicates that frontier situations such as that found in Lower Burma in the late nineteenth century need to be included in Gunnar Myrdal's list of the limited circumstances under which tenants and landless laborers possess upward social mobility. See *Asian Drama*, 2:1060.

45. For a detailed analysis of these trends see Adas, *Burma Delta*, chapter 6.

46. Government of Burma, *Report on the Suspension of Grants in the Hanthawaddy District* (Rangoon, 1910), p. 13.

47. For examples, see C.H. Duffin, *Report of the Second Settlement...of the Bassein District, 1912-13* (Rangoon, 1914), p. 43, and U Tin Gyi, *Report of the Original Settlement Operation in the Labutta Township of the Myaungmya District, 1924-25* (Rangoon, 1926), p. 12.

48. Government of Burma, *Report on the Land Revenue Administration of Burma, 1905-6*, Tables on landholding in Lower Burma.

49. Ibid., *1929-30*.

50. The following discussion of the struggle to enact tenancy legislation from 1890 to 1911 is based on the special reports and enclosures in the Government of Burma *Revenue and Agriculture Proceedings, 1890-1911*.

51. Ibid., vol. 4886 (March 1896), p. 49.

52. India Office Archives, MSS European 254, The Herbert Thirkell White Collection, File 190. Emphasis added.

53. Mya Maung has stressed the absence of these pressures in shaping the Burmese outlook and Burmese responses to economic changes. See "Cultural Value and Economic Change in Burma," *Asian Survey* 4 (March 1964): 575–64.

54. *Asian Drama*, 2:1039.

55. For more detailed discussions of the factors which restrict the innovative capacity of tenants and sharecroppers see ibid., pp. 1065–67; Mellor, *Economics of Agricultural Development*, p. 254; and M.F. Millikan and David Hapgood, *No Easy Harvest: The Dilemma of Agriculture in Underdeveloped Countries* (Boston, 1967), pp. 91–92.

56. Liversage's arguments along these lines, which were made nearly three decades ago, have been largely neglected. See *Land Tenure*, pp. 123–34.

Immigrant Asians and the Economic Impact of European Imperialism: The Role of the South Indian Chettiars in British Burma

THE early debate over the economic impact of European imperialism on the Afro-Asian world centered largely upon the roles played by the European rulers. Both pro- and anti-imperialist writers focused on the introduction and effects of European economic policies and institutions, on the alleged benefits or exploitation that resulted from official and private European economic enterprise, and on the implications of European colonial control for the future economic development of subject areas. In recent years historians and other social scientists, drawing on hitherto neglected sources and applying new techniques of analysis, have undertaken a thoroughgoing reappraisal of the economic effects of European imperialism.[1] One product of this effort has been the increased attention given by scholars to the important roles played by non-Europeans in the economic transformation of colonized areas.

Indigenous groups and non-European immigrants not only served in the armies of conquest and staffed colonial bureaucracies; they also performed economic functions which the Europeans themselves were either unwilling or unable to provide. Among the most vital and controversial roles played in the transformation of precapitalist Asian or African economies were the commercial and entrepreneurial services rendered by foreign immigrants: Indians and Levantines in Africa, Indians and Chinese in Southeast Asia. Through the provision of skills and capital in sectors where the Europeans were reluctant or did not have the manpower to enter, the activities of these groups complemented the efforts of European officials and businessmen to develop the exchange sectors of colonial economies and to stimulate economic growth. By developing transportation and marketing networks, supplying credit for indigenous producers and traders, and investing in local processing industries immigrant Asian minorities established essential links between what had formerly been primarily subsistence economies and the global commercial network which the Europeans had been building since the fifteenth century. The *direct* economic impact of these groups on the indigenous population of colonial areas was normally greater than that of the Europeans for as P. T. Bauer and B. S. Yamey have pointed out:

Michael Adas is Assistant Professor of History at Rutgers University.

[1] M. D. Morris' article, "Towards a Reinterpretation of 19th Century Indian Economic History" in the *Journal of Economic History* 23/4 (Dec. 1963), pp. 606–18, marked the conscious and systematic beginning of this reappraisal. Some of the most important reassessments which have appeared thus far include Dharma Kumar's *Land and Caste in South India* (Cambridge, 1965); Clifford Geertz's *Agricultural Involution* (Berkeley, 1966); and T. R. DeGregori's *Technology and the Economic Development of the Tropical African Frontier* (Cleveland, 1965).

By permeating the economy more extensively than the establishments and activities of the large-scale European mercantile, industrial, mining or plantation concerns, their influence has generally been more widespread and has affected large numbers of the local people directly.[2]

Their extensive contact with the indigenous peoples of the areas where they migrated eventually worked to the detriment of these commercially-oriented groups. With the growth of nationalism and anti-colonialism among Asian and African peoples, the activities of these alien minorities became the object of intense criticism. Indigenous nationalist leaders forgot or ignored their positive contributions as they assailed the immigrant minorities' "strong-hold" over the colony's economy and their alliance with the European overlords as "co-exploiters." As defenseless foreigners who were mainly merchants, bankers and moneylenders, these groups were obvious targets for urban rioters and rural rebels during the turbulent decades of decolonization. In the post-independence period the position of these communities has become increasingly precarious, and at times untenable. Nationalist regimes have imposed legal restrictions on their activities, openly supported their indigenous competitors, and in some instances have confiscated their property and forced them to return to their areas of origin.

The Chettiars of Tamilnad in South India provide one of the most important and illustrative examples of the involvement of Asian immigrant minorities in the development of European colonial economies. Although they were found throughout Southeast Asia and elsewhere, the Chettiars concentrated their overseas operations in Burma which was annexed piecemeal to Britain's Indian Empire between 1826 and 1886. Although Burma was officially part of the Indian empire, it was historically, ethnically, linguistically, and culturally distinct from any area in the Indian subcontinent. Therefore, whatever their legal or technical status, Burma was as much a foreign country for Indian immigrants as Malaya, Ceylon or Indonesia which were not parts of the Indian Empire. Within Burma, Chettiar activities were centered in the Irrawaddy Delta region of Lower Burma where they played major roles as moneylenders and later landlords in the growth of the Burma rice-export economy during the period of British colonial rule.

The high quality of the available statistical and textual materials relating to the history of the Chettiars in Burma allows one to examine in depth the operations of an immigrant Asian group. In addition to the data supplied by annual administrative reports, special government enquiries into agrarian and market conditions, and official proceedings; information on local conditions in Lower Burma is amply provided by a superb, but much-neglected, series of settlement reports. Most vital to an analysis of Chettiar operations in Burma is the data obtained by a special survey, directed by a leading Chettiar in cooperation with the Nattukkottai Chettiars' Association of Burma, which was conducted as part of the broader Burma Banking Enquiry of 1929–30. These documents provide answers to such important questions as why Asian commercial groups migrated to particular areas, how they came to play dominant economic roles in alien societies, what was the nature of their interaction with the indigenous inhabitants of the areas of destination, and in what ways did this interaction change over time and why? The influences of history and family

---

[2] *The Economics of Under-Developed Countries* (Chicago, 1957), p. 107.

life on the roles played by the Chettiars have great bearing on questions relating
to the sources of entrepreneurial attributes and commercial acumen. Their organization and methods of operation, when contrasted with those of the indigenous Burmese, reinforce the observations of a number of social scientists working in other
areas regarding the reasons for the economic dominance of certain minority groups.
Finally, the case of the Chettiars in Lower Burma demonstrates the vital importance
of including non-European factors in any assessment of the economic impact of
European colonial rule.

Long before Lower Burma became a part of the Indian Empire in 1852, the
British were aware of the great potential of the fertile Irrawaddy Delta region as a
source of foodstuffs and raw materials and a market outlet for British manufactured
goods.[3] Prior to 1852, however, they were able to make little use of this potential.
Bans on the export of rice and other commodities, sumptuary laws, and other restrictions imposed by the ruling Konbaung dynasty greatly impeded domestic growth and
held foreign commercial contacts to a minimum. Throughout the Burman period,
the Delta remained a poorly-developed, sparsely populated and subsistence-oriented
backwater of the Konbaung Kingdom. After 1852 the British colonial regime acted
to remove the impediments to growth imposed by the Konbaung rulers and to
promote economic development. The ban on rice exports was lifted, and Burman
sumptuary laws were no longer enforced. The British introduced legal and political
institutions geared to a capitalistic economy, and expended large sums on transportation improvements, embankments, and other public works. Private British investors
built processing plants for rice, which was to become the Delta's predominant
export, and European merchants furnished links with market outlets overseas. British
and Indian merchants also imported the consumer goods that were to prove an
important stimulus to surplus production on the part of Burmese agriculturists.

In terms of the Chettiars' involvement in the Delta economy, one of the most
important changes effected by the British after 1852 was the introduction of a new
system of land tenure. The British replaced the loose, non-contractual, usufructuary
rights (termed *dama-u-gya*) which had prevailed in the Konbaung period with a
tenure system modeled on the *ryotwari* which was dominant in South India. The
chief aim of this new system was to concentrate ownership in the hands of individual cultivator-landholders. However, the new tenure system made it possible for
agriculturists to mortgage their holdings as security for loans obtained from moneylenders and other sources. This practice, which would eventually permit the widespread alienation of land to nonagriculturists, was well-established in Lower Burma
by the 1880s when the Chettiars began to extend their operations into rural areas on
a large scale.

Owing to the existence of a strong and steadily rising demand for Burma's rice
in Europe and other areas, the Irrawaddy Delta's economy expanded rapidly in the
last half of the nineteenth century.[4] Between the mid-1850s and 1900 five million

---

[3] The following summary of economic develop-
ment in the Delta is based upon Michael Adas, *The
Burma Delta: Economic Development and Social
Change on an Asian Rice Frontier, 1852–1941*
(Madison, Wisc., 1974), Chapters 1, 3, 6, and 8.
[4] The indicators of growth cited below were

derived from tables in J. W. Grant, *The Rice Crop
in Burma* (Rangoon, 1932); Cheng Siok-Hwa, *The
Rice Industry of Burma, 1852–1940* (Singapore-
Kuala Lumpur, 1968); and the censuses and administrative reports prepared by the Government
of Burma.

additional acres of rice land were brought into production in Lower Burma, and the amount of rice exported annually from Burma rose from less than two hundred thousand to over two million tons. This growth was supported by a steady rise in the price of paddy from Rs. 45 to Rs. 95 per hundred (46 lb.) baskets at Rangoon. Attracted by the profit and employment opportunities on the booming Delta frontier, immigrants from Upper Burma and immigrants from India and to a lesser extent China contributed to a sharp increase in the population of Lower Burma. Between the 1850s and 1900 the population of the region grew from approximately one to over four million. By the end of the nineteenth century Lower Burma was the premier rice-exporting area in the world and one of the richest provinces of the British Empire.

After the turn of the century the growth of the Delta economy slowed due to a combination of factors including rising competition for export outlets and the diminished availability of unoccupied land suitable for rice cultivation. Although rice exports rose by nearly a million tons between 1900 and 1930 and the area cultivated in Lower Burma increased by over two million acres, rural indebtedness, land alienation, the control gained by middlemen over the surplus produced by the Burmese agriculturists and related disorders gradually undermined the general prosperity which rapid economic expansion had brought to the region in the late nineteenth century. The market slump caused by the Great Depression merely intensified problems that had existed for decades. The economic crisis of the early 1930s gave rise to rural and urban unrest, exacerbated communal tensions and supplied ammunition for nationalist agitators. Although Burma's rice-export situation improved somewhat in the mid- and late-1930s, the problems of massive land alienation, widespread agrarian indebtedness and insolvency, and the poor condition of the Delta's tenant and laboring classes had not been resolved at the time of the Japanese invasion in 1941–42.

The Chettiars played only a marginal role in the early decades of Lower Burma's economic expansion. Europeans dominated foreign trade, transportation, and large-scale processing. Internal marketing was divided between thousands of Burmese "jungle" brokers who purchased paddy from the local producer or rice merchant, and non-Chettiar Indian or European agents who supervised purchasing operations at the rice mills.[5] The provision of credit in the agricultural sector, where the Chettiars would focus their activities beginning in the 1880s, was previously rudimentary and largely in the hands of successful agriculturists, local shopkeepers, and rice merchants in the first decades after 1852. The descriptions of credit institutions, which have appeared in recent works on the Burmese economy in the British period,[6] have dealt almost entirely with conditions in the twentieth century, particularly the 1920s and 1930s. The different government and private agencies, the various types of loans, and the rather well-defined procedures for borrowing and repayment which characterize this period were nonexistent or embryonic in the early years of agrarian development. Since there had been little need for credit or capital accumulation in the predominantly subsistence and natural economy of the Delta in the pre-British period, there

[5] The best discussions of marketing and milling operations in the Delta may be found in Cheng, *Burma Rice Industry*, pp. 48–76, 83–95 and 198–219.

[6] See, for examples, Cheng, *Burma Rice Industry*, pp. 179–93 and Tun Wai, *Currency and Credit in Burma* (Bombay, 1953), pp. 42–82.

were few bankers or moneylenders in Lower Burma at the time of its annexation to the Indian Empire. The capital of existing creditors was devoted primarily to trade, and only marginally, if at all, to agricultural production.

Sources of agricultural credit emerged gradually after the ban on rice exports was lifted and a cash-nexus, market-oriented economy began to develop. Because most agriculturists produced for the market on what Hla Myint has termed a "spare-time" basis in the first decades after 1852,[7] their need for capital was less pronounced than in later decades when most had shifted to dependence on market production. The peasant household continued to produce most of the food and goods required for its subsistence, but extra man hours were spent clearing waste land and harvesting paddy that might formerly have been left to rot for want of market outlets. The early growth of export production was based upon inputs of cheap and abundant land and additional labor, normally generated from within the agriculturist's own family, and not upon large inputs of capital.

If capital were needed for the purchase of new implements or bullocks, or by migrant settlers seeking to open new lands, it was obtained in most cases from indigenous sources.[8] Perhaps the most important sources of credit in the first decades of growth were the cultivator's relatives or neighbors who had managed to save a portion of the profits they had made by marketing their surplus rice. Indigenous professional moneylenders, who were often originally successful cultivators or paddy brokers, extended loans to agriculturists in many areas of the Delta by the 1870s. Most professional moneylenders provided credit on a *ngwedo* basis which meant that the loan was given in cash and both the principal and interest were repaid in cash. Local shopkeepers, who often functioned as rice merchants and moneylenders as well, also provided a major source of credit. Shopkeepers lent on *sabape* terms which meant that they advanced goods or cash to cultivators in the monsoon season and received paddy in repayment after the harvest. The shopkeeper would then market the paddy and use the profits to make further advances in the next cropping season. Lending transactions between neighbors or relatives were normally verbal, without security, and at rates of interest which ranged from 2.5 to 3.33 percent per month. These rates were well below the minimum 4 to 5 percent per month on land security charged by professional moneylenders, or the *sabape* rates charged by shopkeepers which went as high as 10 to 12 percent per month.

Prior to the 1880s the Chettiars confined their banking and moneylending operations largely to Rangoon city and its immediate environs. Although they financed agricultural production indirectly through loans to indigenous moneylenders who in turn lent to cultivators at higher rates of interest,[9] the Chettiars provided few loans directly to agriculturists in this period. This low level of Chettiar involvement in the early expansion of agricultural production contradicts a number of major assumptions regarding their role in Burma's development.

The assertions that the Chettiars played an "essential role in the opening up" of

---

[7] *The Economics of Developing Countries* (New York, 1965), pp. 38–52.

[8] This description of indigenous moneylending operations prior to the 1870s is based upon information in the district settlement reports for Lower Burma relating to this period.

[9] B. A. Parrot, *Report on the Settlement Operations in the Syriam Township, Hanthawaddy District, 1880–1881* (Rangoon, 1881), p. 7. This practice would become a dominant feature of credit provision in later decades.

Lower Burma and that economic advance could not have occurred without them[10] are not supported by the history of the Delta's early growth. In the first three decades after 1852, when the Chettiars were only marginally involved in any aspect of the region's economy, the area under rice cultivation increased by nearly two million acres and rice exports rose from virtually zero to 850,000 tons. The contention that the high rate of growth achieved after 1880 would not have been possible without the large amounts of capital advanced by the Chettiars in the agricultural sector is well founded. The history of the early decades of the Delta's development demonstrates, however, that economic expansion would have occurred, albeit more slowly and on a reduced scale, without the Chettiars.

The contention that "alien" moneylenders controlled most of the Delta's rice land from early in the period of British rule and the related inference that they compelled the participation of the Burmese cultivator in the rice-export economy through an indebtedness-cum-foreclosure cycle[11] are also at variance with historical reality. Burmese agriculturists, the great majority of whom were smallholders, owned all but a small percentage of the occupied area in Lower Burma until the last decade of the nineteenth century.[12] Until the 1880s loans taken by agriculturists from any source were normally small and repaid within a single cropping season. Few landowners fell so deeply in debt that they lost their lands, or were in danger of doing so.[13] Neither the Chettiars nor any other moneylending group, indigenous or alien, compelled Burmese agriculturists to produce for the market. Burmese cultivators participated willingly in the rice-export economy because they judged the material and social returns worth the extra labor involved in producing surplus paddy for sale.

Perhaps the major reason for the limited involvement of the Chettiars in Lower Burma in the early decades of British rule was the low level of the demand for agricultural credit. After the opening of the Suez canal in 1869, however, the need for credit rose sharply. The canal made it possible to supply large quantities of higher-priced husked and even white rice to European markets. In addition, market outlets in Asia expanded as the result of the growth of plantations and a concomitant growth of their laboring forces who were often dependent on imported foodstuffs.[14] These factors led to a great acceleration in the rate of growth of the Burma rice industry. Increasing numbers of cultivators shifted from spare-time to full-time production for the market in order to take the fullest advantage of the rising prices paid

[10] Cheng, *Burma Rice Industry*, p. 187 (quoted portion); N. R. Chakravarti, *The Indian Minority in Burma* (London, 1971), pp. 64 and 67–8; Philip Siegelman, "Colonial Development and the Chettiar," Ph.D. Dissertation, U. of Minnesota, 1962, pp. 9, 17, and 262; and Usha Mahajani, *The Role of the Indian Minorities in Burma and Malaya* (Bombay, 1960), pp. 19–20.

[11] Hans O. Schmitt, "Decolonization and Development in Burma," *Journal of Development Studies* 4/1 (Oct. 1967), pp. 101–3; and J. S. Furnivall, *Colonial Policy and Practice* (New York, 1956), pp. 86–7.

[12] See the tables on land ownership in the Government of Burma, *Reports on the Land Revenue Administration* for the 1880s and 1890s.

[13] The statistics provided by settlement officers

relating to indebtedness showed that as late as the first decade of the twentieth century 60 percent of the cultivators in debt could pay after the next harvest, while only 9.5 percent were "hopelessly" involved or in danger of losing their holdings. A large portion of the remaining 30 percent of cultivators in debt had taken long or medium term loans for major improvements on their holdings or to purchase additional land. These loans were normally repaid in from two to five years and were generally a sign of the borrower's wealth and reliability rather than his insolvency. See also B. O. Binns, *Agricultural Economy in Burma* (Rangoon, 1948), pp. 34–6.

[14] For a more detailed discussion of these trends see Cheng, *Burma Rice Industry*, pp. 12–15.

for paddy. At the same time, however, the cultivator's costs of production and living rose sharply. As competition for paddy land intensified, the price per acre and hence the cost of enlarging his holdings rose. Paralleling the rising cost of land was a general increase in the costs of goods and services in Lower Burma. The cultivator had to buy, at rising prices, items which had once been produced within his own household, such as farm implements and clothes. He also had to purchase firewood, fish, and other commodities that he had once obtained free in a nearby forest or stream. In addition, since the size of most cultivators' holdings had increased beyond the point where they could work them with family labor alone, the employment of wage laborers became a standard feature of rice cultivation and a major cost of production throughout much of the Delta. Rising costs resulted in a heightened demand for capital and agricultural credit, a demand which could not be met by the existing indigenous sources. In response to this demand, the Chettiars began to extend their operations from Rangoon and other urban centers into the rural Delta.

In the 1880s Chettiar firms established branches in the larger villages of rural tracts and in towns along the railway lines and main rivers throughout most of Lower Burma. Chettiar moneylenders began to supply credit directly to cultivators on a large scale, and expanded their role as a source of capital for indigenous moneylenders. During the first decades of the twentieth century Chettiar moneylenders gradually established themselves as the main source of agricultural credit in the rural Delta. The Burma Banking Enquiry Committee reported that special surveys taken in 1929-30 showed that the number of Chettiar firms in Burma had increased from approximately 350 in 1910 to over 1650 in 1930.[15] The Committee found that Chettiar firms provided nearly 60 percent of the crop loans and 45 percent of the long term loans taken by agriculturists in the Lower Burma districts where rice production was concentrated.[16] The importance of Chettiar credit was further indicated by the Committee's estimate that Chettiar loans to all agriculturists in the main rice producing districts totalled from 450 to 500 million rupees, an amount which exceeded by from 30 to 80 million rupees the value of the current rice crop.[17]

Although the total volume of loans extended by the Chettiars came to surpass that provided by indigenous sources,[18] the Burmese continued to play a major role in this field throughout the British period. Professional Burmese lenders, whose numbers the Banking Enquiry Committee set at a minimum of 15,000 in 1930,[19] far outnumbered their Chettiar counterparts. If part-time lenders were included, the difference between the number of indigenous and Chettiar lenders would have been even greater. Burmese participation in moneylending was paralleled by their extensive involvement in the domestic retail and wholesale marketing of a wide range of

---

[15] Government of Burma, *Report of the Burma Provincial Banking Enquiry Committee, 1929-30* (Rangoon, 1930), Vol. 1, pp. 204 and 210-13.

[16] For a district by district breakdown see *ibid.*, Vol. 3, pp. 11-33 and 80-90.

[17] *Ibid.*, Vol. 1, pp. 210-13. The committee appointed to investigate government-sponsored, cooperative credit programs in 1928-29 gave a lower estimate of 250 million rupees lent by Chettiars to agriculturists in Lower Burma. (See, Government of Burma, *Report of the Committee on Cooperation*

in *Burma, 1928-29* [Rangoon, 1929], p. 10). It is probable that the carefully-researched estimate of the Banking Enquiry Committee is more accurate.

[18] The Banking Enquiry Committee estimated that 17 percent of the crop loans and 15 percent of the long term loans extended to agriculturists in the Delta districts were provided by Burmese moneylenders. See *Banking Enquiry Report*, Vol. 3, pp. 11-33 and 80-90.

[19] *Ibid.*, Vol. 1, p. 67.

392

products.[20] This high degree of Burmese participation in moneylending and marketing provides a striking exception to the Southeast Asian norm where the middleman's niches in colonial economies were dominated by immigrant Asian minorities.[21] It also calls into question the widely-held assumption that Theravada Buddhist values, which are held by the great majority of the Burmese population, are inimical to moneymaking activities and the pursuit of material gain because these are identified as sources of insatiable craving and thus evil. This argument has been the most effectively developed by Mya Maung, who emphasizes the importance of Buddhist doctrines such as the Four Noble Truths, which stress nonattachment, and the concept of the impermanence (*anatesa*) of wealth and high status. Maung also argues that the strong leisure-preference of the average Burmese, the low level of economic anxiety which has historically prevailed in Burma, and the low status attached to business pursuits in traditional Burmese society have all impeded extensive or effective entrepreneurial involvement on the part of the Burmese.[22]

The extensive Burmese participation in moneymaking activities in the colonial period suggests that prohibitions regarding the pursuit of profit were (and are) largely doctrinal and not rigidly observed in actual practice. Melford Spiro's fieldwork in Upper Burma provides evidence which supports this supposition. He points out that doctrines such as the Four Noble Truths and impermanence were neither understood nor accepted by the villagers whom he studied.[23] The findings of other anthropologists, like Manning Nash and David Pfanner, indicate that Buddhist values are at most neutral with regard to moneymaking professions. Both conclude that since commercial activities do not involve the taking of life, no social disapproval is attached to them.[24] Furthermore, it is clear that in the capitalist, export-oriented context of the colonial Delta, traditional Burmese attitudes regarding the low status of commercial groups changed considerably. This was true even among the "tradition-abiding rural population" where Maung asserts that these attitudes have been the most entrenched.[25] Burmese cultivators in the Irrawaddy Delta became highly market-oriented, developed a strong taste for imported consumer goods, and increased their enjoyment of traditional pastimes as their incomes permitted. By the last decades of the nineteenth century numerous revenue officials noted the Burmese agriculturist's shift from "peasant to professional grower or paddy purveyor."[26]

[20] See the sections on internal marketing in the settlement reports for Lower Burma or the Government of Burma, *Interim Report of the Riot Enquiry Committee* (Rangoon, 1939), p. 20; and J. S. Furnivall, *An Introduction to the Political Economy of Burma* (Rangoon, 1957 ed.), p. 158.

[21] See, for examples, K. S. Sandhu, *Indians in Malaya: Immigration and Settlement, 1786–1957* (Cambridge, 1969), p. 42 *et passim;* Edgar Wickberg, *The Chinese in Philippine Life, 1850–1898* (New Haven, 1965), especially pp. 67–80; and Alice Dewey, "Capital, Credit and Saving in Javanese Marketing" in R. Firth and B. S. Yamey (eds.), *Capital, Saving and Credit in Peasant Societies* (London, 1964), pp. 230–32. Groups, like the Minangkabau on Sumatra, also provide important exceptions to this general trend.

[22] Mya Maung, "Cultural Value and Economic Change in Burma," *Asian Survey* 4 (March 1964), pp. 757–64. See also Maung's "The Genesis of Economic Development in Burma: The Plural Society" (Ph. D. dissertation, Catholic University of America, 1962), especially, pp. 98–9, 101–2 and 110.

[23] "Buddhism and Economic Action in Burma," *American Anthropologist* 68/3 (October 1966), pp. 1163–65.

[24] Manning Nash, *The Golden Road to Modernity* (New York, 1965), pp. 159–60; and David E. Pfanner and Jasper Ingersoll, "Theravada Buddhism and Village Economic Behavior: A Burmese and Thai Comparison," *Journal of Asian Studies* 21/3 (May 1962), p. 345.

[25] Maung, "Cultural Value," p. 760.

[26] Government of Burma, *Revenue and Agriculture Proceedings*, Vol. 4886, March 1896, no. 5, p. 9. For a detailed discussion of these shifts in peasant attitudes see, Adas, *Burma Delta*, chapter 3 and conclusion.

The large numbers of Burmese engaged in moneylending and internal marketing indicate that the proper questions for the historian to ask with regard to the distribution of positions in finance in the Delta rice industry is not why so few Burmese were involved, but why the Chettiars were able to operate on such a greater scale than the Burmese and how they came to play such an important role in the economy of an alien land. The answers to these questions can be found through an examination of the differences between the Burmese and their immigrant competitors in terms of their previous experiences, social organization, and cultural values.

Throughout most of their recorded history the Chettiars have been extensively involved in commerce and finance, and thus they came to Burma well prepared to assume the middleman's role in the Delta economy. The origins of the Chettiar community, like those of most caste groups in India, are obscure and expressed in legends. It is known, however, that Chettiars were engaged in commerce as early as the period of the Chola dynasty's hegemony in Tamilnad (c. 900–1250). In Chola times they were engaged primarily in maritime trade, but in the sixteenth and seventeenth centuries they began to concentrate on banking and moneylending.[27] The Chettiar caste was of the Vaisya *varna,* which meant that its members were considered twice-born like Brahmans and Ksatriyas and ranked above Sudras (traditionally agriculturists) and outcastes. Because of their great wealth and generous contributions to Hindu temples and charities, the Chettiars had long been a powerful and highly respected community in South India.[28]

Despite the fact that they showed little inclination to learn or adopt Western methods until the twentieth century, Chettiars had had much more extensive contacts than the Burmese with European merchants and shippers in the centuries prior to the Delta's annexation. Chettiars and other mercantile castes had, of course, functioned in rather well-developed market and money economies long before the Europeans had begun to trade in India. However, long centuries of dealing with Europeans, prepared them for extensive involvement in the Delta economy after 1852. Especially important were Chettiar connections with Western banks and joint-stock companies, such as the Imperial Bank of India and the Indian Overseas Bank, which provided them with sources of working capital which were not readily available to Burmese brokers, merchants and moneylenders.[29]

In contrast to the experience gained by the Chettiars through centuries of commercial enterprise, the nature of the pre-British economy in Burma proved a serious handicap for Burmese who became involved in marketing and credit provision after 1852. In the largely subsistence economy of Konbaung Burma, merchants played a marginal role. External commerce by sea was largely in the hands of foreigners; and the overland trade to China was controlled by the Chinese. Internal trade was localized and mainly of a peddling nature. Because there were few ways in which wealth might profitably be invested, there was little impetus to save. In fact, in a society where dacoity was widespread, warfare periodic, and government officials

[27] Edgar Thurston, *Tribes and Castes of South India* (Madras, 1909), Vol. 5, pp. 258–61; A. Appadorai, *Economic Conditions of South India, 1000–1500* (Madras, 1936), Vol. 1, p. 379; and C. H. Rau, "The Banking Caste of Southern India," *Indian Review* (Madras) 8/8 (Aug. 1907). p. 593.

[28] Rau, "Banking Caste," p. 594; and Government of Madras, *Madura (District) Gazetteer* (Madras, 1914), p. 101.
[29] Tun Wai, *Burma's Currency and Credit,* pp. 49–50; and L. C. Jain, *Indigenous Banking in India* (London, 1929), pp. 165–69 and 177.

often rapacious, hoarded wealth was a tempting target. As a result, the level of investment in mercantile or handicraft enterprises was low.

In addition to the limitations imposed by the nature of Konbaung society itself, the isolation of the Burman kingdom placed those Burmese who sought to fill positions in trade or finance after 1852 at a disadvantage vis-à-vis their foreign competitors. The vast majority of Burmese, including members of the small mercantile class, had had only fleeting contacts with foreigners in the Konbaung period. They had almost no knowledge of European business techniques and marketing practices. Even more importantly, no group of Burmese possessed contacts with European banking firms comparable to those of the Chettiars and to a lesser extent the Chinese and other Indian merchants. Consequently, Burmese merchants and moneylenders were normally not able to take advantage of the great capital resources of these establishments.

Centuries of involvement in commercial enterprises had shaped the social patterns and oriented the values of the Chettiar community. The home-life and upbringing of a Chettiar child inculcated values of thrift and self-reliance, and prepared him for a position in a Chettiar firm when he came of age. Chettiar parents were expected to set aside a certain amount of money at the birth of each son. The money with accumulated interest was later used to finance the boy's education. Although Chettiar families normally resided in joint households, each married unit cooked and ate its meals separately. Fixed allotments of food and other provisions were divided among married members of the family annually, and they were expected to use their supplies judiciously so that they would not be caught short. The wives of even the most wealthy Chettiars dressed simply, performed menial household tasks, and wove baskets or spun thread to help pay household expenses. When a Chettiar visited his relatives, he received only his first meal free. If he stayed longer he would be "quietly debited" the cost of the rest of his stay.[30]

Until the age of ten or twelve, Chettiar boys studied in Tamil schools where they learned bookkeeping techniques and the caste's special counting system.[31] At the age of twelve, they went to work as apprentices for Chettiar firms. Boys of rich parents usually remained in Madras, but in firms other than those owned by their parents. Boys from less well-to-do families were normally apprenticed to Chettiar firms abroad. During the period of their apprenticeship, which could last as long as nine years, Chettiar youths received little in the way of theoretical training, for the Chettiars considered experience the best teacher. They also received no salary during the first three years of their service, but were provided with room, board, pocket money, and a bonus at the end of the three years which varied according to the promise they had shown and the distance they were stationed from Madras. If he were successful, the Chettiar youth would begin to work his way up the hierarchy from accountant to cashier after four or five years, and become an assistant or sub-agent in an out-station after seven or eight years. After a year's holiday between the ages of twenty-two and twenty-five, the successful trainee would receive a

---

[30] Thurston, *Tribes and Castes*, Vol. 5, pp. 250–53 and 270; *Banking Enquiry Report*, Vol. 1, p. 192.

[31] Information on Chettiar professional training was derived mainly from the questionnaire pre-

pared by Mr. Vellayan Chettiar for the Banking Enquiry Committee and included in Vol. 2 of the *Banking Enquiry Report*, pp. 129–36. See also Thurston, *Tribes and Castes*, Vol. 5, pp. 252–3; and Rau, "Banking Caste," p. 595.

position as an agent and, if he were talented, eventually become a partner in a Chettiar firm.

There was no group in Burmese society whose family structure and rearing practices were geared to success in commerce to a degree comparable to that of the Chettiars. Although contemporary studies of Burmese village communities suggest that Burmese Buddhist values are not inimical to commercial pursuits, they indicate that Buddhist practices may place considerable limitations on the extent to which an individual can become involved in financial endeavors and on the scale of his operations. These limitations result from the fact that Theravada Buddhist beliefs militate against the economically productive use of wealth. David Pfanner has observed that "the accumulation of wealth as an end in itself is not admired in rural Burma, but the accumulation of wealth for the purposes of merit-making is highly valued."[32] Manning Nash found that rich villagers of Nondwin near Sagaing in the Dry Zone are expected to spend lavishly on Buddhist ceremonies, pagoda and monastery building or repair, and the support of local monks. According to popular Buddhist belief, the rich have the greatest opportunity to make merit by using their wealth for these ends. A survey taken by Nash in Nondwin showed that these expectations were fulfilled in actual practice, for religious donations comprised a far higher percentage of the annual expenditure of rich than of poor peasants.[33]

The information provided by British settlement officers indicates that these patterns were widely followed in Lower Burma in the nineteenth and early-twentieth centuries. Rich agriculturists spent large sums on pagodas and village ceremonies, and rich villages invariably contained ornate teak monasteries and gilded pagodas which were often built by individual patrons.[34] The merit-making syndrome would have greatly hindered effective Burmese participation in money-lending and commerce by diverting the resources of those individuals who were best able to engage in these activities to non-productive (in economic terms) channels.[35] The Chettiars also made large donations to Shaivite temples and charity. However, the scale of their operations and the fact that only a fixed percentage of their profits, termed *magamai*, was given, meant that their commercial activities were not constricted to the extent that merit-making limited Burmese economic investment.

In competition with Burmese moneylenders, the Chettiars also derived great advantage from their superior organization and group solidarity. While most Burmese moneylenders worked as individuals, Chettiars were almost invariably members of firms which were organized in a standard fashion.[36] The firms were

---

[32] Pfanner, "Theravada Buddhism and Economic Behavior," p. 345.

[33] Nash, *Golden Road*, pp. 160–61. See also Pfanner, "Theravada Buddhism and Economic Behavior," p. 348 and Maung, "Cultural Value," pp. 759–60.

[34] See, for examples, James MacKenna, *Report on the Settlement Operations in Myaungmya and Thongwa 1902–3* (Rangoon, 1903), Appendices A and B, p. 118; H. Des Voeux, *Report on the Settlement Operations in Toungoo 1898–99* (Rangoon, 1900), p. 34; and E. A. Moore, *Report on the Revision Settlement Operations in the Thar-rawaddy District, 1901–2* (Rangoon, 1903), p. 7.

[35] This judgement would, of course, have been incomprehensible to the Burmese agriculturist who regarded merit-making as the very best possible long-term investment. See Melford Spiro's excellent article on "Buddhism and Economic Action in Burma," *American Anthropologist* 68 (Oct. 1966), pp. 1163–73; or Maung, "Cultural Value," p. 759.

[36] The best accounts of Chettiar organization and operations in Burma may be found in the *Banking Enquiry Report*, Vol. 1, pp. 194–96 and 200–09, and Vol. 2, pp. 128–36 *et passim*.

owned on a partnership basis by several persons who were usually related. Agents directed the day to day operations of the firms' main branches which were located in the larger towns of the Delta. An agent overseer, who might be one of the proprietors, was stationed in Rangoon or Moulmein to supervise the operations of the firm's branches. Each of the main branches was staffed with cashiers, accountants and clerks. Beginning in the 1880s, *utkades* or out-stations which were run single-handedly by sub-agents were established in villages throughout Lower Burma.

An agent usually remained at his post for three years. Six months before his period of service was to end, his successor joined him in order to familiarize himself with the station's records and clientele. After his term of service ended, the agent returned to Madras where he spent up to three years tending to domestic concerns and working on accounts in the firm's main office. At the end of this period, he returned to Burma to take up a post often, but not necessarily, with the same firm.

Chettiar combinations not only provided superior sources of capital to invest and lend, but they also strengthened community ties which were vital to Chettiar predominance in Burma. Alice Dewey has shown that Chinese success in trade on Java can to a large degree be attributed to the "informal" or non-legal sanctions through which members of the community insure that debts are paid, orders delivered on time, and contracts kept on a continuing and long-term basis. She points out that by reducing the element of risk involved in commercial activities, these sanctions have given the Chinese a decisive edge over the Javanese whose supra-village business ties are "transient" and "intermittent."[37] Through caste and kinship networks and their firm organizations, Chettiars in Burma institutionalized "informal sanctions."

Like the Chinese on Java and other alien minorities, the Chettiars were united by their differences from the indigenous population. The Banking Enquiry Committee observed:

> Existence as a small alien group with frequent blood-relationship and with common economic interests, descent, language, worship and all caste associations, but divided in all these points from the population around them, was sure to generate a feeling of sodality. . . .[38]

Prosperous Chettiars were often partners in several firms, and a firm in financial difficulty was usually given aid by other firms. The caste *panchayat,* which held the power to ostracize caste members, maintained community discipline, upheld Chettiar business codes, and arbitrated disputes. Caste sanctions were so strong that the only security given for capital assigned to Chettiar agents was "an unstamped acknowledgement scratched on a palmyra leaf."[39] To protect themselves from the risk of employing dishonest clerks, the Chettiars hired only persons from Madras whom they knew and trusted. The main Chettiar temple on Mogul Street in Rangoon, which was called the "Chettiar exchange," served as a focal point for the community's activities in Burma. On the upper floor in a large room before the community shrine to Siva, Chettiars held periodic meetings, determined current interest rates, settled disputes, formed common opinions regarding important

---

[37] "Javanese Marketing" in Firth and Yamey (eds.), *Credit in Peasant Societies,* pp. 233–242.

[38] *Banking Enquiry Report,* Vol. 1, p. 194.

[39] P. Siegleman, "Colonial Development," p. 126.

political issues (such as proposed tenancy or land alienation legislation), and exchanged gossip.

Although other Indian commercial groups, such as the Marwaris and the north Indian *banias* and the Chinese, were also active as middlemen in the Delta, none played roles comparable to those of the Chettiars. Proximity was perhaps the crucial advantage the Chettiars had over these groups. Because their homeland in the Madura and Ramnad districts of the Madras Presidency was just across the Bay of Bengal, the Chettiars were in close touch with developments in the Delta and only a rather short journey by steamship away. In moving into Lower Burma, they merely extended the commercial network which they had established throughout much of the Madras Presidency centuries earlier and in Tenasserim before 1852. Lower Burma soon became by far the most important area of Chettiar activity. By contrast, the Chinese were far better established in other areas of Southeast Asia and other Indian commercial groups had focused their operations in East Africa, Ceylon or on the Indian subcontinent itself. In addition, from the cultivator's viewpoint the Chinese offered a less attractive source of credit. Most of the Chinese who extended loans to cultivators were village shopkeepers who lent at the very high *sabape* rates of interest discussed above. Consequently, Chinese loans went mainly to high-risk clients, like landless laborers and tenants, who had little security to offer and little to tie them to a particular locale. In the late 1920s the Chinese provided approximately nine percent of the crop loans taken by Delta agriculturists.[40]

As noted above, private British investors had neither the manpower nor the desire to extend credit on the basis of the myriad, small-scale transactions required in the agricultural sector. The one exception to this general rule was Dawson's bank which was established in 1905. The original purpose of the bank was to assist cultivators in redeeming mortgages which had been offered as security for loans from Chettiar moneylenders. In the early 1920s Dawson's bank also began to make advances for cultivating expenses. Even though it lent at low rates and grew fairly rapidly in the 1920s, Dawson's loans to agriculturists in Lower Burma totaled only seven million rupees per year as late as 1929.[41]

While the colonial government made a number of attempts through agricultural loan funds and co-operatives to provide alternatives to private lenders, their efforts were largely unsuccessful. Government agencies never supplied more than a small fraction of the amount extended by Chettiars or other private lenders. Although government interest rates were considerably lower, private lenders were far more accessible, and private loans were obtained with much less delay and red tape, in larger amounts, and with less severe penalties for default on repayments.[42]

In contrast to the Chettiars, Burmese moneylenders rarely established stable or long-term combinations. As one Burmese moneylender observed, ". . . they have no

[40] *Banking Enquiry Report*, Vol. 1, pp. 81 and 94, Vol. 3, pp. 11–33; sections on agricultural credit in the settlement reports for Lower Burma districts, especially O. M. Rees, *Initial Report on [the] Revision Settlement of the Pyapon District, 1921–25* (Rangoon, 1927), p. 8 and U Tin Gyi, *Report on the Second Revision Settlement of the*

Ma-ubin District, 1925–28 (Rangoon, 1929), pp. 15 and 21–22.

[41] Tun Wai, *Currency and Credit*, pp. 78–82; and *Banking Enquiry Report*, Vol. 2, p. 98.

[42] The best discussion of government lending efforts in the secondary literature may be found in Cheng, *Burma Rice Industry*, pp. 190–97.

relations beyond mutual rivalry and dislike."[43] Given their lack of organization and the other handicaps discussed above, it is remarkable that so many Burmese participated successfully in trade and credit provision in the Delta rice industry. One factor that may explain their ability to survive was the informal division of clientele that had developed between Burmese and Chettiar lenders by the 1880s. Chettiars lent mainly to reliable persons who could offer good security. Burmese moneylenders, on the other hand, who had a better knowledge of local customs and a personal acquaintance with prospective customers, often gave loans to persons Chettiars had turned down.[44] The scale of their operations and their lower "risk premium," due to the nature of their clientele, were the major factors behind the Chettiars' ability to extend credit at lower rates than their Burmese counterparts. As the Chettiars extended their operations throughout the rural Delta, they forced indigenous moneylenders in most areas to scale down their rates. In the first decades of the twentieth century, the average rate charged by professional moneylenders on standard *ngwedo* loans, which were taken on land security, had fallen from over 4-5 percent to 1.25-3 percent per month.[45]

The position of indigenous moneylenders was also enhanced by the fact that they were able to borrow from the Chettiars. In the last decades of the nineteenth century, the Chettiars became a major source of working capital for professional Burmese moneylenders, as well as indigenous paddy brokers, rice merchants, large landlords, and other groups who engaged in credit provision on a part time basis. The indigenous lender would borrow from a Chettiar firm at an average interest rate of 2 percent per month, and lend to cultivators at 3 or 4 percent.[46] The Chettiar gained because larger transactions simplified his bookkeeping operations, and because established moneylenders and landlords were safer clients than smallholders. For the indigenous lender, the Chettiar agent provided a link with the great capital reservoirs of the Chettiar firms and through them with European-owned banks. This pattern meant that through most of the British period, the spread of Chettiar operations contributed substantially to, rather than impeded, the growth of an indigenous moneylending class.

Despite the great attention given to the Chettiars' role as large-scale landholders in the secondary literature on Burma in the British period, they controlled less than 6 percent of the occupied area in Lower Burma as late as 1930.[47] The evidence supplied by British and Burmese settlement officers supports the statements of the Nattukottai Chettiars' Association that they did not want land, and that they foreclosed on mortgages, which were provided by most of their cultivator-clients as security, only when no other way could be found to reclaim their loans. The Chettiars also attempted to sell the holdings gained through foreclosure as soon as possible. They sought to keep their capital fluid and had no desire to become involved in extensive landholding in an alien and potentially hostile land.[48] Burmese

---

[43] *Banking Enquiry Report*, Vol. 2, p. 97.

[44] Govt. of Burma, *Revenue and Agriculture Proceedings*, Vol. 8633, Nov. 1911, p. 496 *et passim*; and *Banking Enquiry Report*, Vol. 1, p. 78.

[45] *Ibid.*, p. 4; and *Banking Enquiry Report*, Vol. 1, pp. 78–80, Vol. 2, p. 106 *et passim*, and Vol. 3, pp. 11–33.

[46] *Ibid.*, Vol. 7237, May 1906, pp. 25–6; and the sections on credit provision in the settlement

reports for this period.

[47] Govt. of Burma, *Report of the Land and Agriculture Committee* (Rangoon, 1938), Pt. 2, p. 39.

[48] Govt. of Burma, *Revenue and Agriculture Proceedings*, Vol. 4886, March 1896, pp. 36–7; Vol. 7238, Aug. 1906, p. 63 and Vol. 7237, May 1906, pp. 25–6; and Mahajani, *Role of the Indian Minorities*, p. 178.

moneylenders, on the other hand, were viewed by many government officials as "dangerous landgrabbers" who were anxious to acquire large estates through foreclosures.[49] Although this reputation was deserved in some instances, it is probable that most indigenous lenders, like the Chettiars, were forced to take over holdings when it became clear that their loans would not be repaid. The fact that Burmese moneylenders generally extended credit to less reliable customers than the Chettiars may best explain the higher incidence of foreclosures in transactions involving indigenous lenders.

Due in part to the nature of their lending operations, the Chettiars initially avoided becoming deeply involved in the struggle over land control that intensified in Lower Burma in the first decades of the twentieth century. Because Burmese lenders and Chinese shopkeepers serviced most of the borrowers who were likely to default on their payments, a high percentage of the land alienated by cultivator-owners fell into the hands of these groups. In addition, indigenous landlords increasingly provided credit for their own tenants, and shopkeepers lent to landless laborers.[50] Thus, the Chettiars had little contact with these potentially hostile groups. If it were necessary for a Chettiar to foreclose on a client's mortgage, he did so through the courts, thereby minimizing direct confrontations with his debtors. Until the second decade of the twentieth century, when the unoccupied, cultivable land ran out in most areas of the Irrawaddy Delta,[51] dispossessed cultivators had the option of migrating to frontier areas and claiming new holdings. In any case, prior to the 1920s it was relatively rare for Chettiars to foreclose on the mortgages of their clients.[52] In most cases the Chettiar was content to collect the interest due on his loans year after year and leave the principal unpaid.[53]

The spread of land alienation and the growing indebtedness of Delta agriculturists were symptoms of serious disorders which increasingly dominated the economy of Lower Burma in the last decades of British rule. A full discussion of the factors which caused these disorders clearly lies beyond the scope of this essay, but some mention should be made of those factors which had the greatest bearing on the position of the Chettiars in Burma.[54] Since the expansion of rice production in Burma had been based primarily upon added inputs of land and labor rather than major technological innovations, the closing of the rice frontier was one of the underlying determinants of the agrarian crisis. In the face of continuing population growth, the unavailability of cultivable, unoccupied land drove up land prices thereby limiting the ability of cultivator-owners to add to their holdings (and productivity) or start anew should they lose their original lands. The closing of the frontier also resulted in a growing surplus of tenants and laborers which undermined the once strong bargaining position of these groups. Recurrent market slumps, due largely to international conditions, reduced the income the producer received for his surplus production, while a high rate of inflation increased his costs of cultivation and living. The combinations and collusive buying practices of rice

---

[49] *Ibid.*, Vol. 7237, May 1906, pp. 25–6 and 89–92 and Vol. 7238, Aug. 1906, p. 63.

[50] For a detailed discussion of these trends see Adas, *Burma Delta*, Chapter 6.

[51] *Ibid.*

[52] Excepting the years following the world-wide credit crisis which began to affect Burma in 1907.

See Thomas Couper, *Report on Indebtedness in the Thaton District* (Rangoon, 1911), pp. 10–11.

[53] J. R. Andrus, *Burmese Economic Life* (Stanford, 1948), p. 77.

[54] The following summary is based on Adas, *Burma Delta*, Chapters 6, 7 and 8.

merchants and millers, especially those of the big Rangoon firms, further reduced the income of the rice producer.

As more and more landlords and cultivator-owners defaulted on loan payments, the Chettiars were forced to foreclose on mortgages and assume the proprietorship of increasing amounts of paddy land which they could no longer easily sell. In the late 1920s the widespread defaulting of their clients also led to the failure of a number of Chettiar firms due to their inability to repay loans taken from European banks and other non-Chettiar sources.[55] The market slump and subsequent crisis of the Delta economy caused by the Great Depression of the 1930s completely undermined the Chettiars' already uneasy position in Burma. The amount of credit they were able or willing to provide decreased sharply, and they were forced to call in the principal on loans which they had been content to collect only interest on for years. The inability of many Burmese smallholders and large landlords alike to repay their loans meant that the Chettiars were compelled to foreclose on mortgages offered as security. Thus, their capital became increasingly fixed in landholding at a time when the profits from rice production and the price of land were falling sharply. By 1937, Chettiars controlled 25 percent of the total occupied area in Lower Burma, and nearly 50 percent of the land alienated to non-agriculturists.[56]

Their growing role as landlords increased the Chettiars' vulnerability to Burmese nationalist criticisms. Although Burmese nationalist leaders also protested against the continued influx of large numbers of Indian laborers into Burma, they often singled out the Chettiars in their polemical assaults on the Indian community. The Chettiars' singular appearance and alien customs, their wealth and social exclusiveness made them a likely scapegoat. They were blamed for many of Burma's economic woes and soon became the "butt of the cartoonist" and "Public Enemy No. 1."[57] In the mid-1920s, Burmese agriculturists, prompted by nationalist leaders, formed *Sibwaye Athins* (development associations) whose purpose was to forcibly compel the Chettiars to reduce debts owed by Burmese cultivators and eventually to abandon their operations in Burma entirely.[58] In the turbulent thirties, their *pucca* agency-dwellings with their ornate teak trim and iron-barred windows became major targets for wandering dacoits, agrarian rebels, and urban rioters. In the last years before the Japanese invasion in 1941-2, the Burma Legislative Council passed several agrarian relief measures aimed at reducing tenants' rental rates and reclaiming for the smallholder land that had been alienated to Chettiars and Burmese landlords. There were provisions for compensation, but these measures were cut short by the imposition of Japanese rule and the flight of the Chettiars and most of the Indian population from Burma. After independence, the lands held by the Chettiars were nationalized and the debts owed them cancelled by the Burmese regime. To this date only minimal compensation has been received by the Chettiars. They have been forced to write off as a loss most of their investments in Burma whose value was estimated at 750,000,000 rupees in the late 1920s.[59]

---

[55] *Banking Enquiry Report*, Vol. 2, p. 89; and the *Rangoon Gazette*, 8 December 1929, p. 12.

[56] *Land and Agriculture Report*, Pt. 2, p. 39.

[57] G. E. Harvey, *British Rule in Burma, 1824-1942* (London, 1946), p. 55. See also the excerpts from Burmese vernacular papers reprinted in the Government of Burma, *Interim Report of the Riot Enquiry Committee* (Rangoon, 1939), pp. 35-36;

and Mahajani, *Role of the Indian Minorities*, p. 21.

[58] John Cady, *A History of Modern Burma* (Ithaca, 1958), p. 252.

[59] N. Chakravarti, *Indian Minority*, pp. 61, 67-8, 162-63 and 177-78. The grievances of the Chettiars and their associations' claims are discussed in Mahajani, *Role of the Indian Minorities*, pp. 68-69 and 174-79.

The Chettiars' responsibility for the crisis of the Delta rice-export economy has been a matter of considerable controversy. A close examination of their operations in Burma reveals, however, that neither as landlords nor as moneylenders were they the "hard-hearted lot" who were guilty of "swindling, cheating, deception and oppression,"[60] that many of their critics have pictured. The Banking Enquiry Committee and numerous government officials concluded that in both of their major capacities in Burma, the Chettiars dealt with their clients and tenants or laborers in a manner no worse, and often quite better, than their indigenous counterparts. As moneylenders they extended credit to all races on equal terms, and at rates that were generally lower than those of their competitors. Although these rates would be considered high by Western standards, it is important to note that in the capital-scarce economies of the developing world, interest rates are normally higher than those in developed areas. This is particularly true of rates on loans in the agricultural sector, where there is a high risk of illiquidity and default, and where handling costs are high due to the large number of small transactions.[61]

Perhaps the most detrimental aspect of the Chettiars' operations in Burma was their tendency to overlend. If a prospective client could offer adequate security, Chettiars would grant large loans without any attempt to determine the borrower's actual needs or the reasons why he was taking the loan. There is some evidence which suggests that Chettiars also encouraged cultivators to overborrow or to take loans when they had no economic reasons to do so.[62] Consequently, the cultivator-owner, who frequently had a rather imperfect understanding of the workings of a money economy, often borrowed beyond his means or needs. In many cases, particularly during times of economic decline like the late 1920s and 1930s, the cultivator would be unable to keep up his interest payments on the loan. Eventually the Chettiar would be forced to foreclose on the mortgage which the cultivator had offered as security, thereby contributing to the spread of land alienation and the decline of the peasant proprietor-based agrarian system that the British had striven to establish in the late nineteenth century.

It is impossible and unnecessary to apportion the blame for the decline of the Delta rice-export economy among the major participants in its development: Europeans, Chettiars and other Indian groups; Burmese, and Chinese. The problem of what went wrong cannot be solved with reference to any one group. The roles of each and their interaction must be analyzed within the context of the Delta economy as a whole. It is clear, however, that the Chettiars' critics have overstated their responsibility for the economic disorders which became so pronounced in the last decades of British rule, just as their defenders have overstated the Chettiars' role in the Delta's early growth. Nevertheless, the Chettiars' activities in Burma underscore the importance of detailed studies of the involvement of non-European immigrant minorities in the colonial and post-colonial economies and societies of the Afro-Asian world. Much of the internal strife between indigenous and immigrant communities which has been characteristic of emerging nations can be traced to this involvement.

---

[60] These statements were made by a Karen witness before the Banking Enquiry Committee. See *Report*, Vol. 1, p. 189.

[61] Bauer and Yamey, *Economics of Underdeveloped Countries*, pp. 115-17.

[62] *Land and Agriculture Report*, Part 3, p. 78.

XIV

The Annex of the Raj:
The Anglo-Indian Interlude in Burmese History
c. 1826-1941

One of the most striking features of the history of Burma in the post-World War II era has been the extent to which its leaders have sought to isolate the new nation from the rest of the world. While nationalist leaders in most of Britain's Asian empire buffered the transition from colonial to independent status through membership in the British Commonwealth, the Burmese brusquely rejected the British offer to join the Commonwealth, despite the considerable economic, military and political advantages that membership provided. The leaders of the AFPFL, who struggled to assert the new state's control over rebellious minorities and political factions in the decade after independence were, relative to the military regime that followed, open to international exchanges and aid and continuing foreign investment, including that by Indian businessmen who continued to play a major role in the economy.[1] But under the Ne Win regime, which, following a stint as a "caretaker" government, seized power from U Nu and the civilian politicians in 1962, Burma steadily reduced its outside contacts and commitments and closed in on itself.

From non-alignment and neutrality, then fashionable among Third World leaders, the Burmese moved to outright isolation. A once-booming export economy was reduced to a shadow of its former self. As state planners intended, foreign investment dried up in the harsh climate generated by military dictatorship and the Burmese determination to forge their own path to socialism.[2] Cultural exchanges with other nations dwindled. Scholarly research by foreigners was confined to a handful of specialists who maintained personal contacts with the military leaders or whose work was in fields like archaeology and the early periods of Burmese history that were regarded remote enough from current realities to be innocuous. Few places in Burma were accessible even to the most stalwart of tourists. Cities like Rangoon, where visitors were allowed, served as the pretext for numerous journalists to launch into rather predictable accounts of the lack of even the most minimal "modern" facilities in isolated Burma and to chronicle the steady deterioration of the famous haunts and imperial monuments of the late-lamented Raj.

Though many Third World nations in the post-colonial era have displayed an understandable wariness with regard to contacts with the superpowers as well as their former colonial rulers, none has surpassed Burma in its determined retreat into isolation. Explanations for this response have varied, but two basic suppositions inform much of the speculation on this point. Burma's retreat from the world, it is argued, is quite consistent with its longstanding tradition of xenophobia and mirrors attempts by earlier rulers to shut their kingdom off from the world. The pronounced expansionist tendencies of Burmese dynasties, their extensive contacts with both neighboring rulers and those more distant like China, as well as Burma's receptivity to outside cultural influences and its active participation since early times in the Indian Ocean trading network, all render the

XIV

xenophobic interpretation highly questionable. This is especially true when Burma is compared to China or Japan, which were much more cut off from outside influences for longer periods of time than Burma and yet have been major forces in the international struggles of the postwar world. As Victor Lieberman has shown, from the sixteenth century the contacts of various burmese peoples with the merchants and adventurers of the expansive European powers were extensive and influential in shaping the history of the region as a whole.[3]

In addition to xenophobia, Burma's determined retreat into isolation is blamed on the "traumatic" effects of colonization on the Burmese people. Thus, the hostility of the Burmese to outsiders and foreign influences is linked to political and social turmoil brought on by the collapse of the Burmese export-oriented economy in the Great Depression and the gradual but perhaps more unsettling decline of Burmese culture as exemplified by decay within the Buddhist Sangha.[4] Once again, however, if Burma's colonial experience is viewed in a comparative context, the explanation offered for its retreat from the world is problematic. British colonial rule in Burma was a good deal milder and less exploitative than French colonization in Algeria or Vietnam, the early decades of Belgian control in the Congo, or British conquest and settlement in areas like Kenya and Rhodesia. Yet none of the nations that emerged from these other colonial contexts has closed in on itself to the extent that Burma has. In fact, Algeria, Kenya and Rhodesia (Zimbabwe), which suffered the shocks of both imperial domination and occupation by European settlers, have been among the most engaged of post-colonial societies in international and regional affairs and exchanges.

Despite the fact that colonialism was considerably more benign in Burma than in many other areas, an examination of the experience of the Burmese peoples under British rule reveals an added dimension of colonization that goes a long way to explaining their determination to close themselves off from the world in the post-colonial era. Like Kenya and Rhodesia, Burma was twice colonized. But unlike them, the second wave was not tens of thousands of European farmers but rather well over a million Indians from officials and policemen, to merchants and factory and farm laborers. This second colonization was in many ways the more traumatic and threatening. The Indians not only migrated, and in many cases settled, in unprecedented numbers, but they came to dominate many sectors of the colonial economy and administration. Burma's formal annexation to Britain's Indian empire across the Bay of Bengal initiated an era of foreign domination in which the interests of the Province were consistently subordinated to those of the larger empire. Even Burma's nationalist movement developed in the shadow of its earlier and much larger counterpart in India, and Burmese nationalist leaders soon concluded that their struggle involved the expulsion not only of the British but, even more critically, the colonizers' Indian allies and camp followers. At the peak of the Indian influx in the early 1920s, there were over a million Indians resident in the Province as a whole and these made up over ten percent of the population in some areas. It is not surprising then that many Burmese leaders feared that their small and historically under-populated land would be overwhelmed by migrants from their giant and over-populated neighbor to the west. Though the xenophobia of certain Burmese leaders and parties can not entirely be dismissed as a factor. Burma's double colonization and the very formidable threat to the Burmese people and culture posed by decades of virtually unrestricted migration and Indian sub-imperialism can be seen as one of the prime causes of Burma's postwar retreat into isolation.

Though angry British merchants, clamoring for free access to the markets and resources of Burma and myopic, even arrogant, Burmese monarchs did much to bring on the conflicts that led to the piecemeal conquest of Burma between 1826 and 1888,[5] all prompted British officials in India to view the region as yet another turbulent frontier that must be pacified, if necessary at the cost of annexation. The threat of attack or the spread of social unrest from regions ruled by Indian princes that bordered on areas to which British control had brought "peace and good government" had been a key justification for British expansion within the Indian subcontinent from the middle decades of the eighteenth century. By the first decades of the nineteenth century, Burma had become, in the mind of English East India Company officials, one of these turbulent frontiers. Its step-by-step reduction was seen as essential to peace and security in the eastern portions of the empire. Thus, Burma fell victim to imperialist aggression not so much because of calls for international free trade by British merchants, though these did much to bring on specific crises, but because it had the misfortune to border on Britain's Indian domains and appeared to fit the logic of expansion into the turbulent frontier.

Even the techniques that the British had employed since the mid-eighteenth century with regard to truculent Indian princes were applied, with very little success, to Burma. Methods of informal control from flattery to gunboat diplomacy, which had long been preferred to costly annexations, were first attempted. The British sought, again with very little success, to reduce successive Burman monarchs to what was in effect the status of subordinate allies akin to those they had earlier created through varying forms of "alliances" with the princes of India.[6] As had been the case in the expansion of the empire within the subcontinent, when the Kon-baung rulers understandably spurned British attempts to dominate them informally, the British concluded that they had no choice but to make war and to annex Burma outright to the Indian empire.

But the fatal Indian connection that led to Burma's colonization went much deeper than the imperatives of the turbulent frontier. The merchants and sea captains, who became embroiled in disputes with Kon-baung officials, sailed from Calcutta and other Indian ports and many served the East India Company. The timber and other raw materials they sought were very often intended for the India market or for the use of the Company. Long before the first Anglo-Burman war in 1824-1826, British travellers and officials had viewed Burma's potential as a colonial possession in terms of India's needs. In 1811, for example, William Francklin wrote of the great potential of Burma as a source of raw materials and foodstuffs for India *and* a market outlet for both European and Indian manufacturers. He noted the great fertility of the Irrawaddy delta region of lower Burma and found that its presence offered "great consolation" in the face of the ever-present threat of famine in the heavily populated provinces of Bengal. To enhance the insurance against calamity that Burma might provide, Francklin urged the British to do all they could to promote the advance of agriculture in the region.[7] Decades later, Henry Bell argued that if the fertile provinces of southern Burma were annexed to the Indian empire they would serve as a formidable

XIV

buffer to the famines that periodically ravaged the subcontinent.[8] Shortly after the region was annexed in 1852, East India Company officials at Calcutta set to work on schemes to promote migration to the new territories from heavily populated districts in eastern and southern India.[9]

The armies that conquered Burma in the three Anglo-Burman wars that were fought between 1824 and 1886 were made up mainly of Indian troops. Their commanding officers were in the pay of the East India Company in the first two conflicts and of the Government of India in the final clash. The Kon-baung domains were transformed piecemeal into an annex of the British Raj, one of many Provinces of the vast Indian empire. Though British administrators occupied the top posts in the colonial administration and the military and police forces, many upper level and most of the intermediate positions were staffed by civil servants and officers drawn from various parts of the Indian empire. By the 1930s, nearly thirty percent of those engaged in public administration were Indian, and over forty-five percent of the security forces were made up of Indian recruits.[10] Throughout the colonial era, internal security in Burma, particularly in times of crisis, as well as external defense were dependent on the Indian army.[11] For the great majority of the Burmese, the Indian presence was magnified by the fact that Indian or Anglo-Indian assessors, surveyors, policemen and census takers were much more likely to be in daily contact with the peasants and urban laborers than higher ranking British officials. Thus, the second or Indian wave of colonization was much more apparent to the Burmese than British overlordship in the Province.

The influx of Indian administrative and military personnel foreshadowed the reliance of the colonizers on Indian precedents in the governance of the new territories. The administrative organization itself was patterned after those which had evolved over nearly a century in India. Though the architects of the Boat and Gymkhana clubs indulged in decorative flourishes that were decidedly Burmese, the great government buildings of Rangoon–the Secretariat, Government House and the High Court–were patterned after the "great utilitarian pile[s] of Victorian brick"[12] that in a motley blend of imagined gothic, Italianate and "Moorish" styles dominated nineteenth-century Indian urban centers from Bombay to Calcutta. The physical reordering of the Burmese political landscape was based on Indian prototypes. Like India, Burma was divided into districts with British District Officers at their heads. Cadastral surveys were undertaken by British and Indian engineers trained in Indian engineering colleges. Successive Burma censuses were conducted in conjunction with and on the same pattern as those in India, complete with detailed breakdowns of caste and religious configurations.

Perhaps most critically for the majority of the Burmese people, from the 1880s, indigenous residential patterns in the rural areas–which for most of southern Burma, at any rate, were based on circles of small hamlets–were fundamentally reorganized on the model of the (often imagined) prototypical Indian village.[13] Central to this transformation was the reduction in the colonial period of local Burman notables, who had often been staunch defenders of "village" interests in the pre-colonial era, to the status of government functionaries or "headmen" on the Indian model. This shift not only rendered local administrative arrangements alien and artificial, it turned key intermediaries between the former Burman rulers and the peasant population into enemies of the people and prime targets in times of rural unrest.[14]

The application of Indian precedents was particularly intense in the relatively underpopulated southern districts of Burma. There East India Company officials, who were well schooled in the abstract principles of Bentham and the Utilitarian philosophers, saw an opportunity to create a political economy that was genuinely based on peasant smallholder production. For decades their attempts to create such a system had been frustrated in one region of India after another by the resistance of entrenched landholding elites and the Indian caste hierarchy. In the 1850s, British revenue officials viewed lower Burma as a tabula rasa, free from the deep-seated traditions and complexities that had frustrated their designs in India. They applied, with virtually no consideration for Burmese givens, the land tenure and revenue system that was then in favor in India, the *ryotwari*.[15] Though the architects of Burma's agrarian economy clearly had the interests of the ordinary cultivators in mind, the social and economic system they promoted ignored or rode roughshod over indigenous social structures and cultural arrangements, including Buddhist religious and educational institutions. In the decades of rapid expansion and general prosperity of the late-nineteenth century, few noticed the toll the alien system was taking on Burmese social and cultural life. When the economy turned sour, this deterioration became a major rallying call for Burmese leaders who wished to stir up indigenous resistance to the British and Indian domination.

At the same time that the *ryotwari* was being introduced, the British opened Burma to foreign trade and immigration as part of their overall scheme to remake Burma as a model of laissez-faire, market-oriented colonialism. Their aims meshed nicely with the earlier version of Burma as a key supplier of food for India and as an outlet for its surplus population. Much of the spectacular increase in export trade from Burma was directed toward India though, in the first decades after 1852, a high percentage of the leading export product–rice–went to Great Britain and Europe. By the early twentieth century, however, India and Ceylon had become the main market for Burma rice, and by the 1930s their share of Burma's exported rice crop had reached nearly sixty percent.[16] The great post-conquest expansion of the market economy in Burma also attracted Indian investors, mill owners, merchants and moneylenders. It set into motion a massive movement of capital that Lenin never dreamed of in his analysis of the workings of the capitalist-imperialist world order. Indian entrepreneurs and financiers were perhaps the greatest beneficiaries of the annexation of Burma to the Indian Raj. Though Europeans controlled the largest banking houses, shipping firms and processing plants throughout the colonial era, Indians again dominated at the intermediate levels. Very often Indian moneylenders, particularly the Chettiars, served as the major source of capital for local traders and moneylenders who were predominately Burmese. This meant that Indian, not European, capital financed the great expansion of cultivation and rice export that occurred from the last decades of the nineteenth century. Burmese who sought to operate large rice or timber mills or export firms inevitably came into competition with Indian owners, not European mercantile establishments. Burmese rice merchants competed with Indians and, to a much lesser extent, Chinese. By the last decades of the nineteenth century, Indian moneylenders and speculators had also

XIV

established themselves as substantial landholders through much of lower Burma.[17]

The movement of Indian entrepreneurs and capital to Burma was paralleled by a massive influx of Indian migrant laborers into both the urban centers and rural districts of Burma. In keeping with the vision held by British administrators in India of Burma as an ideal safety valve for overcrowded and famine-prone Indian districts, no restrictions were placed on Indian immigration during virtually the whole period of colonial rule. In fact, though earlier officials had expressed misgivings, none until James Baxter issued his 1941 *Report on Indian Immigration*, strongly urged meaningful restrictions on Indian entry into Burma. By the early decades of the twentieth century, hundreds of thousands of seasonal and permanent migrants crossed back and forth over the Bay of Bengal each year. Tens of thousands took up permanent residence in Burma. In the peak year of 1914, the influx of Indians into Burma surpassed those leaving by 143,000; as late as 1928, the *net* migration of Indians into the Province reached 94,000.[18] By the late 1920s, there were over a million Indians in all of Burma, over 600,000 concentrated in the market-oriented districts of lower Burma alone.

Just as they did in administration, marketing and processing, Indians competed with indigenous ethnic groups for positions as dock hands and street sweepers, tenants and landless laborers. In some areas in the Irrawaddy delta, they also claimed their own smallholdings and established communities that were exclusively or preponderantly Indian.[19] This meant that at all social levels from the upper realms of the civil service to the lowliest coolie, Indians were in competition and intense contact with the Burmese. As long as the economy was buoyant and steadily expanding, migrants and indigenous peoples managed to coexist with surprisingly little friction despite (or perhaps because of) minimal social and cultural interchange. When the economic pie began to shrink, especially after World War I, Burmese awareness of and hostility toward the Indian immigrant community rose sharply.

In the early 1900s, the closing of the land frontier in most districts of Lower Burma and growing external competition for a slowing international demand for Burma exports, particularly rice, set the stage for the economic dislocations and social tensions that dominated the final decades of British rule. Intensifying competition between Indians and Burmese at virtually all occupational levels and social strata both fed Burmese nationalism and was exacerbated by it. In the early stages of agrarian slowdown, the importance of the India connection was again dramatically and perniciously demonstrated. The handful of British officials who sought to introduce measures for debt relief, the restriction of land alienation and tenancy control in the 1890s and early 1900s were vehemently opposed by both powerful Indian landholding and financial groups within Burma and their allies in India proper. Though Burmese landlords and moneylenders often also opposed agrarian legislation, the financial clout of Indian merchants and moneylenders again and again proved decisive in frustrating reform efforts.[20] The decision that in effect brought an end to the salvage efforts was made by the Governor General of India, Lord Minto, not the Governor of Burma, Sir Herbert T. White. And in killing what was to be the last land alienation act introduced before the Great Depression, Minto acted out of concern for the situation in India not in the interests of the colonized people of Burma. In instructing White to put an end to the struggle to enact agrarian reform legislation, Minto emphasized that:

> *Even if the Alienation Act is required in Burma, its introduction would cause a certain amount of uneasiness in other provinces* [he specifically referred to the Punjab and Bihar] *where similar legislation has been threatened, and it is advisable to avoid anything of this sort at present.*[21]

As it turned out, the agrarian legislation campaign was the last chance for the British to shore up a crumbling peasant proprietor economy. From the late 1890s, smallholder indebtedness, land alienation, rent-racked tenants and rapacious landlords became ever more prevalent features of the colonial economy and social order in Burma. Relative prosperity and communal coexistence gave way to cutthroat competition, increasing communal tensions and, by the late 1920s, communal violence. Because Burma had been twice colonized, Burmese nationalists had to organize the drive for independence at two levels: the first and more studied against the British, the second against the large and powerful Indian immigrant community. The mounting importance of the latter struggle goes far toward explaining first Burmese ambivalence and later their outright hostility toward linking the fate of the Province to an alliance between Burmese parties and the much larger and more highly developed Indian Congress Party. The Indian "problem" was also at the root of incessant factional squabbles about the extent to which Burma should also enjoy the concessions that Gandhi and the Congress politicians were wresting from the British overlords—whether Burma should march in step with India to independence or forge a separate path.[22]

By the late 1920s, the popular struggle for independence among the Burman majority had become as much or more anti-Indian than anti-British. This trend is manifested not only in the horrific communal riots that erupted in both urban and rural Burma in 1931 and again in 1938, but also in the widespread anti-Indian assaults that were associated with the series of agrarian uprisings that broke out in the early 1930s. By the last years of British rule, assaults on the Indian community at all social levels had reached epidemic proportions. It is fitting that economic grievances and ethnic hostility are often hard to separate, as in the case of attacks on Indian moneylenders, in determining motives for communal conflict. From the viewpoint of the Burmese peasant or urban worker, the two were inseparable.[23] The fact that Indian policemen and troops were brought in to put down the peasant uprisings and quell the communal riots only served to heighten the Burmese awareness of their double colonization and the growing threat of Indian dominance. From the early 1930s, the restriction of Indian immigration and limitation of Indian economic activities became major rallying points for Burmese nationalist leaders at virtually all points of the political spectrum. As it became increasingly clear that the days of the British colonizers in both India and Burma were numbered, the struggle to reverse the process of Indianization in Burma loomed as large, particularly in the popular mind, as the drive for independence. Abruptly and brutally, the issue was decided by the Japanese invasion of Burma, which brought the death of tens of thousands and the flight of hundreds of thousands of Indians, who followed the British in their retreat from Burma, and the severing of economic and migratory links between the Province and the subcontinent.

Burma was, of course, not the only British colony to receive large numbers of Indian migrants. But the speed and harshness with which the Indian populations of former colonies like Kenya and Uganda were expelled after independence suggests just how great a threat India posed in the minds of nationalist leaders in areas where the Indian connection had been significant. Because Burma, with a pre-colonial population not much greater than either of these areas, absorbed a far greater number of Indian migrants and was far more dominated by Indian administrators and financiers, the dangers of demographic innundation and cultural extinction were all the more pronounced. Until government records and personal memoirs from the post-colonial era become available, it will be difficult to judge with any precision how much influence these fears had on the Burmese retreat from the world. But in weighing the lingering legacy of the second and infinitely more pervasive wave of colonization, one can do well to remember a cartoon that was included in Thein Maung's highly emotional assessment of *The Indian Immigration Problem in Burma,* which was published in the late 1930s. The caption reads, "Crowded out by the guests, such is the lot of the Burmese." The illustration shows a smallish Burmese in traditional garb perched precariously on the edge of a long bench. The rest of the bench is occupied by six husky foreigners. One is British, one Chinese. The remaining four are clearly Indian.

Notes

1. Robert H. Taylor, *The State In Burma,* Honolulu, 1987, pp. 244-72

2. In fact, Michael Aung Thwin has argued that the main purpose of the retreat into isolation was to allow the Burmese to develop their unique blend of Buddhism and Socialism. See the *Bulletin of Concerned Asian Scholars* (1984).

3. "Europeans, Trade, and the Unification of Burma, c. 1540-1620," *Oriens Extremus* 27:2, pp. 203-26 (1980)

4. These themes were emphasized by anthropologists like David Pfanner and John Brohm who conducted field work in Burma in the "open" 1950s, and by Donald Smith who wrote an early and influential postwar account of religion and politics in Burma.

5. These factors are covered in depth by Oliver B. Pollack, *Empires in Collision,* Westport, Connecticut, 1979, and Charles Keeton, *King Thebaw and the Ecological Rape of Burma,* Delhi, 1974. For a view of the process of conquest and annexation from the perspective of the Burmese court, Maung Htin Aung's *History of Burma,* New York, 1967 remains useful.

6. On the workings of the British alliance systems, see H.H. Dodwell, *Dupleix and Clive,* London, 1920; P.E. Roberts, *India Under Wellesley,* London, 1929.

7. *Tracts, Political, Geographical and Commercial: on the Dominions of Ava, and the North Western Parts of Hindustan,* London, 1911, pp. 31, 34

8. *An Account of the Burman Empire,* Calcutta, 1852, p. 57

9. *Government of Burma, Report on the Administration of the Province of Pegu,* 1855-56, Rangoon, 1856, paragraph 237

10. Taylor, *State in Burma,* pp. 111-112, 127

11. *Ibid.*, p. 122

12. *Ibid.*, p. 71

13. Daw Mya Sein, *Administration of Burma: Sir Charles Crosthwaite and the Consolidation of Burma,* Rangoon, 1938, pp. 81-115, 161-75; and Albert Moscotti, *British Policy and the Nationalist Movement in Burma,* Honolulu, 1974, pp. 6-8

14. Albert Moscotti, *British Policy in Burma,* pp. 42-6; and *Government of Burma, The Origins and Causes of the Burma Rebellion (1930-32),* Rangoon, 1934, pp. 3-6, 15

15. Michael Adas, "The Ryotwari in Lower Burma: The Establishment and Decline of a Peasant Proprietor System," in R.E. Frykenberg, ed., *Land Tenure and Peasant in South Asia,* New Delhi, 1977, pp. 100-110

16. Cheng Siok-Hwa, *The Rice Industry of Burma 1852-1940,* (Singapore, 1968), p. 201

17. On these developments see Cheng Siok-Hwa, *Rice Economy,* chapters four and seven; and Michael Adas, *The Burma Delta: Economic Development and Social Change on an Asian Rice Frontier, 1852-1941,* Madison, Wisconsin, 1974, chapters four and five.

18. Adas, *Burma Delta* p. 163 and chapter seven

19. *Ibid.*, chapters six and seven

20. The struggle for agrarian reform legislation can be traced in great detail in the special reports and enclosures in the Government of Burma, *Revenue and Agriculture Proceedings,* 1890-1911.

21. India Office Archives, MSS European 254, The Herbert Thirkell White Collection, File 190, my emphasis

22. The intricacies of the final stages of the independence struggle are ably unravelled in Taylor, *State in Burma,* chapter three.

23. On the anti-Indian assaults, see Taylor, *ibid.*; and Adas, *Burma Delta,* chapter eight.

Ethnic Pluralism and Conflict on the Frontiers of South Asian Migration

It has been a quarter of a century since Ronald Robinson and John Gallagher's seminal work *Africa and the Victorians: The Climax of Imperialism* was first published. Though that study and their related essays on "informal empire" have sparked lively, often highly productive debates and numerous studies on specific aspects of the late-nineteenth-century spurt of European imperialist expansion, surprisingly little attention has been devoted to the implications of the premise on which Gallagher and Robinson built their interpretation of the origins of the scramble for Africa. They argue that the "decisive motive" for British territorial acquisitions in Africa was an official concern to protect the routes that connected Great Britain to India. The decision to send British troops into Egypt in 1882, which Gallagher and Robinson view as the prime mover of the scramble sequence, was forced on a reluctant Liberal cabinet by the threat of the collapse of the puppet Khedival regime and the dangers that potential French intervention in Egypt posed for the vital Suez "lifeline" to India. The British were motivated, they conclude, not by a desire to build a new empire in Africa, but by the necessity of protecting the empire they already possessed in India.[1]

Given India's importance in their interpretive scheme, it is disconcerting that Gallagher and Robinson devote so little attention to its roles in the maintenance of British global power and domestic prosperity. Some

---

[1]   London, 1961, esp. pp. 11-15, 463-7.

passing remarks about India as an outlet for British investment capital and manufactured goods are tacked onto a rather brief discussion of India's role as England's Indian "Barrack in the Oriental Seas," which they judge to be an "essential supplement to British seapower."[2] This rather cursory summary and the African focus of much of the rest of *Africa and the Victorians* go a long way to explaining the neglect of the Indian factor in the debates and monographs generated by the sequence of partition presented in the work.[3] Gallagher and Robinson not only greatly understate the significance of India in the British imperial structure, they distort its position by viewing it as a passive field for British economic enterprise and a recruiting ground for the British military. In the first instance, they ignore a wide range of vital roles that Indians played at all levels of the global imperial edifice in British colonies from South and Southeast Asia to East Africa, the Middle East and the Pacific, and even the Caribbean. In the second, they obscure the complexities and reciprocities of the Indians' relationship with their British overlords and the Indians' energetic involvement in the imperial enterprise. Not only were the loyalty and services of diverse Indian ethnic and social groups essential to the growth and maintenance of the empire, Indians reaped substantial financial and status rewards through their positions in or connections to the British imperial establishment.

There were two basic dimensions to the multifaceted involvement of Indian migrants in the British empire. The first was political and military. Gallagher and Robinson's remarks about the Asian barracks touch upon this dimension, but do not begin to do justice to the prodigious contribution of Indians in the conquest and administration of the empire. Indian troops often made up the bulk of the expeditionary forces that conquered new territories in East Africa or Southeast Asia and forced open kingdoms like China whose

---

[2]   Ibid., pp. 11-14.
[3]   Much of the criticism of *Africa and the Victorians* has centered upon the authors' contention that the 1882 intervention was the event that triggered and shaped the partition throughout Africa. See, for examples, C. W. Newbury, "Victorians, Republicans, and the Partition of Africa," or Jean Stengers, "L'imperialisme colonial de la fin du XIXe siècle: mythe ou realité," *Journal of African History* 3/3 (1962), pp. 493-501 and 469-91 respectively.

rulers were resistant to British overtures for trading or diplomatic links.[4] They garrisoned these areas until indigenous forces could be recruited and trained, and usually remained in substantial numbers as in effect elite reserve forces whom the British considered the most reliable in emergency situations. Indians also migrated to take up positions as policemen in the new possessions, and Indian reinforcements were invariably called in when serious social disturbances erupted (or threatened) or the British were challenged politically by indigenous movements of resistance. Interestingly, though Indians did much of the fighting and repressing, African or Southeast Asian epics of primary resistance or revolt against colonialism stress the setbacks of legendary British commanders and the firepower of maxim guns rather than the courage and tenacity of Indian troops that in the end were decisive. In times of severe crisis and threat to the British empire as a whole, as, for example, during the period of the Great War, Indian soldiers served on fronts throughout the empire and in Europe itself, and fought the bulk of Britain's battles in the Middle East and East Africa.

As conquest gave way to consolidation, Indian influences were felt at virtually all levels of administration. Though often a source of misinformation and wrong-headed decisions, Indian precedents shaped British colonial policies in Africa and Southeast Asia on issues ranging from relations with indigenous princes and legal codes to land tenure systems and village organization. The British governors, commissioners and district officers of the new colonies had frequently served in India before taking up their new assignments, and that experience colored their perception of colonial peoples, influenced their administrative techniques, and shaped the "imperial style" adopted by officials of diverse origins throughout the empire. Subordinate Indian administrators, clerks, surveyors, and tax collectors proved essential to British efforts to govern in newly annexed areas, particularly in the early decades of occupation when Indians possessed a facility with English and a familiarity of British bureaucratic ways that were rarely found among newly colonized peoples. The impact of Indian administrators was a good deal more lasting than their

---

[4]   In fact the Indian role in this regard was the reverse of the rather naive conviction of Chinese historians in the late 1950s that the Mutiny was an effort by the Indians to aid Chinese resistance to the British in the late 1850s, See Yu Sheng-wu and Chang Chen-kun, "China and India in the Mid-Nineteenth Century," P.C. Joshi, ed., *Rebellion 1857* (New Delhi, 1957), pp. 241-55.

XV

contributions as soldiers, and there is good reason to believe that the former produced more lasting hostility on the part of subordinated peoples. As surveyors, tax collectors, and census takers, Indians were not only in direct contact with newly colonized peoples in far larger numbers than the British, they were perceived to be the main agents of bureaucratic measures aimed at breaking down the barriers to effective state control over the local community. If the British greatly overestimated how much they knew about village affairs and peasant productivity in India and elsewhere,[5] they vastly exceeded the Asian or African rulers who preceded them in the degree to which they were able to subvert the autonomy of the local community and integrate acephalous peoples into a centralized bureaucratic hierarchy.

In the extension of imperial control, the Indian experience and Indians themselves played additional, but rarely noted roles. Engineering and surveying skills gained by both British and Indian civil servants in spanning the vast Indian subcontinent with railways were put to good use in Burma and East Africa. Indian laborers were recruited to build roads and railways, most notably the vital Uganda railway, that allowed the British to open the interior of East Africa to European settlement and market production,[6] and the port facilities that invariably served as the foci of British efforts to integrate new colonial possessions into the larger empire and world market economy. Indian laborers were also often prominent among the stevedores and coolies who manned the wharves and processing plants of the new port cities, as well as the steam and sailing ships that carried the bulk of the "country" or local trade of the Indian Ocean.

If Indian soldiers and subordinate administrators were essential to the British in their formidable task of governing a rapidly expanding and bewilderingly diverse empire, the Indians in turn made good use of the political stability and protection that the imperial presence provided and the new communication links that were established to facilitate overseas emigration and enterprise. Indians had, of course, travelled and migrated throughout the Indian Ocean region long before the British appeared at the end of the sixteenth

[5]   As the many essays of Clive Dewey and other historians have shown in recent decades. See, for example, Dewey, "Patwari and Cahukidar: Subordinate Officials and the Reliability of India's Agricultural Statistics," in Dewey and A. G. Hopkins, *The Imperial Impact in Africa and South Asia* (London, 1979).
[6]   H. S. Morris, *The Indians in Uganda* (London, 1968), p. 8.

century. They had established trading communities in the Persian Gulf area, on Africa's Swahili coast, and throughout Southeast Asia. They had also migrated in substantial numbers as settlers to northern Ceylon, Arakan and southern Burma.[7] But Indian overseas migration increased dramatically under the British Raj, particularly in the nineteenth century. Poor records, seasonal movements, and temporary or multiple migration make it difficult to estimate the total flow from South Asia to other areas in the empire with any accuracy. But a recent and careful calculation by Hugh Tinker places just the number of South Asians who have settled permanently overseas at upwards of five million. As the numbers of South Asians still residing overseas in 1970 provided by Tinker illustrate, Indian migrants strongly favored colonies under British control as areas of destination. Though Indians were found in non-British areas, the Chettiers in Vietnam, for example, or the mercantile communities and descendants of the railway construction workers in Madagascar, an overwhelming proportion of Indian migrants at all levels went to work or settle in British colonial dependencies.[8]

The late-nineteenth-century explosion of overseas emigration from South Asia was preceded by waves of indentured laborers who went to work the declining plantations of the British Caribbean when recently liberated slave laborers from Africa understandably proved reluctant to work as wage earners on the estates where they had once been held in bondage.[9] Though British imperial control did not grant Indians immunity from discrimination or even violent assaults by the indigenous peoples or rival immigrant communities, a comparison of the Indian experience with the even larger movement of Chinese overseas makes the advantages of the British imperial umbrella readily

---

[7]   A very large, and at times contentious, literature h as developed on early Indian overseas migration and influence. The best works include the fine studies by George Coedes, especially *The Making of South-East Asia* (English ed., Berkeley, 1966) and *The Indianized States of Southeast Asia* (English ed., Honolulu, 1968).

[8]   *The Banyan Tree: Overseas Emigrants from India, Pakistan and Bangladesh* (Oxford, 1977), pp. 10-12.

[9]   The best general studies of this movement are Hugh Tinker, *A New System of Slavery: The Export of Indian Labour Overseas 1830-1920* (London, 1974), esp. chapter one; and W. Kloosterboer, *Involuntary Labour since the Abolition of Slavery* (Chicago, 1967).

6   ETHNIC PLURALISM AND CONFLICT

apparent.[10] Indian migrants enjoyed reasonably predictable and uniform political arrangements and policies that were frequently aimed at encouraging their immigration to other areas within the empire. The Chinese were subject to the whims of often hostile potentates or European colonizers who had few ties to the Chinese in their areas of origin and no vested interest in encouraging their migration. Overseas Indians worked within sociocultural systems that protected private property, promoted hard work and ambition, and where some attempt (athough often appallingly little) was made to regulate working conditions and wages. The absence of these givens in many of the areas where the Chinese migrated led to arbitrary seizures of their property, inhuman working conditions, and periodic anti-Chinese pogroms, which officials of the governments in question did little to suppress and in some instances actually initiated or joined.[11]

The second main dimension of the Indian alliance with British colonizers was economic. Indian economic roles in the British empire were even more divers than their political and military ones, and involved far larger numbers of Indian migrants. Indians both followed and facilitated the spread of the global market economy under the aegis of formal and informal British domination. Indian and British merchants and investors based in India provided capital, entrepreneurial skills, and processing machinery that were in short supply in many of the areas that came under British rule in the late-nineteenth century. Indian merchants and moneylenders supplied the local, small-scale sources of credit, the consumer incentives, and the small-scale marketing services that were essential to British designs to bring promising, but previously little developed, areas into production for the world market.[12] Indian laborers made it possible for the British to revive old plantation areas in the Caribbean and Mauritius, open new plantation areas in Natal and Fiji,

---

[10]   For superb studies of the Chinese experience see G. W. Skinner, *Chinese Society in Thailand* (Ithaca, 1957) and Edgar Wickberg, *The Chinese in Philippine Life, 1850-1898* (New Haven, 1965)

[11]   As, for example, the Dutch massacre of the Chinese in Batavia in 1740. See H. J. De Graaf, *Geschiedenis van Indonesie* (The Hague, 1949), pp. 253-6.

[12]   For case studies of Indian activities in different colonial settings, see K. S. Sandhu, *Indians in Malaya* (Cambridge, 1969); Michael Adas, *The Burma Delta* (Madison, 1974), and F. & L. Dotson, *The Indian Minority of Zambia, Rhodesia and Malawi* (New Haven, 1968).

expand estate cultivation in Assam and Ceylon, and bring new crops like rubber into estate production in Malaya.[13] Indian migrant laborers from overcrowded districts like Bengal and those of the Tamil south eagerly took up positions that indigenous peoples refused or lacked the numbers to fill.[14] Though some British officials expressed a preference for Chinese over Indian laborers,[15] through most of the empire Indian migrants were the favored source of cheap, dependable labor. The connections between the spread of Indian traders and laborers were often close. In British colonies in central Africa, for example, Gujarati shopkeepers and hawkers followed migrant laborers. The laborers in turn strove to set up their own retail businesses, and with some success, for by the 1950s some four-fifths of the Indians who had migrated as laborers were engaged in trade.[16]

British imperial needs and the willingness of millions of Indians at a variety of caste levels to migrate overseas made for a splendid symbiosis, perhaps the largest and most profitable alliance between colonizer and colonized in all history. The British gained manpower to staff their police forces and bureaucracies, tend their plantations, and settle sparsely populated areas. British bankers and merchants were assisted by Indian moneylenders and shopkeepers, who were willing to deal in credit transactions that were too small to be economical for European banks and to pedal the cheap wares wholesaled by Indian and British mercantile firms to the most remote hamlets of the empire. Indian castes specializing in commercial and financial endeavors, such as the Chettiars of Tamilnad and the *vanis* of Gujarat and

[13] In addition to the sources cited in footnote nine and Sandhu, ibid., see M. W. Roberts, "Indian Estate Labour in Ceylon during the Coffee Period (1830-1880)," *Indian Social and Economic History Review* 3/1 (1966), pp. 1-52 and 3/2 (1966), pp. 101-36; A. C. Mayer, *Peasants in the Pacific* (Berkeley, 1991), chapter one; and L. M. Thompson, *Indian Immigration into Natal* (Cape Town, 1952).
[14] See, for example, Sandhu's discussion of different responses of South Indians and Malays to plantation work in Malaya(*Indians in Malaya*, pp. 51 ff.).
[15] See Government of India, *Report on the Administration of Burma 1857-58* (Rangoon, 1858), paragraph 177; and Government of India, *Secret and Political Correspondence*, India Office Records, range 201, vol. 15, 20 Feb., 1857, no. 842. For misgivings about the employment of what were regarded as more truculent Chinese, see Sandhu, ibid., pp. 53-4.
[16] F. & L. Dotson, *Indian Minority*, pp. 27, 33, 58.

Maharashtra, found lucrative outlets for capital investment throughout the empire. These castes were responsible for a significant movement of capital within the British empire that Lenin never dreamed existed. Indian castes, such as the Kayasthas, with a penchant for literacy and government service found opportunities for employment greatly enhanced by British imperial annexations in Africa and Southeast Asia. Peoples like the Sikhs and Gurkhas, whom the British deemed martial and consequently recruited heavily into their Indian armies, found plenty of opportunities to show their mettle in the many punitive actions, frontier wars and wars of conquest that the Raj was called upon to fight in the name of the larger empire. Finally, millions of impoverished peasants, landless laborers, and un- or under-employed urban workers found jobs, and in some cases unoccupied lands that they could settle and claim, in overseas in British dependencies. In perhaps hundreds of thousands of instances, they also found opportunities for social advancement that were closed to them in their impoverished and caste-ridden home districts. Their expectations were wonderfully captured by a Paraiyan laborer who accidentally collided with a Brahmin while disembarking at Rangoon. He informed the angry Brahmin, who was berating him for his carelessness and its polluting consequences, that he had left his caste behind in India and would not take it up again until he returned to Madras. Decades later, the children of Indians who had migrated to Africa recalled the feelings of revulsion that they had felt upon encountering caste divisions and prohibitions during visits to their ancestral villages in India.[17] Employment and investment opportunities in British overseas colonies also helped sustain parents and siblings or wives and children who remained behind in overcrowded and famine-prone villages. The extent of the capital flow generated by the earnings of returning Indian migrant laborers and remittances sent home by laborers and merchants or landlords has never been determined. Amounts clearly varied by social group, with some laborers able to spare only negligible amounts while moneylending castes funneled millions of rupees to their home districts or other overseas branches of their financial networks. Without detailed enquiries into the amounts remitted and variations at different levels of the Indian migrant community, the impact of funds transmitted by overseas Indians on living standards in the

---

[17]   Government of India, *Census of the Madras Presidency, 1911* (Madras, 1912), p. 26; and Dotsons, ibid., pp. 324-5.

subcontinent itself is hard to gauge. But there can be little doubt that rupees from relatives overseas helped reduce malnutrition or stave off starvation among the laboring castes in many regions, and greatly enhanced the investment opportunities of prosperous castes like the Chettiars and *vanis*.

The extensive and multifaceted migration of Indians within the expanding British empire meant that peoples in a remarkably large number of areas were twice colonized — formally by the British, informally, but often in greater depth and more enduringly, by the Indians. The diversity of the peoples in the areas into which the Indians moved combined with the great variability of migrant flows to different regions gave rise to widely varying patterns of multi-ethnic and, using categories devised in the nineteenth century, multi-racial societies within the British empire. Controversies that have raged for decades over the meaning and application of the concept of the plural society, which J. S. Furnivall first proposed in the 1940s to characterize these societies, underscore their great differences.[18] Relatively small, mainly mercantile, Indian communities in east and central Africa contrast with Indian communities in Trinidad or Guyana that are descended from indentured laborers and make up near majorities or majorities of the total populations of these areas. In Malaya, Indians competed with Chinese immigrants or their descendants at all levels as well as with the indigenous Malays. In Burma, in addition to hundreds of thousands of laborers and thousands of merchants and moneylenders, Indians came to settle permanently on the land. In South Africa, the growth of an Indian community, which presently numbers over three-quarters of a million, further fragmented a society divided between white and black and colored, between Boer and British, between Zulu, Xhosa and Basuto. In all instances divisions have been rooted in cultural differences, but as H. Hoetink has stressed in his writings on plural societies in the Caribbean, somatic differences shape daily interaction and inter-community relations.[19] Significant differences within communities are obscured by the sharp demarcation between groups who perceive themselves to be culturally and

---

[18]   For contributions to the debate see the essays in *Pluralism in Africa*, edited by Leo Kuper and M. G. Smith (Berkeley, 1971); R. S. Bryce-Laporte, "M. G. Smith's Version of Pluralism," *Comparative Studies in Society and History* 10/1 (1967), pp. 114-20; and Adas, *Burma Delta*, esp. chapter five.

[19]   "The Concept of Pluralism as Envisaged by m. G. Smith," *Caribbean Studies* 7/1 (1967), pp. 36-43 and *The Two Variants in Caribbean Race Relations* (London, 1967).

10   ETHNIC PLURALISM AND CONFLICT

racially distinct.[20]

The advantages that diverse Indian social groups gained from the British imperial connection were not won without considerable cost. The links between British colonizers and Indian immigrants did not escape the notice of the indigenous peoples in newly colonized areas. Initially, however, resentment of the Indians tended to be muted and, if it surfaced, focused on their social and economic positions. Furnivall's vision of plural societies, at least in their initial stages, as hierarchies in which different ethnic groups gravitated to different occupational niches and thus complemented rather than competed with each other[21] often bore little resemblance to the actual realities in the areas where Indians migrated. To begin with, the indigenous peoples were usually relegated to the lower strata of the social pyramid, where the overwhelming majority were laborers or cultivators. In areas like east Africa and Malaya, where the recruitment of Indian migrant labor was prompted in part by the refusal of indigenous peoples to work British estates, the latter were left outside or on the periphery of the growing capitalist sector. In this phase there were usually more than enough places for workers and peasant producers. But if the indigenous peoples sought to move into other levels of the colonial social hierarchy, which contrary to Furnivall's assumptions they often did, they faced stiff Indian competition. The history of the military and bureaucracy of colonial societies with respect to this competition remains to be written, but much work has been done on Indian (and Chinese and Lebanese)[22] dominance of the middle range of the mercantile and financial sectors of colonial societies.

As a result of centuries of involvement in the very sophisticated market systems that had developed in South Asia, groups like the Chettiars and Marwaris had built credit and trading institutions, networks of dependence and

---

[20]   R. S. Morris, "Indians in East Africa: A Study in a Plural Society," *British Journal of Sociology* 7/3 (1956), pp. 207-9.

[21]   "The Political Economy of the Tropical Far East," *Journal of the Royal Central Asian Society* 29/3 (1942), p. 198.

[22]   See the works cited by Skinner and Wickberg above, and R. B. Winder, "The Lebanese in West Africa," *Comparative Studies in Society and History* 4 (1961-2), pp. 292-333. For a fine recent study of a number of trade diasporas, see Philip Curtin, *Cross-Cultural Trade in World History* (London, 1984).

reciprocity, and a procedural consistency that gave them great advantages over established or aspiring merchants and moneylenders in British dependencies beyond India. They had also established longstanding connections with British mercantile firms and banking houses that greatly facilitated their purchase of goods for retail, and enhanced their access to capital for loans, land purchase and speculation.[23] In areas like Malaya and Indonesia, Indian merchants and moneylenders encountered competition from migrant groups, most notably the Chinese, with similar advantages, including at times links to British firms in Canton, Hong Kong ,and Shanghai. Similar but far weaker rivals faced them on the east African coast, but in the African interior from Kenya to Natal, Indians gained such extensive control over retail trade and money lending that some British administrators advocated special education programs that would allow Africans to claim a share of the positions in these sectors.[24] In areas like Burma where economic expansion in the early colonial period was very rapid, less well-connected and organized indigenous shopkeepers, buyers and moneylenders survived the Indian influx and grew in numbers and wealth. But the great majority of Burmese engaged in commerce or finance worked at the lowest and local level with small-scale transactions. In fact, many Burmese served as buyers, lenders and hawkers for Chettiar or Chinese firms.[25] The one area in which the Burmese appear to have held their own was in processing, where Burmese mill owners employed more workers than Indian owners did throughout the colonial period. Indians, however, like the Chinese and Europeans, controlled a far greater share of the mills than the percentage they made up of the population. Indians and Chinese also controlled a substantial share of the middle-sized mills, while British owners nearly monopolized the largest, leaving the Burmese mainly with those mills employing less than one

---

[23]   On these patterns see Adas, "Immigrant Asians and the Economic Impact of European Imperialism: The Role of the South Indian Chettiars in British Burma," *Journal of Asian Studies* 23/3 91974), pp. 385-401.

[24]   T. F. Victor-Buxton, "Missionaries and Education in East Africa," *Journal of the Africa Society* 8 (1908-9), p. 287. In the 1960s, the Dotsons estimated that the Indians still controlled seventy-five percent of the retail trade of the former British colonies of central Africa and Rhodesia. *Indian Minority*, p. 3.

[25]   Adas, *Burma Delta*, chapter 5.

hundred workers.[26]

    These patterns help to explain why in many of the British colonies to which Indians migrated, they came to be perceived by the indigenous peoples as the central agents of both colonial domination and the spread of the market economy.   When colonial economies stagnated or fell into depression, increasing numbers of African or Southeast Asian peasants and workers fell into debt to Indian shopkeepers and moneylenders. In some areas, Indian moneylenders, often reluctantly, became landlords as well, as a result of the necessity of foreclosing on land offered as security for loans that cultivators could not repay. Though their lending policies were often more lenient than indigenous merchants or moneylenders, and Indian landlords were usually no more rapacious than their Burmese counterparts, cultural and physical differences made it easier to single out Indians and overstate their abuses. Indians came to be stereotyped as a "hard-hearted lot," who are guilty of "swindling, cheating, deception and oppression."[27]   This tendency was enhanced by the fact that in economies where employment opportunities for laborers or tenants were increasingly scarce, large numbers of Indian migrants were competing for the available jobs. Because they were often willing to work for wages that Burmese or Malays considered beneath subsistence, and at jobs that indigenous peoples had once spurned but now sought, Indians were seen by the masses of laborers and peasants in overseas dependencies as a much more immediate and direct threat than the British overlords. In areas like Burma, Ceylon and to some extent Malaya, where hundreds of thousands of Indians had migrated on a permanent basis, hostility arising from competition for work was reinforced by fears that an unchecked flood of migrants from much more densely populated Indian districts would someday overwhelm the rather sparse populations of island and mainland Southeast Asia. Nowhere were these fears more vividly expressed than in a cartoon in a Burmese vernacular newspaper that depicted a diminutive Burmese peasant being pushed off a long bench occupied by a Chinese, an Englishman (replete with pipe and pith helmet) and *four* large Indians representing various types of

---

[26]   Cheng Siok-Hwa, *The Rice Industry of Burma* (Kuala-Lumpur, 1968), pp. 82-93.

[27]   Government of India, *Report of the Burma Provincial Banking Enquiry Committee, 1929-30* (Rangoon, 1930), vol. 1, p. 189.

migrants from South Asia.[28]

As economic competition intensified, the spread of nationalist sentiment hardened the divisions between Indians and the indigenous peoples of the areas where they had migrated.[29]   At the mass level, appeals to nationalist identity sharpened perceptions of cultural and racial differences, and emphasized the inter-communal nature of competition and alleged exploitation. But it was at the upper levels of colonial societies that the emerging sense of nationalism did the most to erode, in some cases irreparably, the fragile bonds that held together the plural societies that Indian immigration had brought into being. As the power of the British overlords came under assault and receded, not only the common leadership but the institutions, laws and values that Furnivall and others[30] have rightly seen as the grid that held such polyglot and artificial social structures together was weakened or shattered. Besieged first in India and increasingly in the empire as a whole, British officials were tempted to play one ethnic group off against another or deflect hostility to the Indian minority — a temptation they did not always resist. Nationalism drove indigenous leaders searching for mass support to increasingly inflammatory attacks on the Indian minority, which was pilloried for its special relationship with the British, condemned for draining other colonies through remittances of earnings and profits to India, and pictured as both wealthy and exploitative (as in the case of Indian landlords and moneylenders) and a threat to the jobs and livelihood of indigenous cultivators and urban workers. In many instances these anti-Indian campaigns were far from disinterested, for the indigenous elites, who themselves were often from landowning, mercantile and

---

[28]   Printed in Thein Maung, *Immigration Problem of Burma* (Rangoon, 1939), p. 22. Though less understandable in terms of the small numbers of Indians who migrated to Africa, fears that the local population would be swamped there as well surfaced in British settler and African writings. See, for example, N. H. Wilson, The Central African Dilemma (n.p., 1954).

[29]   For sample case studies see Leo Despres, "The Implications of Nationalist Politics in British Guiana for the Development of Cultural Theory," *American Anthropologist* 66/5 (1964), pp. 1051-77; Sandhu, *Indians in Malaya*, pp. 229-30; F. & L. Dotson, *Indian Minority*, pp. 32-40; Adas, *Burma Delta*, chapter eight; and Hilda Kuper, "'Strangers' in Plural Societies: Asians in South Africa and Uganda," in Kuper and Smith, eds., *Pluralism in Africa*, esp. pp. 262ff.

[30]   Leo Kuper, "Plural Societies, Perspectives and Problems," in ibid., pp. 11-13, 15.

professional families, had much to gain from the weakening or ouster of their Indian competitors. Nationalist rhetoric aimed at Indian immigrant groups transformed wary cooperation at the upper social levels of colonial plural societies, where as Steven Morris has observed[31] the most significant interaction between communities occurred, into hostile confrontation. This shift occurred at a time when the British were increasingly less willing or able to bridge the rifts between subject ethnic groups.

Indian responses to changing conditions and the global retreat of their British allies varied widely from one colonial dependency to the next, and the Indian leadership within a given colony was often divided on the course to pursue. Attempts to forge nationalist alliances between Indian and African or Southeast Asian leaders came to little despite the potential a common front offered. In many cases the timing was wrong. Indian nationalism was simply too advanced relative to that in east Africa or Malaya for meaningful alliances to be made. In other instances, Indian efforts to cement nationalist cooperation between colonies floundered on the fears of less numerous and politically sophisticated peoples that British dominance would be replaced by Indian. In Burma, for example, these fears led to the ultimate defeat of the once-ascendant anti-Separationist faction, which sought to tie Burma's drive for independence closely to India's.[32]

Indian strategies were everywhere muddied by deep ambivalence regarding the British retreat: pride in the emergence of an Indian nation and leaders of world renown, on one hand, and anxiety about their future status in overseas areas once nationalist leaders had come to power, on the other. Again and again, Indian efforts at rapprochement with African or Southeast Asian leaders were stymied both by suspicions aroused by their financial and political ties to the Congress Party or other political organizations in India itself, and their tendency in times of crisis to retreat to time-tested British alliances for protection. But the Indian affinity for the British had come to be more than just a matter of self-advancement or defense. Indians had imbibed many of the ideas and attitudes professed by their British masters and allies, and come to share the sense of superiority and civilizing mission that are normally considered the monopoly of European colonizers. The Dotsons' survey of

---

[31]   Morris, "Indians in East Africa," p. 210.
[32]   John Cady, *A History of Modern Burma* (Ithaca, 1965), pp. 298-302 & chapter ten.

Indians in Zambia, Rhodesia and Malawi in the 1960s, for example, found that the Indians considered the Africans "illiterate and incomprehensible savages" who were incapable of self-rule.   Perhaps more significantly, Indian respondents voiced some of the central tenets of the civilizing mission ideology in their contention that the Africans were wanting in culture, had childlike mentalities and were incapable of logical deductions, were lazy and lacking in foresight, and were self-indulgent and morally reprobate.[33]

George Orwell's stereotypic depiction of Doctor Veraswami in *Burmese Days* wonderfully captures the extent to which educated Indians, particularly those in the service of the empire, had come to view other colonized peoples from the perspective of the dominant Westerners. At one point Veraswami chides the protagonist Flory for his cynical views on the British imperial mission. "My friend," Veraswami protests, "it iss pathetic to me to hear you talk so. It iss truly pathetic. You say you are here to trade: Of course you are. Could the Burmese trade for themselves? Can they make machinery, ships, railways, roads? They are helpless without you. What would happen to the Burmese forests if the English were not here? They would be sold immediately to the Japanese, who would gut them and ruin them. Instead of which, in your hands, actually they are improved."[34] The attitudes uncovered in surveys like the Dotsons', and satirized by Orwell, reinforced by ancient Indian color preferences and pride in their own civilization, go a long way to account for the arrogance and condescension that Indians were often accused of doing little to conceal in their dealings with Africans and Southeast Asians.[35]

Alliances between Indian migrant groups and other colonized peoples were also blocked by fundamental divergences between Indian interests and those of African or Southeast Asian peoples.   Indian landlords and moneylenders in Burma, for example, lobbied for decades from the 1890s onwards to prevent the passage of land alienation and tenancy legislation that they viewed as a potential threat to their economic position in the province.

---

[33]   F. & L. Dotson, *Indian Minority*, pp. 262-8, 320.
[34]   New York, 1963 ed., pp. 34-44; quoted portion, p. 37.
[35]   One of the more candid discussions of the persistence of these attitudes can be found in Nirad C. Chaudhuri, *The Autobiography of an Unknown Indian* (Bombay, 1951), pp. 123-30. For African reactions, see F. & L. Dotson, *Indian Minority*, pp. 325ff.

XV

Though successful in blocking the legislation,[36] their efforts inevitably increased the hostility felt towards them by Burmese laborers and cultivators, who stood to gain from proposed limitations on mortgage liability and limits on the share of the crop a landlord could demand from his tenants. In east and central Africa, Indian migrants were caught between white settlers, determined to defend the enclaves that they had established in British territories, and African majorities increasingly resistant to European rule and economic dominance. Assailed by the settlers, who often viewed them as dangerous rivals, and fearful of African reprisals if they refused to support their nationalist efforts, the Indians usually opted, though often tentatively, for alliances with African nationalists. Once their British protectors had withdrawn, however, the Indians frequently became the targets of African politicians resentful of the Indians' lukewarm support and prominent social and economic positions.[37]

As the nationalist revolt intensified and the British moved, at times with unseemly haste, to extricate themselves from one colony after another, Indians overseas became more than just rhetorical targets. Because of their isolation in village shops and extensive involvement in cash transactions, Indian merchants and moneylenders had long been a like prey for dacoits. In Burma raids on Indian shops by indebted peasants or those who had lost their land through Indian foreclosures sometimes took on the characteristics or social banditry.[38] In periods of economic crisis and nationalist agitation, ethnic clashes increased in number and virulence. In central and east Africa, where the numbers of Indian immigrants were low relative to Ceylon or southeast Asia, boycotts or attacks aimed at Indian shopkeepers appear to have been initially prompted more by opportunity than deep-seated hostility arising from a sense that Indians were exploiters. As one African informant candidly admitted to the Dotsons, African leaders were sensitive to the Indian charge that they had done nothing to harm the indigenous peoples, but concluded that they had to "get back" at the British "somehow." By the late 1950s, African

---

[36]   See the Government of Burma, *Land and Agriculture Proceedings* (India Office Records), 1890-1911, *passim*.

[37]   F. & L. Dotson, *Indian Minority*, pp. 321, 324, 334-5.

[38]   Michael Adas, "Bandits, Monks, and Pretender Kings: Patterns of Peasant Resistance in Colonial Burma, 1886-1941," in R. Weller & S. Guggenheim, eds.,*Power and Protest in the Countryside* (Durham, 1982), pp. 96-7.

aggression came to be more directed at the Indians themselves rather than as surrogates for British administrators or settlers. The epidemic of arson incidents that was a central feature of the 1959 Emergency in Nyasaland was entirely aimed at Indian shops. Violent assaults on Indians, which indigenous policemen did little to discourage, were fanned by calls in the nationalist press for the Indians to return home. As one Indian emigre observed, in the crisis the Indian community was like a drum that African leaders beat to mobilize anti-colonial resistance.[39]

In areas like Burma, Ceylon, and British Guyana, where large communities of Indians had become established, periodic clashes grew in the period of decolonization and the post-colonial era into extended conflicts exhibiting all the ugly features of race wars. In Burma, sporadic raids on Indian shops and the homes of Indian landlords grew in the late 1920s and 1930s into an extended and violent conflict between Burmese and Indians. Indians, including agricultural and urban workers, were major targets of the agrarian rebellions that spread through much of the colony as the depression slump in the rice market took its toll. In 1930 and again in 1938, communal riots, beginning in Rangoon, spread to many of Burma's urban centers. Pitched battles were fought between Indian and Burmese laborers and crowds of Burmese led by political *pongyis* launched vicious assaults against Indian residential districts, which the colonial police and military professed they did not have the manpower to cover. In the charred wreckage of Indian squatter huts in Rangoon, or later in Mackenzie in Guyana or the highlands of Sri Lanka, the Indian migrant experience reached its nadir. Maurice Collis's recollections of the aftermath of the 1930 riots in Rangoon convey a sense of the savagery and cruelty associated with crowds engaged in communal conflicts:

> The corpses had been removed, but everything reeked of blood; boxes had been broken open, their contents looted or slashed; the very walls dripped blood; little pictures of the gods had not escaped destruction.[40]

---

[39]   F. & L. Dotson, *Indian Minority*, pp. 330-33; and H. Kuper, "'Strangers' in Plural Societies," pp. 265-70.

[40]   *Trials in Burma*, pp. 159-60.

XV

The denouement in Burma was equally painful and symbolic. As many as four hundred thousand Indian refugees fled with the retreating British-Indian armies before the Japanese onslaught in 1941.[41] Thousands of Indians died of starvation or simply exhaustion in the flight from the overseas area that more than any other they had labored and given their capital to transform from an underdeveloped frontier into a model enclave of the global market economy.

The post-colonial fate of Indian overseas communities has been as varied as the societies to which they immigrated and the composition of the Indian migrant flow. In Trinidad, Guyana, Mauritius, Malaya and Fiji, they have reached a modus vivendi with indigenous and other immigrant groups. In South Africa, they perch precariously between a white minority, increasingly inclined to co-opt them with "second class" status, and the black majority, determined to resist the poverty and powerlessness that are its own fate as third class subjects of the apartheid regime. In much of east Africa and in Burma, the bulk of the Indian minority fled as indigenous assaults mounted and their British protectors withdrew, or they were expelled after independence. In Sri Lanka, violent Tamil separatism and Sinhalese discrimination and reprisals raise fears of yet another "race" war on the frontiers of Indian settlement. Whatever the outcome of communal interaction in these contrasting plural societies, their global distribution and continued existence stand as the legacy of one of the largest movements of population in human history, and reminders of one of the most remarkable alliances between colonizer and colonized ever recorded.

---

[41]   Hugh Tinker, "A Forgotten Long March: The Exodus from Burma, 1942," *Journal of Southeast Asian Studies* 4/1 (1975).

XVI

Market Demand Versus Imperial Control: Colonial Contradictions and the Origins of Agrarian Protest in South and Southeast Asia

In the decades since the end of the Second World War, the study of peasant protest and agrarian revolution in Asia has been transformed from a peripheral sub-field, dominated by a handful of scholars and ex-colonial officials, into one of the central concerns of theoreticians, comparativists, and area specialists in virtually every social science discipline. At the most superficial level, this transformation has resulted from a fascination with the global repercussions of the victorious Communist-led peasant revolutions in China and Vietnam.

Many of the scholars—American, Asian, and European—who are engaged in the current discourse on peasant unrest came of age as intellectuals in the turbulent decades of revolutionary upheaval in post-war China and Vietnam's long struggle against foreign domination and rule by indigenous elites. More fundamentally, however, the growth of interest in peasant societies and movement was spurred by the rapid change and agrarian unrest that was associated with the era of decolonization. The centrality of social conflict in the Marxist ideologies that have exerted such a great influence in the emerging states of Asia, and the implicit assumptions of fundamental change and disruption in the tradition/modernity approach to societal development that has come to be regarded by some as a counter to the Marxist challenge, gave great impetus to the study of the sources of rural and urban unrest, of the conditions that made for revolution, and often of the measures needed to prevent them. The credibility of both approaches was in turn enhanced by their emphasis on change, conflict, and social unrest. A vast literature devoted to the "passing of traditional societies," "transitional" groups and institutions, political "disequilibrium," and "revolutions of rising expectations" provides dramatic testimony to the centrality of these concerns. The growing importance of social history and social anthropology which made long-neglected groups—workers, women, the elderly, peasants—the focus of their inquiry gave added importance to the study of agrarian protest. Though much work has been done on rural social structures and economic systems that is not directly related to peasant protest, a disproportionate share of the literature on the Asian countryside has been devoted to the study of peasant unrest.

The growth of interest in peasant societies and movements has produced much that is positive. It has resulted in a relative abundance of well-researched and detailed case studies in a field where reliable data, much less insightful analysis, was often difficult to locate several decades ago. These studies have made major contributions to our understanding of the organization and dynamics of agrarian systems over much of the Asian world. Our theoretical gains with regard to agrarian societies or peasant protest have on the whole been more modest, but existing theories have been tested or reformulated to take into account our greatly improved knowledge, and a number of important debates have been generated. There has also been a necessary reorientation for our approaches from elite- and Western-centric perspectives and political concerns to peasant views and responses and broader social and economic issues. As several scholars have recently argued both implicitly and explicitly, however, this reorientation may have gone too far (Skocpol 1979; Paige 1975). An exclusive or preponderant emphasis on peasant concerns or a neglect of the critical roles of elite groups, whether they be European or Asian, has made for distortions, inaccuracies, and an incompleteness about much of this work that will have to be corrected by coming generations of scholars. The peasant-centric approach has also rendered much of the work that has been done somewhat tedious, increasingly inbred, and aimed at tiny groups of specialists. These tendencies have restricted the audience and blunted the impact of much of the important, recent work on peasant societies.

Although it has resulted in impressive advances in our understanding of peasant conditions and responses, the growing emphasis in the literature on agrarian societies in Asia and elsewhere on protest and rebellion and the conditions which give rise to these has distorted, I believe, our perception of the experience and reactions of the vast majority of agriculturists in the colonized world. The now commonplace assumption that the colonial age was everywhere a time of rapid change, disruption, and disorientation, which in turn produced frequent and widespread agrarian unrest, has gained acceptance as the result of a tendency, often unconscious, to generalize too readily from the experience of peasant groups in China and Vietnam, or turbulent frontier zones like the Panjab in India, the West Coast of Sumatra, or Lower Burma. Though we may well have overstated the extent of the transformations occurring in these societies and the degree of protest involvement by different peasant groups, we have certainly given disproportionate attention to these patterns in our attempts to develop general models to explain the peasant experience or rural resistance and protest in the Afro-Asian world. We have also tried to force the historical experience of societies where change was much more gradual, the persistence of pre-colonial institutions and ideas much more pronounced, and the incidence of overt protest rare into the change/conflict models that have come to dominate the literature on agrarian societies. This trend is perhaps most dramatically illustrated by the growing numbers of books and articles, by specialists working on India in a variety of disciplines, devoted to incidents or movements of rural protest. Though the actual "movements" described often amount to little (Jha 1977; Robb 1977; Kling 1966), the extensive coverage given to rural unrest in recent years provides a striking contrast with Barrington Moore's choice nearly two decades ago of India as a counter case—a society where massive poverty and oppression had produced little in the way of overt protest, much less revolution.

Our growing emphasis on socioeconomic disruption and peasant protest has led to a serious neglect of the "negative cases"—those agrarian situations where political and social transformations were less dramatic than we have come to assume and where the spread of agrarian production for the domestic or export market has generated little in the way of sustained protest on the part of cultivating groups. This neglect is particularly serious because the evidence produced to date indicates that these situations were over-whelmingly in the majority. With relatively rare exceptions, peasants have endured (depending on which theory of protest causation one employs) oppression, exploitation, grinding poverty, relative deprivation, the violation of custom and ethical codes, anomie, and alienation. Despite the prevalence of conditions that the models and theories of a growing cadre of social scientists postulate must have driven them to rebellion, there has been a surprising paucity of peasant protest movements in the Afro-Asian world.

The persistence, despite the coming of colonial rule, of long standing systems of social control and effective peasant defenses and non-confron-tational modes of protest, rather than innate docility or habitual submission, can best explain the paucity of agrarian risings in the colonial and post-colonial eras in most of the Afro-Asian world. Despite the vision of relentless change and upheaval that has come to be accepted for the colonial era, in many peasant societies, especially those in densely-populated core areas like Bihar in India and Dutch-ruled Java which are the focus of this essay, the impact of European conquest and rule was far less dramatic and far less extensive, particularly at the village level, than recent approaches to colonized peasant societies would lead us to assume. In fact, colonial administrators in these areas deliberately fashioned political economies that promoted preservation, not innovation, security and stability, not risk-taking and rapid change. They sought to shield the areas they ruled from the social upheavals and disruption that they believed would result from too rapid and extensive an exposure to the forces for the global economy. They advocated colonial policies that were aimed at shoring up pre-colonial political institutions, social hierarchies, and patterns of economic exchange based primarily on personal interaction and patron-client bonds, rather than Western European capitalist principles of competition, contracts, and the cash nexus.

For decades the systems that colonial administrators created by incorporating pre-colonial elites, institutions, and symbols into an overarching bureaucratic grid staffed at the highest levels by Europeans, succeeded in limiting change and reducing rural unrest to a minimum. In the last decades of the nineteenth century, however, internal problems and external pressures—demands for reform emanating from Holland and Britain and global market forces—resulted in changes in Bihar, Java, and other similarly ruled Asian core regions, that undermined the systems of colonial control that had been so carefully fashioned. These forces also brought into being new social groups and competing interests that would ultimately bring about an end to European rule. Ironically, however, despite their struggles to end European domination, these groups were careful to preserve, though with significant modifications, the systems of dependence and control that had made centuries of European rule possible. Thus, though they rose up in protest, nationalist agitators—with the exception of important, but minority, radical elements—strove not to destroy the systems which had made possible their rise to prominence, but to "reform" or alter them in ways that would eliminate foreign and weaken indigenous rivals and provide even greater opportunities for them to enhance their wealth and power.

Although Bihar and different areas on Java passed under colonial rule at different times, the transition to European control had little immediate impact upon and went largely unnoticed by the peasants who made up the vast majority of the populations in these regions. In some cases, recalcitrant princes or regional lords were overthrown by the alien conquerors and there were some shifts in the power exercised by local notables and their dependents as they vied for the favor of indigenous leaders allied to the Europeans and occasionally European officials themselves. Little else changed—in some cases for decades. The European overlords, who assumed the responsibility for the governance of these areas in the late eighteenth or early nineteenth centuries, had neither the strength nor the desire to rule them in depth. The British, confidently citing the ideas of the "classical" economists on the advantages of an improving gentry (Guha 1963; Stokes 1959), conceded local authority and control to a motley collection of Bengali and Bihari ex-officials and local notables who were granted landlord status in the Western sense for the first time. Their titles, which ranged from *zamindar* and *jotedar* to *maharaja* and *taluqdar*, and the complex gradation of regional lords and petty notables that had existed in the pre-colonial period were largely retained, though the specific families and kin groups that controlled these positions changed substantially in some areas (Cohn 1969).

In Java, the Dutch also chose to rule though the pre-colonial aristocracy or *priyayi*. In contrast to Bengal and Bihar, the regents, as the Dutch labelled their *priyayi* subordinates, and lower level members of the indigenous administrative corps, were not granted landlord status as such. During the period of the Cultivation System, (1830–c.1870), some were "paid" in part for their services by grants of control over the surplus from specified areas of land (Deventer 1865–6:vol. 2, 141 ff). Nonetheless, for many decades, and in some areas for well over a century, the regents and their client subordinates dominated rural administration, often with only minimal supervision by Dutch officials (Sutherland 1973:chs. 1, 2; Burger 1948–9:390–398; Furnivall 1939:123–126, 141–142). As in most other densely populated Asian areas were European colonizers worked out similar arrangements with indigenous elite groups), petty officials and local notables, who had shared authority in the pre-colonial era, retained, and often improved upon their positions, in the early decades of colonial rule.

In both Java and Bihar the European colonizers enlisted the aid of indigenous elite groups not only because of personnel and resource shortages, but also because by retaining the long-established Javanese or Indian lords and notables they preserved, virtually intact highly developed and well-tested systems of social control. By incorporating indigenous elites into the colonial administrative grid the Europeans gained the institutional and ideological means to pacify and extract revenue on a regular basis from a large portion of the peasantry at various levels from occupant tenants and smallholders to landless laborers. Patron-client networks in different guises, which had formed the backbone of the pre-colonial political economy and had been essential to the maintenance of wealth and authority at all levels, were now drawn into the colonial bureaucratic structure.

In Bihar, as in other lowland areas of India, patron-client links were embedded in the caste hierarchy that had long formed the central and in many ways the defining element in Indian culture and civilization. By elevating patron or *jajman* caste groups to the status of landowners in the Western legal sense, which they had not been previously, and attaching them as political allies and revenue collectors to the British Raj, the colonizers greatly enhanced these groups already considerable control over *kamin* or client caste groups, including tenants, laborers, and village artisans.[1] Patron-client dependency and reciprocity were critical elements in the colonial formula for social control. By buttressing the ancient *jajman* system and caste organization generally, the British, often quite deliberately, reinforced the vertical orientation and compartmentalization that were key characteristics of pre-colonial patron-client systems. The often asserted notion that colonialism and the spread of capitalism and the market system atomized peasant societies and gave rise to competition, individualism, and the primacy of self-interest in the rural sphere, makes little sense when applied to societies like those found in Java and India. Social and economic exchanges were already compartmentalized and identity constricted by patron-client networks of dependency that promoted family and kinship orientations and cooperation. These webs of dependence also greatly impaired, if not altogether blocked, the emergence of even the feeblest sense of class consciousness or organization. Through calculation or instinct, colonial officials came to view these networks of dominance and exchange as essential props for the maintenance of stability and control in the rural sphere.

In Java, from the early 1700s when the Dutch began to assume control of the agrarian hinterland beyond their port centers on the north coast,

XVI

94

they sought whenever possible to incorporate the *kawula-gusti* patron-client chains of the *priyayi* aristocracy and local leaders into the administrative hierarchy of the colonial regime. At the village level, and usually through the patronage powers exercised by their regional Javanese allies, the Dutch mobilized labor and extracted resources in collaboration with the *lurahs* or village headmen and the *sikeps* or prominent, usually land controlling families, within each peasant community. The acquiescence of these groups to Dutch rule was essential to control the great mass of the peasantry. (Deventer 1865–6:vol.2, 201; Kartodirdjo 1972:83–7; Onghokham 1975:161–76).

In both Java and India, the cooperation of regional and local elites meant that those groups that had had the broadest and strongest horizontal links, normally operating through kinship lineages or, in India, caste connections (Fox 1971), were firmly drawn into the colonial establishment, thereby eliminating (or at least greatly reducing) the potential for large-scale and widespread risings against European rule. The fact that these groups had often dominated military affairs in the pre-colonial era and that they often retained their weapons and ability to forcibly back up the demands they made of subordinate cultivators at various levels rendered their alliance with the colonizers all the more essential (Deventer 1865–6:vol.2, 201ff). As the British learned in the Indian "mutiny" of 1857–58 (Raj 1965:19–40; Metcalf 1964, 1979) and the Dutch in the Java War of 1825–30 (Palmer 1960:214ff; Schrieke 1966:219ff) when threatened aristocrats and landed groups led tens of thousands of retainers into open rebellions, indigenous elite groups were potent sources of leadership for resistance against colonial rule (Niel 1969:272–3). The co-option of these groups meant that a possible catalyst for dissidence was transformed into a bulwark of social control in the countryside.

In terms of regular revenue extraction and internal repression on a day-to-day basis, the adherence of indigenous elites was essential to the maintenance of colonial rule. Their private forces of armed retainers, which usually included local toughs or *goondas* in India and *jagos* in Java, meant that landlords and local notables could themselves quell disturbances mounted by disgruntled tenants or laborers through a variety of methods that ranged from crop confiscation and ejection to arson, torture, and murder.[2] European courts and laws based on private property and the sanctity of written contracts further buttressed the power of landlords and local officials (Harcourt 1977:332; Robb 1979:110; Kling 1966:51), but through most of the colonial period threats and violent reprisals proved the most expedient means of dealing with village "trouble makers."

The colonizers' decision to exercise their rule through indigenous elite groups at various levels meant that in Bihar and Java institutions and ideas that had given legitimacy to pre-colonial rulers and officials remained effective means of social control (Low 1973:18–21). This pattern contrasts sharply with the fate of elites and institutions in frontier zones like Lower Burma, where they were swept aside or Cochin China, where they were discredited

XVI

by defeat and collaboration (Adas 1982; Marr 1971:chs. 2,3). In Java experienced Dutch officials stridently rejected suggestions that the status or powers of the *priyayi* be curbed or their roles reduced. Numerous writers argued that the continuance of Dutch rule was impossible without the cooperation for the regents and village. Dutch authors asserted that these indigenous officials possessed an aura of legitimacy and inspired a depth of peasant loyalty that could never be acquired by the Dutch themselves or even by Javanese administrators whom the Dutch appointed, no matter how well the latter were trained. Dutch officials also came to regard regents and other *priyayi* administrators, and the elaborate symbols and rituals of rule which they wielded, as the most potent antidotes to message of sedition and revolt preached by Muslim teachers and holymen (Boeka 1904; Deventer 1865–6:201–208). In fact, the Dutch were so impressed by the splendor and pageantry of the Javanese "theater state"[3] that they themselves adopted the use of gilded umbrellas and other symbols of Javanese authority (Di Nijs 1961, relevant photos). Though the position and powers of the regent allies of the Dutch varied by region and time period in the nineteenth century, their posts became hereditary and they persisted as the symbolic, if not the actual, locus of political authority in rural Java (Sutherland 1973:ch. 2; Palmier 1960).

If the pageantry was less grand in Bihar and the British somewhat less inclined to wield the physical symbols of Indian power, the role of indigenous allies in legitimizing European colonial rule was no less critical. The British periodically held lavish regional and all-India *durbars* to bolster ritually their ties to indigenous lords. But more than etiquette and elaborate costumes were necessary for the maintenance of an official's or estate owner's legitimacy. Donations to local temples and village shrines, the repair and construction of irrigation works, and dramatic gestures of material generosity were expected of those who exercised local power and claimed a share of the cultivator's harvest or his labor services. In Bihar, as in other areas of India, when these obligations were not fulfilled, cultivators grew resentful to the demands of the landlord class and at times openly challenged their authority.[4] Through much of the nineteenth century, however, the British and Dutch preservation of indigenous social hierarchies insured the persistence of peasant acceptance of stratification and inequities in wealth and power as part of the natural order of things—a view which Louis Dumont (1970) has argued has historically been essential to social cohesion and control in India, and, implicitly, in most pre-industrial societies.

Although patron-client ties and shared cultural values bound the peasant populations of areas like Java and Bihar to indigenous elites in a way they could never have been attached to alien European rulers, the exchanges between landed groups and indigenous bureaucrats and the mass of the cultivators heavily favored the form and were often harshly exploitative. Effective checks on excessive elite demands in the pre-colonial era were largely logistical. If ethical, these buffers were personalized and renegotiated with each encounter, rather than embedded in abstract moral codes, though pious injunctions about the welfare of the peasantry certainly existed. Thus, the fact that indigenous lords retained or increased their authority in the early decades of European rule in itself tells us little about the impact of colonialism on cultivating groups at various levels. Paternalist and patron-client ties could be used in ways that were as oppressive and exploitative as those based on impersonal contracts and cash payments. In social systems where patron-client reciprocity comprised the matrix of economic exchanges and socio-political cohesion, the consciousness of subordinate cultivating groups (as Marx n.d.:18–21 has argued, the cultivating classes as a whole) was highly constricted. Their vertical orientation and social compartmentalization meant that it was rare for tenants or laborers to reorganize effectively for bargaining or resistance to the oppressive exactions of landlords or local officials even within a single village. Geographical and occupational mobility were normally limited, and legal means of cultivator redress of grievances—beyond reliance on precedents established by longstanding custom—were virtually non-existent. Protest, on the rare occasions when it took the form of riot or rebellion, was almost always in support of the cultivators' patron or their patron's lord. Protest against their patrons occurred only in the most desperate circumstances and normally involved flight into the wilderness or (preferably) the transfer of the cultivators' allegiance and services to another patron official, religious leader, or bandit chief (Adas 1982:226–239).

Although ruling through the indigenous elites greatly reduced the costs to the British and Dutch of maintaining internal order, it also greatly limited the amount of control which European or European-trained administrators could exert at the village level. In fact, the level of day-to-day contact between European officials and the peasant population was so minimal under regimes that are conventionally classified as those exhibiting direct rule, that one might well conclude that the standard direct/indirect categorization misleads than informs by concealing critical differences within each type and making too sharp a distinction between them. Because ongoing social control was left to indigenous elites and institutions, British and Dutch intervention in local affairs was sporadic and confined to intermittent tours of inspection and occasions where conflict or peasant unrest threatened serious disturbances. The colonizers routinely responded to the latter situations by stationing extra police or regular military forces in the affected areas (BPP). Thus, the overwhelming edge in military technology, organization, and communications which the Europeans possessed by the mid nineteenth century normally played only a passive role in the maintenance of colonial control. It provided the ultimate guarantee of the authority of the Europeans and their indigenous allies, not the omnipresent force that is central to Frantz Fanon's (1968) Manichaean vision of the colonial world. It could, however, be employed with devasting effect when the Europeans' allies or the colonial regime itself were threatened.

The limits to the control over local affairs that the Europeans were able to exercise were most strikingly revealed by the poor quality of colonial population, revenue, and crop yield statistics. In both Bihar and Java, records keeping and revenue collection were left in the hands of village notables and petty functionaries. Because revenue demands in Bihar (and Bengal and Orissa) were fixed by the terms of the Permanent Settlement of 1782 which the British struck with those rural elite groups who would come to make up the landlord class, British officials had little to do with the gathering and compilation of statistics at the village level. These figures were, of course, the basis for all records keeping relating to rural areas throughout the colonial period. Village crop and population statistics were kept either by high caste, literate *patwaris* or low caste, illiterate *chaukidars* depending on the area in question. For different reasons both groups subordinated the demands of supra-village elite groups to village interests. *Patwaris* were normally related to or closely allied with the dominant, land-controlling caste groups within the village they served. Therefore, the consistent under-reporting of population totals and crop production, and hence the amount of services or produce that had to be yielded up to non-village landlords or officials, enriched both the *patwaris* and the dominant caste families in the village. In villages where low caste *chaukidars* were in charge of crop and revenue records, high caste families found it relatively easy, and perhaps less costly than alliances with *patwaris*, to bribe and browbeat these untrained and impoverished functionaries who were usually treated like menial servants (Dewey 1979:280–286; Robb 1979:102–103, 108–110; *BAR* 1916; 12, 1917:9).

Because the Permanent Settlement barred increases in the revenue demands made by the British, the periodic settlements and revenue revisions that gave the British a much clearer, though by no means wholly accurate, impression of the productivity and manpower resources of areas ruled in greater depth like Burma, Maharashtra, and the Panjab were non-existent in Bihar. Thus, as British revenue officials freely conceded, agrarian statistics were, on the whole, little more than "absurd guesses" through most of the period of British rule (Dewey 1979:283).

In Java, where village headmen and their kin and client allies monopolized records keeping, revenue collection, and census counts, the Dutch and their Javanese and Chinese allies literally had to "dicker" with village leaders to set the amount of revenue due. In the absence of cadastral surveys (which were not carried out until the last decades of the nineteenth century), assessments were "arbitrary and inexact" and village heads were "unusually successful" in disguising the extent of village cultivation and the productivity of the are cropped (Niel 1964:358). A recent estimate based on a careful study of the reports on the working of the Cultivation System in the middle decades of the nineteenth century reveals that on average only 70–75 percent of the population and land cultivated were actually reported in the 1830s and 1840s (Niel 1972:98, 108–109; also Vitalis 1851:2–3). To avoid increases in crop delivery demands or labor services, village and district heads simply neglected to list population growth that resulted from in-migration or natural increase or new lands that came into cultivation. Because the Dutch, like the British in India, did not have the trained personnel to check local returns in a rigorous manner, most reports went un-challenged even though European officials and the regents were well aware that they were riddled with inaccuracies and deliberate attempts to deceive (Fasseur 1978:16, 21–22, 61–62, 98–99; Onghokham 1975:155–156, 212, 216; J. L. V. 1855:6).

In both Java and Bihar alliances struck with indigenous elite groups and the colonizers' failure to intervene effectively at the village level resulted in large losses of revenue to the European overlords. Due to severe shortages of trained administrators and the obsession with low costs of governance exhibited by the officials and legislators who increasingly shaped colonial policy from the European metropolis, there appeared to be no viable alternatives. To effect change at the local level or extract greater revenues, the colonizers had to put pressure on the indigenous elites that had made their low cost rule possible. As the Dutch were reminded by the Java War and the British by the "mutiny," to press these groups too hard, or even worse to attempt to displace them, endangered the longstanding hierarchies of dependence and control that gave some semblance of legitimacy to European rule (Robb 1979:110).

The loss of revenue that resulted from the inefficiency of ruling largely through indigenous elite groups was, as was intended, offset to a considerable degree by the low level of peasant unrest. Compared to the turbulent frontier zones like Lower Burma and the Mekong Delta region of Vietnam, where the collapse of the indigenous order and far-reaching social and economic changes severely eroded the efficacy of pre-colonial systems of social control, overt peasant resistance was rare in Java and Bihar. This contrast is even more striking if one takes into account the fact that the population of Bihar and Java, both in density and in absolute terms, was far greater than that in Lower Burma or Cochin China, where peasant risings were far more frequent. In part this difference can be attributed to the contrasting fates of the elites and symbols of legitimacy in each region. Equally critical, however, to the lower level of overt resistance to colonial rule in areas like Bihar and Java was the persistence beneath the highest levels of administration of pre-colonial systems of social control and revenue extraction. The survival of indigenous elites and institutions, especially at the village level, meant that most modes of ongoing defense and non-confrontational resistance that cultivating groups had devised in the pre-colonial period to buffer elite demands and check oppression remained viable well into the colonial era, they were usually small-scale and infrequent. Rather, the great majority of the cultivators continued to rely on evasive techniques of defense and protest. Thus, Judith Brown's (1972:464) contention that Indian peasants, before the emergence of Gandhi, had no protest alternatives other than rioting, not only gives undue emphasis to confrontational modes of agrarian resistance, it conveys a distorted image of the nature of the social and political framework in which peasants acted and the economic conditions to which they responded.

As in the pre-colonial period, poor records and the failure of the bureaucracy to penetrate to the village level left ample openings for concealment and evasion which had long been the first line of peasant defense. The complex maze of rights and sub-rights to the land that had evolved over the centuries in Bihar and Java made it possible for local officials and village notables in charge of tax collection or labor recruitment to baffle even the most diligent landlords' agents in Bihar or revenue officials in Java. Even in areas where landlords employed overseers or relatives to check up on local conditions, crop returns were grossly under-reported, newly cultivated fields went unrecorded, and the actual state of land control in the village—which in Bihar was normally dominated by tenants and not landowners—remained largely a mystery to supra-village elites, most especially the Europeans. When villages were assessed on a communal basis, as was the case in Java during the period of the Cultivation System, concealment and collusion worked to the advantage of the village as a whole. In both Java and Bihar, however, these modes of peasant defense best served the interests of the dominant land and records controlling groups in the village just as they had in the precolonial period. In some instances (Deventer 1865–6: vol. 2, 195; Vitalis 1851: xiv, 18) the weak control exerted by the colonial overlords led to extortion and excessive demands by petty officials who were not above resorting to torture and force to have their way. As the ties between groups of high caste tenants in Bihar and *sikep* families in Java and subordinate cultivating groups shifted from paternalist, patron-client links to contractual exchanges, tax and labor service evasion increasingly shielded and enriched locally dominant families and ambitious market producers, often at the expense of the great majority of the village dwellers (Robb 1979:119; Fasseur 1978:21–22, 86; Niel 1972; 98, 105).

Because unclaimed arable land and local shortages of labor persisted into the first decades of the twentieth century, flight and migration remained viable peasant defenses against elite oppression, as they had been in the pre-colonial era. In Java disgruntled cultivators migrated, at times *en masse*, from areas where the burdens of the Cultivation System were too great to those where labor and production demands were lighter. Of the crops introduced by the Dutch, indigo was the most demanding in terms of time and labor. The movement of populations from areas where indigo was grown to coffee or sugar growing areas, or those outside the Cultivation System entirely, is particularly notable (Elson 1978:26; Niel 1972:103; Fasseur 1978:39, 53). In some instances dissident cultivators fled into areas still ruled by Javanese lords, albeit under Dutch tutelage (Vitalis 1851:46). In times of soaring rice prices and famine, which were arguably linked to the substitution of export for subsistence crops (Elson 1978:15–16, 22; Soest 1869:3, 109ff, 165ff; 206–207, Pierson 1868:33–34, 152; Vitalis 1851:21, 35, 42, 55–57), there were large-scale migrations from areas where excessive Dutch quotas had resulted in famine conditions (Fasseur 1978:85, 88; Vitalis 1851:xi, 4).

As the most recent major study of the Cultivation System demonstrates (Fasseur 1978), migration was the Javanese peasants' major form of defense against and resistance to the changes and increased burdens which colonial demands introduced into the countryside. Peasant families—including well-to-do households—migrated to escape arrogant officials, increased labor demands, or excessive tribute quotas. The use of migration both as a defense and an act of protest is the most clearly illustrated by instances where peasants who had fled their home villages returned when official abuses ceased or revenue quotas were lowered. In some cases peasants who had fled migrated yet again when officials in the district to which they had first moved tried to force them to perform labor services similar to those which they had originally resisted (Soest 1869:3, 205). In some instances peasant migrants explicitly stated that the reason for their flight was a protest of government demands. Cultivators who had migrated from the Japara region in northeast Java in the late 1840s informed government officials who inquired into the causes for their flight that in addition to customary services they were required to transport sugar cane and firewood—extra services for which they received no wages. They complained that demands linked to the Cultivation System were so heavy that they had little time to cultivate the fields on which they grew the crops for their own subsistence (Soest 1869:3, 205; Vitalis 1851:xiv, 4). Peasants who fled from areas subject to the Cultivation System in the neighboring districts of Demak and Grobgan in the 1850s voiced similar complaints about government demands for tobacco production. The refugees brazenly declared to inquisitive Dutch officials that they had migrated to protest excessive labor demands and that they would not return to their home districts until forced tobacco cultivation there was ended (Pierson 1868:154–155).

In Bihar, as in Java, flight was a major mode of peasant defense. At times large tracts were left virtually deserted by cultivators fleeing special taxes by Indian landlords or the forced exactions of European planters. In the late nineteenth century, British revenue officials remarked on the stronger bargaining position and consequently the better conditions enjoyed by Bihari tenants who lived in areas where uncultivated arable land, and thus the option of flight, was still available (Robb 1979:105). Until the first decades of the twentieth century the possibility for cultivators who worked estates located in the northernmost areas of the district. Marriage alliances with families living in Nepal and the rather meager material possessions of most Bihari tenants and laborers facilitated this movement which severely undercut the productive capacity of affected estates. As in Java, when conditions improved in the area of departure or overly zealous estate agents were dismissed, large numbers of cultivators would return to their home districts (Henningham 1979:55; O'Malley 1907:38–39).

Labor shortages in some areas (particularly those where new lands were being brought into cultivation for the first time) and the consequent competition of land controlling groups for seasonal and long-term workers meant that some possibilities existed for tenants and laborers to escape exploitation by transferring their services to competing landholders (Sinha 1918:18–19, 26–27; Ray 1973:114, 116–117; Robb 1979:113–114; Kumar 1968:45, 47). Though available evidence indicates that this was a preferred mode of peasant defense in the pre-colonial era (Adas 1981:229–232), the rather infrequent mention of it in the available sources makes it difficult to determine if it remained preferred by cultivators to the high risks preferred by cultivators to the high risks and great labor involved in settling unoccupied areas. Its infrequent mention may be due to the fact that wage and contract labor made the severing of landlord and tenant or laborer ties a good deal easier and much more common than in the pre-colonial period and thus it attracted little in the way of special attention.

Because colonial laws and land tenure systems were loaded heavily in favor of landowning and official groups, and resort to court actions was too expensive for most cultivators, legal avenues of grievance redress were seldom employed until the first decades of the twentieth century. The likelihood that tenants or laborers would turn to the local magistrate with their complaints was also limited because the rural police were almost invariably in collusion with or at least under the control of landholders, headmen, and other local notables. The response of one old man to Gandhi's inquiry in Champaran, Bihar, in 1917 vividly dramatizes the peasants' well-founded mistrust of legal channels of redress. This man who had lost his lands and had had his house pulled down by the local landlord's toughs, reported that when he went to the magistrate to complain of his brutal treatment he was rudely dismissed with a clear threat of bodily harm if he should persist with his complaints. The lesson, he concluded, was clear— "all *topiwallahs* (officials) are the same (Prasad 1949:15). A similar attitude was displayed by peasants in north central Java who were migrating to avoid excessive labor demands. When asked by Dutch officials why they had not taken their complaints to local Javanese officials, they responded incredulously that the option simply was not possible for the "little man" or *wong tjilik* (Pierson 1868:155).

Although tenants and laborers avoided the courts and police, they often resorted to petitions and processions of protest to the residences of government officials; these had been standard modes of peasant dissidence in the pre-colonial era (Kling 1966:68, 168; O'Malley 1938:83–85; Henningham 1979:63, 65–66; Kartodirdjo 1973:25, 28–29; Vitalis 1851:46; Fasseur 1978:47). Work refusals are also recorded and these were sometimes combined with protest processions (Pierson 1868:150). Because this sort of dissidence struck at the very heart of the colonial revenue system, it was usually dealt with harshly by colonial officials. At times, however, protest demonstrations or work refusals prompted investigations of local conditions, some concessions to dissident cultivators, and in a number of instances the dismissal or demotion of offending officials (Vitalis 1851:11–13).

The failure of peasant defensive tactics or non-confrontational modes of protest periodically led to the eruption of overt, at times violent, riots or rebellions. Until the first decades of the twentieth century, however, rural disturbances appear to have been surprisingly infrequent, small-scale, and short-lived in both Bihar and Java. Banditry or dacoity was endemic to many areas of both regions (*BPP*, Criminal Caste Reports: *passim*; Sinha

XVI

1918:18–19: Onghokham 1975: 231ff; Siau Giap 1968:111–112; Anon. 1861:289–300), but it is difficult to determine the extent to which it was a symptom of social unrest or merely a continuation of the pattern of professional, often hereditary, criminality that was associated with certain social groups in the pre-colonial era. In fact, in many areas bandit gangs remained in collusion with and often linked by kinship ties to local notables and indigenous officials (Vitalis 1851:6–7)—a pattern that had been widespread in the pre-colonial period. Colonial officials understandably tried to play down the degree to which criminal activities were linked to peasant discontent, but in certain instances in both Java and Bihar, clear connections existed between poor economic conditions, cultivators' distress, and increases in banditry and other criminal activities. Due, however, to the much greater risks involved in banditry in the colonial period, when the police and military were better trained and armed than in the pre-colonial era, it is probable that vandalism, arson, crop destruction and theft, and other forms of sometimes violent, but short-term and clandestine reprisal, became the preferred modes of peasant resistance to excessive demands by landlords and tax collectors. Unfortunately, though some of the more notorious incidents involving these forms of protest were recorded in police records (O'Malley 1938:833, 87, 89; Kling 1966:88, 93; Onghokham 1975:226, 230) most were too minor to come to the attention of colonial officials. As a result, it is impossible to estimate how important arson or vandalism became as modes of peasant response—though as I shall argue below, they became widespread in the turbulent first decades of the twentieth century.

Given the large agrarian populations of both Bihar and Java and the long time span during which these areas were under colonial rule, rioting or more sustained agrarian risings were far rarer than our conflict-oriented models of peasant societies would lead us to assume. Though there were disturbances in some parts of Bihar during the Indian "Mutiny" of 1857–58, the most serious challenges to British rule during the crisis in the district came in highland tribal areas, not in the densely populated lowlands where, as in Bengal, most of the rural elite groups and the cultivators subordinate to them remained loyal to the colonial regime or at least refused to support the rebel cause (Majumdar 1963:140–44; Datta 1957). Despite British charges that the district was one of the main centers of Muslim fundamentalist Wahhabite activity (Sen 1957:245–247), there is little evidence that this resulted in overt or violent challenges to colonial rule.[5] Hindus, who made up a large majority of the district's population, would, of course, have had little sympathy for such efforts. In fact, the available evidence suggests that social tensions were more often released through communal clashes than protest against the colonial overlords or their landlord allies. Paralleling these communal disturbances were innumerable petty squabbles between different villages or tenant holders over field boundaries, stray cattle, water rights, and crop shares (*BPP*, 1911–1931, passim). Other than protest aimed at-European indigo planters, which will be discussed in more detail below, there is not evidence of major violent risings against the British until the decades of crisis in the early twentieth century. This absence of overt protest provides eloquent testimony to the effectiveness of the British strategy of ruling as much as possible through indigenous elites and institutions.

In Java peasant risings were more frequent than in Bihar, but, relative to the large population ruled, surprisingly few and generally quite feeble. Ironically, despite the greater concern of the Dutch to preserve and themselves adopt the symbols and rituals that had given political legitimacy to the Javanese *priyayi*, conspiracies and peasant risings focusing on the alien and infidel nature of Dutch rule posed a far more serious challenge in Java than in Bihar. The greatest threat to Dutch rule was posed by the risings that were touched off by the spillover of the widespread rebellion led by Prince Dipanagara between 1825 and 1830 which extended beyond the princely states to the north coast residencies and east-central Java. After the rebellion, which had been led by a mix of threatened *priyayi* officials and Muslim religious figures, the Dutch consciously, and by and large successfully, placated *priyayi* resistance by guaranteeing the position of the princes and restoring much of the power and status that the *bupati* regents had lost in the era of reform under Daendels and Raffles in the first decades of the nineteenth century.[6]

Muslim dissidents, however, could not be mollified or coopted by the infidel and secular-minded Dutch. Muslim teachers (*kyais*) and holymen became, therefore, the main foci of anti-colonial resistance in the years after the Java War. Their determination to overthrow the Dutch was exacerbated by the anti-Muslim policies pursued by the Netherlands Indies regime and by contact between Javanese Muslims and Middle Eastern Muslim fundamentalist and revivalist movements through the *hadj* to Mecca (Anon. 1891:1768–1776). The fact that the great majority of Javanese were at least nominally Muslim, in contrast to Bihar where Muslims were in the minority, gave the threat which Muslim holymen and religious teachers appeared to pose for the Dutch added potency. The fears of Dutch officials and planters, which often bordered on paranoia (Shoemaker 1896) were not entirely without foundation, as was demonstrated by periodic risings in west and central Java led by Muslim religious figures. In some instances these risings, which were usually brief and localized, resulted in the deaths of Dutch planters and their families or *priyayi* officials. Most of these outbursts involved small groups of peasants led by Muslim teachers or holymen who, like Dipanagara, relied on amulets, eschatological prophecies, and their ability to inspire fanatical devotion on the part of their followers to rally (Cary 1979:87–91; Kartodirdjo 1966, 1973; Vitalis 1851:8–9). Fortunately for the Dutch, all of these rebellions were small-scale affairs and thus easily suppressed.[7] Therefore, despite the disproportionate attention given in recent years to overt protest in nineteenth century Java, the study of social control and the persistence of pre-colonial modes of non-confrontational defense and protest is of much greater relevance if we are concerned with the condition and responses of the great majority of the rural Javanese population.

If colonial officials had only to maintain the patchwork combinations of European and indigenous officials and institutions that constituted most colonial regimes, it is reasonable to argue that European imperialist dominance would have been far more enduring than it has proven to be. The Indian Civil Service or the Netherlands Indies Binnenlands Bestuur did not operate in a vacuum, however, but were forced to take into account policy directives predicated on the needs and demands of their respective European metropolises, and the requirements of an ever-expanding global market economy. These external forces generated changes that colonial officials often welcomed initially as beneficial for the colonized peoples, but came eventually to regard as fundamentally disruptive to the systems of social control that had so painstakingly been put together in the early decades of European rule. Attempts to improve and extend bureaucratic control of levy new taxes, the spread of new forms of economic activity, and dramatic shifts in demographic patterns produced new social groups and divisions that threatened the alliances on which the Europeans had based their rule and undermined the centuries-old networks of dependence and modes of defense upon which European global dominance had been based.

Many of the administrative changes that upset the fragile balance between European control and intervention and the continued dominance of indigenous elite groups that had been established in the late eighteenth and early nineteenth centuries, were brought about in response to needs and conditions within the colonies themselves. In all cases, however, ideas and demands emanating from Britain and Holland impinged to a greater and greater extent on the formulation of administrative and revenue policy. Proponents of social reform and the cause of the laboring classes in Europe often extended their campaigns to colonial questions involving the peasantry and urban workers (Fasseur 1978: chs. 4,6; Das 1964). By late nineteenth century liberal, socialist, or even reform conservative standards, the social and political systems produced by the Permanent Settlement in Bihar or the Cultivation System in Java were exotic anachronisms riddled with corruption, inefficiency, and openings for the exploitation of the cultivating classes. Scandals in Java that spread to Holland and debates in the Hague were decisive in the Dutch decision to abandon the Cultivation System and inaugurate the highly touted Liberal Policy. Though British officials in India usually acted more on their own initiative than did the Dutch in Java, the heightened sense of responsibility that was enshrined, however hypocritically, in the *"mission civilisatrice"* gave important impetus to efforts to introduce agrarian reforms in the late nineteenth century.

Bureaucratic reform at the most basic level meant better trained administrative personnel which in the late nineteenth century was synonymous with the rapid expansion of Western-language educational institutions among the colonized peoples. This trend gave rise to the new urban-based elite groups that would eventually wrest power from the European overlords and some of their indigenous allies, but its effects were not really felt in rural Bihar or Java until the first years of the twentieth century. Of more immediate significance were the series of agrarian reform bills that were put into effect in India and Java in the late nineteenth century and the growing involvement of colonial officials in local affairs. Though intended to check only the most serious abuses of landlord groups and indigenous officials, agrarian reform measures often provided the basis for fundamental challenges by subordinate groups to the longstanding dominance of indigenous elites. The ability of estate owners in Bihar or local and regional officials in Java to levy special taxes, turn troublesome tenants off their lands, or manipulate the local judiciary or constabulary was restricted at a time when the financial position and authority of these groups were under assault from other quarters (Robinson 1971:314, 328–329; Robb 1979:11).

Most critically, agrarian bills and judicial reforms could provide effective legal buffers for smallholder, tenant, and laboring classes for the first time. The rise of the vernacular press in both Bihar and Java, and the protracted and often polemical struggles that were necessary to enact these reforms, also served to instill an awareness on the part of cultivating groups of their legal rights. Though landlord interests continued to dominate court actions, increasing evidence from different areas in India indicates that court suits had also become a weapon of tenants and smallholders under certain conditions. In Madras, for example, disgruntled tenants used barrages of court cases to wear down financially strapped landlords to the point where rent demands became too expensive to collect (Baker 1976:27–29). More commonly, tenants, often allying themselves with urban-based lawyers connected to the Congress Party and other nationalist organizations, used the courts to challenge the levying of special taxes or gifts by landlords or to establish their claims to occupancy tenant status which gave them secure tenure and other special privileges as a result of the land reform bills of the late nineteenth century (Sengupta 1971:195).

In addition to agrarian reform, there were major efforts in the late nineteenth century in both Java and Bihar to increase the reach of the colonial bureaucracy and promote its involvement in local affairs in the rural areas. In part these initiatives, as well as the economic innovations discussed below, were the responses of financially troubled regimes. As inflation, the need for additional personnel, and soaring military expenses made it increasingly difficult to balance colonial budgets, European administrators sought new ways to raise revenues and insure that a greater share of what they claimed as their due actually reached the imperial coffers. Though income taxes that were introduced in India as one way of keeping up with expenses affected mainly urban groups, they indirectly fueled rural unrest. These taxes, which were linked to the spread of local self-government, angered mercantile and landholding interests that increasingly sought to rally mass support among rural cultivators for their anti-colonial campaigns (Robinson 1971:324–325; Pandey 1978). In both Java and Bihar village dwellers were more directly affected by sanitation campaigns, drives to inoculate peasant families and livestock against disease, efforts to improve roads and build bridges while the colonizers saw these as essential to improvements in rural welfare, they were often regarded by peasants as bothersome sources of extra demands for labor and resources (Furnivall 1956:430–432).

XVI

In some cases the tightening of administrative control clearly worked against the interests of subordinate cultivating groups. In their effort to set aside additional forest reserves and improve surveillance over those already established, for example, colonial administrators deprived the peasant populations which lived in areas near woodlands of free firewood and timber for construction, as well as a wide variety of supplementary foods and medicinal plants. In both Bihar and Java (Benda and Castles 1969:212, 221; Henningham 1979:59, 60, 63) access to forest zones and the right to use tree products in cultivated areas became major sources of friction between government officials or landlords and smallholders, tenants, and landless laborers. More pervasive, however, was peasant anxiety about or overt hostility towards government efforts, through special inquiries and regular census counts to gain more accurate estimates of the population, land resources, and landholding patterns in the areas under colonial control. Peasants rightly perceived that these efforts were a vital threat to many of their most potent means of defense against excessive government and elite demands. As a result, despite some improvements in records collecting, government efforts to upgrade the quality of their data on rural conditions were largely frustrated—again by a shortage of personnel and funds and especially local collusion and concealment (J. L. V. 1855:6–7; Fasseur 1978:62; Dewey 1979:302ff).

As important as administrative reforms and land tenure legislation were in eroding the systems of social control which had upheld colonial rule in Java and Bihar through most of the nineteenth century, their impact was far less extensive and disruptive than the market forces that increasingly penetrated these areas from mid-century onwards. A steadily rising demand in industrializing Europe and later North America for foodstuffs (coffee, tea, sugar, groundnuts, rice) and industrial crops (jute, hemp, palm oil, indigo, cotton) gave impetus to a global communications and transport revolution that began to have significant effects on Java and Bihar in the 1840s and 1850s. In the same period there was a related and rapid spread of the production of export crops in colonized areas under a wide variety of production systems ranging from the plantation zones of Sumatra and Assam to the smallholder economies of Ghana and Minangkabau. In most instances the demand for tropical produce was complemented by a need to find new market outlets for cheap consumer goods and, on a more selective and limited basis, investment capital.[8] Roads, canals, and railway lines were constructed, first in India, and later in Southeast Asia, Africa, and the Middle East, to link crop producing areas to port outlets where improved sailing vessels and, increasingly, steamships could carry them to Europe, North America, and, by the 1890s, Japan for processing, consumption, and sometimes reshipment (Harnetty 1972; Allen and Donnithorne 1957). For most crops[9] the last decades of the nineteenth century were an era of steadily rising demand and, as a result, increasing prices. These conditions drew growing numbers of cultivators throughout the colonial world deeply into production for domestic and overseas markets. Though often viewed as essential concomitant of European imperialist expansion and proudly touted by its defenders as an index of the benefits bestowed by colonial rule, this involvement ultimately did much to break the hold which the European colonizers and their indigenous allies had maintained over rural Asia for most of the nineteenth century.

Some colonial officials voiced concern over the disruptive effects of the rapid spread of market production. In both Java and Bihar this concern appeared to be well-founded, in view of the close association that had already been observed in the early and mid-nineteenth century between agrarian unrest and the presence of European-run estates producting for the export market in each area. In Java the *Particuliere Landerijen* or private estates leased to Europeans or Chinese had been the target of peasant uprisings and labor protest with a frequency that was far out of proportion to the small numbers of Javanese cultivators involved in crop production for these enterprises (Kartodirdjo 1973: ch.2). In Bihar disputes between European indigo planters and the Indian laborers and tenants who worked the lands these entrepreneurs leased from Indian landlords were virtually the only agrarian disturbances in the district in the late nineteenth century (Misra 1967). In neighboring Bengal this connection was even more pronounced and indigo disturbances more frequent and far more serious (Kling 1966).

As export production spread beyond the European and great landlord estates, however, the threats which market involvement posed for systems of colonial control in Java and Bihar multiplied rapidly. A new class of market-oriented, relatively prosperous cultivators emerged in each area. For Bihar, and elsewhere in India, this process has been studied in some detail. In Bihar occupancy tenants, usually from high caste groups, appear to have been the main beneficiaries of increased involvement in market production and to have concentrated their efforts on cultivating foodstuffs for sale both domestically and overseas (Fisher 1979:122–128; Charlesworth 1979; Kumar 1968:45, 54–55; Robinson 1971:319–320).

Much less work has been done on the emergence of market-oriented farmers in Java, in part because of the hold which Clifford Geertz's (1966) brilliantly argued concepts of agricultural involution and shared poverty have exercised over a generation of scholars of Indonesian history. In recent years, however, many of Geertz's ideas have been challenged (Kano 1980). As a result, there is a growing body of evidence which indicates, though by no means conclusively, that the levelling process which Geertz pictured for rural Java as a consequence of the Cultivation System and Liberal Policy was by no means all-inclusive (Elson 1978:7–8, 24–25, 30). In some areas of Java, at least (Tjeribon, Semerant, Bagelen), local notables and land-controlling families not only amassed considerable holdings, but achieved positions of wealth and power through a combination of production for the market and their roles as the intermediaries in negotiations between village communities and Dutch entrepreneurs or revenue collectors. From the first years after the imposition of the Cultivation System, dominant families in the areas where it was introduced reaped great profits from the cuts they were given for tribute produce collected, the control they gained over village lands, and their monopoly of lucrative, local administrative posts (Vitalis 1851:10; Niel 1969:269–270, 274–275; 1972:98, 104–105). Thus, in part at least, the social stratification and divisions between landed and landless classes that characterize rural Java today had their roots in the changes in the island's political economy effected by the Dutch in the middle of the nineteenth century (Elson 1978:20–21, 28–29; Onghokham 1975:201, 206–208). Though the Dutch intended to limit the direct involvement of the Javanese peasantry in the market economy through the introduction of the quasi-tribute Cultivations System, the use of cash payments for produce delivered, and the introduction of export crops on a vast scale frustrated the colonizer's aims and revived and expanded the inland marketing network that had been in decline for decades (Fasseur 1978:36–37; Kartodirdjo 1978:88–89).

However small the numbers of cultivators involved, the growth of a market-oriented class of farmers in Bihar and Java proved increasingly troublesome for colonial regimes that rested on alliances with indigenous elites and the preservation of paternalistic networks of dependency and exchange. In Bihar and other areas of India market-oriented tenants, and in some regions smallholders, vied with European estate managers and Indian landlords for control over land, water rights, and labor. For landless laborers or sharecroppers, the rise of market-oriented tenants, and in some regions smallholders, vied with European estate managers and Indian landlords for control over land, water rights, and labor. For landless laborers or sharecroppers, the rise of market-oriented production meant an increased potential for geographical and occupational mobility within Bihar, which complemented the more limited outlets for work which migration overseas or to the plantations of Assam and towns of Bengal had long provided (Zachariah 1964:200ff; Government of India, *Emigration Proceedings*, [hereafter cited as *EP*] 1875). though it is difficult to know whether the living standard of the laboring classes improved or declined, given population increases and presumably growing competition for jobs and inflation through much of the late nineteenth century, their gains in mobility meant a loss of control on the part of landlord groups.[10] The great increase in cash cropping and the shipping of market produce outside of the areas where it was grown also meant local shortages of food. These were often blamed for famine and price inflation and thus became sources of rural discontent and at times outbursts of protest (Robinson 1971:319). Though these patterns need to be explored in greater depth, they appear to suggest the relevance of some aspects of E.P. Thompson's (1971) formulation of the moral economy in the Indian context.

As the late nineteenth century boom gave way in the 1890s and early 1900s to bad weather, poor harvests, declining world market demands, and tightening credit, the market farmers' resentment of and rivalry with European planters and Indian landlords intensified. Market fluctuation that now affected the great majority of Bihari cultivators produced a no-win situation for the beleaguered colonial administration. Food price increases, which were essential to the continued prosperity and contentment of market farming groups, worked to the detriment of landless, wage earning laborers who thus became a potential source of rural unrest. On the other hand, when food prices declined, to the delight of the laboring classes, market-oriented cultivators faced ruinous debts and sharp drops in their standard of living.

The combination of transport shortages, market disruptions, inflation, and social dislocation that struck India during and right after the First World War (Saini 1978:161–173) drove many market producers to support organized protest in Bihar that came to be focused on Mohandas Gandhi's personal, not mass, *satyagraha*. If recent authors on the subject are correct (Pouchepadass 1974; Henningham 1976:68–69), agrarian agitation in Champaran was not a groundswell struggle of impoverished tenants and sharecroppers as it has traditionally been pictured (Prasad 1949; Datta 1957). Gandhi's main allies in the province and the main beneficiaries of his highly publicized campaign against the European indigo planters were the market-oriented tenants who had seen their gains of the late nineteenth century all but wiped out during the war years. Their struggle with the European planters and Indian landlords over what crops should be grown was intensified by population increases which restricted the amount of land available for market production, drove up the purchase price and rental rates on land already under cultivation, and rendered migration and the clearing of new lands no longer a viable option in most areas of the province. As a result, acts of vandalism, arson, and crop destruction increased sharply in the Champaran period and after—despite Gandhi's message of non-violent protest. Petitions and government inquiries also played a prominent role, but work and rent refusals, land seizures, and violent clashes with police and estate agents became frequent and widespread relative to any period prior to World War I, (Misra 1963:102–103, 116, 132, 140, passim; Prosad 1949:passim). Recent work done on Gandhi's equally famous *satyagrahas* in Gujarat demonstrates that the patterns of market farmer support and shifts to confrontational modes of protest found in Bihar were not isolated or exceptional, but widespread (Hardiman 1977; Charlesworth 1979).

Gandhi's mass appeal in the Indian countryside appears to have resulted from different reasons at different social levels. For illiterate and impoverished laborers and non-occupancy tenants, he was a holyman or *sahdu* and, some authors have argued a messiah. These groups turned out in the tens of thousands to perform *darshan*, ritual and religious obeisance, to the frail figure who lived as simply as they did, preached a message they could understand, and convinced them that he was working to improve the conditions under which they had lived their lives—though it is doubtful that they understood his political goals or his tactics (Pouchepadass 1974:83–84; Hardiman 1977:59ff). For the emerging market farmer classes of Bihar, Gujarat, and other provinces, Gandhi was an ally in their struggles against entrenched landlords and British planters and officials. Gandhi and his Congress Party lieutenants provided a focus and the organizational framework

XVI

that the competitive and independent-minded minority of tenant and small-holder farmers had sorely lacked in the pre-World War I period. In their view, Gandhi supplied both effective channels of communication with the British and potent tactics for protest should the colonizers resist the farmers' demands. The appeal of Gandhian tactics was all the stronger for peasant groups because some of the principles that underlay passive resistance and civil disobedience had considerable affinity with the modes of defense and protest that had long been employed by Indian cultivators (Spodek 1971; Pandey 1978: 173; Hardiman 1977:62–63).

The appeal of Gandhian techniques and the Congress Party for the emerging farmer class can also be traced to the former's non-revolutionary political aims. Though British planter competition and official restrictions were to be eliminated and Indian landlord rivals weakened, the mixed system of market opportunities and patron-client dependencies in which cash farming groups had achieved prosperity was to be preserved. At the same time, Gandhi and other prominent Congress politicans preached class unity, abhorred violence, and promoted alliances between all Indian groups and classes, including the landlords, who were to become the main targets of more radical movements like the *kisan sabhas* in Bihar and the neighboring United Provinces. The co-option or dissolution of these latter movements, which best represented the interests of poor tenants and landless laborers, became major challenges for Gandhi, Nehru, and other socially-committed Congress leaders from the 1920s onwards. Their success rendered the Indian nationalist "revolution" a process of accommodation and limited adjustments, rather than radical upheavals. Though their wealth and status were somewhat reduced and their power restricted, the landlords and dominant caste groups survived (Low 1973:209–211). With the departure of the British, they came increasingly into cooperation with urban politicians and market-oriented farmers out of their mutual concern to shore up badly battered systems of patronage, dependence, and social control (Pandey 1978; Dhanagare 1975; Huawe 1961).

For Java detailed studies of nationalist agitation in the early decades are not available as they are for India on the rural sources of support for Gandhi and the Congress Party.[11] It is difficult to trace with any certainty the links between the emergence of a market-oriented class of cultivators and the spread of nationalism. Sartono Kartodirdjo, who has written the most detailed account to date on the spread of the Sarekat Islam movement to the rural areas of Java, has surprisingly little to say about which social groups actively supported this first wave of nationalist agitation among the rural masses. For the mass of rural dwellers, Sarekat Islam and especially its quasi-messianic leader, Tjokroaminioto, may have had much the same meaning as Gandhi, the holyman, and the Congress Party (Kartodirdjo 1973:ch. 5; Dahm 1969:32–39). The origins of the Sarekat Islam movement in the Indonesian mercantile classes and its anti-Chinese and heavily economic thrust, may well have meant that it was a rallying point for disgruntled, market-oriented landholders in the years of shipping shortages, inflation, and increased exactions during the decade of the First World War. This connection would appear to be reinforced by recent evidence of involvement by prosperous market farmers in the Tjimareme and Afdeelng B disturbances and other localized protest movements aimed against the *priyayi* and the Dutch regime in this period (Chong 1973:22–25; Kartodirdjo 1973:63, 93, 99).

Several general conclusions emerge from this overview of the nature of colonial control systems and rural protest in Java and Bihar. Most striking is the discovery that there was a paucity of confrontational or violent protest at any social level. It is also notable that the most impoverished groups in both of these societies rarely protested in any form, and when they did it was usually in support of rich and powerful patrons. Their quiescence demonstrates in part the strength of the systems of social control and village defense that the Europeans largely preserved after these areas came under colonial rule. Their lack of overt resistance also reflects, as Eric Wolf (1969:289–290) has argued, their deep dependence on other, especially land-controlling groups and the precarious nature of their existence on the edge of subsistence.[12] The fact that well-to-do, market-oriented peasants were those who supported the most strongly confrontational protest movements in both Java and Bihar—even though these were usually led by religious figures— also lends support to Wolf's contention that "middle" peasants are those who are most able and likely to mount sustained movements of protest. Though the "middle" peasants in Bihar were mainly tenants, they had secure control over the lands they worked and had deeply committed themselves to production for the market. Like their landholder counterparts in Java, and in contrast to the groups studied by Wolf, they sought not revolution but limited changes and reforms that would improve their competitive advantage and counter the adverse effects of market reverses and new bureaucratic demands.

If the sharply contrasting fates of societies where these groups threw in their lot with the forces of revolution is indicative, their decisions in Bihar and Java to ally themselves with parties stressing class cooperation and preservation may well have been decisive for the outcome of the Indian and Indonesian nationalist struggles against European colonial dominance.

Notes

1. There is a surprising paucity of secondary studies on caste in rural Bihar. The best source of information on population composition by caste remains the Indian census reports beginning in 1881. For published accounts that are more accessible, see the various Bihar district gazetteers, especially those compiled by L.S.S. O'Malley. See also Brown 1972:55–58. The best account of caste as a patron-client system based on fieldwork in north Indian remains Lewis 1965: esp. chapter two.

2. The role of force in local control in the colonial period has been studied for many regions in India. For Bihar, see Robb (1979:100–101, 115), Jha (1977:550–551), Henningham (1979:69), *BPP*, (1914:vol. 9546, 6). For other areas in India see Government of Bihar and Orissa (hereafter *BPP*), *Bihar Police Proceedings* (Sengupta

1971:197–201), Hardiman (1977:53, 59), Washrook (1976:42, 151 et passim), Kling (1966:52–54). For examples from Java see, Onghokham (1975:65–66), Vitalis (1851:4–6).

3. For the most elaborate discussion of this concept which Clifford Geertz introduced nearly two decades ago, see his recent work (Geertz 1980). In contrast to Geertz's argument that the Balinese built power and authority to support the pomp and splendor of the court (esp. p. 13), the Dutch clearly sought to make use of the pomp and splendor of their Javanese princely "allies" to bolster their legitimacy and control.

4. For the best discussion of these patterns in the Indian context, see Baker 1976:22–26. For Bihar, see Henningham (1979:59–65).

5. Though a militant, puritanical Muslim sect repeatedly stirred up dissidence among the peasants of parts of Bengal in the mid-nineteenth century (Kling 1966:61, 68).

6. The fullest account of the Java War in print remains Louw and Klerck (1894–1909, 6 vols.). On the *priyayi* restoration see Palmier (1960) or Schrieke (1966). For post-rebellion disturbances that the Dutch argued were linked to the Java War, see Cary (1979:88–89), Deventer (1865–6:vol. 2, 468–469, 471–474).

7. Deventer (1865:vol. 2, 468–474) discusses a number of minor disturbances or rebellious plots that appear to have been mainly linked to official excesses or new government demands. No religious overtones are discussed in Deventer's account, but his analysis of rebel motives and activities is too brief and sketchy for one to be certain that religious motivations were not important.

8. Although the motives for late nineteenth century expansion have been the subject of one of the most heated (and productive) of all historical debates for some decades, major works by authors like D.C. Platt, Hans-Ulrich Wehler, and William A. Williaams have firmly established the importance of a need for raw materials, markets and to a much lesser extent investment outlets in the mix of reasons for that great burst of empire building.

9. For important exceptions, see Hopkins (1973), especially chapter four.

10. Even though the evidence for these patterns is very scanty, Peter Robb (1979:112) has suggested that laborers preferred contracts to paternalistic arrangements.

11. For well-to-do peasant involvement in risings in the mid and late nineteenth century, see Kartodirdjo (1973:47, 51–53, 63, 93, 99).

12. A different view of the implications for protest of the subsistence peasants' precarious position is developed in Scott (1976).

References

Adas, M. 1981. "From Avoidance to Confrontation: Peasant Protest in Precolonia and Colonial Southeast Asia," *Comparative Studies in Society and History*, 23:217–247.

──── . 1982. "Bandits, Monks and Pretender Kings: Patterns of Peasant Protest in Colonial Burma, 1826–1941," in R. Weller and S. Guggenheim, eds., *Power and Protest in the Countryside: Studies of Rural Unrest*, Durham: Duke University Press.

Allen, G. C., and A. Donnithorne. 1957. *Western Enterprise in Indonesia and Malaysia*, London: Allen and Unwin.

Anonymous. 1861. "Binnenlandsche onlusten op Java," *Tijdschrift voor Nederlandsch Indie* 23:289–300.

Anonymous. 1891. "De wording en het verloop van de Tjilegonsche troebelen in Juli 1888," *De Indische Gids*, 13:1137–1206.

Baker, C. 1976. "Tamilnad Estates in the Twentieth Century," *Indian Social and Economic History Review*, 13:1–44.

Benda, H., and L. Castles. 1969. "The Samin Movement," *Bijdragen tot de Taal-, Landen Volkenkunde*, 125:207–240.

Boeka, pseud. 1904. "De Hoofden op Java: een studie," *De Indische Gids*, 26:331–361, 516–544.

Brown, J. 1972. *Gandhi's Rise to Power: Indian Politics 1915–1922*, Cambridge: Cambridge University Press.

Burger, D. H. 1948–9. "Sturctuurveranderingen in de Javaanse samenleving," *Indonesie*, 2:381–398.

Cary, P. 1979. "Rich Peasants and Poor Peasants in Late Nineteenth Century Maharashtra," in C. Dewey and A. G. Hopkins, eds., *The Imperial Impact in Africa and South Asia*, London: Institute of Commonwealth Studies.

Cheong, Y. M. 1973. *Conflicts within the Priyayi: World of the Parahyangan in West Java, 1914–1927*, Singapore: Institute of Southeast Asian Studies.

Cohn, B. 1969. "Structural Change in Indian Rural Society, 1596–1885," in R. E. Frykenberg, ed., *Land Control and Social Structure in Indian History*, Madison: University of Wisconsin Press.

Dahm, B. 1969. *Sukarno and the Struggle for Indonesian Independence*, Ithaca: Cornell University Press.

Das, M. N. 1964. *India under Minto and Morley*, London: Allen and Unwin.

Datta, K. K. 1957a. *Agrarian Unrest against British Rule in Bihar, 1831–1859*, Patna: Government of Bihar.

———. 1957b. *History of the Freedom Movement in Bihar*, Patna: Government of Bihar.

Deventer, S. V. 1865–66. *Bijdragen tot de kennis van het landelijk stelsel op Java*, Zalt-Bommel: J. Norman en zoon, 3 vols.

Dewey, C. 1979. "Patwari and Chaukidar: Subordinate Officials and the Reliability of India's Agricultural Statistics," in C. Dewey and A. G. Hopkins, eds., *The Imperial Impact in Africa and South Asia*, London: Institute of Commonwealth Studies.

Dhanagare, D. N. 1975. *Agrarian Movements and Gandhian Politics*, Agra: Agra University Press.

Di Nijs, E. B. 1961. *Tempo doeloe: Fotographische Documenten uit het oude Indie*, Amsterdam: *Querido*.

Dumont, L. 1970. *Homo Hierarchius: The Caste System and Its Implications*, London: Weiedenfeld and Nicolson.

Elson, R. E. 1978. *The Cultivation System and "Agricultural Involution"*, Clayong, Victoria: Monash University Press.

Fanon, F. 1968. *The Wretched of the Earth*, New York: Grove Press.

Fasseur, C. 1978. *Kultuurstelsel en Koloniale Baten: De Nederlandse Exploitatie van Java 1840–1860*, Leiden: University of Leiden Press.

Fisher, C. 1979. "Planters and Peasants: The Ecological Contest of Agrarian Unrest on the Indigo Plantations of North Bihar, 1820–1920," in C. Dewey and A. G. Hopkins, eds., *The Imperial Impact in Africa and South Asia*, London: Institute of Commonwealth Studies.

Fox, R. 1971. *Kin, Clan, Raja and Rule: State-Hinterland Relations in Pre-Industrial India*, Berkeley: University of California Press.

Furnivall, J. S. 1939. *Netherlands India: A Study of Plural Economy*, Cambridge: Cambridge University Press.

———. 1956. *Colonial Policy and Practice*, New York: New York University Press.

Geertz, C. 1966. *Agricultural Involution: The Process of Ecological Change in Indonesia*, Berkeley: University of California Press.

——. 1980. *Negara: The Theatre State in Nineteenth Century Bali*, Princeton: Princeton University Press.

Government of Bihar and Orissa. *Reports on the Administration of Bihar and Orissa, 1915-1920*, London: India Office Records.

——. *Bihar Police Proceedings, 1911/12-1924/5*, London: India Office Records.

Government of India. *Emigration Proceedings*, Vol. 932, 1875, No. 8. London: India Office Records.

Guha, R. 1963. *A Rule of Property for Bengal*, Paris: Moulton.

Harcourt, M. 1977. "Kisan Populism and Revolution in Rural Indian: The 1942 Disturbances in Bihar and East United Provinces," in D. A. Low, ed., *Congress and the Raj*, London: Heinemann.

Hardiman, D. 1977. "The Crisis of the Lesser Patidars: Peasant Agitations in Kheda District, Gujarat, 1917-34," in D. A. Low, ed., *Congress and the Raj*, London: Heinemann.

Harnetty, P. 1972. *Imperialism and Free Trade: Lancashire and India in the Mid-Nineteenth Century*, Vancouver: University of British Columbia Press.

Hauser, W. 1961. "The Bihar Provincial Kisan Sabha, 1929-42: A Study of an Indian Peasant Movement," Ph.D. Dissertation, University of Chicago.

Henningham, S. 1976. "The Social Setting of the Champaran Satyagraha: The Challenge of an Alien Elite," *Indian Economic and Social History Review*, 13:59-73.

——. 1979. "Agrarian Relations in North Bihar," *Indian Social and Economic History Review*, 14:53-75.

Hopkins, A. G. 1973. *An Economic History of West Africa*, New York: Columbia University Press.

Jha, H. 1977. "Lower-Caste Peasants and Upper-Caste Zamindars in Bihar (1921-25): An Analysis of Sanskritization and Contradiction between Two Groups," *Indian Social and Economic History Review*, 14:549-559.

J. L. V. 1855. "Bijdrage tot de kennis der residentie Madioen," *Tijdschrift voor Nederlandsch Indie*, 17:1-17.

Kano, H. 1980. "The Economic History of Javanese Rural Society: A Reinterpretation," *Journal of the Developing Economies*, 17:3-22.

Kartodirdjo, S. 1966. *The Peasants' Revolt of Banten in 1888*, The Hague: Njhoff.

——. 1972. "Agrarian Radicalism in Java," in C. Holt, ed., *Culture and Politics in Indonesia*, Ithaca: Cornell University Press.

——. 1973. *Protest Movements in Rural Java*, Singapore: Oxford University Press.

Kling, B. 1966. *The Blue Mutiny: The Indigo Disturbances in Bengal, 1859-62*, Philadelphia: University of Pennsylvania Press.

Kumar, R. 1968. "The Rise of the Rich Peasants in Western India," in D. A. Low, ed., *Soundings in South Asian History*, Berkeley: University of California Press.

Lewis, O. 1965. *Village Life in Northern India*, New York: Vintage.

Louw, P., and E. S. de Klercke. 1894-1909. *De Java-Oorlog van 1825-1830*, 6 vols. The Hague: Nijhoff.

Low, D. A. 1973. *Lion Rampant*, London: Cass.

Majumbar, R. C. 1963. *The Sepoy Mutiny and Revolt of 1857*, Calcutta: K. L. Mukhopadhyay.

Marr, D. 1972. *Vietnamese Anticolonialism*, Berkeley: University of California Press.

Marx, K. and F. Engels. n.d. *The First Indian War of Independence 1857-1859*, Moscow: Foreign Languages Publishing House.

Metcalf, T. R. 1964. *The Aftermath of Revolt: India, 1857-1870*, Princeton: Princeton University Press.

———. 1979. *Land, Landlords, and the British Raj*, Berkeley: University of California Press.

Misra, B. B. 1963. *Select Documents on Mahatma Gandhi's Movement in Champaran 1917-1918*, Patna: Government of Bihar.

Misra, G. 1967. "Indigo Plantations and the Agrarian Relations in Champaran during the Nineteenth Century," *Indian Social and Economic History Review*, 3:332-357.

Moore, B., Jr. 1966. *Social Origins of Dictatorship and Democracy: Lord and Peasant in the Making of the Modern World*, Boston: Beacon.

Niel, R. V. 1964. "The Function of Land Rent under the Cultivation System in Java," *Journal of Asian Studies*, 23:357-375.

———. 1969. "The Introduction of the Government of Sugar Cultivation in Pasuruan, Java, 1830," *Journal of Oriental Studies*, 7:261-276.

———. 1972. "Measurement of Change under the Cultivation System in Java, 1837-1851," *Indonesia*, 14:89-109.

O'Malley, L. S. S. 1907. *Champaran District Gazetteer*, Patna: Government of Bihar and Orissa.

———. 1938. *Champaran District Gazetteer*, Patna: Government of Bihar and Orissa.

Oonghokam. 1975. "The Residency of Madiun Priyayi and Peasant in the Nineteenth Century," Ph.D dissertation, Yale University.

Paige, J. 1975. *Agrarian Revolution: Social Movements and Export Agriculture in the Underdeveloped World*, New York: The Free Press.

Palmier, L. 1960. "The Javanese Nobility under the Dutch," *Comparative Studies in Society and History*, 2:197-227.

Pandey, G. 1977. "A Rural Base for Congress: The United Provinces, 1920-1940," in D. A. Low, ed., *Congress and the Raj*, London: Heinmann.

———. 1978. *The Ascendancy of the Congress in Uttar Pradesh*, Delhi: Oxford University Press.

Pierson, N. G. 1868. *Het Kultuurstelsel: Zes Voorlezingen*, Amsterdam: Van Kampen.

Pouchepadass, J. 1974. "Local Leaders and the Intelligensia in the Champaran Satyagraha (1917): A Study in Peasant Mobilization," *Contributions to Indian Sociology*, 8:67-87.

Prasad, R. 1949. *Satyagraha in Champaran*, Ahmedabad: Navajivan Publishing House.

Raj, J. 1965. *The Mutiny and the British Land Policy in North India*, New York: Asia Publishing House.

Ray, R and R. Ray. 1973. "Officials and Non-Officials and Leaders in Popular Agitation: Shahabad 1917 and Other Conspiracies," in B. N. Pandey, ed., *Leadership in South Asia*, New Delhi: Oxford University Press.

Robb, P. 1977. "Officials and Non-Officials as Leaders in Popular Agitation: Shahabad 1917 and Other Conspiracies," in B. N. Pandey, ed., *Leadership in South Asia*, New Delhi: Oxford University Press.

———. 1979. "Hierarchy and Resources: Peasant Stratification in Late Nineteenth Century Bihar," *Modern Asian Studies*, 13:97-126.

Robinson, F. C. R. 1971. "Consultation and Control: The United Provinces's Government and Its Allies, 1860-1906," *Modern Asian Studies*, 5:313-336.

Saini, K. G. 1978. "The Economic Aspects of India's Participation in the First World War," in D. C. Ellinwood and S. D. Pradhan, eds., *India and World War I*, Columbia: South Asian Books.

Schrieke, B. 1966. "The Native rulers," in *Indonesian Sociological Studies*, The Hague: Van Hoeve.

Scott, J. C. 1976. *The Moral Economy of the Peasant*, New Haven: Yale University Press.

Sen, S. N. 1957. *Eighteen Fifty-Seven*, New Delhi: Government of India.

Sengupta, K. K. 1971. "Agrarian Disturbances in Nineteenth Century Bengal," *Indian Social and Economic History Review*, 8:192–212.

Shoemaker, W. J. 1896. "Het Mohammedaansche fanatisme," *De Indische Gids*, 20:1517–1537.

The Siau Giap. 1968. "The Samin and Samat Movements in Java: Two Examples of Peasant Resistance," *Revue du sud-est asiatique*, 1:63–77, 107–113; 2:303–310.

Sinha, R. 1918. *The Law of the Landlord and Tenant in Bengal and Bihar*, Calcutta: R. Cambray and Co.

Skocpol, T. 1979. *States and Social Revolutions: A Comparative Analysis of France, Russia and China*, Cambridge: Cambridge University Press.

Spodek, H. 1971. "On the Origins of Gandhi's Political Methodology: The Heritage of Kathiawad and Gujarat," *Journal of Asian Studies*, 30:361–372.

Stokes, E. 1959. *The English Utilitarians and India*, Oxford: Oxford University Press.

Sutherland, H. 1973. "Pargreh Pradja: Java's Indigenous Administrative Corps and Its Role in the Last Decades of Dutch Colonial Rule," Ph.D. dissertation, Yale University.

Thompson, E. P. 1971. "The Moral Economy of the English Crowd in the Eighteenth Century," *Past and Present*, 50:76–136.

van Soest, G. H. 1869. *Geschiedenis van het Kultuurstelsel*, H. Nijgh, 3 Vols.

Vitalis, L. 1851. *De Invoering, werking en gebreken van het stelsel van Kultuurs op Java*, Zalt-Bommel: Norman en zoon.

Washbrook, D. 1976. *The Emergence of Provincial Politics: the Madras Presidency, 1870–1920*, Cambridge: Cambridge University Press.

Wolf, E. 1969. *Peasant Wars of the Twentieth Century*, New York: Harper and Row.

Zachariah, K. C. 1964. *A Historical Study of Internal Migration in the Indian Sub-Continent, 1901–1931*, Bombay: Asia Publishing House.

INDEX

This index includes names, places and major themes. The location references refer to the chapter numberings in roman numerals followed by the page reference within the chapter; an 'n' indicates a mention in the notes; *passim* indicates that there are frequent mentions of the subject in one chapter. Filing order is letter-by-letter. Names of contemporary historians and writers have been included where they make a significant contribution to the debate in question. Chinese names are indexed under their family names without a comma; Burman and Vietnamese names have been inverted. References and notes have not been indexed unless they contain discussion of significant points. Publications are represented in italics.

For Product Safety Concerns and Information please contact our EU
representative GPSR@taylorandfrancis.com
Taylor & Francis Verlag GmbH, Kaufingerstraße 24, 80331 München, Germany

www.ingramcontent.com/pod-product-compliance
Lightning Source LLC
Chambersburg PA
CBHW070901270326
41926CB00057B/2272